The Hawkins' Voyages During The Reigns Of Henry Viii, Queen Elizabeth, And James I, Issue 57

The Hakluyt Society.

REPORT FOR 1878.

REPORT FOR 1878.

THE Hakluyt Society has to mourn the loss of its President, Sir David Dundas, who held that post for six-and-a-half years.

Sir David Dundas was the eldest surviving son of Robert Dundas, Esq., of Ochtertyre, in Perthshire. Born in 1799, he was a Queen's Scholar at Westminster, whence he was elected off as a Student of Christ Church, Oxford, where he graduated M.A. in 1822. He was called to the Bar at the Inner Temple on February 7th, 1823, and went the Northern Circuit. In April 1840, he was appointed a Queen's Counsel, Solicitor-General on July 10th, 1846, and was knighted on February 4th, 1847. He resigned the office of Solicitor-General in March 1848, and was Judge-Advocate General from May 19th, 1849, until 1852. On June 29th, 1849, Sir David Dundas was sworn of the Privy Council. In 1840, he was elected Member of Parliament for Sutherlandshire, which seat he held until 1852, and again from May 1861, until May 1867. He was also a Trustee of the British Museum.

Sir David was an active Member of the Hakluyt Society from its foundation. He presided at a meeting of the Council on the 15th of November, 1853, for the first time, and was ever afterwards a constant attendant, presiding at twenty-eight of the meetings. He never edited a volume for the Society, but was ever ready with advice and assistance, sparing no trouble in making researches; while his fine library, which contained many works bearing on the Society's objects, was always at the service of editors. His great knowledge of books relating to early voyages and travels rendered his services as a Member of the Council invaluable. On June 3rd, 1863, Sir David Dundas succeeded the Marquis of Lansdowne as one of the Vice-Presidents; and, after the lamented death of Sir Roderick Murchison, who had presided since the foundation of the Society in 1847, Sir David was unanimously elected to be the second President of the Hakluyt Society, on the 20th of November 1871. He continued to fulfil the duties of that post until his death on the 30th of March 1877, and his sound practical judgment, as well as his fund of useful and interesting information, made his presence always most acceptable. The last time he attended a meeting of the Council was a very few days before his decease, namely, on the 13th of March 1877.

Since the last Report, in 1874, the Society has lost several other active and useful Members. Among these are Rear-Admiral Sherard Osborn, C.B., Commodore J. G. Goodenough, R.N., C.B., C.M.G., The Hon. Frederick Walpole, M.P., Sir William Stirling Maxwell, Bart., the Earl of Sheffield, and the Bishop of St. Davids.

On the 19th of June 1877, Colonel Henry Yule, R.E., C.B., was unanimously elected to be the third President of the Hakluyt Society.

Since the last Report in 1874, the following volumes have been issued to Members:—

I. The First Voyage round the World by Magellan. Translated from the Accounts of Pigafetta and other contemporary writers, accompanied by original documents, with notes and an introduction, by Lord Stanley of Alderley.

II. The Captivity of Hans Stade of Hesse, in A.D. 1547-1555, among the Wild Tribes of Eastern Brazil. Translated by Alfred Tootal, Esq., of Rio de Janeiro, and annotated by Richard F. Burton.

III. The Second Edition of the Three Voyages of William Barents to the Arctic Regions (1594, 1595, and 1596). By Gerit de Veer: the first edition, edited by G. Charles T. Beke, Phil.D., in 1853; the second edition, with an introduction, by Lieut. Koolemans Beynen, of the Royal Netherlands Navy.

IV. The Commentaries of the great Afonso Dalboquerque, second Viceroy of India. Translated from the Portuguese edition of 1774, with notes and an introduction, by Walter De Gray Birch, F.R.S.L.

V. The Second Volume of the Commentaries of Dalboquerque.

VI. The Voyages of Sir James Lancaster, Kt., to the East Indies, with Abstracts of Journals of Voyages to the East Indies during the Seventeenth Century, preserved in the India Office; and the Voyage of Captain John Knight (1606) to seek a North-West Passage. Edited by Clements R. Markham, C.B., F.R.S.

Two Volumes are in the printer's hands, and will shortly be issued, namely:—

The Third Volume of the Commentaries of Afonso Dalboquerque; and

The Second Edition of the Observations of Sir Richard Hawkins, to which will be added the Voyages of his grandfather William Hawkins, of his father Sir John Hawkins, and of his cousin William Hawkins, thus forming a monograph on the naval services of this family of distinguished Elizabethan seamen: edited, with an introduction, by Clements R. Markham, C.B.

Several volumes have been undertaken by Editors, and are making progress. Mr. W. A. Tyssen Amherst is engaged upon the translating and editing of the Journal of the Pilot Gallego, and other documents relating to the Voyages of Mendaña. Mr. R. C. Groves is editing Rosmital's Embassy to the Courts of England and Spain in 1466. Lord Stanley of Alderley will translate and edit the NARRATIVE OF THE PORTUGUESE EMBASSY TO ABYSSINIA in 1520, by Father Francisco Alvarez. Mr. Clements Markham has undertaken to edit, and collate with the original Spanish, the (1603) translation of Acosta's NATURAL HISTORY OF THE WESTERN INDIES; and Captain A. H. Markham, R.N., will edit a monograph of JOHN DAVIS, including his Three Arctic Voyages, his Voyage with Cavendish, his Seamen's Secrets, his World's Hydrography, his Voyage to the East Indies with the Dutch Fleet, and his last Voyage with Michelborne. These volumes will meet the just demands of subscribers down to the end of the year 1880.

The Council have great pleasure in being able to report that there has been a satisfactory increase in the number of Members. In 1873 there were 214, in 1874 the number was 228, and it is now 248. The funds are in a healthy state.

The following six Members retire from the Council:—

CAPTAIN PORCHER, R.N. (deceased)
HENRY H. HOWORTH, ESQ.
CAPTAIN CRUTTENDEN.
W. E. FRERE, ESQ., C.M.G.
AUGUSTUS W. FRANKS, ESQ.
EDWARD THOMAS, ESQ., F.R.S.

The three latter are proposed for re-election, and the names of the following gentlemen are proposed for election:—

COLONEL SIR WILLIAM L. MEREWETHER, K.C.S.I., C.B.
LORD ARTHUR RUSSELL, M.P.
LIEUT.-GENERAL SIR J. H. LEFROY, K.C.M.G., C.B.

Statement of the Accounts of the Society from Jan. 1874, *to Feb.* 1876.

Balance at the Bankers at the last Audit	£586	13	11	Mr. Richards for Printing	£641	6	6
Received by Bankers, Jan. 1874, to Jan. 1876	835	17	0	Mr. Weller for Maps	38	14	11
				Mr. Saunders for a Map	31	2	6
				Mr. Prætorius for Photo-lithography	12	12	0
				Mr. Coote for Transcriptions ..	9	0	4
				Mr. Baynes for Translations ..	4	14	9
				Mr. Dalziel for Wood-engraving	15	6	0
				Messrs. Spencer for Photo-lithography	20	3	0
				Mr. Handcock for Calendaring E. I. Log Books	10	10	0
				Wymans & Sons for Lithography	7	15	6
				Mr. Quaritch. Purchase of a Society's volume out of print	3	3	0
				Stamps	0	5	0
					794	13	6
				Balance at the Bankers....	627	17	5
	£1,422	10	11		£1,422	10	11

Examined and approved, *March* 18*th*, 1878.

LINDESAY BRINE,
A. H. MARKHAM.

Statement of the Accounts of the Society from Feb. 1876, *to May* 1877.

Balance left at the Bankers (Feb. 1876)	£627	17	5	Mr. Richards for Printing	£292	17	6
Received by Bankers, Feb. 1876, to May 1877	449	5	0	Mr. Handcock for Calendaring E. I. Log Books............	46	4	0
				Mr. Prætorius	58	16	0
				Mr. W. R. Wilson—Index......	5	0	0
				Petty Cash	5	0	0
				The Autotype Company.........	14	9	8
					422	7	2
				Balance at the Bankers	654	15	3
	£1,077	2	5		£1,077	2	5

Examined and approved, *March* 18*th*, 1878.

LINDESAY BRINE,
A. H. MARKHAM.

THE

HAKLUYT SOCIETY.

1879.

THE HAKLUYT SOCIETY, which is established for the purpose of printing rare or unpublished Voyages and Travels, aims at opening by this means an easier access to the sources of a branch of knowledge, which yields to none in importance, and is superior to most in agreeable variety. The narratives of travellers and navigators make us acquainted with the earth, its inhabitants and productions; they exhibit the growth of intercourse among mankind, with its effects on civilisation, and, while instructing, they at the same time awaken attention, by recounting the toils and adventures of those who first explored unknown and distant regions.

The advantage of an Association of this kind consists not merely in its system of literary co-operation, but also in its economy. The acquirements, taste, and discrimination of a number of individuals, who feel an interest in the same pursuit, are thus brought to act in voluntary combination, and the ordinary charges of publication are also avoided, so that the volumes produced are distributed among the Members (who can alone obtain them) at little more than the cost of printing and paper. The Society expends the whole of its funds in the preparation of works for the Members; and since the cost of each copy varies inversely as the whole number of copies printed, it is obvious that the members are gainers individually by the prosperity of the Society, and the consequent vigour of its operations.

Gentlemen desirous of becoming Members of the Hakluyt Society should intimate their intention to the Secretary, MR. CLEMENTS R. MARKHAM, C.B., F.R.S., 21, *Eccleston Square, S.W.*, or to the Society's Agent for the delivery of its volumes, MR. RICHARDS, 37, *Great Queen Street, Lincoln's Inn Fields;* when their names will be recorded, and on payment of their subscription of £1 : 1 to Mr. Richards, they will receive the volumes issued for the year.

New Members have, at present (1879), *the privilege of purchasing the publications of the Society for previous years for £25 12s. 6d.* Members wishing to purchase back volumes may, with the consent of the Council, be supplied with them at the rate of 10s. each volume, when they require any number less than one quarter of the whole series, and at the rate of 8s. 6d. a volume when they require any number more than a quarter of the whole series.

The Members are requested to bear in mind that the power of the Council to make advantageous arrangements will depend in a great measure on the prompt payment of the subscriptions, which are payable in advance on the 1st of January, and are received by MR. RICHARDS, 37, Great Queen Street, Lincoln's Inn Fields. Post Office Orders should be made payable to MR. THOMAS RICHARDS, at the *West Central Office, High Holborn.*

WORKS ALREADY ISSUED.

1—The Observations of Sir Richard Hawkins, Knt.,

In his Voyage into the South Sea in 1593. Reprinted from the edition of 1622, and edited by Capt. C. R. DRINKWATER BETHUNE, R.N., C.B.
Iſſued for 1848. *(First Edition out of print. See No.* 57.*)*

2—Select Letters of Columbus.

With Original Documents relating to the Diſcovery of the New World. Translated and Edited by R. H. MAJOR, Esq., of the Britiſh Muſeum.
Iſſued for 1849. *(First Edition out of print. See No.* 43.*)*

3—The Discoverie of the Empire of Guiana,

By Sir Walter Raleigh, Knt. Edited, with copious Explanatory Notes, and a Biographical Memoir, by SIR ROBERT H. SCHOMBURGK, Phil. D., etc.
Iſſued for 1850.

4—Sir Francis Drake his Voyage, 1595.

By Thomas Maynarde, together with the Spaniſh Account of Drake's attack on Puerto Rico. Edited from the Original MSS. by W. D. COOLEY, Esq.
Iſſued for 1850.

5—Narratives of Early Voyages

Undertaken for the Diſcovery of a Paſſage to Cathaia and India, by the Northweſt, with Selections from the Records of the worſhipful Fellowſhip of the Merchants of London, trading into the Eaſt Indies; and from MSS. in the Library of the Britiſh Muſeum, now firſt publiſhed; by THOMAS RUNDALL, Esq.
Iſſued for 1851.

6—The Historie of Travaile into Virginia Britannia,

Expreſſing the Coſmographie and Commodities of the Country, together with the manners and cuſtoms of the people, gathered and obſerved as well by thoſe who went firſt thither as collected by William Strachey, Gent., the firſt Secretary of the Colony; now firſt Edited from the original manuſcript in the Britiſh Muſeum, by R. H. MAJOR, Esq., of the Britiſh Muſeum.

Iſſued for 1851.

7—Divers Voyages touching the Discovery of America

And the Iſlands adjacent, collected and publiſhed by Richard Hakluyt, Prebendary of Briſtol in the year 1582. Edited, with Notes and an introduction, by JOHN WINTER JONES, Esq., of the Britiſh Muſeum.

Iſſued for 1852.

8—A Collection of Documents on Japan.

With a Commentary by THOMAS RUNDALL, ESQ.

Iſſued for 1852.

9—The Discovery and Conquest of Florida,

By Don Ferdinando de Soto. Tranſlated out of Portugueſe by Richard Hakluyt; and Edited, with notes and an introduction, by W. B. RYE, Esq., of the Britiſh Muſeum. *Iſſued for* 1853.

10—Notes upon Russia,

Being a Tranſlation from the Earlieſt Account of that Country, entitled Rerum Muscoviticarum Commentarii, by the Baron Sigiſmund von Herberſtein, Ambaſſador from the Court of Germany to the Grand Prince Vaſiley Ivanovich, in the years 1517 and 1526. Two Volumes. Tranſlated and Edited, with Notes and an Introduction, by R. H. MAJOR, Esq., of the Britiſh Muſeum. Vol. I. *Iſſued for* 1853.

11—The Geography of Hudson's Bay.

Being the Remarks of Captain W. Coats, in many Voyages to that locality, between the years 1727 and 1751. With an Appendix, containing Extracts from the Log of Captain Middleton on his Voyage for the Diſcovery of the North-west Paſſage, in H.M.S. "Furnace," in 1741-2. Edited by JOHN BARROW, Esq., F.R.S., F.S.A.

Iſſued for 1854.

12—Notes upon Russia. Vol. 2.

Iſſued for 1854.

13—Three Voyages by the North-east,

Towards Cathay and China, undertaken by the Dutch in the years 1594, 1595, and 1596, with their Diſcovery of Spitzbergen, their reſidence of ten months in Novaya Zemlya, and their ſafe return in two open boats. By Gerrit de Veer. Edited by C. T. BEKE, Esq., Ph.D., F.S.A.

(First Edition out of print. See No. 54.) *Iſſued for* 1855.

14-15—The History of the Great and Mighty Kingdom of China and the Situation Thereof.

Compiled by the Padre Juan Gonzalez de Mendoza. And now Reprinted from the Early Tranſlation of R. Parke. Edited by SIR GEORGE T. STAUNTON, Bart. With an Introduction by R. H. MAJOR, Esq. 2 vols.

Iſſued for 1855.

16—The World Encompassed by Sir Francis Drake.

Being his next Voyage to that to Nombre de Dios. Collated, with an unpubliſhed Manuſcript of Francis Fletcher, Chaplain to the Expedition. With Appendices illuſtrative of the ſame Voyage, and Introduction by W. S. W. VAUX, Esq., M.A. *Iſſued for* 1856.

17—The History of the Tartar Conquerors who subdued China.

From the French of the Père D'Orleans, 1688. Tranſlated and Edited by the EARL OF ELLESMERE. With an Introduction by R. H. MAJOR, Esq.

Iſſued for 1856.

18—A Collection of Early Documents on Spitzbergen and Greenland,

Confifting of: a Tranflation from the German of F. Martin's important work on Spitzbergen, now very rare; a Tranflation from Isaac de la Peyrère's Relation de Greenland; and a rare piece entitled 'God's Power and Providence fhowed in the miraculous prefervation and deliverance of eight Englifhmen left by mifchance in Greenland, anno 1630, nine months and twelve days, faithfully reported by Edward Pelham." Edited, with Notes, by ADAM WHITE, Esq., of the Britifh Mufeum.

Iffued for 1857.

19—The Voyage of Sir Henry Middleton to Bantam and the Maluco Islands.

From the rare Edition of 1606. Edited by BOLTON CORNEY, Esq.

Iffued for 1857.

20—Russia at the Close of the Sixteenth Century.

Comprifing "The Ruffe Commonwealth" by Dr. Giles Fletcher, and Sir Jerome Horfey's Travels, now firft printed entire from his manufcript in the Britifh Mufeum. Edited by E. A. BOND, Esq., of the Britifh Mufeum.

Iffued for 1858.

21—The Travels of Girolamo Benzoni in America, in 1542-56.

Tranflated and Edited by ADMIRAL W. H. SMYTH, F.R.S., F.S.A.

Iffued for 1858.

22—India in the Fifteenth Century.

Being a Collection of Narratives of Voyages to India in the century preceding the Portuguefe difcovery of the Cape of Good Hope; from Latin, Perfian, Ruffian, and Italian Sources, now firft tranflated into Englifh. Edited, with an Introduction by R. H. MAJOR, Esq., F.S.A.

Iffued for 1859.

23—Narrative of a Voyage to the West Indies and Mexico,

In the years 1599-1602, with Maps and Illuftrations. By Samuel Champlain. Tranflated from the original and unpublifhed Manufcript, with a Biographical Notice and Notes by ALICE WILMERE.

Iffued for 1859.

24—Expeditions into the Valley of the Amazons

During the Sixteenth and Seventeenth Centuries: containing the Journey of Gonzalo Pizarro, from the Royal Commentaries of Garcilaffo Inca de la Vega; the Voyage of Francifco de Orellana, from the General Hiftory of Herrera; and the Voyage of Criftoval de Acuna, from an exceedingly fcarce narrative written by himfelf in 1641. Edited and Tranflated by CLEMENTS R. MARKHAM, Esq. *Iffued for* 1860.

25—Early Indications of Australia.

A Collection of Documents fhewing the Early Difcoveries of Auftralia to the time of Captain Cook. Edited by R. H. MAJOR, ESQ., of the Britifh Mufeum, F.S.A. *Iffued for* 1860.

26—The Embassy of Ruy Gonzales de Clavijo to the Court of Timour, 1403-6.

Tranflated, for the firft time, with Notes, a Preface, and an Introductory Life of Timour Beg. By CLEMENTS R. MARKHAM, Esq.

Iffued for 1861.

27—Henry Hudson the Navigator.

The Original Documents in which his career is recorded. Collected, partly Tranflated, and Annotated, with an Introduction by GEORGE ASHER, LL.D.

Iffued for 1861.

28—The Expedition of Ursua and Aguirre,

In search of El Dorado and Omagua, A.D. 1560-61. Tranflated from the "Sexta Noticia Hiftoriale" of Fray Pedro Simon, by W. BOLLAERT, Esq.; with an Introduction by CLEMENTS R. MARKHAM, Esq.

Iffued for 1862.

29—The Life and Acts of Don Alonzo Enriquez de Guzman.

Tranflated from a Manufcript in the National Library at Madrid, and edited, with Notes and an Introduction, by CLEMENTS R. MARKHAM, Esq.
Iffued for 1862.

30—Discoveries of the World by Galvano,

From their firft original unto the year of our Lord 1555. Reprinted, with the original Portuguefe text, and edited by VICE-ADMIRAL BETHUNE, C.B.
Iffued for 1863.

31—Marvels described by Friar Jordanus,

Of the Order of Preachers, native of Severac, and Bifhop of Columbum; from a parchment manufcript of the Fourteenth Century, in Latin, the text of which has recently been Tranflated and Edited by COLONEL H. YULE, C.B., F.R.G.S., late of H.M. Bengal Engineers.
Iffued for 1863.

32—The Travels of Ludovico di Varthema

In Syria, Arabia, Perfia, India, etc., during the Sixteenth Century. Tranflated by J. WINTER JONES, Esq., F.S.A., and edited, with Notes and an Introduction, by the REV. GEORGE PERCY BADGER.
Iffued for 1864.

33—The Travels of Cieza de Leon in 1532-50

From the Gulf of Darien to the City of La Plata, contained in the firft part of his Chronicle of Peru (Antwerp 1554). Tranflated and edited, with Notes and an Introduction, by CLEMENTS R. MARKHAM, Esq.
Iffued for 1864.

34—The Narrative of Pascual de Andagoya.

Containing the earlieft notice of Peru. Tranflated and edited, with Notes and an Introduction, by CLEMENTS R. MARKHAM, Esq.
Iffued for 1865.

35—The Coasts of East Africa and Malabar

In the beginning of the Sixteenth Century, by Duarte Barbofa. Tranflated from an early Spanifh manufcript by the HON. HENRY STANLEY.
Iffued for 1865.

36—Cathay and the Way Thither.

A Collection of all minor notices of China, previous to the Sixteenth Century. Tranflated and edited by COLONEL H. YULE, C.B. Vol. 1.
Iffued for 1866.

37—Cathay and the Way Thither. Vol. 2.
Iffued for 1866.

38—The Three Voyages of Sir Martin Frobisher.

With a Selection from Letters now in the State Paper Office. Edited by REAR-ADMIRAL COLLINSON, C.B.
Iffued for 1867.

39—The Philippine Islands.

Moluccas, Siam, Cambodia, Japan, and China, at the close of the 16th Century. By Antonia de Morga. Translated from the Spanish, with Notes, by LORD STANLEY of Alderley. *Iffued for* 1868.

40—The Fifth Letter of Hernan Cortes.

To the Emperor Charles V, containing an Account of his Expedition to Honduras in 1525-26. Translated from the Spanish by Don Pascual de Gayangos.
Iffued for 1868.

41—The Royal Commentaries of the Yncas.

By the Ynca Garcilasso de la Vega. Translated and Edited, with Notes and an Introduction, by CLEMENTS R. MARKHAM, Esq. Vol. 1.
Iffued for 1869.

42—The Three Voyages of Vasco da Gama

And his Viceroyalty, from the Lendas da India of Caspar Correa; accompanied by original documents. Translated and Edited by the LORD STANLEY of Alderley. *Iſſued for* 1869.

43—Select Letters of Christopher Columbus,

With other Original Documents, relating to his Four Voyages to the New World. Tranſlated and Edited by R. H. MAJOR, F.S.A., etc. 2nd Edit. *Iſſued for* 1870.

44—History of the Imâms and Seyyids of 'Omân,

By Salîl-Ibn-Razîk, from A.D. 661-1856. Tranſlated from the original Arabic, and edited, with Notes, Appendices, and an Introduction, continuing the Hiſtory down to 1870, by GEORGE PERCY BADGER, F.R.G.S. *Iſſued for* 1870.

45—The Royal Commentaries of the Yncas. Vol. 2. *Iſſued for* 1871.

46—The Canarian,

Or Book of the Conqueſt and Converſion of the Canarians in the year 1402, by Meſſire Jean de Bethencourt, Kt. Compoſed by Pierre Bontier and Jean le Verrier. Tranſlated and Edited, with Notes and an Introduction, by R. H. MAJOR, F.S.A. *Iſſued for* 1871.

47—Reports on the Discovery of Peru;

Tranſlated and Edited, with Notes and an Introduction, by CLEMENTS R. MARKHAM, C.B. *Iſſued for* 1872.

48—Narratives of the Rites and Laws of the Yncas;

Tranſlated from the original Spaniſh Manuſcripts, and Edited, with Notes and an Introduction, by CLEMENTS R. MARKHAM, C.B., F.R.S. *Iſſued for* 1872.

49—Travels to Tana and Persia,

By Joſafa Barbaro and Ambrogio Contarini; Edited by LORD STANLEY of Alderley; and Narratives of other Italian Travels in Perſia, Tranſlated and Edited by CHARLES GREY, Esq. *Iſſued for* 1873.

50—Voyages of the Zeni

To the Northern Seas in the Fourteenth Century. Tranſlated and Edited by R. H. MAJOR, F.S.A. *Iſſued for* 1873.

51—The Captivity of Hans Stade of Hesse in 1547-55

Among the Wild Tribes of Eaſtern Brazil; tranſlated by ALBERT TOOTAL, Esq., and annotated by RICHARD F. BURTON. *Iſſued for* 1874.

52—The First Voyage Round the World by Magellan.

Tranſlated from the Accounts of Pigafetta and other contemporary writers. With Notes and an Introduction by Lord STANLEY of Alderley. *Iſſued for* 1874.

53—The Commentaries of the Great Afonso Dalboquerque,

Second Viceroy of India. Tranſlated from the Portuguese Edition of 1774; with Notes and Introduction by WALTER DE GRAY BIRCH, Esq., F.R.S.L. Vol. I. *Iſſued for* 1875.

54—Three Voyages to the North-East.

Second Edition of Gerrit de Veer's Three Voyages to the North East by Barents. Edited, with an Introduction, by Lieut. KOOLEMANS BEYNEN, of the Royal Dutch Navy. *Iſſued for* 1876.

55—The Commentaries of the Great Afonso Dalboquerque. Vol. 2. *Iſſued for* 1875.

56—The Voyages of Sir James Lancaster.

With Abstracts of Journal of Voyages preserved in the India Office, and the Voyage of Captain John Knight to seek the N.W. Passage. Edited by CLEMENTS R. MARKHAM, C.B., F.R.S. *Iſſued for* 1877.

57—Second Edition of the Observations of Sir Richard Hawkins, Kt.,
In his Voyage into the South Sea in 1593, with the Voyages of his grandfather William, his father Sir John, and his cousin William Hawkins. Edited by CLEMENTS R. MARKHAM, C.B., F.R.S. *Issued for* 1877.

OTHER WORKS UNDERTAKEN BY EDITORS.

Rosmital's Embassy to England, Spain, etc., in 1466. Edited by R. C. GRAVES, Esq.

The Journal of the Pilot Gallego, and other Documents relating to the Voyages of Mendaña. Translated and edited by W. A. TYSSEN AMHERST, Esq.

The Natural History of the Western Indies, by Father Joachim Acosta. Edited by CLEMENTS R. MARKHAM, C.B., F.R.S.

Father Francisco Alvarez. Narrative of the Portuguese Embassy to Abyssinia. 1520. Translated and Edited by Lord STANLEY of Alderley.

The Voyages of John Davis, and his Works on Navigation. Edited by Captain A. H. MARKHAM, R.N.

A Manuscript History of Bermuda, in the British Museum (*Sloane*, 750). Edited by Lieut.-General SIR J. HENRY LEFROY, K.C.M.G., C.B.

WORKS SUGGESTED TO THE COUNCIL FOR PUBLICATION.

Inedited Letters, etc., of Sir Thomas Roe during his Embassy to India.

John Huigen van Linschoten. Discourse of a Voyage unto the East Indies; to be reprinted from the English translation of 1598.

The Topographia Christiana of Cosmas Indicopleustes.

Bernhard de Breydenbach, 1483-84, A.D. Travels in the Holy Land.

Felix Fabri, 1483. Wanderings in the Holy Land, Egypt, etc.

El Edrisi's Geography.

Voyage made by Captain Jaques Cartier in 1535 and 1536 to the isles of Canada, Hochlega, and Saguenay.

Ca da Mosto. Voyages along the Western Coast of Africa in 1454: translated from the Italian text of 1507.

Leo Africanus.

J. dos Santos. The History of Eastern Ethiopia. 1607.

Joam de Castro. Account of a Voyage made by the Portuguese in 1541, from the city of Goa to Suez.

John and Sebastian Cabot. Their Voyages to America.

Willoughby and Chancellor. Their Voyages to the North-east, with the Voyages of Burroughs, Pett, and Jackman; and the Embassy of Sir Dudley Digges to Russia.

Icelandic Sagas narrating the Discovery of America.

The Voyages of the Earl of Cumberland, from the Records prepared by order of the Countess of Pembroke.

La Argentina. An account of the Discovery of the Provinces of Rio de la Plata from 1512 to the time of Domingo Martinez de Irala; by Ruiz Diaz de Guzman.

The Four Epistles of A. G. Busbequius, concerning his Embassy into Turkey, done into English 1694.

LAWS OF THE HAKLUYT SOCIETY.

I. The object of this Society shall be to print, for distribution among its members, rare and valuable Voyages, Travels, Naval Expeditions, and other geographical records, from an early period to the beginning of the eighteenth century.

II. The Annual Subscription shall be One Guinea, payable in advance on the 1st January.

III. Each member of the Society, having paid his Subscription, shall be entitled to a copy of every work produced by the Society, and to vote at the general meetings within the period subscribed for; and if he do not signify, before the close of the year, his wish to resign, he shall be considered as a member for the succeeding year.

IV. The management of the Society's affairs shall be vested in a Council consisting of twenty-one members, viz., a President, two Vice-Presidents, a Secretary, and seventeen ordinary members, to be elected annually; but vacancies occurring between the general meetings shall be filled up by the Council.

V. A General Meeting of the Subscribers shall be held annually. The Secretary's Report on the condition and proceedings of the Society shall be then read, and the Meeting shall proceed to elect the Council for the ensuing year.

VI. At each Annual Election, six of the old Council shall retire, of whom three shall be eligible for re-election.

VII. The Council shall meet when necessary, for the dispatch of business, three forming a quorum, including the Secretary, and the Chairman having a casting vote.

VIII. Gentlemen preparing and editing works for the Society, shall receive twenty-five copies of such works respectively, and an additional twenty-five copies if the work is also translated.

RULES FOR THE DELIVERY OF THE SOCIETY'S VOLUMES.

I. The Society's productions will be delivered without any charge, within three miles of the General Post Office.

II. They will be forwarded to any place beyond that limit, the Society paying the cost of booking, but not of carriage; nor will it be answerable in this case for any loss or damage.

III. They will be delivered by the Society's agent, Mr. Thos. Richards, 37, Great Queen Street, Lincoln's Inn Fields, to persons having written authority of subscribers to receive them.

IV. They will be sent to the Society's correspondents or agents in the principal towns throughout the kingdom; and care shall be taken that the charge for carriage be as moderate as possible.

LIST OF MEMBERS

OF THE

Hakluyt Society.

Admiralty (The) 2 *copies.*
Advocates' Library, Edinburgh.
Allen, C. F. R., Esq.
Allen, Mr. E. G., Henrietta-street, Covent Garden.
All Souls College, Oxford.
American Geographical Society.
Amherst, W. A. Tyssen, Esq., Didlington Hall, Brandon.
Antiquaries, the Society of.
Army and Navy Club, 36, Pall Mall.
Asay, E. G., Esq., Chicago, U.S.
Athenæum Club, Pall Mall.
Badger, Rev. Dr. G. Percy, D.C.L., F.R.G.S., 21, Leamington-road Villas, W.
Bain, James, Esq., 1, Haymarket.
Bank of England Library and Literary Association.
Barrow, J., Esq., F.R.S., F.S.A., 17, Hanover-terrace, Regent's Park.
Berlin, the Royal Library of.
Bethell, W., Esq., Rise, Hull.
Bethune, Admiral C. R. Drinkwater, C.B., of Balfour, 19, Cromwell-road.
Bibliothèque du Depôt de la Marine.
Birch, W. de G., Esq., British Museum.
Birmingham Library (The).
Birmingham Central Free Library.
Bombay Asiatic Society.
Boston Athenæum Library.
Bowdoin College, Brunswick, Maine, U.S.
Boston Public Library.
Boyveau, Madame, Paris.
Bremen Museum.
Brevoort, J. C., Esq., New York.
Brine, Captain Lindesay, R.N., 25, Montagu-street, W.
British Museum *(copies presented).*
Brooklyn Library, Brooklyn, U.S.
Brown, J. A., Esq., 3, Newcastle-place, Clerkenwell.
Brown, Mrs. J. C., Providence, U.S.
Brown, General J. Marshall, Portland, U.S.
Brown, W. H., Esq., Chester.
Bunbury, E. H., Esq., 35, St. James's-street.
Burns, J. H., Esq., Kilmahew, Dumbartonshire.
Burton, Captain Richard F., H.M. Consul, Trieste.
Caley, A. J , Esq., The Crescent, Norwich.
Cambridge University Library.
Canada, The Parliament Library.
Canada (Upper) Department of Public Instruction for.
Cannon, Charles, Esq., British Museum.
Carlton Club, Pall Mall.
Chicago Public Library.
Christiania University Library.
Christie, Jonathan Henry, Esq., 9, Stanhope-street, Hyde-park-gardens.
Cincinnati Public Library.
Clark, J. W., Esq., Scroope House, Cambridge.
Colgan, N., Esq., Dublin.
Collinson, Admiral Sir Richard, K.C.B., The Haven, Ealing.

Colomb, Captain, R.N., Harrow.
Colonial Office (The), Downing-street.
Congress, Library of, United States.
Coomes, M., Esq., 141, Regent-street.
Cooper, Lieut.-Col. E. H., 42, Portman-square, W.
Copenhagen Royal Library.
Cordeiro, Professor Luciano, Lisbon.
Cotton, R. W., Esq., Woodleigh, Forde Park, Newton Abbot.
Crawshay, George, Esq., Haughton Castle, Hexham.
Cresswell, Frank J., Esq., Bank House, King's Lynn.
Cruttenden, Captain C. J., 16, Talbot-road, Bayswater.
Danish Naval Library.
Deane, Charles, Esq., Boston, U.S.
De Clifford, Lord, 3, Carlton House-terrace.
Derby, The Earl of, 25, St. James's-square.
Dismorr, James Stewart, Esq., 42, Windmill-street, Gravesend.
Donald, C. D., Esq., jun., 196, Bath-street, Glasgow.
Drummond, A. S., Esq.
Ducie, Earl of, 16, Portman-square, W.
Dundas, Lieutenant Colin M., R.N., 2, Belgrave-crescent, Edinburgh.
Dunedin Athenæum, per W. G. Parsons, Esq.
Duprat, the Viscount, Consul-General of Portugal
EDINBURGH, Captain H.R.H. the Duke of, R.N., K.G.
Elias, N., Esq.
Elliot, Sir Walter, K.C.S.I., Wolflee, Hawick, N.B.
Ellis, Sir Barrow, K.C.S.I, India Office, S.W.
Ely, Miss, Philadelphia.
Forbes, Captain C. J. F. Smith, Deputy Commissioner, Shwegyeen, British Burmah.
Foreign Office (The).
Franks, Augustus W., Esq., F.R.S., F.S.A., 103, Victoria Street, S.W.
French Geographical Society.
Frere, W. E., Esq., C.M.G., Bitton Rectory, Bristol.
Frere, The Right Hon. Sir H. Bartle, Bart., G.C.B., G.C.S.I., Cape Town.
Galignani, Messrs, Paris.
Glasgow College.
Goodison, Rev. John, U.S.A.
Grey, Charles, Esq., India Office, S.W.
Grosvenor Library, Buffalo, U.S.A.
Göttingen University Library.
Hailstone, Edward, Esq., Walton Hall, Wakefield.
Hankey, Captain F. B., R.N., Oaklands, Cranleigh, Guildford.
Harcourt, Egerton Vernon, Esq., Whitwell Hall, York.
Harker, Turner James, Esq., Edenbridge, Kent.
Harper, E. A., Esq., Rio de Janeiro.
Harvard College, Cambridge, Massachusetts.
Hatchard & Co., Messrs., 187, Piccadilly.
Hellwald, Frederick de, Office of the *Ausland*, Augsburg.
Harvey, F. A. Dudley, Esq, Chesterford, Saffron Walden.
Hippisley, A., Esq., Shanghai.
Hodges, J., Esq.
Horner, J. F. Fortescue, Esq., Mells Park, Somersetshire.
Horrick, Mrs. Perry, Beau Manor Park, Loughborough.
Hoskins, Commodore A. H., R.N.
Howard, Hon. Charles, M.P.
Hull Subscription Library.
Hutcheson, David, Esq.
Imperial Library, Paris.
India Office (20 *copies*).
Jenner, Thomas, Esq., Brixton.
Jones, Joseph, Esq., Abberley Hall, Stourport.

Jones, J Winter, Esq , F S.A., British Museum.
Kensington, Science and Art Department.
King's Inns Library, Dublin.
Krämer, Messrs., Rotterdam.
Lefroy, Lieut.-General Sir J. Henry, C.B., K.C.M G., 82, Queen's-gate, S.W.
Lenox, James, Esq., New York.
Liverpool Free Public Library.
London Institution, Finsbury-circus.
London Library, 12, St. James's-square.
Luyster, A. L., Esq., 10, Silver Street, W.C.
Lynch, Thomas Kerr, Esq., 31, Cleveland-square, W.
M'Calmont, Robert, Esq., 87, Eaton-square.
Mackenzie, John W., Esq., Royal Circus, Edinburgh.
Mackern, George, Esq , Buenos Ayres.
Macmillan, A., Esq., 16, Bedford-street.
Macmillan & Co., Cambridge.
Major, R H., Esq., F S.A.. British Museum.
Malcolm, W. Elphinstone, Esq., Burnfoot, Langholm, Carlisle.
Manchester Public Free Libraries.
Mantell, Walter, Esq., New Zealand.
Markham, Colonel, Melton Mowbray.
Markham, Clements R , C.B., F.R S , 21, Eccleston-square, S.W.
Markham, Captain Albert H., R.N , F.R.G S., 21, Eccleston-square, S.W.
Massachusetts Historical Society, Boston.
Massachusetts State Library, Boston.
Massie, Admiral T. L., R.N., Chester.
Mayne, Captain, R.N., C.B
Melbourne, Public Library of.
Merewether, Colonel Sir William L., C.B., K.C.S.I., India Office.
Mitchell Library, Glasgow.
Moresby, M. F., Esq., R.N., Exmouth.
Morgan, E. Delmar, Esq., 15, Rowland-gardens, South Kensington.
Morrow, Robert, Esq., Halifax, Nova Scotia.
Munich Royal Library.
Murchison, Kenneth, Esq., Ashurst Lodge, East Grinstead.
Murphy, H. C., Esq., Brooklyn, U.S
Murray, John, Esq., F.R.G.S , Albemarle-street.
Nattali & Bond, Messrs., New Bond Street, W.
Newcastle-upon-Tyne Literary and Scientific Institute.
New Zealand General Assembly Library.
Nicholl, John Cole, Esq , Merthyr Mawr, Bridgend, S. Wales.
Nicholson, Sir Charles, Bart , D C.L., 26, Devonshire-place, W.
Northbrook; The Earl of, G.C.S.I., Stratton, Micheldever Station.
Nutt, Mr. D., Strand.
Ommanney, Admiral Sir Erasmus, C B., F.R.S., The Towers, Yarmouth, Isle of Wight.
Ontario, Education Department.
Oriental Club, Hanover-square.
Ouvry. F., Esq , F.S A , 66, Lincoln's Inn Fields.
Paine, W Dunkley, Esq., Cockshutt Hill, Reigate.
Parker, Messrs., Strand.
Peabody Institute, Baltimore, U.S.
Pearson, Rev J. B., Emanuel College, Cambridge.
Pearson, John F., Esq., Buenos Ayres.
Peckover, Alexander, Esq., Harecroft House, Wisbech.
Pennsylvania, Historical Society of, Philadelphia, U S.
Phillimore, Charles B., Esq., F.R.G.S., Hurley Manor House, Great Marlow.
Plowden, W. H. Chicheley, Esq., F.R S., Ewhurst Park, Basingstoke.
Portico Library, Manchester.
Portland, His Grace the Duke of.
Powis, Earl of, 45, Berkeley-square.

Quebec Literary and Historical Society.
Ransom, Edwin, Esq., Kempstone, Bedfordshire.
Rawlinson, Major-General Sir H., K.C.B , 21, Charles-street, Berkeley-square.
Reed, F. J., Esq., Hassness, Cockermouth.
Reform Club.
Richards, Commodore, H.M.S. *Boadicea*, Cape of Good Hope.
Rigge, G. W., Esq., Washington, U.S.
Roberts, Jos., Esq., 12, Bond-street, Leeds.
Robson, J. R., Esq., Worcester Lodge, New-road, Shepherd's Bush.
Royal Geographical Society, 1, Savile Row, W. *(copies presented)*.
Rushout, The Hon Miss, Burford House, Tenby.
Russell, Lord Arthur, M.P., 4, Audley-square, W.
Ryder, Admiral Alfred, R.N., 5, Victoria-street, Westminster.
Rye, W. B., Esq , British Museum.
San Francisco, Mercantile Library at.
Shanghai Library.
Silver, S. W., Esq., 66, Cornhill.
Simpkin, Marshall, & Co., Messrs., Stationers' Hall Court.
Somers, Earl, 33, Princes-gate, Hyde Park.
Sotheran, Messrs. H. & Co., Strand.
South African Public Library.
South Australian Legislative Library.
Spottiswoode, William, Esq., F.R.S., 50, Grosvenor-place.
Stanley, Lord, of Alderley, Alderley Park, Congleton.
St. Andrew's University.
Stevens, Mr. B. F., 4, Trafalgar-square.
Stibbs, Edward, Esq., 10, Monmouth-road, Westbourne-grove.
Stockholm, Royal Library of.
Strasburg University Library.
Stuart, Alexander, Esq., New York.
Stuart, M. J. Shaw, Esq , Calcutta.
Stuart, R. L., Esq., New York.
Stubbs, Captain Edward, R.N., Liverpool.
Suckling, Samuel, Esq.
Thomas, Edward, Esq., F.R.S., Athenæum Club.
Thomas, R. Gerard de Visme̱s, Esq., 4, Albert Street, Victoria Square, S.W.
Timmins, J., Esq., Elvetham Lodge, Birmingham.
Tolbort, T. W. H., Esq., 19, Westbourne Park-road.
Tolstoy, George, Esq., St. Petersburg.
Toronto University.
Travellers' Club, 106, Pall Mall.
Trinity College, Cambridge.
Trinity Corporation, Tower-hill.
Trübner, Herr Karl.
Trübner, Nicholas, Esq , Ludgate Hill.
Union Society, Oxford.
United Service Institution, Scotland Yard.
Vefyk, His Excellency Ahmed Effendi, Constantinople.
Vienna Imperial Library.
Watkinson Library, Hartford, Connecticut, U.S.
Webb, Captain John Sydney, The Trinity House.
Webb, William Frederick, Esq., Newstead Abbey.
Wellington, The Duke of, K.G., Apsley House, Piccadilly.
Wigan Public Library.
Williams, T., Esq., 8, Gray's Inn-square.
Wilson, Edward S., Esq., 6, Whitefriar-gate, Hull.
Wilson, Major-General J., 28, Market Place, Salisbury.
Worcester, Massachusetts, Free Library.
Yule, Colonel H., C.B.

WORKS ISSUED BY

The Hakluyt Society.

THE HAWKINS' VOYAGES.

ETC.

No. LVII.

SIR JOHN HAWKINS KT.

FROM A BASSO RELIEVO IVORY BUST IN POSSESSION OF THE REVD BRADFORD DEAN HAWKINS.

John Hawkyns

(AUTOGRAPH FROM A FACSIMILE IN THE ARCHÆOLOGIA, Vol. XXXIII.)

THE

HAWKINS' VOYAGES

DURING

THE REIGNS

OF

HENRY VIII, QUEEN ELIZABETH,

AND JAMES I.

Edited, with an Introduction,

BY

CLEMENTS R. MARKHAM, C.B., F.R.S.

LONDON:

PRINTED FOR THE HAKLUYT SOCIETY.

MDCCCLXXVIII.

T. RICHARDS, PRINTER, 37, GREAT QUEEN STREET.

COUNCIL

OF

THE HAKLUYT SOCIETY.

CONTENTS.

CONTENTS.

ERRATUM.

At page 13 *(note)*, *for* "11,430", *read* "12,370".

INTRODUCTION.

THE *Observations of Sir Richard Hawkins in his Voyage into the South Sea* was the first volume issued by the Hakluyt Society, in 1847. It was edited by Admiral C. R. Drinkwater Bethune, C.B.; and most of his valuable foot-notes in the first edition have been retained, especially those explaining old sea terms and Spanish phrases. Some of the Admiral's notes have been omitted as having become obsolete, or from other considerations. As the first edition is now out of print, it has become necessary to reproduce it. The Council decided that the present volume should be made more complete, by including the narratives of the voyages of Sir Richard's grandfather William, of his father Sir John, and of his cousin William Hawkins. It is, therefore, intended to be a monograph of the naval enterprises of the great Elizabethan navigators of the name of Hawkins.

The first of that name made three voyages to Brazil in the time of Henry VIII, and was one of our earliest naval pioneers. The second was closely connected with the history of our navy, both as a gallant commander at sea and as an able administrator on shore, during upwards of thirty eventful years. The third was a worthy emulator of his father's fame; while the fourth is among the first founders of the success of the East India Company.

The cradle of the naval Hawkinses was certainly in Devonshire,[1] the county of Drake and Oxenham, of Grenville and Davis, of Raleigh and Gilbert, and of so many other Elizabethan naval worthies. In the reign of Henry VII, John Hawkins and his wife Joan, daughter of William Amydas of Launceston, were living at Tavistock, and their son William Hawkins is the first of the three generations of famous seamen.[2]

We owe our slight knowledge of the first WILLIAM HAWKINS to the research of Hakluyt. He tells us that old Mr. William Hawkins of Plymouth was a man of wisdom, valour, experience, and skill in sea causes, and that he was much esteemed and beloved by King Henry VIII. He was one of the principal sea captains in the west of England in his time, and made three adventurous voyages to the coast of Brazil, an account

[1] The name of Hawkins, it has been suggested, may be derived from Hawking, in the hundred of Folkestone. There was an Osbert de Hawking in the reign of Henry II, from whom descended Andrew Hawkins of Nash Court, near Faversham, in the time of Edward III, according to one statement. Another account derives Andrew Hawkins from Holderness, and marries him to Joan de Nash, an heiress. A family of Hawkins of Nash Court, flourished there until the end of the last century. (See *Halsted's Kent*, iii, p. 4.)

But Hawkins is a common name, and it is more probably derived from the Dutch Huygen; in common with Hodge, Hodgson, Hodgkinson, Hoskins, Huggins, Hoggins, Hewson, and the like.

[2] The Hawkins ancestry is given by Prince in his *Worthies of Devon*, p. 472, who had it from William Harvey, Clarencieux; entry of 1565, when the arms were granted to John Hawkins.

of two of which, taken from Hakluyt, will be found at pages 3 and 4 of the present volume. William Hawkins married Joan, daughter of William Trelawney, and had two sons, John and William, who entered upon the sea service with great advantages, owing to the wealth and experience of their father.

The date of the birth of JOHN HAWKINS is not certain, but the inscription on his monument, formerly in the church of St. Dunstan's-in-the-East, gives his age at the time of his death in 1595, as "six times ten and three". If this is correct, he was born in 1532.[1] Hakluyt tells us that he made divers voyages to the Canary Islands in his youth, where he obtained much information respecting the trade with the West Indies. He heard, among other things, that there was a great demand for negroes at St. Domingo, and that they could easily be obtained from the coast of Guinea. He resolved to make trial of this trade, and, having communicated his plan to several influential friends in London, he received liberal support. Among those who were adventurers for this voyage, was Mr. Benjamin Gonson, of Sebright Hall, near Chelmsford, and Treasurer of the Navy, who, probably before the ship sailed, became the father-in-law of the gallant young commander of the expedition.

John Hawkins, when he undertook the voyage in 1562, was in about his thirtieth year; and he was then married to Katharine Gonson,[2] daughter of

[1] 1520 is the date usually given, but on no authority.

[2] William Gonson was Treasurer of the Navy in the reigns of Henry VIII, Edward VI, and Mary. He bought Sebright Hall,

the Treasurer of the Navy, by whom he had a son Richard.

The first expedition of John Hawkins, consisting of three good ships, was very successful, though a cargo which he sent to Cadiz in charge of his second in command, Captain Hampton, was confiscated. An order was also sent to the Indies, by the Spanish Government, that no English vessel was to be allowed to trade there in future. The account of this voyage, taken from Hakluyt, will be found from pages 5 to 7 of the present volume. Hawkins returned in September 1563.

No blame attaches to the conduct of John Hawkins in undertaking a venture which all the world, in those days, looked upon as legitimate and even as beneficial. It was in 1517 that Charles V issued royal licences for the importation of negroes into the West Indies, and in 1551 a licence for importing 17,000 negroes was offered for sale. The measure was adopted from

in the parish of Great Badow, near Chelmsford. His son Benjamin Gonson, of Sebright Hall, was also Treasurer of the Navy from 1553 to 1573, when he was succeeded by his son-in-law, John Hawkins. He died on November 21st, 1577, leaving a son, Benjamin, born in 1551, and a daughter, Katharine, the first wife of Sir John Hawkins. This second Benjamin Gonson left only four daughters, co-heiresses. One of them, Anne, married Giles Fleming. Another, Thomasine, was the wife of Christopher Browne of Sayes Court (son of Sir Richard Browne, Clerk of the Green Cloth to Queen Elizabeth), who died, aged 70, in 1645. Their son, Sir Richard Browne of Sayes Court (Deptford), died in 1683, aged 78, leaving an only daughter, Mary, the wife of John Evelyn, F.R.S., the author of *Sylva*. Evelyn lived at Sayes Court from 1652 till 1686.

philanthropic motives, and was intended to preserve the Indians. It was looked upon as prudent and humane, even if it involved some suffering on the part of a far inferior race. The English were particularly eager to enter upon the slave trade, and by the treaty of Utrecht in 1713 England at length obtained the *asiento*, giving her the exclusive right to carry on the slave trade between Africa and the Spanish Indies for thirty years. So strong was the party in favour of this trade in England, that the contest for its abolition was continued for forty-eight years, from 1759 to 1807. It is not, therefore, John Hawkins alone who can justly be blamed for the slave trade, but the whole English people during 250 years, who must all divide the blame with him.

John Hawkins sailed on his second voyage in 1564, in the good ship *Jesus of Lubeck*, of 700 tons, returning in the autumn of the following year. He was accompanied by several gentlemen adventurers, and one of them, named John Sparke, wrote the narrative published by Hakluyt. It will be found from pages 8 to 64 of the present volume, and is followed by an account of the succour given by Hawkins to a distressed French colony in Florida, which Hakluyt translated from the French work of M. Laudonnière, printed in Paris in 1586.[1] Mr. Sparke is somewhat diffuse,

[1] See pages 65 to 69. When Hakluyt was Chaplain to the English Embassy in Paris, he discovered a manuscript account of Florida, and published it at his own expense in 1586. It is dedicated to Sir Walter Raleigh. The attention this book excited in France encouraged Hakluyt to translate it, and the English ver-

but he gives many interesting details respecting the various places, in Africa and the West Indies, that were touched at, including a full account of Florida.

The third voyage was undertaken in 1567, and had a most disastrous termination. It was on this occasion that Hawkins and Francis Drake first served together. Drake is called the kinsman of Hawkins by his biographers, and he certainly appears to have been born in a cottage on the banks of the Tavy, while the Hawkinses came originally from Tavistock, so that the two families were near neighbours. Francis was about ten years younger than Hawkins. His father was persecuted under the Six Articles Act, and fled into Kent, where he became the vicar of Upnor, and the son served his apprenticeship in the Medway, and in short voyages to Zeeland. But young Francis, as soon as he had the means, returned to his native county, and had made at least one voyage (with Captain Lovell in 1565-66) to the West Indies before he joined the expedition of Hawkins. The latter commanded his old ship, the *Jesus of Lubeck*, while Drake was in a little

sion was published in London in 1587. The title is: "A notable historie containing foure voyages made by certayne French captaines into Florida, wherein the great riches and fruitefulnes of the countrey, with the manners of the people, hitherto concealed, are brought to light; written, all saving the last, by Monsieur Laudonnière, who remained there himself, as the French King's Lieutenant, a yere and a quarter; newly translated out of the French into English by R. H." (London, 1587, 4to.)

The portion relating to Hawkins was inserted by Hakluyt in his *Principal Navigations*, following Hawkins's second voyage. It is this portion which is reprinted in the present volume.

vessel called the *Judith* (of 50 tons). The sad story of this voyage, as given in Hakluyt, was written by John Hawkins himself, and will be found from pages 70 to 81 of the present volume. After the treacherous attack of the Spaniards at San Juan de Ulloa, two vessels only escaped, the *Minion*, with Hawkins on board, and the *Judith*;[1] but there was not sufficient food for so large a number of men crowded into two small vessels, and their case seemed almost hopeless. At length half the number, a hundred out of two hundred, volunteered to land on the coast of Mexico, so as to save the rest. They were put on shore, and their more fortunate comrades, after suffering great hardships, arrived in England on January 25th, 1568.[2]

It is remarkable that Hawkins never mentions Drake's name throughout his narrative. His letter to Mr. Secretary Cecil,[3] describing his misfortunes, is dated on the day of his landing in Mounts Bay.

The fate of the unfortunate men who were put on shore in Mexico was most cruel. They were sent to the capital, and were at first treated with humanity. But in 1571 a tribunal of the Inquisition was established in Mexico, the English castaways were seized and shockingly maltreated, and several tortured and most inhumanly mutilated. Some were burnt, and a few were sent to Spain, and left to die of hunger in

[1] See page 78.

[2] The introduction of tobacco into England after this voyage is attributed to Hawkins by Stow, and also by John Taylor, the Water Poet, in his *Prosaical Postscript* to the *Old old, very old man, etc.* (4to., 1635).

[3] Given by Barrow, in his *Life of Sir Francis Drake*, p. 10.

the Archbishop of Seville's dungeons. Three escaped, and the tale of their wrongs excited the utmost indignation throughout England. The narratives of these survivors, David Ingram, Job Hartop, and Miles Philips, are given by Hakluyt;[1] and no one who peruses them can be surprised at the hatred of the English against the Spaniards in those days. John Hawkins was extremely anxious about the fate of his unhappy men, and when tidings of their treatment began to reach England he sought every means to be revenged upon the Spanish nation. He intended to go out in search of his men, but was prevented. He then determined to try what cunning would do, apparently deeming intrigue and deceit to be justifiable against such a foe.

But there never was a more absurd calumny than that promulgated by Dr. Lingard and others, to the effect that Hawkins consented to betray his country for a bribe from Spain. Lingard[2] refers us to an agreement made at Madrid on August 10th, 1571, between the Duke of Feria,[3] on the part of Philip II, and George Fitzwilliam on the part of John Hawkins, by

[1] *Principal Navigations*, pp. 557 to 560. Philips reached England in 1582, and Hartop not until 1590.

[2] *History of England*, v, p. 481 (*n*).

[3] Gomez Suarez de Figueroa y Cordova, fifteenth Conde de Feria, was created Duke of Feria in 1567. He was envoy in England when Queen Mary died, and married her maid of honour, Jane, daughter of Sir William Dormer, by Mary, sister of Sir Henry, and aunt of Sir Philip Sydney. He died at the Escurial, on Friday, September 7, 1571, less than a month after the signature of the above imaginary document. His son, born in 1559, succeeded as second Duke.

which the latter was to transfer his services to Spain, bringing with him sixteen of the Queen's ships fully equipped with 420 guns, in consideration of an amnesty for past offences, and monthly pay of 16,987 ducats. This pretended agreement may be found in the Spanish Archives. The calumny lies in Dr. Lingard's conclusion from it, and in his additional statements which are as follows. "The secret was carefully kept, but did not elude suspicion. Hawkins was summoned, and examined by order of the Council. Their lordships were, or pretended to be, satisfied, and he was engaged in the Queen's service." Lingard adds that Hawkins tendered hostages to Spain for his fidelity. All these supplementary statements are untrue. The simple fact was that Hawkins was trying to deceive and entrap the Spaniards, with the full knowledge and approval of the English Government from the first. This is proved beyond doubt by Cecil's correspondence. It was not very clean work and it ended in failure, but it is false that Hawkins was ever untrue to his country. A more loyal and devoted subject never lived. His whole life was one of zealous devotion to the service of his Queen.[1] His Spanish intrigue was

[1] Lingard quotes, as his authority for the above calumny, *Gonzalez*, 116, *Memorias*, vii, 351, 360, 364, 367, 368, a formidable array!

These references are calculated to confuse the reader, sometimes being given as "*Memorias*", then as "*Gonzalez*", in another place "*From the documents at Simancas*". On the return of Ferdinand VII, in 1815, the archives were entrusted to Don Tomas Gonzalez, who restored them to order at Simancas. In the seventh volume of the *Memorias de la Real Academia de la Historia* (4to., Madrid,

undertaken with the object of rescuing his unfortunate men by a resort to guile, as he could not do so by force. Their miserable condition must have haunted him, and

1832) was published a contribution entitled, "Apuntamientos para la historia del Rey Don Felipe Segundo de España por lo tocante a sus relaciones con la Reina Isabel de Inglaterra desde el año 1558 hasta el de 1576, por Tomas Gonzalez, Canonigo de Placencia." There is an English version: "Documents from Simancas relating to the reign of Elizabeth (1558-1568), translated from the Spanish of Don Tomas Gonzalez, and edited by G. Spencer Hall, F.S.A., Librarian to the Athenæum (1865)."

It is to the *Apuntamientos* of Gonzalez that Lingard alone refers. As for his reference at p. 351 there is no mention of Hawkins there. At p. 357 there is a statement that "Achins" had solicited to be allowed to enter Philip's service, offering to make great discoveries; that he sent Fitzwilliam to the King to offer to re-establish the Catholic religion in England, and that Philip received the proposals well, but required details as to the mode and form of executing them. At p. 360 it is stated that Fitzwilliam, having reported this reply, returned to Spain with assurances of promptitude from "Achins" and other disaffected persons. At p. 364 is the detailed agreement between the Duke of Feria and Fitzwilliam on the part of "Achins". At p. 367 there is nothing about Hawkins. At p. 368 an interview is reported between Don Gueran de Espés, the Spanish Ambassador in England, and John Hawkins.

The whole of Lingard's portentous mare's nest, built out of these Spanish references, is exploded by Cecil's correspondence, which proves that Hawkins was fooling the Spaniards, with the full knowledge and approval of the English Government. The aim of Hawkins was to obtain the release of the prisoners. Cecil's object was to unravel Spanish plots.

It was with Cecil's secret permission that Hawkins sent Fitzwilliam to Spain, and that he himself had an interview with Don Gueran de Espés, the Spanish Ambassador. See Froude's *History of England*, x, cap. xxi, pp. 259-270. The letters of Hawkins to Lord Burleigh at p. 264 (*n.*) and p. 269, finally dispose of Lingard's accusation.

he felt that any means that offered a chance of liberating them was justifiable.

After his three voyages, John Hawkins justly stood high with the Government, as a resolute and experienced sea captain. In 1565 a coat of arms was granted to him, with an augmentation in August 1571.[1]

ARMS.—*Sable*, on a point wavy a lion passant *or*. In chief 3 bezants. Augmentation: on a canton *or* an escallop between two palmer's staves *sable*.

CREST.—Upon a wreath *argent* and *azure* a demi-Moor proper bound and captive, with amulets on his arms and ears *or*.

In 1573 Hawkins succeeded his father-in-law as Treasurer of the Navy, and commenced a useful, but very anxious and laborious administrative career on shore. But he still occasionally served afloat. In 1570

[1] The grant in 1565 was by William Harvey, Clarencieux. The augmentation was granted by Robert Cook, Clarencieux, in 1571.

his son tells us that he was Admiral of the fleet of Queen's ships then riding in Catwater, and that he fired upon a Spanish ship for not lowering her topsails.[1] In a letter dated February 23rd, 1573, from Charles IX to La Motte Fénélon, a complaint is made against "Haquin" (Hawkins) for being joined with certain French rebels in the neighbourhood of the Isle of Wight, to the number of twelve or thirteen ships, with which they carried munitions and provisions from England to Rochelle.[2]

The civil employments of John Hawkins must, however, have absorbed most of his time. Besides the Treasurership of the Navy, he was also Treasurer of the Queen's Majesty's Marine Causes, and in the same year he succeeded Mr. Holstock as Comptroller of the Navy. He was a keen reformer of dockyard abuses, and Sir William Monson says that he introduced more useful inventions and better regulations into the navy than any of his predecessors. Stow tells us that Hawkins was the first that invented the cunning stratagem of sail nettings for ships in fighting, and he also devised chain pumps for ships.

In 1581 he had a severe illness,[3] but he had recovered

[1] See p. 118.

[2] But this may refer to his brother, William Hawkins.

[3] On October 30, 1581, he wrote to T. Smythe that he would be glad to join in Sir Francis Drake's enterprise, but was hardly able to overcome the debt he owes Her Majesty, and keep his credit. His sickness, too, continually abides with him, and every second day he has a fit. More like to provide for his grave than to encumber himself with worldly matters. *E. I. Colonial*, 1513-1616, p. 68.

in 1583, when we find him busily engaged making investigations for the reduction of the expenses of the navy, and encountering much opposition. For fifteen months the officers at Chatham took "hardness and courage to oppose themselves against him", yet he there made a saving of over £3,200, while adding to the efficiency of the fleet. His correspondence with Sir Julius Cæsar, the Judge of the Admiralty, shows that he paid close attention to all branches of naval expenditure, detecting and putting a stop to many abuses. This good service naturally made him enemies. Mr. Borowe, who was ousted, "made a book against him", and in 1583 there were articles drawn up "against the injuste mind and deceitful dealings of John Hawkins".[1] Among those whom he found out conniving at abuses were Sir William Winter and the Master Shipwright Baker, who of course became his bitter enemies, and he had a controversy with Mr. Peter Pett, the shipwright, touching his accounts. Winter wrote—"When he was hurte in the Strande and made his will he was not able to give £500. All that he is now worth hath byn drawne by deceipte from her Majesty." These calumnies received no credit, and Hawkins never lost the confidence of his Government.

In 1584 we find him consulting with Peter Pett as to a project for improving Dover harbour. In December 1585 he submitted books to Lord Burleigh with lists of her Majesty's ships, their tonnage, and estimates for outfit; and he represented the expediency of increasing the seamen's pay. He also sent in a state-

[1] *Lansdowne MSS.*, vol. lii, cap. 43, fol. 109.

ment of the management of the navy from 1568 to 1579, with his scheme for its future government by commissioners.

During all these years of active civil employment John Hawkins lived in a house in the parish of St. Dunstan's-in-the-East, with his office at Deptford. He lost his first wife, the mother of his son, when she was only thirty-two years of age, and married secondly Margaret, daughter of Charles Vaughan, Esq., of Hergest House, Herefordshire, by Elizabeth, daughter of Sir F. Baskerville. This lady was bed-chamber woman to the Queen.

In 1587 the intention of Spain to invade England was manifest, and a Council consisting of Lord Charles Howard, Hawkins, Drake, and Frobisher, got the English fleet in readiness to meet its formidable adversary. Hawkins was appointed Vice-Admiral, hoisting his flag on board the *Victory*; and after the dispersion of the Spanish Armada he received the honour of knighthood. Then came the anxious and troublesome business of paying off the fleet. "I pray God", he wrote to Burleigh, "I may end this account to her Majesty's and your Lordship's liking, and avoyd myne owne undoing, and I trust God will so provyde for me as I shall never meddell with soche intrycatte matters more." In 1590 he got away to sea again, in a fleet commanded by himself and Sir Martin Frobisher, with orders to do all possible mischief on the coast of Spain. But the Plate fleet was warned in time, and remained in the Indies. None of the enemy's ships appeared, and the expedition came back without any results.

Sir John Hawkins, on his return, reminded Elizabeth that "Paul planteth and Apollos watereth, but God giveth the increase." "God's death!" exclaimed the Queen, "this fool went out a soldier, and is come home a divine!"

In the year 1588 Sir John, aided by Drake, instituted a fund for maimed and worn out mariners, which was long known as the "chest at Chatham". This fund was the forerunner of Greenwich Hospital. Thus actively and laboriously employed, on shore and afloat, Sir John Hawkins became grey in the service of his country. Edmund Spenser, when he drew likenesses of the chief sea captains of England, in his "*Colin Clout's come home again*", speaks of old Hawkins as Proteus, "with hoary head and dewy dropping beard". His end was heroic. In 1593 he had, with some difficulty, obtained a commission for his dearly loved son Richard,[1] when he set out on his adventurous voyage to the South Sea in the good ship *Dainty*. Then came the sad news that his boy was a prisoner in the hands of the Spaniards.

There can be no doubt that old Sir John undertook his last fatal voyage with a broken heart, in the faint hope of rescuing his son.

An expedition was decided upon to sail for the West Indies under the command of Sir John Hawkins and

[1] Oct. 1593. "Commission to Richard Hawkins to attempt some enterprise with a ship, bark, and pinnace, against the King of Spain, upon the coasts of the West Indies, Brazil, Africa, America, or the South Seas, reserving to the Crown one-fifth of treasure, jewels, or pearls." *Calendar of State Papers. Domestic.* 1591-94, p. 276.

Sir Francis Drake, in 1595. The Queen furnished five ships, but she drove a hard bargain with her old Treasurer of the Navy. She was to have a third of the booty, and Sir John was to victual the fleet at his own charge. He did his part well, being, as Sir T. Gorges reported from Plymouth to Robert Cecil, "an excellent man in those things, and sees all things done orderly." Nombre de Dios was the destination of the fleet, but Hawkins died at sea, off Puerto Rico, on the 21st of November 1595.[1]

So ended the life of Sir John Hawkins, one of the best of Elizabeth's great sea captains, and the terror of the Spaniards.[2] He was a thorough seaman, and an able and upright administrator; endowed with great courage and unfailing presence of mind; "merciful," says Maynarde, "and apt to forgive, and faithful to his word". Stow, in his *Chronicle*, speaks of him as a very wise, vigilant, and true-hearted man.

On July 9th, 1596, the disbursements of Sir John Hawkins in his last voyage, were delivered by Robert Langford, Deputy Treasurer, in the name of his widow Margeret Hawkins, at £18,661, which was declared to be not more than his third part. His watery grave was far away within the tropics, but a handsome tomb to his memory was erected on the north side of the chancel of St. Dunstan's-in-the-East,[3] which was his place of

[1] Drake also died during this disastrous voyage, on the 28th of January 1596.

[2] They called him "Juan Achines".

[3] Destroyed in the great fire. The present church was built by Sir Christopher Wren; and the tomb has disappeared.

worship during many years. It bore the following inscription—

> "Johannes Hawkins, Eques Auratus, clariss. Reginæ Marinarum causarum Thesaurarius. Qui cum XLIII annos muniis bellicis et longis periculosisque navigationibus, detegendis novis regionibus, ad Patriæ utilitatem, et suam ipsius gloriam, strenuam et egregiam operam navasset, in expeditione, cui Generalis præfuit ad Indiam occidentalem dum in anchoris ad portum S. Joannis in insula Beriquena staret, placide in Domino ad cœlestem patriam emigravit, 12 die Novembris anno salutis 1595. In cujus memoriam ob virtutem et res gestas Domina Margareta Hawkins, Uxor mœstissima, hoc monumentum cum lachrymis posuit."

His widow survived until 1621. Stow tells us[1] that she hung a "fair table" by the tomb, fastened in the wall, with these verses in English:—

> "Dame Margaret,
> A widow well affected,
> This monument
> Of memory erected,
> Deciphering
> Unto the viewer's sight
> The life and death
> Of Sir John Hawkins, *Knight*,
> One fearing God
> And loyal to his Queen,
> True to the State
> By trial ever seen,
> Kind to his wives,
> Both gentlewomen born,
> Whose counterfeits
> With grace this work adorn.

[1] *Survey of London*, vol. i, lib. ii, p. 45 (ed. 1720).

Dame Katharine,
The first, of rare report,
Dame Margaret
The last, of Court consort,
Attendant on
The chamber and the bed
Of England's Queen
Elizabeth, our head
Next unto Christ,
Of whom all princes hold
Their scepters, States,
And diadems of gold.
Free to their friends
On either side his kin
Careful to keep
The credit he was in.
Unto the seamen
Beneficial,
As testifieth
Chatham Hospital.
The poor of Plymouth
And of Deptford town
Have had, now have,
And shall have, many a crown.
Proceeding from
His liberality
By way of great
And gracious legacy,
This parish of
St. Dunstan standing east
(Wherein he dwelt
Full thirty years at least)
Hath of the springs
Of his good will a part
Derived from
The fountain of his heart,
All which bequests,

With many moe unsaid,
Dame Margaret
Hath bountifully paid.
Deep of conceit,
In speaking grave and wise,
Endighting swift
And pregnant to devise,
In conference
Revealing haughty skill
In all affairs ;
Having a worthie's will
On sea and land,
Spending his course and time
By steps of years
As he to age did climb.
God hath his soul,
The sea his body keeps,
Where (for a while)
As Jonas now he sleeps ;
Till He which said
To Lazarus, Come forth,
Awakes this knight,
And gives to him his worth.
In Christian faith
And faithful penitence,
In quickening hope
And constant patience,
He running ran
A faithful pilgrim's race,
God giving him
The guiding of His grace,
Ending his life
With his experience
By deep decree
Of God's high providence.
His years to six times
Ten and three amounting,

The ninth the seventh
Climacterick by counting.
Dame Katharine,
His first religious wife,
Saw years thrice ten
And two of mortal life,
Leaving the world the sixth,
The seventh ascending.
Thus he and she
Alike their compass ending,
Asunder both
By death and flesh alone,
Together both in soul,
Two making one,
Among the saints above,
From troubles free,
Where two in one shall meet
And make up three.
The Christian knight
And his good ladies twain,
Flesh, soul, and spirit
United once again;
Beholding Christ,
Who comfortably saith,
Come, mine elect,
Receive the crown of faith."

There is a basso-relievo ivory bust of Sir John Hawkins[1] in the possession of the Reverend Bradford Denne Hawkins, Rector of Rivenhall, near Witham, in Essex, who informs me that it came to his father by inheritance, from Dr. Denne, Archdeacon of Rochester and Rector of Lambeth in the last century.

I can only hear of one portrait of Sir John Hawkins. It was at Kirtling in Cambridgeshire, the seat of the

[1] See the frontispiece to the present volume.

Lords North, and on the dismantling of the house in 1802 it was sold. In 1824 it came into the hands of a Mr. Bryant, whose brother sold it to Mr. R. S. Hawkins of Oxford in 1866. It is a portrait on panel, kit-cat size, of a man in armour, with small head, dark brown hair and yellowish beard, and the hand resting on a helmet. The face has a strong family resemblance to that of the ivory basso-relievo bust. Above the shoulder of the figure are reeds, a rock, and waves, and the following motto:—"*Undis arundo vires reparat cædensque fovetur funditus at rupes en scopulosa ruit.*" The present owner inclines to the belief that it is a portrait of the son Sir Richard, and not of Sir John Hawkins.

The will of Sir John Hawkins was proved in December 1596.

RICHARD HAWKINS, the only son of Sir John, was brought up to a sea life from a boy, and his father's position and circumstances must have given him special advantages. For his father and uncle, the two brothers John and William, were men of considerable means, at one time owning thirty sail of good ships.[2] Richard was born at about the time of his father's first Guinea voyage in 1562. His mother died when she was only thirty-two, so that the boy became his father's constant companion at an early age, and his reminiscences went back to a childhood spent at Plymouth and Deptford, amongst ships and dockyards. Thus, in his *Observations*,[3] he calls to mind how, he being of

[1] Reference 26 and 50, Drake.

[2] Stow's *Chronicle*, p. 806 (1631).

[3] P. 118.

tender years, there came a large fleet of Spaniards into Plymouth Sound, bound for Flanders to fetch Queen Anne of Austria, last wife of Phillip II.[1] "They entred without vayling their top-sayles or taking in of their flags; which my father Sir John Hawkins (Admiral of a fleet of her Majesties ships then ryding in Cattwater) perceiving, commanded his gunner to shoote at the flagge of the Admirall, that they might thereby see their error; which, notwithstanding, they persevered arrogantly to keepe displayed, whereupon the gunner at the next shot, lact the admiral through and through, whereby the Spaniards tooke in the flags and top-sayles, and so ranne to anchor." In this masterful school was young Richard Hawkins brought up. At the age of twenty, "being but young and more bold than experimented",[2] he made his first long voyage to the West Indies in 1582, with his uncle William Hawkins of Plymouth. During the voyage he displayed boldness and sagacity which showed that he had the makings of a good officer and seaman. On one occasion the captain of one of the vessels named the *Bonner* reported her to be leaky and unseaworthy, and it was arranged that the stores and provisions should be taken out of her, the men divided among the other ships, and the hull sunk or burnt. Richard suspected that the captain of the *Bonner* made the matter worse than it really was. So he volunteered, with as many men as would stand by

[1] This fixes the date 1570. But here is some confusion, for he mentions that Sir John's ship was the *Jesus of Lubeck*, and she was lost in 1567.

[2] P. 212.

him, to take her home, and his uncle consented; but this shamed the captain, who resolved to stand by her. Thus he saved the vessel to the owners, and was commended for his resolution. During the voyage he visited the Margarita pearl fishery.[1]

From his return in 1583 to the equipment of the fleet to withstand the Spanish Armada in 1588, Richard Hawkins was constantly employed on sea service. His father had married again, as already mentioned, to a lady of whom her step-son speaks as "religious and most virtuous and of very good understanding";[2] so that his home relations were probably undisturbed. In 1588 he commanded the *Swallow* in the fleet which opposed the Spanish Armada; and in the end of the same year, with the consent and help of his father, he prepared for a voyage to China and India by way of the straits of Magellan and the South Sea, with the object of discovering and surveying unknown lands, and reporting upon their inhabitants, governments, and on the commodities they yield, and of which they are in want. With this object he caused a ship to be built in the Thames, between 300 and 400 tons, "pleasing to the eye, profitable for stowage, good of sayle, and well-conditioned." His step-mother craved the naming of the ship and called her the *Repentance*. Richard often asked her reason for bestowing upon his ship so uncouth a name, but he could never get any other satisfaction than that "*Repentance* was the safest ship we could sayle in, to purchase the haven of heaven". Queen Elizabeth afterwards passed by, on her way to

[1] See page 314.

[2] See page 90.

Greenwich Palace, and, causing her bargemen to row round the ship, disliked nothing but her name. She christened her anew, and ordered that henceforth she should be called the *Daintie.* Other duties delayed the voyage, and in the meanwhile the *Daintie* was usefully employed in the Queen's service, but in April 1793 all things were in readiness, and the young adventurer prepared to sail on his great enterprise.

Richard Hawkins was now in about his thirtieth year; and he already had a wife and children. He had married a short time previously a lady whose Christian name was Judith, but I have not yet succeeded in ascertaining to what family she belonged.[1] He was already an experienced sea captain, and had seen much service. He was a man of resource, observant and eager to adopt every new improvement or good suggestion. Devoted to his profession, his whole mind was wrapped up in its interests, he paid close attention to every detail, and nothing seemed to escape him. Thus his *Observations* are a perfect storehouse of valuable information of all kinds, and every incident of the voyage leads him off into reminiscences of former experiences, or into statements of facts and observations gathered from others. The *Observations of Sir Richard Hawkins* will be found from pages 89 to 329 of the present volume.

On the 13th of June 1593, Richard Hawkins, having taken his unhappy last leave of his father,

[1] He mentions his wife's father as having assisted him with money, at p. 107.

sailed from Plymouth on board the *Daintie*,[1] accompanied by the *Fancy* pinnace of 60 tons,[2] and a victualler named the *Hawk*. The most noteworthy event during the voyage across the Atlantic was the sighting of land of which Hawkins believed himself to be the first discoverer, and which he named "Hawkins's maiden-land". This was on the 2nd of February 1594, in latitude, according to Hawkins, about 49°·30′ S.[3] Hawkins wrote from memory, and fortunately he is corrected, as regards his latitude, by one of his officers named Ellis,[4] who tells us that the land was in 50° S. and about fifty leagues off the Straits of Magellan. Without doubt they sighted the Falkland Islands, but the group had already been discovered by John Davis, the great Arctic Navigator, in August 1592. Davis reached Berehaven on June 11th, 1593, and Hawkins sailed from Plymouth on June 13th, so that Hawkins was not aware of the previous discovery. Passing through the Strait of Magellan, the *Daintie* ranged up the west coast of South America, encountered a Spanish fleet off Chilca, from which she was separated

[1] His officers were—

Richard Hawkins	(*General*).		
John Ellis.........	(*Captain*).		
Hugh Cornish ...	(*Master*).	See pp.	106, 235, 294.
Henry Couston..	(*Volunteer*).	„	106, 218, 294.
William Blanch...	(*Master's Mate*).	„	200, 299.
Hugh Mairs	(„ „).	„	310.
Thomas Saunders	(*Servant*).	„	xxix, 308.

[2] Her captain, Tharlton, basely deserted Hawkins off the River Plate, and went home. See page 184.

[3] See p. 188.

[4] Purchas, iv, p. 1415.

by a gale of wind, and anchored in the bay of Atacames on June 10th, 1594.

Hawkins was now on the coast of the province of Quito, a little to the north of the equator. Atacames Bay is in 0°·57′·30″ N. To the left is Cape San Francisco, off which Sir Francis Drake captured his rich prize the *Cacafuego* on March 1st, 1579. To the right is the mouth of the great river of Santiago, and the bay of San Mateo.

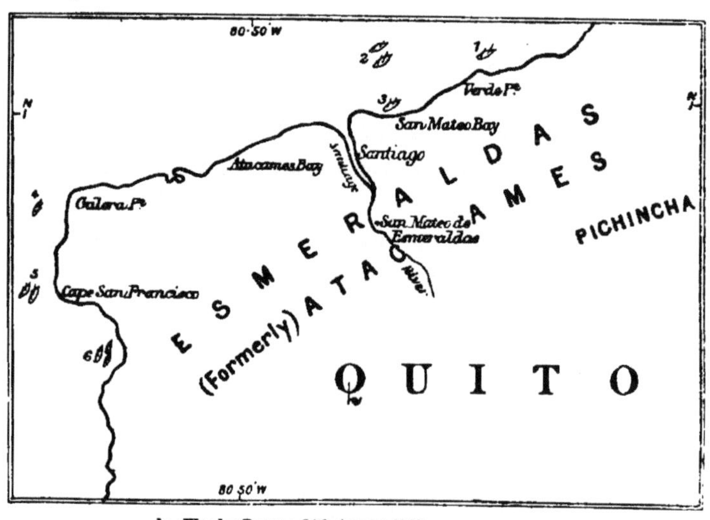

1.—Woodes Rogers, 24th August 1709.
2.—Naval Action, Hawkins and Castro, 22nd June 1594.
3.—Hawkins, 16th June 1594.
4.—Cook and Dampier, 25th December 1685.
5.—Drake and the *Cacafuego*, 1st March 1579.
6.—Dampier, etc., in Canoes, 19th April 1681.

It is a coast which was much frequented by Dampier and the buccaneers in the end of the following century. On the 14th of June[1] Hawkins was in the Bay of San

[1] He says May; but this is an obvious error. See pages 266 and 267, and compare page 308.

Mateo. On the 17th he was about to make sail and leave the coast of South America, when the Spanish fleet, under the command of Don Beltran de Castro, came round the point.[1] Hawkins fought a most gallant action, and did not surrender until he had received several wounds, was quite over-matched, and the ship was sinking. He also gives a most spirited and interesting account of it, interspersed with remarks on naval discipline, gunnery, and seamanship.[2] After three days' hard fighting the gallant young Englishman surrendered to superior force on the 22nd of June, 1594. The Spanish commander, Don Beltran de Castro, a humane and honorable man, granted quarter, and promised that Hawkins and his people should be allowed to return to their own country.[3] Don Beltran received young Hawkins with great courtesy and kindness, and accommodated him in his own cabin. The prize was taken to Panama, where she arrived on the 9th of July, the distance from San Mateo being 500 miles, a very slow passage. She was re-christened the *Visitacion*.

I have inserted, after the *Observations of Sir Richard Hawkins*, a Spanish account of the naval action between our hero and Don Beltran de Castro,[4] which I have translated from the life of the Marquis of Cañete,

[1] See page 269. [2] See pages 271 to 312.

[3] Saunders says that Don Beltran swore by God Almighty, and by the order of Alcantara, whereof he had received knighthood, and in token whereof he wore on his breast a green cross, that he would give them their lives with good entreaty.—Purchas, iv, p. 1410. [4] See pages 333 to 349.

Viceroy of Peru, by Dr. Don Christobal Suarez de Figueroa.[1] Readers will thus be able to form a judg-

[1] Dr. Don Christobal Suarez de Figueroa was a man of some literary fame in his day. Cervantes celebrated him in the *Viaje al Parnaso*, and in *Don Quijote* (iv, p. 272). His poems are published with eulogy in the *Parnaso Español*, of Sedano. He was born at Valladolid in 1578, his father having been a Gallician advocate of small means. At seventeen, after studying in his native town, he went to Italy, and obtained the degree of Doctor in one of the universities of Lombardy. The Governor of Milan then gave him the post of auditor of a body of troops sent on an expedition to Piedmont. During the next twenty-seven years he was a judge, a governor, and accountant of troops in Lombardy, Naples, and Spain. He devoted his spare time to literature, especially to studying Italian works. In 1602 he published his first book, a translation in Castilian verse of the pastoral poem of Guarini, entitled *El Pastor Fido*. Cervantes praised this translation. When Don Quixote comes to Barcelona (part 2, cap. lxii) he visits a printing press, and makes a long dissertation on the bad translations that were then appearing in Spain. But he excepts the *Pastor Fido* from his censures. In 1609 Suarez de Figueroa published the most famous of his works, *La Constante Amarilis*, a pastoral novel. In 1612 appeared his heroic poem, entitled *España defendida*. These works gained a high reputation for their author. In 1599 the Marquis of Cañete had died, after having been treated with shameful ingratitude for all his services. Moreover, he had not received justice from Ercilla in his *Araucana*, so that his heirs considered that a narrative of his life ought to be published. They applied to Suarez de Figueroa to undertake the work, and the family papers were entrusted to him, including the correspondence of the Marquis. The result was the work entitled *Hechos de Don Garcia Hurtado de Mendoza, cuarto Marques de Cañete*, which was printed in 1613. It, however, never reached a second edition until it appeared in the fifth volume (pages 1 to 206) of the *Colleccion de Historiadores de Chile y documentos relativos a la Historia Nacional*, a work published in seven volumes at Santiago in 1864. After completing this biography, Suarez de Figueroa published other books, in-

ment from the accounts of both sides. They agree on all material points. Hawkins wrote from memory, and many years after the event; while Suarez de Figueroa, although he was not an actor in the scenes he describes, had the great advantage of having at his disposal all the official and other documents formerly in the possession of the Viceroy of Peru at the time.

Hawkins and his fellow prisoners were taken to Payta, and thence to Lima. Hawkins was at first treated with kindness and consideration by the Marquis of Cañete, then Viceroy of Peru; and his servant Saunders says that he was beloved for his valour, by all brave men in those parts. He was received, says Saunders, by all the best of the country, and carried by them to a princely house all richly hanged, the which he had to himself. But afterwards he was claimed by the Inquisition, and suffered much anxiety and annoyance. The Viceroy delayed entire compliance with the requisition of the Holy Office on the ground that he had no instructions. Nevertheless, within six or seven days of his arrival at Lima, Hawkins was

cluding *El Pasajero, advertencias utilisimas a la vida humana*, written in the form of dialogues, and giving the biography of the author. In this work he confesses that his character is frivolous, that he is imprudent and a murmurer, and he attacks Cervantes, who had praised him, and who died in 1617, the year *El Pasajero* was published. Suarez de Figueroa was never in America. He was living in 1624. The best account of his life is by Don Diego Barros Arana, the editor of the Chilian volume. The *Constante Amarilis* went through three editions, the last at Madrid (8vo.) 1781. Ticknor gives some account of the works of Christobal Suarez de Figueroa in his *History of Spanish Literature*, ii, 305, 432, 463, 464, 141 *(n.)*, iii, 46, 169 *(n.)*, 92.

carried by a Father to the "Holy House", to rest there till they heard what should be done with him. The honour of Don Beltran de Castro, who had promised that Hawkins and his people should be allowed to return to England, was also compromised. The Marquis wrote to Philip II for orders, and received a very ambiguous reply, dated December 1595. The King wrote:—"You understand that he (Hawkins) is a person of quality. In this matter I desire that Justice may be done conformably to the quality of the persons."[1] This loop-hole probably enabled the Viceroy to defy the Inquisition, and Hawkins was sent to Spain, by way of Panama in 1597, after a detention of three years at Lima. Purchas gives two interesting extracts from letters written by fellow captives of Hawkins. The first is *A brief note written by Master John Ellis, one of the captains with Sir Richard Hawkins in his voyage through the Strait of Magellan, begunne the ninth of April* 1593, *concerning the said strait and certaine places on the coast and inland of Peru.*[2] Ellis made a journey from Lima across the Andes to Guamanga and Cuzco. He was the first Englishman who ever visited the ancient capital of the Yncas, which he describes as being as "big as Bristol, having a castle on a hill with stones of 20 tons weight strangely joined together without mortar". Purchas next gives two letters from T. Saunders,[3] servant to Sir Richard Hawkins, addressed to his father, Sir John, from the prison

[1] See page 348.

[2] Purchas, iv, lib. VII, cap. 6, page 1415.

[3] *Ibid.*, page 1016.

at San Lucar. Saunders speaks of one Master Lucas, who was condemned to the galleys by the Holy Office and sent to Nombre de Dios, where he died.

Sir Richard was sent to Spain in a galleon which touched at Terceira, in the Azores. A fleet under the Earl of Essex[1] chased her into the roads, and she did not escape without loss, for the splinters from the English shot killed and wounded a dozen Spaniards.[2] The galleon, with Hawkins on board, then continued its voyage to Seville, and in the *Observations* there is an account of a curious accident which befell two ships at anchor in the river, owing to a Spanish punctilio.

Sir Richard was thrown into prison at Seville, in defiance of the terms of his surrender, and was dishonourably detained for several years. Don Beltran de Castro was indignant at a breach of faith which compromised his honour, and persistently protested against

[1] This expedition of 1597, under Essex, is known as the "Island Voyage"; and an interesting account of it is given by Sir Francis Vere, in his *Commentaries* (p. 45). The Cadiz Expedition was in 1596. The object of the "Island Voyage" was to destroy the Spanish ships at Ferroll and Coruña, and to intercept the galleons coming from the Indies, on board of one of which was the captive Sir Richard Hawkins. The commanders of the English fleet were the Earl of Essex, the Earl of Southampton, Lord Mountjoy, Lord Thomas Howard, Sir Francis Vere, Sir William Monson, and Sir Walter Raleigh. They plied between the Islands of Graciosa and Terceira, in the Azores, until a great ship was sighted, and then a fleet of twenty sail. The Spaniards got safely into the Terceira anchorage, where they were so well defended by land batteries that the English could not attack them without extreme hazard. Essex landed on the Island of St. Michael's, had a skirmish with some Spanish troops, and then returned to England.

[2] See page 304.

it, but for a long time without avail. In May 1598[1] a letter to Cecil reported that Hawkins was still kept in the castle at San Lucar, as a hostage for Spaniards in England. Another letter from Lisbon reported that Captain Hawkins escaped out of the castle of Seville in September 1598, but was taken, thrust into a dungeon, and great store of irons put upon him.[2] In the following year the unhappy captive managed to send a message to England. One Deacon, Sir Richard's servant, was passed over by Martin de Marseval from St. Jean de Luz, and enabled to get on board a British vessel of St. Ives in the Breton port of Conquet, in August 1599.[3] In April 1600 Richard Cooke, another messenger, brought news of the captive, taking a passage in the *Diana* of Portsmouth.

By one of these channels Hawkins made a touching appeal to Queen Elizabeth, his letter being dated April 1st, 1598. He wrote from his prison in Seville, asking for compassion in the name of his father's services, who sacrificed his life for his Queen. He added that he himself had spent fifteen years in her service without pay or recompense, knowing that she had infinite charges while he had a good estate ; and he urged that he was in danger of perpetual imprisonment unless her powerful hand was reached out. The letter concludes with a pitious appeal in the name of his wife and children. In 1599 he was removed to Madrid.[4]

[1] *Calendar of State Papers, Domestic*, 1598-1601, p. 43.

[2] *Ibid.*, p. 97.

[3] *Ibid.*, p. 303.

[4] Lysons (*Magna Britannia*, vi, *Devonshire*, part ii, 1822) says that there was a tradition in the Hawkins family that Sir Richard,

His next letter is dated from the Court Prison at Madrid, on October 23rd, 1599, and addressed to Sir Henry Nevill, the English Ambassador at Paris. He tells him that he is the unfortunate son of Sir John Hawkins; that he fought for three days and nights and was wounded in six places; that most of his men were killed and wounded, and that he surrendered when the ship was ready to sink. The Spanish general sent his glove as a pledge to give life and liberty; but he had been detained lest he should return and molest the Spaniards. Most of his people had been freed long ago. He entreated the Ambassador to intercede with the Queen for him. "I and my father", he concluded, "ever since we could bear arms, spent time and substance in her service."[1]

The dishonorable detention of Richard Hawkins at last excited the indignation of a more powerful man

when a prisoner in Seville, captivated the heart of a Spanish lady, and that the circumstance of the lady's attachment and his fidelity to his wife gave occasion to the well known ballad of "The Spanish Lady's Love" in Percy's *Reliques* (ii, p. 256). The ballad is said to have been written by Hawkins, and it is also stated that the gold chain presented to him by the lady was carefully handed down as an heirloom in the family, and was lately in possession of Mrs. Ilbert Prideaux, a female descendant. The claim is absurd, as the Englishman in the ballad was an officer in the expedition of Essex. The Pophams of Littlecote also claimed the lover, but the Bowles family have proved that he was one of the Bolles of Scampton (see *Illingworth's History of Scampton*, p. 397 (n.) and Mr. Charles Long, a high authority on such matters, concurred. Sundry jewels belonging to the Spanish lady came into the possession of the Lees of Coldrey, where Mr. Charles Long saw them.

[1] *Ibid.* p. 333.

than Don Beltran de Castro. The credit of his release is due to the Count of Miranda,[1] who declared, if a prisoner was detained whose liberty had been promised, no future agreement could ever be made, because faith in Spanish honour would be destroyed. His views prevailed, and Richard Hawkins at length returned to England, after a dreary captivity of nearly eight years.[2]

It was a sad home-coming. The brave old father gone, the estates of both ruined, and long years of the prime of life utterly wasted. Richard Hawkins settled down, with his wife and children, in

[1] The first Count of Miranda was Don Diego Lopez de Zuñiga, second son of the Count of Placencia and Ledesma. He was a great military leader in the days of Juan II and Enrique IV, and received his creation from the latter. Don Pedro, the second Count of Miranda, served in the Granada war, and Don Francisco, the third, was Viceroy of Navarre, under Charles V, and a Knight of the Golden Fleece. He married Maria Henriquez de Cardenas, and was succeeded by Francisco, fourth Count of Miranda, a nobleman of rare virtue and great authority. His son, Don Pedro, died at Madrid, in 1572, of a kick from a horse, leaving three daughters. Maria, the eldest, was Countess of Miranda in her own right, and married her uncle Juan, who was Captain General of Cataluña, Viceroy of Naples, President of the Royal Council of Castille, and of the Councils of State and of War. It was this nobleman who insisted upon the liberation of Richard Hawkins. Philip III created him Duke of Peñaranda.

[2] *Gulielmi Camdeni annalium rerum Anglicarum et Hibernicarum regnante Elizabetha*, iii, p. 683. "Verum visum Hispanis, ad deterrendum ne alii in Australe mare penetrarent, hanc servitatem adhibere, donec Comes Mirandæ Concilii Præses pronunciaret, illum dimittendum, eo quod in rebus bellicis promissa a regiis ducibus deliberate sub conditione facta sint servanda, alias neminem deditionem unquam facturum."

one of the most secluded combes between Dartmouth and the Start Point. The road from Dartmouth to Slapton leads southwards along the coast, with the sea generally in sight, first up a very steep hill to Stoke Fleming, then down to the little hamlet of Blackpool in a shingly bay, up again to Street, and down to the long reach of Slapton Sands, which extends for several miles, almost to the Start. The "sands" are in reality a steep bank of fine shingle, within which there is a fresh water lake called the Ley, about three miles long, full of roach and pike, and frequented by water fowl of all kinds. A causeway leads across the Ley and over the hill, down into the pretty little village of Slapton. The church has a low tower and spire, a nave separated from the two aisles by four arches, and good perpendicular windows. There is a very richly carved wooden rood screen across the chancel and others across each aisle, with grapes and vine leaves carved along the upper borders. Old glass from other windows has been collected in a south chancel window, consisting of coats of arms of the Bryan family (or three piles *azure*). Near the church, and in the hollow where the village is built, there is a tall ivy-covered tower of the fourteenth century, part of a chantry founded by Jane, the wife of Sir Guy de Bryan, K.G.[1] Slapton was originally the property of the Bryan family. In the time of Henry VIII it was sold to Edward Ameredith, and his son

[1] Sir Guy de Bryan was the last Knight of the Garter created in the reign of Edward III.

John sold Slapton and Pole to Sir Richard Hawkins.[1]

CHANTRY TOWER AT SLAPTON.

From Slapton church a pretty Devonshire lane leads up for a quarter-of-a-mile to Pole, where is the site of the old residence of the Bryans, Amerediths, and Hawkinses, in a secluded hollow, with many fine trees. No ruins remain now, and the site is occupied by a modern house and farm buildings. From the lane leading down from Pole to Slapton there is a view of the sea,

[1] From the son of Sir Richard Hawkins Pole and Slapton passed into the possession of the Luttrell family, who sold the estates to Mr. Nicholas Paige. The ruins of the old mansion at Pole were taken down in 1800. William Paige, son of Nicholas, had a daughter, who married Mr. Bastard. The property now belongs to Mr. Richard Bastard.

with Start Point in the distance. It was here that Sir Richard Hawkins lived during the last twenty years of his life, with his wife and family; passing down the lane to Slapton church every Sunday, and doubtless recounting his adventures and sufferings to friends and relations during many a summer stroll and winter evening in the old house at Pole.

SLAPTON CHURCH.

But Sir Richard Hawkins was very far from being an idle man in his Devonshire home. He was knighted by James I, was appointed Vice-Admiral of Devon, and was often at Plymouth on business connected with his office. In March 1605 we find him sequestering a Spanish prize laden with Brazil wood and sugar, which was driven into Salcombe bay.[1] In June 1608 he is corresponding with the Earl of Nottingham respecting some pirates, and discussing a question of Admiralty jurisdiction;[2] and in September of the same year mention is made of his active prosecution of pirates, in his office of Vice-Admiral of Devon.[3]

He was also engaged in projects for a new voyage of discovery. In March 1614 there was a proposal before the Governors of the East India Company for carrying out a favourite scheme of Sir James Lancaster to send a ship through Magellan's Straits to the Solomon Islands, and it was suggested that Sir Richard Hawkins should have the command.[4] He was generally held to be of "courage, art, and knowledge" to attempt such enterprise.[5] There is a letter from Sir Richard himself to the Company on this subject, dated July 16th, 1614.[6] He réferred to a discovery formerly made by him, and to his desire to undertake another voyage to the Straits in person. A Committee was appointed to confer with Sir James Lancaster on the subject, and then to treat with Sir Richard, but with orders not to meddle with his ship, which was very old. He offered,

[1] *Calendar of State Papers, Domestic*, 1603-1610, p. 207.

[2] *Ibid.*, p. 437.

[3] *Ibid.*, p. 457.

[4] *Calendar of State Papers, Colonial* (*East India*), 1513-1516, p. 706.

[5] *Ibid.*, p. 711.

[6] *Ibid.*, p. 306.

with others, to join the Company in adventuring £20,000 for a voyage to the South Sea.

Nothing appears to have come of this negotiation, which shows, however, that Hawkins was as eager and zealous as ever in the cause of geographical discovery. In July 1620 we find Sir Richard Hawkins going, in command of the *Vanguard*, as Vice-Admiral of a fleet of twenty ships, under Sir Robert Mansell as Admiral, for suppressing Algerine pirates;[1] and in October a special commission was issued to Hawkins, to be Admiral in case of Mansell's death.[2] Then comes a letter announcing the end. "Sir Robert Mansell and his crew are ill-paid and Sir Richard Hawkins, the Vice-Admiral, has died of vexation."[3] This is in a letter from the Lord Chamberlain to Sir Dudley Carlton dated April 17th, 1622. He was seized with a fit, it is said, when actually in the chamber of the Privy Council on business connected with his command. His will, dated on April 16th, 1622, was proved by his widow on June 13th of the same year. He is described as of Slapton in Devonshire, and owner of the manor of Pole, as well as of a house called Pryvitt, at Alverstoke in Hampshire.[4] His widow followed him to the grave in 1629, and lies buried in the north aisle of Slapton Church.[5] A

1 Letter from Rowland Woodward to Francis Windebank. *Cal. of State Papers, Domestic*, 1619-1623, p. 159.

2 *Ibid.*, p. 182.

3 *Ibid.*, p. 280.

4 For copy of Sir Richard's will, see page xlvii.

5 For descendants of Sir Richard Hawkins, see page l.

slate slab, with an inscription round it, marks the spot, but one side and part of both ends are obliterated. There remains :—

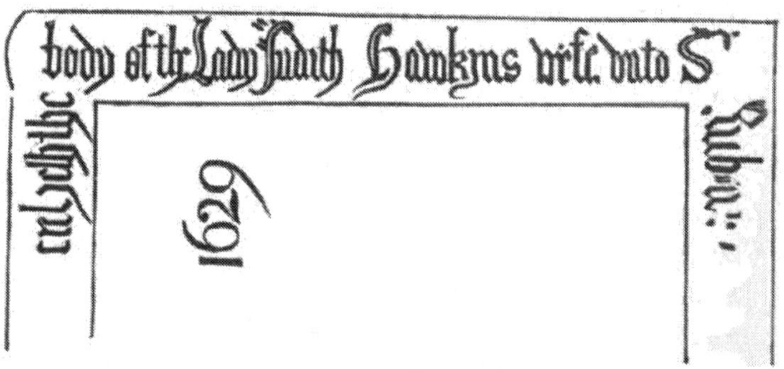

Sir Richard Hawkins was actually passing his work through the press, at the time of his very sudden death ; and it was published immediately afterwards with a dedication to Charles, Prince of Wales, by the author, and a short notice by another hand. The following is the entry in the Register of Stationers' Hall :—[1]

"1622,

"24 Julii.

"Master John Jaggard[2]	entred for his copie under the handes of Wilson and Master Gilwyn a book called *The discipline of the sea historie, in the observations which Sir Richard Hawkins made in his South Sea voyage, anno domini,* 1593, *vj.*"

The actual title page of the work, published by

[1] *Arber's Transcript of the Stationers' Register*, iv, p. 38.

[2] Master Jaggard had been Warden of the Stationers in 1619.

Jaggard in 1622, will be found at page 83 of the present volume. Purchas, in his *Pilgrims*, reprinted the *Observations of Sir Richard Hawkins* in a mutilated form—"once before published, now reviewed and corrected by a written copie, illustrated with notes, and in divers places abbreviated".[1] The reprint of the Hakluyt Society is from the original edition of 1622. Admiral Burney devotes an interesting chapter to the voyage of Sir Richard Hawkins.[2] A poetical relation of the voyage is preserved in the British Museum, composed by William Ridley in his nineteenth year.

Sir Richard intended to have given an account of his long imprisonment, and of Peru and Tierra Firme, Terceira, and Spain, in a second part, as he informs us at the end of his *Observations* (see p. 329). Death prevented the accomplishment of this intention, and the loss of the promised second part is a serious and irreparable loss to history. For we possess no account of Peru during that period, written by an observant foreigner.

Another distinguished seaman of this family was William, brother of Sir John and uncle of Sir Richard Hawkins. He was not only an adventurous sea captain but also a large owner of ships, and in 1568 his Plymouth cruisers were the terror of the Spaniards.[3] In

[1] IV, lib. vii, cap. v, pages 1367 to 1415.

[2] *A Chronological History of the Voyages and Discoveries in the South Sea or Pacific Ocean*, by James Burney (London, 1806) part II, chap. ix, pages 118 to 133.

[3] Froude's *History of England*, ix, p. 363.

1582 he made the voyage to the West Indies, with his nephew Richard, which has already been referred to. He died on the 7th of October 1589, having had eleven children by two wives, and his brother Sir John put up a monument to his memory (now removed) in the church of St. Nicholas at Deptford, with the following inscription:—[1]

> "Sacræ perpetuæque memoriæ Gulielmi Haukyns de Plimouth armigeri; qui veræ religionis verus cultor, pauperibus præcipue naviculariis munificus, rerum nauticarum studiosissimus, longinquas instituit sæpe navigationes; arbiter in causis difficilissimis æquissimus, fide, probitate, et prudentia singulari. Duas duxit uxores, e quarum una 4, ex altera 7 suscepit liberos. Johannes Haukyns, eques auratus, classis regiæ quæstor, frater mœstissimus posuit. Obiit spe certa resurgendi 7 die mensis Octobris anno domini 1589."

Several of the sons of William Hawkins of Plymouth were sailors or merchants.[2] But the most famous was he who bore the same name as his father. We first hear of WILLIAM HAWKINS *(junior)* as Lieutenant-General of Fenton's fleet in 1582. He had previously been in some voyage to Magellan's Straits, and also in the West Indies.[3] Edward Fenton, a Nottinghamshire man, was appointed by Martin Frobisher as captain of the *Gabriel* in the second Arctic voyage of 1577, and he also accompanied Frobisher in the third voyage as

[1] Thorpe's *Registrum Roffense*, p. 946.

[2] Charles Hawkins was certainly a son. He was an adventurer of £600 in the sixth East India Company's voyage. Giles, Nicholas, and Roger were also probably sons. Giles was a factor, who died at Bantam in 1615.

[3] See p. 401.

Rear-Admiral in the *Judith.* Four years afterwards Fenton was selected, by the Earl of Leicester, to command an expedition nominally to discover the north-west passage. The Queen contributed two of her ships. One was the galleon *Leicester* of 400 tons with Fenton on board as general. The other was the *Bonaventure* of 300 tons, commanded by Luke Ward, as Vice-Admiral. There were also the *Francis* of 40 tons, under Captain John Drake, with William Markham as master; and the *Elizabeth* pinnace. The instructions were ambiguous and absurd. Fenton was to discover the north-west passage if it was to be found south of 40° N., but he was not to go north of that parallel, and he was to visit the Moluccas. But he was not to pass the Straits of Magellan. In short, he was to discover the north-west passage by going round the Cape of Good Hope to the East Indies, and enriching himself and his employers by trade and plunder.

The journal of the voyage was kept by Mr. Maddox, the chaplain of the *Leicester;* and William Hawkins also kept a journal which is now in the British Museum (*MSS. Otho,* E viii), but much mutilated by fire. What can be deciphered will be found at pages 353 to 363 of the present volume. The expedition sailed in May 1582, and on July 20th the coast of Guinea was sighted. It appears to have been a most unhappy cruise, and the journal of Hawkins is full of complaints of the ill treatment he received from Captain Fenton. It is clear that Fenton wanted to abandon the voyage at a very early period, and that most of the officers protested against it. The *Francis* reached the river Plate, where she was wrecked, but the crew were saved and kept among the savages for fifteen months. The other ships entered the port of St. Vincent in Brazil, where an action was fought with a Spanish fleet by moonlight, and next morning, until both sides were weary. The English then made the best of their way home; and the *Leicester* arrived at Kinsale on June 14th, 1513. On reaching the Downs Fenton broke out in violent abuse of Hawkins, calling him a knave, a villain, and a boy; and the voyage ended in mutual reproaches. It was an utter failure. Fenton, however, does not appear to have lost any credit.[1]

We do not hear of William Hawkins again until 1607; but he appears to have been in the Levant, and to have learnt Turkish; for he could converse in that language. In 1607 he was captain of the *Hector* in the third voyage set forth by the East India Company. Captain Keelinge, in the *Dragon*, was general of the voyage. Purchas gives an abstract of Keelinge's Journal occupying eighteen pages,[2] and another abstract of the Journal of Captain Hawkins of the same length.[3] In my Introduction to the *Voyages of Sir James Lancaster*, I have stated that the manuscript of the Journal of

[1] Fenton commanded the *May Rose*, of 600 tons, in 1588, in the fleet for opposing the Spanish Armada, and he had a distinguished share in the subsequent operations. He afterwards lived at Deptford, and died there in 1603. Roger, Earl of Cork, who married his niece, erected a monument to his memory in the church of St. Nicholas.

[2] IV, cap. vi, p. 188.

[3] III, cap. vii, p. 206.

Hawkins was lost.[1] It should be in the collection of East India Company's logs in the India Office. It has since been found among the manuscripts in the British Museum (*Egerton MS.* 2100); but much injured by damp. All that can be deciphered will be found at pages 364 to 388 of the present volume. This is followed by the interesting account of the "occurrents which happened in the time of his residence in India", and the "briefe discourse of the strength, wealth, and government, with some of the customs of the *Great Mogol*", reprinted from Purchas.[2]

The journey of William Hawkins to Agra, and his residence at the court of Jehanghir, may be looked upon as the opening scene in the history of British India. The Emperor induced the English captain to marry the daughter of Mubarik Khan, a Christian Armenian; and when Hawkins was dismissed from Agra in November 1611, he took his native wife with him. They got safely on board Sir Henry Middleton's ship in the following January, and proceeded to Bantam, whence they sailed for England in the *Thomas,* arriving at Saldanha Bay on April 21st, 1613. The *Thomas* sailed from Saldanha Bay on May 21st, 1613, and here the letter (or report) of Hawkins to the company terminates abruptly.[3] He died on the passage from the Cape, and was buried in Ireland.[4]

Mrs. Hawkins, alone amongst strangers, was left in a

[1] Page viii.

[2] III, cap. vii, p. 206.

[3] See page 418.

[4] *Calendar of State Papers, Colonial (East India),* 1608-1616.

very forlorn condition. But she had one diamond worth £2000, and smaller ones worth £4000, so that she had no difficulty in finding another husband. In 1614 she married Gabriel Towerson,[1] who had been in the voyage of Captain Saris and brought home the *Hector*. In 1617 Captain and Mrs. Towerson went out to India again, and visited Agra; where the lady remained with her relations. Towerson went home, and in 1620 he was appointed Principal Factor at the Moluccas, where he was judicially murdered, after suffering inhuman treatment from the Dutch, on February 27th, 1623. He was the chief victim in the Massacre of Amboyna.

I have to thank Mr. Coote of the British Museum for the careful and intelligent way in which he transcribed two very illegible manuscripts; the Reverend Bradford Denne Hawkins for a photograph of his bust of Sir John Hawkins; the Reverend R. Antrim for information respecting Slapton; and Mr. Fortescue Moresby, R.N., for sketches of the church and priory at Slapton, and for the copy of the inscription on the Lady Hawkins's tombstone in Slapton church.

[1] The Company presented her with a purse of 200 Jacobuses, as a token of their love, upon a general release being given by her.

WILL OF SIR RICHARD HAWKINS.

In the name of God Amen the sixteenth day of Aprill 1622 in the twentieth yeare of the raigne of our Sovraigne Lord James by the Grace of God Kinge of England Fraunce and Ireland Defender of the Faith and of Scotland the fyve and fyftith I Sir Richard Hawkins of Slapton in the Countye of Devon Knight beinge sicke and weake in bodye but of pfect mynde and memory blessed be God therefore doe hereby make ordayne and declare this to be my last Will and Testament in manner and forme followinge. First and principalle I commend my soule unto Almightie God my Maker Redeemer and Sanctifier hoping and beleeving assuredly that through the only merritts death and resurrection of Jesus Christ I shall obtayne full and free remission and pardon of all my sinnes and be made ptaker of eternall life and happiness in the kingdome of heaven with God's elect for ever And I comitt my body to the earthe from whence it came and after my bodye buried my will and minde is that all suche debts as I shall owe to any p'son or p'sons at the tyme of my decease be first well and trulie satisfied And touching the orderinge and disposinge of all such lands grounds tenements goods and chattells as it hathe pleased Almightie God to blesse mee with in this life I give and bequeathe the same in manner and forme following Item I give unto Judith my well beloved wife (for and duringe the terme of her naturall life) all that my Mannor or Lordshipp of Poole in the Parishe of Slapton in the County of Devon with all mills lands grounds messuages cottages tenements and hereditaments with their and every of their appurtennes to the said Mannor or Lordshipp of Poole now belonging or in any wise app'teyninge And likewise I give and bequeath unto the said Judith my wife (for and duringe the tearme of her naturall life) all other my lands and tenements cottages and hereditaments with the appertennes situate lyeinge and being in or about Plymouth in the Countye of Devon Neverthelesse and uppon this condition followeinge that she shall yearelye duringe soe longe tyme as my sonne John Hawkins shall remaine and dwell with his said mother allowe and paie unto my said sonne twentie pounds per annum of lawfull money of England And if it shall happen that he shall hereafter be minded to lyve from her and betake himself to some other place of aboade or otherwise to travaile or to betake himself to lyve either at the Innes of Courte or at the universities of Oxford or Cambridge then to paie unto my said sonne John and his assignes during all such time as hee shall live from her as aforesaid the yearlie some of fortie pounds of lawfull money of England at fower of the most usual feests or termes in the yeare by even and equall por'cons Item I give and bequeath ymediatlie from and after the decease of my said wife Judith all the said Mannor howse or Lordship called Poole with all mills lands grounds messuages cottages tenements and hereditaments with theire and every of theire appurten'ces in the Parish of Slapton and all other my said lands tenements cottages and hereditaments with th' app'tences lyeinge and being in or about Plymouth in the County of Devon aforesaid with the reverc'on and rever'cons thereof unto my said sonne John Hawkins with all and singular my goods chattells utensils and household stuffe whatsoever Provided always that my said wife may have and enjoy use occupie and possesse the same goods and chattells during her life without any interup'con or lett of my said sonne John or of any others by his pcurement Item I give and bequeathe to my sonne Richard Hawkins and to his heires for ever all that messuage or tenement with th' app'tences called Pryvitt scituate lyeinge and beinge in Alverstoke in the Countye of South[t] with all lands and grounds thereunto belonginge or in any wise apperteyninge Item I give and bequeathe to Margaret Hawkins my daughter (over and above a hundred pounds legacie given her by her grandmother and a jewell of twentye pound value) the some of one hundred pounds of lawfull mony of England Item I give and bequeathe to my daughter Joane Hawkins one hundred and twenty pounds and to my youngest daughter Mary the like some of one hundred and twentye pounds All which said three severall legacies of somes of money by me given unto my said three daughters as afforesaide I will shal be paid them at sixteene yeares of age or daye of marriage which shall first happen and to be receaved and had out of my owne entertaynmt due to me from the King's Ma'tie for my last service and imployment don by me at Argeire And if any of my said daughters shall happen to decease or dep'te this transitorie lyfe before they shall happen to come or attayne to their severall ages of sixteene yeares or daye of marriage as aforesaid then I will that the parte and porc'on of any of them so dyeinge or deceasinge as aforesaide shall remayne and come unto the others surviving and overlyving p'te and p'te alike by even and equall por'cons also for the further advancement and encrease of my said daughters porcons as aforesaide I doe equallie giue to amongst my said daughters the some of one hundred and fiftie pounds due to me by Sir Henry Thynn Knight to be paid them when and so soone as my Executrix hereafter named shall happen to recover and receave the same And I make and ordayne the said Judith my lovinge wife sole and only Executrix of this my last Will and Testament and I renounce and revoke all former Wills by me formerly made In witness whereof I the said Sir Richard Hawkins have hereunto sett my hand and seale the said sixteenth day of Aprill 1622 in the twentith yeare of the raigne of our said

Soveraigne Lord King James over England France and Ireland Richard Hawkins Sealed and delyvered in the presence of us Thos Button Jo Gifford Josias Shute and Robert Holyland Sr

Proved June 13th, 1622, by Dame Judith Hawkins.

DESCENDANTS OF SIR RICHARD HAWKINS.

Sir Richard Hawkins, by his wife Judith, had five children, John, Richard, Margaret, Joan, and Mary.

The eldest son, John, succeeded to Slapton on the death of his mother in 1629. He married Hester . . . . and had three sons, Robert who died in 1644, John born in 1639 and died in 1642, and John born in 1643.

There is reason to believe that John, born in 1643, was the same John Hawkins who settled at Great Milton in Oxfordshire in 1682, having previously married Mary, daughter of Edward Dewe, of Islip, who was the son of Richard Dewe of Abingdon, by Elizabeth daughter of Tesdale, the Founder of Pembroke College at Oxford. For this John of Great Milton bore the same arms and crest as Sir Richard Hawkins.

John Hawkins of Great Milton, by Mary Dewe, had 14 children, born between 1681 and 1698. The eldest, William Hawkins, was a Serjeant at Law, and author of *Pleas of the Crown.* He had two sons, William and Philip, Fellows of Pembroke College, who left issue, and a daughter Mary, married to William Ram. The second son of John Hawkins of Great Milton was also named John.

This second son had a son William, who married Susannah, daughter of Thomas Grant by Susannah his wife, who was niece of Bishop Bradford. Their son, Samuel Hawkins, was born in 1757, and died in 1839. By his wife Sarah, daughter of Charles Calland, Esq., he left two sons, John Croft and Bradford Denne.

John Croft Hawkins was born in 1798 and, after being in the navy, entered the Bombay Marine in 1816. He served in the Persian Gulf at the reduction of Ras-el-Khaimah, and in 1821 against the Benu-Bu-Ali tribe. He became a Lieutenant in 1824, and Commander in 1831. He made a remarkably rapid overland journey through Persia to India in 1832, for which he received the special thanks of the Board of Control. In 1838 he surveyed the Euphrates as far as Hit; and was promoted to the rank of Captain in 1839. He was Commodore in the Persian Gulf, and performed acts of great personal daring: first in bringing a noted piratical chief to terms; and secondly in diving to run a line through the ring of an anchor, which greatly contributed to save H.M.S. *Fox*. Sir Henry Blackwood spoke of the skill and energy of Commodore Hawkins as never surpassed by any seaman. He thrice received the thanks of the Home, and seven times of the local Government. He died at Bombay in 1851. Commodore Hawkins was one of the most distinguished naval officers in the Indian Service.

Bradford Denne Hawkins, born in 1799, entered holy orders, and is Rector of Rivenhall near Witham, in Essex. He married Sarah, daughter of Robert Hopkins, Esq., of Tidmarsh House in Berkshire; and has a son, Robert Samuel Hawkins, of 18, Norham Gardens, Oxford, who was born on July 11th, 1832, and married Lucy Sybil, daughter of Sir Thomas Tancred, Bart. They have issue.

Burke, in his *Landed Gentry*, gives a genealogy by which Sir John Hawkins, the author of *The History of Music* (born 1719, died 1789) is made to be a descendant of John, the eldest son of Sir Richard Hawkins. But there is internal evidence of this genealogy being apocryphal. This Sir John's father was a house carpenter, respecting whose ancestry there is no evidence whatever.

Richard Hawkins, the second son of Sir Richard Hawkins, settled at Slapton and had a son Nicholas, who was born in 1639. John Hawkins, the son of Nicholas, was settled at Kingsbridge in Devonshire, and was a Captain of Militia in 1703. His son Richard Hawkins of Kingsbridge died in 1742, leaving two sons, John and Richard.

Richard Hawkins, the second son, was also of Kingsbridge, and died there in 1778, leaving a son, Richard Hawkins of Kingsbridge, who died in 1836. This last Richard had two sons, namely Major John Hawkins, of the E.I.C. Engineers, who died in 1831 leaving four children; and Captain Abraham Mills Hawkins, R.N., who had two sons—John Mills Hawkins in the 52nd Light Infantry, and Christopher Stuart Hawkins, Esq., of Alston near Plympton in Devonshire.

THE VOYAGE

OF

WILLIAM HAWKINS

(1530),

AND THE

THREE VOYAGES

OF HIS SON

SIR JOHN HAWKINS

(1562-1568).

A Voyage to Brasill, made by the worshipfull *M. William Haukins of Plimmouth, father to* sir Iohn Haukins, Knight, now liuing, in the yeere 1530.

Olde M. William Haukins of Plimmouth, a man for his wisdome, valure, experience, and skill in sea causes much esteemed, and beloued of King Henry the eight, and being one of the principall Sea Captaines in the West partes of England in his time, not contented with the short voyages commonly then made onely to the knowen coastes of Europe, armed out a tall and goodlie ship of his owne, of the burthen of 250. tunnes, called the Pole of Plimmouth wherewith he made three long and famous voyages vnto the coast of Brasill, a thing in those days very rare, especially to our Nation. In the course of which voyages he touched at the Rieur of Sestos,[1] vpon the coast of Guinea, where he trafiqued with the Negroes, and tooke of them Oliphants' teeth, and other commodities which that place yeeldeth: and so arriuing on the coast of Brasil, used there such discretion, and behaued himselfe so wisely with those sauage people, that he grew into great familiarite and friendship with them. Insomuch that in his 2. voyage, one of the sauage kings of the Countrey of Brasill was contented to take ship with him, and to be transported hither into England: whereunto M. Haukins agreed, leauing behinde in the countrey as a pledge for his safetie and returne againe, one Martin Cockeram of Plimmouth. This Brasilian king

[1] Rio Cestos, in 5° 30′ N., on the Grain Coast of Guinea.

being arriued, was brought up to London, and presented to King Henry 8. lying as then at Whitehall: at the sight of whome, the king and all the Nobilitie did not a little marueile, and not without cause: for in his cheekes were holes made accordinge to their sauage manner, and therein small bones were planted, standing an inche out from the said holes, which in his own Countrey was reputed for a great brauerie. He had also another hole in his nether lippe, wherein was set a precious stone about the bignesse of a pease: all his apparell, behauiour, and gesture, were very strange to the beholders.

Hauing remained here the space almost of a whole yere, and the king with his sight fully satisfied, M. Haukins, according to his promise and appointment, purposed to conuey him againe into his Countrey: but it fell out in the way, that by change of ayre and alteration of diet, the saide Sauage king died at sea, which was feared woulde turn to the loss of the life of Martin Cockeram, his pledge. Neuerthelesse, the Sauages being fully perswaded of the honest dealing of our men with their Prince, restored againe the said pledge, without any harm to him, or any other man of the companie: which pledge of theirs they brought home againe into England, with their shippe fraighted, and furnished with the commodities of the Countrey. Which Martine Cockeram, by the witnesse of sir Iohn Haukins, being an officer in the towne of Plimmouth, was liuing within these fewe yeeres.

I have bene informed by M. Anthony Garrard, an ancient and worshipful marchant of London, that this voyage to Brasil was frequented by Robert Reniger, Thomas Borey, and diuers other wealthie marchants of Southampton, about 50 yeeres past, to wit, in the yeere 1540.

The First Voyage of the right worshipfull and valiant *knight, sir Iohn Haukins, now treasurer of* her Maiesties nauie Royall, made to the West Indies 1562.

Master Iohn Haukins hauing made diuers voyages to the yles of the Canaries, and there by his good and vpright dealing being growne in loue and fauour with the people, informed himself amongst them by diligent inquisition, of the state of the West India, whereof he had receiued some knowledge by the instructions of his father, but increased the same by the aduertisements and reports of that people. And being amongst other particulars assured that Negroes were very good marchandise in Hispaniola, and that store of Negroes might easily be had upon the coast of Guinea, resolued with himselfe to make trial thereof, and communicated that deuise with his worshipfull friends of London: namely, with sir Lionel Ducket,[1] sir Thomas Lodge,[2] M. Gunston,[3] his father-in-lawe, Sir William Winter, M. Bronfield, and others. All which persons liked so well of his intention, that they became liberall contributers and adventurers in the action. For which purpose there were 3. good shippes immediately prouided. The one called the Salomon of the burthen of 120. tunne, wherein M. Haukins himselfe went as Generall; the 2. the Swallow, of 100 tunnes,

[1] Lord Mayor of London in 1573. Sir Lionel was an Adventurer in Frobisher's three Arctic voyages.

[2] Sir Thomas Lodge, son of William Lodge of Cresset, in Shropshire, was a Governor of the Russia Company in 1561; Lord Mayor in 1563. He was of the Grocers' Company.

[3] Benjamin Gonson, Treasurer of the Admiralty, 1553-70.

wherein went for Captaine M. Thomas Hampton: And the 3. the Ionas, a barke of 40. tunnes, wherein the Master supplied the Captaine's roome: in which small fleete, M. Haukins tooke with him not aboue 100. men, for feare of sickenesse, and other inconueniences, whereunto men in long voyages are commonly subiect.

With this company hee put off and departed from the coast of England in the moneth of October 1562, and in his course touched first at Teneriffe, where he receiued friendly intertainement. From thence hee passed to Sierra Leona,[1] upon the coast of Guinea, which place by the people of the countery is called Tagarin, where he stayed some good time, and got into his possession, partly by the sword, and partly by other meanes, to the nomber of 300. negroes at the least, besides other marchandises, which that Country yeeldeth. With this praye he sailed ouer the Ocean sea vnto the Island of Hispaniola, and arriued first at the port of Isabella: and there hee had reasonable utterance of his English commodities, as also of some part of his Negroes, trusting the Spaniards no further, then that by his owne strength he was able still to master them. From the port of Isabella he went to Porte de Plata, where he made like sales, standing always vpon his gard: from thence also hee sailed to Monte Christi,[2] another port on the north side of Hispaniola, and the last place of his touching, where he had peaceable trafique, and made vent of the whole nomber of his Negroes: for which he received in those 3. places by way of exchange, such quantitie of marchandise, that he did not onely lade his owne 3. shippes with hides, ginger, sugers, and some quantitie of pearles, but he fraighted also two

[1] Discovered by Pedro de Cintra in 1462, who named the mountain "Sierra Leona" on account of the roaring of the thunder, which is constantly heard on its cloud-enveloped summit.

[2] Isabella, Port Plata, and Monte Christi, were all ports on the north shore of Hispaniola or St. Domingo.

other hulkes with hides, and other like commodities, which he sent into Spaine.[1] And thus leauing the Island, hee returned and disimboked, passing out by the Islands of the Caycos,[2] without further entring into the bay of Mexico, in this his first voyage to the West India. And so with prosperous successe and much gaine to himselfe, and the aforesaide adventurers, he came home, and arriued in the moneth of September 1563.

[1] He sent his second in command, Captain Hampton, to Cadiz to dispose of this merchandise; but the cargo was confiscated, and Hawkins thus lost half his profits. An order was also sent to the Indies that no English vessel should be allowed to trade there.

[2] The Caicos Bank, north of St. Domingo.

The voyage made by the worshipful M. Iohn Haukins, *Esquire, now Knight, Captaine of the Iesus of Lubek,* one of her Maiesties shippes, and Generall of the Salomon, and her two barkes going in his companie to the coast of Guinea, and the Indies of Noua Spania, being in Affrica, and America: begun in An. Dom. 1564.

October 18. MASTER Iohn Haukins with the Iesus of Lubek, a shippe of 700. and the Salomon, a ship of 7. score, the Tiger, a bark of 50. and the Swallow of 30. tunnes, being all well furnished with men to the nomber of one hundreth, threescore and tenne, as also with ordinance, and victuall requisite for such a voyage, departed out of Plimmouth the 18. day of October, in the yere of our Lord 1564, with a prosperous winde; at which departing, in cutting the foresaile, a marueilous misfortune happened to one of the officers in the shippe, who by the pullie of the sheat was slaine out of hande, being a sorrowfull beginning to them all. And after their setting out tenne leagues to the sea, he met the same day with the Minion, a ship of the Queenes Maiesties, whereof was Captaine Dauid Carlet, and also her consort, the Iohn Baptist of London, being bounde to Guinea also, who hailed one the other after the custome of the Sea, with certaine pieces of ordinance for ioy of their meeting; which done, the Minion departed from him to seeke her other consort, the Merline of London, which was a starne out of sight, leauing in M. Haukins companie the Iohn Baptist, her other consort.

The Minion, the John Baptist, and the Merline, bound for Guinea.

Thus sayling forwards on their way with a prosperous winde until the 21. of the same moneth, at that time a great storme arose, the winde being at Northeast about 9. a clocke in the night, and continued so 23. houres together, in which storme M. Haukins lost the companie of the Iohn Baptist aforesaid, and of his pinnesse called the Swallow, his other 2. shippes being sore beaten with the storme. The 23. day the Swallow, to his no small reioicing, came to him againe in the night, 10. leagues to the Northward of Cape Finister, he having put roomer not being able to double the Cape, in that there rose a contrary winde at Southwest. The 25. the wind continuing contrary, he put into a place in Gallicia, called Ferroll, where hee remained fiue dayes, and appointed all the Masters of his shippes an order for the keeping of good companie in this manner: the small shippes to be alwayes a head and a weather of the Iesus, and to speake twise a day with the Iesus at least: if in the day the Ensigne bee ouer the poope of the Iesus, or in the night two lightes, then shall all the shippes speake with her. If there be three lights aboord the Iesus, then doeth she cast about: If the weather be extreme, that the small shippes cannot keep companie with the Iesus, then all to keep companie with the Salomon, and foorthwith to repaire to the Island of Teneriffe, to the Northward of the road of Sirroes: If any happen to any misfortune, then to shewe two lights, and to shoote off a piece of Ordinance. If any loose companie, and come in sight againe, to make three yawes, and strike the Myson[1] three times: Serue God dayly, loue one another, preserve your victuals, beware of fire, and keepe good companie.

The 26. day the Minion came in also where he was for the reioicing whereof hee gave them certaine pieces of Ordinance, after the courtesie of the Sea, for their welcome, but the Minion's men had no mirthe, because of their consort, the Merline, whome, at their departure from M. Haukins vpon the coast of England, they went to seeke: and having mette with her, kept companie two dayes together, and at

[1] Mizen.

last by misfortune of fire (through the negligence of one of their gunners) the powder in the gunners' roome was set on fire, which with the first blast stooke out her poope, and therewithall lost three men, besides many sore burned (which escaped by the Brigandine being at her sterne), and immediately, to the great losse of the owners, and most horrible sight to the beholders, she sanke before their eyes.

The 30[1] day of the Moneth M. Haukins with his consorts and companie of the Minion, hauing nowe both the Brigandines at her sterne, wayed ancre, and set saile on their voyage, hauing a prosperous winde thereunto.

The fourth of Nouember they had sight of the Islande of Madera, and the sixt day of Teneriffe, which they thought to haue bene the Canaries, in that they supposed themselves to haue bene to the Eastward of Teneriffe, and were not: but the Mynion being a three or foure leagues ahead of vs, kept on her course to Teneriffe, hauing better sight thereof than the others had, and by that meanes they parted companie. For Master Haukins and his companie went more to the West, vpon which course, having sailed awhile, he espied another Island, which he thought to be Teneriffe, and being not able, by the meanes of the fogge upon the hils, to discerne the same, nor yet to fetch it by night, went roomer, untill the morning, being the 7. of November, which as yet he could not discerne, but sailed along the coast, the space of two howres, to perceaue some certaine marke of Teneriffe, and found no likelihood thereof at all, accompting that to be, as it was in deede, the Isle of Palmes:[2] and so sailing forwards, espied another Island, called Gomera,[3] and also Teneriffe, with the which he made, and sailing all night, came in the morning the next day to

The Isle of Palmes. Gomera and Teneriffe.

[1] 20th in edition of 1810.

[2] Palma, the north-westernmost of the Canaries.

[3] Gomera, south-east from Palma, the island from which Columbus sailed.

the port of Adecia,[1] where he found his pinnesse which had departed from him the sixt of the moneth, being in the weather of him, and espying the pike of Teneriffe all a high, bare thither. At his arriual, somewhat before he came to anker, he hoysed out his shippe's pinnesse rowing a shoare, intending to haue sent one with a letter to Peter de ponte, one of the Gouernours of the Island, who dwelled a league from the shoare: but as he pretended to haue landed, suddenly there appeared vpon the two pointes of the roade men leuelling of basses and harquebusses to them, with diuers others to the number of 80. with halberts, pykes, swordes, and targets, which happened so contrairie to his expectation that it did greatly amase him, and the more, because he was nowe in their danger, not knowing well how to auoide it without some mischiefe. Wherefore he determined to call to them, for the better appeasing of the matter, declaring his name, and professing himself to be an especiall friend to Peter de ponte, and that he had sundry things for him, which he greatly desired. And in the meane time, while he was thus talking with them, whereby he made them to hold their hands, he willed the marriners to rowe away, so that at last he gat out of their danger: and then asking for Peter de Ponte, one of his sonnes being Signior Nicholas Ponte, came foorth, whome he perceauing, desired to put his men aside, and he himself would leape a shoare, and common with him, which they did: so that after communication had betweene them of sundry things, and of the feare they both had, Master Hawkins desired to haue certaine necessaries prouided for him. In the meane space, while these things were prouiding, he trimmed the maine mast of the Iesus, which in the storme aforesaid was sprong: here he soiourned 7. daies, refreshing himselfe and his men. In the which time Peter de ponte, dwelling at S.

[1] Adexe, on the west side of the island of Teneriffe.

Cruz,[1] a Citie 20. leagues off, came to him and gaue him as gentle entertainment as if he had been his own brother. To speak somewhat of these Islands, being called in olde time Insulae fortunatæ, by the meanes of the florishing therof, the fruitfulness of them doeth surely exceede farre all other that I haue hearde of: for they make wine better than any in Spaine, they haue grapes of such bignes, that they may be compared to damsons, and in taste inferiore to none: for sugar, suckets, raisons of the Sunne, and many other fruits, abundance: for rosine and raw silke, there is great store, they want neither corne, pullets, cattell, nor yet wilde fowle: they have many Camels also, which being yong, are eaten of the people for victuals, and being olde, they are used for carriage of necessaries: whose propertie is as he is taught to kneele at the taking of his loade, and unloading againe; his nature is to ingender backward, contrairie to other beastes: of understanding very good, but of shape very deformed, with a littie bellie, long mishapen legges, and feete very broade of flesh, without a hoofe, all whole, sauing the great toe, a back bearing up like a molehill, a large and thinne neck, with a little head, with a bunch of hard flesh, which nature hath giuen him in his breast to lean vpon. This beast liueth hardly, and is contented with strawe, and stubble, but of force strong, being well able to carry 500. weight. In one of these islands called "de Fierro"[2] there is, by the reportes of the inhabitants, a certaine tree[3] that raineth continually, by the dropping whereof the inhabitants and cattel are satisfied with water, for other water haue they none in all the Island. And it raineth in such abundance that it were incredible vnto man to beleeue such a vertue to be in a tree, but it is

"De Fierro."

[1] Santa Cruz is on the north-east side of Teneriffe.

[2] Ferro is the south-westernmost of the Canaries.

[3] See a very full account of this tree in the volume on the conquest of the Canaries, by Bethencourt, edited by Mr. Major (1872), p. 125 (*note* .

knowen to be a diuine matter, and a thing ordained by God, at whose power therein, we ought not to maruell, seeing he did by his prouidence, as we read in the Scriptures, when the children of Israell were going into the land of promise, feed them with Manna from heauen, for the space of 40. yeeres. Of the trees aforesaid, we saw in Guinea many, being of great height, dropping continually, but not so abundantly as the other, because the leaues are narrower, and are like the leaues of a peare tree. About these Islands are certaine flitting Islands, which haue bene oftentimes seene, and when men approched neere them, they vanished; as the like hath bene of these Islands now knowen, by the report of the Inhabitants, which were not founde of long time one after the other. And therefore it shoulde seeme he is not yet borne, to whome God hath appointed the finding of them. In this Island of the Teneriffe there is a hill called the Pike, because it is picked, which is in height by their reports, 20. leagues,[1] hauing both winter and summer aboundance of snowe in the top of it: this pike may be seene in a cleere day 50. leagues off, but it showeth as though it were a blacke clowde a great height in the element. I have heard of none to be compared with this in height, but in the Indias I have seen many, and in my iudgment not inferiour to the pike, and so the Spaniards write.

Trees dropping water in Ginney.

The pike of Teneriffe.

The 15 of Nouember, at night, we departed from Teneriffe and the 20. of the same wee had sight of 10. Caruels, that were fishing at sea, with whome we would haue spoken, but they fearing vs, fled into a place of Barbarie, called Cape de las Barbas.

Cape de Barbas.

The 20. the shippes pinnesse, with two men in her, sailing by the shippe, was ouerthrown by the ouersight of them that were in her, the wind being so great that before they were espied, and the ship had cast about for them, she was driuen halfe a league to leeward of the pinnesse, and had lost sight of her, so that there was

[1] The Peak of Teneriffe is 11,430 feet above the sea.

small hope of recouerie, had not God's helpe, and the Captaines diligence bene, who hauing well marked which way the pinnesse was by the Sunne, appointed 24. of the lustiest rowers in the great boate to rowe to windewards, and so recouered, contrary to all men's expectations, both the pinnesse and the men sitting vpon the keele of her.

Cape Blanco. The 25. he[1] came to Cape Blanco,[2] which is vpon the coast of Affrica, and a place where the Portingals doe ride that fishe there, in the moneth of Nouember especially, and is a very good place of fishing for Pargoes, Mullet, and Dogge fishe. In this place the Portingals haue no holde for their defense, but haue rescue of the Barbarians, whome they entertaine as their souldiers, for the time of their being there, and for their fishing vpon that coast of Affrica, doe pay a certaine tribute to the King of the Moores. The people of that part of Affrica are tawnie, hauing long haire, without any apparell, sauing before their priuie members. Their weapons in warres, are bowes, and arrowes.

The 26. we departed from S. Auis Baye, within Cape Blanco, where we refreshed ourselues with fishe, and other necessaries: and the 29. we came to Cape Verde, which lieth in 14. degrees, and a halfe. These people are all blacke, and are called Negroes, without any apparell, sauing before their priuities: of stature goodly men, and well liking, by reason of their foode, which passeth all other Guyneans for kine, goates, pullin, rise, fruits, and fishe. Here we tooke fishes with heades like Conies, and teeth nothing varying, of a iollie thickness, but not past a foote long, and is not to be eaten without flaying or cutting of his head. To speak somewhat of the sundry sortes of these Guyneans. The people of Cape Verde, are called Leophares, and counted the goodliest men of al other, sauing the Manicongoes, which do inhabite on this side the cape de Buena Speranza. These Leophares haue warres against the Ieloffes,[3] which

Cape Verde in 14 degrees.

[1] *We* in edition of 1810.

[2] In 21° N.

[3] Jaloffs, the people of Senegal.

are borderers by them: their weapons are bowes and arrowes, targets, and short daggers, darts also, but varying from other Negroes: for whereas the other use a long dart to fight with in their hands, they carry fiue or sixe small ones a piece, which they cast with. These men also are more ciuil than any other, because of their dailie traffike with the Frenchmen, and are of nature very gentle, and louing: for while we were there, we tooke in a Frenchman, who was one of the 19. that going to Brasill, in a Barke of Diepe, of 60. tunnes, and being a sea boord of Cape De Verde, 200. leagues, the plankes of their barke with a sea brake out upon them so suddenly, that much a doe they had to saue themselves in their boates: but by God's prouidance, the wind being westerly, which is rarely seene there, they got to the shoare, to the Isles Braues, and in great penurie got to Cape Verde, where they remained sixe weekes, and had meate and drinke of the same people. The said Frenchman hauing forsaken his fellowes, which were three leagues off from the shoare, and wandring with the Negroes too and fro, fortuned to come to the water-side, and communing with certaine of his countreymen, which were in our ship, by their perswasions came away with vs: but his entertainement amongst them was such that he desiried it not, but through the importunate request of his Countreymen, consented at the last. Here we staid but one night, and part of the day: for the 7. of December wee came away, in that pretending to haue taken Negroes there perforce, the Mynions men gaue them there to vnderstand of our comming, and our pretence, wherefore they did auoide the snares we had laid for them.

The 8. of December we ankered by a small Island, called Alcatrarsa, wherein at our going a shoare, we found nothing but sea-birds, as we call them Ganets, but by the Portingals called Alcatrarses, who for that cause gaue the said Island the same name. Herein halfe of our boates were laden with yonge and olde fowle, who not being vsed to the sight of men, flew so about vs, that wee stroke them downe with poles. In this place, the two ships riding, the two barkes, with their boates, went into an Island of the Sapies, called La Formio, to see if they could take any of them, and there landed to the number of 80. in armour, and espying certaine, made to them, but they fled in such order into the woods, that it booted them not to followe, so going on their way forward til they came to a riuer which they could not passe ouer, they espied on the other side two men, who with their bowes and arrowes shot terribly at them. Whereupon we discharged certaine harquebusses to them againe, but the ignorant people waied it not, because they knewe not the danger thereof: but vsing a maruelous crying in their fight, with leaping, and turning their tailes, that it was most strange to see, and gaue vs great pleasure to behold them. At the last, one being hurt with a harquebusse vpon the thigh, looked vpon his wound, and wist not howe it came, because he could not see the pellet. Here Master Hawkins perceauing no good to be done amongst them, because we could not finde their townes, and also not knowing how to goe into Rio Grande[1] for want of a Pilot, which was the very occasion of our comming thither: and finding so many sholes, feared with our great ships to goe in, and therefore departed on our pretended way to the Idols.[2]

The 10. of December, hauing a northeast wind, with raine, and storme, which weather continued two daies together, was the occasion that the Salomon and Tyger lost our companie: for whereas the Iesus and pinnesse ankered at one of the Islands, called Sambula, the 12. day, the Salomon and Tiger came not thither, till the 14. In this Island we staied certaine daies, going every day a shoare,

The Island called Sambula.

[1] The Rio Grande was discovered in 1460 by Cadamosto, and is now called the Jeba, in 11° 50′ N.

[2] Ilhas dos Idolos, in 9° 35′ N.

to take the Inhabitants with burning, and spoiling their townes, who before were Sapies, and were conquered by the Samboses, Inhabitants beyond Sierra Leona.

The Samboses had inhabited there 3 yeeres before our coming thither, and in so short space haue so planted the ground, that they had great plentie of mill, rise, rootes, pompions, pullin, goates, of small frye dried, euery house full of the countrey fruite planted by God's prouidence, as Palmito trees, fruites like dates, and sundry other in no place in all that countrey so aboundantly, whereby they liued more deliciously then other. These inhabitants haue diuers of the Sapies, which they tooke in the warres, as their slaues, whome onely they keepe to till the ground, in that they neither haue the knowledge thereof, nor yet will work themselues, of whom wee tooke many in that place, but of the Samboses none at all, for they fled into the maine. Al the Samboses haue white teeth as wee haue, far vnlike to the Sapies, which doe inhabite about Rio grande, for their teeth are all filed, which they doe for a brauerie, to set out themselues, and doe iagge their flesh, both legges, armes, and bodies, as workmanlike as a Jerkinmaker with vs pinketh a ierkin. These Sapies be more ciuil then the Samboses, for whereas the Samboses liue most by the spoile of their enemies, both in taking their victuals and eating them also, the Sapies doe not eat mans flesh, vnless in the warres they be driuen by necessitie thereunto, which they haue not vsed, but by the example of the Samboses, but liue onely with fruitt, and cattel, whereof they haue great store. This plentie is the occasion that the Sapies desire not warre, except that they be therevnto prouoked by the inuasions of the Samboses, whereas the Samboses for want of foode, are inforced thereunto, and therefore are not woont onely to take them that they kill, but also keepe those that they take, vntill such time as they want meate and then they kill them. There is also another occasion

The Sambose.

Sapies.

that prouoketh the Samboses to warre against the Sapies, which is for couetousnes of their riches. For whereas the Sapies haue an order to burie their dead in certaine places appointed for that purpose, with their golde about them, the Samboses diggeth vp the ground to haue the same treasure, for the Samboses haue not the like store of golde, that the Sapies haue. In this Island of Sambula,[1] we found about 50. boates, called Almadyes, or Canoas, which are made of one peece of wood, digged out like a trough, but yet of a good proportion, being about 8. yardes long, and one in bredth, hauing a beake head, and a sterne very proportionably made, and on the outside artificially carued, and painted red, and blewe: they are able to carry 20. or 30. men, but they are about the coast able to carry three score and vpwards. In these Canoas they rowe standing vpright, with an ower somewhat longer then a man, the ende whereof is made about the breadth and length of a man's hand, of the largest sort. They rowe very swift, and in some of them foure rowers, and one to steere, make as much way as a paire of oares in the Thames of London. Their Townes are prettily divided, with a maine streete at the entering in, that goeth thorough their Towne, and another overthwart streete, which maketh their townes crosse waies: their houses are built in a rank very orderly in the face of the streete, and they are made round, like a doue cote, with stakes set full of Palmito leaues, insteede of a wall: they are not much more than a fathome large, and two of heighth, and thatched with Palmito leaues very close, other some with reede, and ouer the roofe thereof, for the better garnishing of the same, there is a rounde bundle of reede pretily contriued like a louer:[2] in the inner part, they make a loft of stickes, whereupon they lay all their prouision of victuals: a place they reserue at their entrance for the kitchin, and the place they lie in is diuided with certaine mats artificially made with the rine

The forme of their townes.

[1] Probably the modern Sherboro Island, in 7° 30′ N. [2] Bower?

of Palmito trees: their bedsteedes are of small staues, laide along, and raised a foote from the ground, vpon which is laide a matte, and another vpon them when they list: for other couering they haue none. In the middle of the Towne there is a house, larger and higher then the other, but in form alike, adioyning vnto the which, there is a place made of four goode stancions of woode, and a rounde roofe ouer it, the grounde raised round with claye, a foot high, vpon the which floore were strawed many fine mats: this is the consultation house, the like whereof is in all Townes, as the Portingals affirme: in which place, when they sit in Counselle, the King or Captaine sitteth in the middes, and the Elders vpon the floore by him: (for they give reuerence to their Elders,) and the common sorte sitte round about them. There they sitte to examine matters of theft, which if a man be taken with to steale but a Portingall clothe from another, he is sold to the Portingals for a slaue. They consult also, and take order what tyme they shall go to warres: and as it is certainly reported by the Portingals, they take order in gathering of fruites in the season of the yeere, and also for receiuing of Palmito wine, which is gathered by a hole cutte in the toppe of a tree, and a gorde set for the receauing thereof, which falleth in by droppes, and yieldeth freshe wine againe within a moneth, and this diuided, part and portion like to euery man, by the iudgment of the Captaine and Elders, euery man holdeth himself contented: and this surely I iudge to be a very good order, for otherwise, where scarcitie of Palmito is, euery man would haue the same, which might breede great strife: but for such things, as euery man doth plant for himselfe, the sower thereof reapeth it to his own vse, so that nothing is common but that which is vnset by man's hands. In their houses there is more common passage of Lizardes like Euats, and other greater, of black and blewe colour, of neere a foot long, besides their tailes, then there is with

Mise in great houses. The Sapies and Samboses also, vse in their wars bowes and arrowes, made of reedes, with heads of yron poisoned with the iuce of a Cucumber, whereof I haue had many in my handes. In their battels they haue target men, with broade wicker targets, and dark with heades at both endes, of yron, the one in forme of a two-edged sworde, a foote and a halfe long, and at the other ende, the yron long of the same length, made to counter-pease it, that in casting, it might flee level, rather than for any other purpose, as I can iudge. And when they espie the enemie, the Captaine to cheer his men crieth, *Hungry*, and they answere *Heygre*, and with that euery man placeth himselfe in order, for about euery target man three bowe-men will couer themselves, and shoote as they see aduantage, and when they giue the onset they make such terrible cryes that they may be heard two miles off. For their beleefe, I can heare of none that they haue, but in such as they themselues imagine to see in their dreames, and so worshippe the pictures, whereof we saw some like vnto Diuels. In this Island aforesaide, we soiourned vnto the one and twentieth of December, where hauing taken certain Negroes, and of their fruites, rise, and mill, as we could well carry away (whereof there was such store that we might have laden one of our Barkes therewith), we departed, and at our departure diuers of our men being desirous to goe a shoare, to fetch Pompions, which having prooued, they found to be very good, certaine of the Tygers men went also, amongst the which there was a Carpenter, a yong man, who with his fellows hauing fet many, and carried them downe to their boates, as they were ready to depart, desired his fellowes to tarry, while he might goe vp to fetch a few which he had layed by for himselfe, who being more licorous than circumspect, went up without weapon, and as he went vp alone, possibly being marked of the Negroes that were vpon the trees, espying him what he

The extreme negligence of one of the companie.

did, perceauing him to be alone, and without weapon, dogged him, and finding him occupied in binding his Pompions together, came behind him, overthrowing him, and straight cut his throat, as he afterwards was found by his fellowes, who came to the place for him, and there found him naked.

The two and twentieth the Captaine went into the Riuer, called Callowsa, with the two Barkes, and the Iohns pinnesse, and Salomons boate, leauing at anker in the Riuers mouth the two shippes, the Riuers being twentie leagues in, where the Portingals roade: he came the fiue and twentieth, and dispatched his busines, and so returned with two Carauels, loaden with Negroes. The Riuer Callowsa.

The 27 the Captaine being aduertised by the Portingals, of a Towne of the Negroes, called Bymba, being in the way as they returned, where was not onely great quantitie of golde, but also that there were not aboue fortie men, and a hundred women and children in the Towne, so that if he would giue the aduenture vppon the same, he might gette a hundreth slaues: with the which tydings hee beeing gladde, because the Portingals should not thinke him to bee of so base a courage, but that he durst to giue them that, and greater attempts: and being thereunto also the more prouoked with the prosperous successe he had in other Islands adiacent, where he had put them all to flight, and taken in one boate 20. together, determined to stay before the Towne three or foure howres, to see what he could doe: and therefore prepared his men in armour, and weapon together, to the number of fortie men well appointed, hauing to their guides certaine Portingals, in a boate, who brought some of them to their death: we landing boate after boate, and diuers of our men scattering themselues, contrarie to the Captaines will, by one or two in a companie, for the hope they had to finde golde in their houses, ransacking the same, in the meane time the Negroes came The towne Bymba. Portingals not to be trusted.

vppon them, and hurte many, beeing thus scattered, whereas if fiue or sixe had bene together, they had bene able, as their companies did, to giue the overthrowe to 40. of them, and being driuen downe to take their boates, were followed so hardly by a route of negroes, who by that tooke courage to pursue them to their boates, that not onely some of them, but others standing a shoare, not looking for any such matter, by meanes that the Negroes did flie at the first, and our companie remained in the towne, were suddenly so set vpon, that some with great hurte recouered their boates: other some not able to recouer the same, tooke the water, and perished by meanes of the oaze. While this was a doing, the Captaine, who with a dosen men went thorough the Towne, returned, finding 200. Negroes at the water side, shooting at them in the boates, and cutting them in peeces, which were drowned in the water, at whose coming they ranne all away: so he entered his boates, and before he could put off from the shore, they returned againe, and shot very fiercely, and hurt diuers of them. Thus wee returned backe, somewhat discomforted, although the Captaine in a singular wise manner, with countenance very cheerful outwardly, as though he did little weigh the death of his men, nor yet the great hurt of the rest, although his heart inwardly was broken in peeces for it, done to this ende, that the Portingals, being with him, should not presume to resist against him, nor take occasion to put him to further displeasure or hinderance, for the death of our men: having gotten by our going ten Negroes and lost seven of our best men, whereof Master Field, Captaine of the Salomon, was one, and we had 27. of our men hurt. In the same howse, while this was a doing, there happened at the same instant, a meruelous miracle to them in the shippes, who roade ten leagues to seaward, by many sharks or Tuberons, who came about the ships, among which one was taken by the Iesus, and foure by the

Want of circumspection in our men.

Salomon, and one very sore hurt, escaped: and so it fell out of our men, whereof one of the Iesus men, and foure of the Salomons were killed, and the 5. hauing 20. wounds, was rescued, and scaped with much adoe.

The 28. they came to their ships, the Iesus and the Salomon, and the 30. departed from thence to Taggarin. Taggarin.

The first of Januarie, the two barkes, and both the boates forsooke the ships, and went into a riuer, called the Casseroes, and the 6. hauing dispatched their busines, the two barkes returned, and came to Taggarin, where the two ships were at anker. Not two daies after the comming of the two shippes thither, they put their water caske a shoare, and filled it with water, to season the same, thinking to haue filled it with fresh water afterward: and while their men were some a shoare, and some at their boates, the Negroes set vpon them in the boates, and hurt diuers of them, and came to the caskes, and cut off the hoopes of twelue butts, which lost us 4. or 5. dayes time, besides great want we had of the same: soiourning at Taggarin, the Swallowe went up the riuer about her traffike, where they saw great townes of the Negroes, and Canoas, that had three score men in a peece: there they vnderstood of the Portingals, of a great battell, betweene them of the Sierra Leona side, and them of Taggarin: they of Sierra Leona had prepared 300 canoas to inuade the other. The time was appointed not past 6. daies after our departure from thence, which we would haue seene, to the intent we might haue taken some of them, had it not been for the death and sicknes of our men, which came by the contagiousness of the place, which made vs to make haste away.

January. The riuer of Casserroes. Very great Canoas.

The 18. of Januarie at night, we departed from Tagarrin, being bound to the West Indiaes, before which departure certaine of the Salomons men went a shoare, to fil water in the night, and as they came a shoare with their boate, being ready to leape a land, one of them espied a Negroe in a

The contagion of the countrey of Sierra Leona.

white coate, standing upon a rocke, being ready to haue receaued them, when they came a shoare, hauing in sight of his fellowes also, eight or nine, some in one place leaping out, and some in another, but they hid themselves straight againe: whereupon our men doubting they had bene a great companie, and sought to haue taken them at more aduantage, as God would, departed to their shippes, not thinking there had bene such a mischiefe pretended toward them as then was in deede. Which the next day we understood of a Portingall, that came downe to vs, who had traffiked with the Negroes, by whome he understoode, that the King of Sierra Leona had made all the power he could, to take some of vs, partly for the desire he had to see what kind of people we were, that had spoiled his people at the Idols, whereof he had news before our comming, and as I iudge also, vpon other occasions prouoked by the Tangomangoes, but sure we were that the armie was come downe, by means that in the euening we sawe such a monstrous fire, made by the watring place, that before was not seen, which fire is the onely mark for the Tangomangoes to know where their armie is alwaies. If these men had come downe in the euening, they had done vs great displeasure, for that we were a shoare filling water: but God, who worketh all things for the best, would not haue it so, and by him wee escaped without danger, his name bee praysed for it.

Tangomangoes.

Februarie.

The 29. of the same moneth, we departed with all our ships from the Sierra Leona, towards the West Indias, where for the space of 21. daies, wee were becalmed, hauing nowe and then contrarie windes, and some Ternados amongest the same calme, which happened to vs very ill, being but reasonably watered, for so great a companie of Negroes, and our selues, which pinched us all, and that which was worst, put vs in such feare, that many neuer thought to haue reached to the Indias, without great death of Negroes, and of themselves: but Almightie God, who neuer suffereth his elect to perish, sent vs the sixteene of Februarie, the ordinarie Briese, which is the Northwest winde, which never left us, till we came to an Island of the Cannybals, called Sancta Dominica, where we arriued the ninth of March, vpon a Satturday: and because it was the most desolate place in all the Island, we could see no Cannybals, but some of their houses, where they dwelled, and as it should seeme, forsooke the place, for want of freshe water, for we coulde finde none there but raine water, and such as fell from the hils, and remayned as a puddle in the dale, whereof we filled for our Negroes. The Cannybals of that Island, and also others adiacent, are the most desperate warriers that are in the Indias, by the Spaniards report, who are neuer able to conquer them, and they are molested by them not a little, when they are driuen to water there in any of those Islands: of very late, not two moneths past, in the said Islande, a Carauell being driuen to water, was in the night sette upon by the Inhabitants, who cutte their cable in the halser, whereby they were driuen a shoare, and so taken by them and eaten. The greene Dragon of New-hauen whereof was Captaine one Bontemps, in Marche also, came to one of those Islands, called Granado, and being driuen to water, could not doe the same, for the Cannybals, who fought with him very desperately two daies. For our part also, if we had not lighted vpon the deserted place in all the Island, we could not haue missed, but should haue bene greatly troubled by them, by all the Spaniards reportes, who make them Deuils in respect of men.

Dominica Island.

March.

Cannyballs exceeding cruell, and to be auoided.

The tenth day, at night, we departed from thence, and the fifteenth had sight of nine Islands, called the Testigos: And the sixteenth of an Island, called Margarita, where we were entertayned by the Alcalde, and had both beeues and sheepe given us, for the refreshing of our men: but the Gouernour of the Island would neither come to speake with

The Testigos Islands.

Margarita Island.

our Captaine, neither yet give him any licence to traffike: and to displease vs the more, whereas wee had hired a Pilot, to haue gone with vs, they would neither suffer him to goe with vs, but also sent worde by a Carauell out of hand, to Santo Domingo, to the Viceroy, who doth represent the King's person, of our arriuall in those parts, which had like to haue turned vs to great displeasure, by the means that the same Viceroy did send word to Cape de la Vela, and to other places along the coast, commanding them by the vertue of his authoritie, and the obedience that they owe to their Prince, no man should traffike with vs, but should resiste vs with all the force they could.[1] In this Island, notwithstanding that we were not within foure leagues of the Towne, yet were they so afraid, that not only the Gouernour himselfe, but also all the Inhabitants forsooke their Towne, assembling all the Indians to them, and fled into the mountains, as we were partly certified, and also saw the experience ourselves, by some of the Indians comming to see vs, who by three Spaniards a horseback passing hard by vs, went vnto the Indians, hauing euery one of them their bowes, and arrowes, procuring them away, who before were conuersant with vs. Here perceauing no traffike to be had with them, nor yet water for the refreshing of our men, wee were driuen to depart the twentieth day, and the two and twentieth, we came to a place in the mayne, called Kenimnawo, whither the Captaine going in his pinnesse, spake with certaine Spaniards, of whome he demanded traffike, but they made him answere, they were but souldiers newly come thither, and were not able to buy one Negroe: whereupon he asked for a watring place, and they pointed him a place two leagues off, called Sancta Fee, where we found maruellous goodly watring, and commodious for the taking in thereof: for that the fresh water came into the Sea, and so our shippes had aboord the shoare 20. fathome water.

[1] Don Antonio de Osorio was President and Captain-General of San Domingo in 1564.

Neere about this place, inhabited certaine Indians, who the next day after we câme thither, came downe to vs, presenting mill and cakes of bread, which they had made of a kinde of corne called Maise, in bignes of a pease, the eare whereof is much like to a teasell, but a span in length, hauing theron a number of graines. Also they brought downe to vs which we bought for beades, pewter whistles, glasses, kniues, and other trifles, Hennes, Potatoes and pines. These potatoes be the most delicate rootes that may be eaten, and doe far exceede their passeneps or carets. Their pines be of the bignes of two fistes, the outside whereof is of the making of a pineapple, but it is soft like the rinde of a coucomber, and the inside eateth like an apple, but it is more delicious than any sweete apple sugred. These Indians be of colour tawnie like an Oliue, hauing every one of them both men and women, haire all blacke, and no other colour, the women wearing the same hanging down to their shoulders, and the men rounded, and without beards, neither men nor women suffering any haire to growe in any part of their body, but daily puls it off as it groweth. They goe all naked, the men couering no part of their body but their yard, vpon the which they weare a gourd or piece of cane, made fast with a threede about his loins, leauing the other parts of their members vncouered, whereof they take no shame. The women also vncouered, sauing with a cloth which they weare a handbreadth, wherewith they couer their privities both before and behind. These people be very small feeders, for trauelling they carry but two small bottels of gourdes, wherein they put in one the iuice of Sorrell, whereof they haue great store, and in the other flowre of their Maise, which being moist, they eate, taking sometime of the other. These men carie euery man his bowes and arrowes, whereof some arrowes are poisoned for warres, which they keepe in a cane together, which cane is of the bignesse of a mans

The vse of Sorrell.

arme, other some with broad heades of iron wherewith they strike fishe in the water: the experience thereof we sawe not once nor twise, but daily for the time we taried there, for they are so good archers that the Spaniards for feare thereof arme themselues and their horses with quilted canuas of two inches thicke, and leaue no place of their bodie open to their enemies, sauing their eyes, which they may not hide, and yet oftentimes are they hit in that so small a scantling: their poison is of such a force, that a man being stricken therewith, dieth within foure and twentie howres, as the Spaniards doe affirme, and in my iudgment it is like there can bee no stronger poyson as they make it, vsing thereunto apples which are very fair, and red of colour, but are a strong poison, with the which together with venemous Bats, Vipers, Adders, and other serpents, they make a medley, and therewith anoint the same.

The making of their poison.

The maners of the yong women.

The Indian women delight not when they are yong in bearing of children, because it maketh them haue hanging breasts, which they account to bee great deforming in them, and vpon that occasion while they be yong, they destroy their seede, saying that it is fitted for olde women. Moreouer, when they are deliuered of childe, they goe straight to washe themselues, without making any further ceremonie for it, not lying in bed as our women doe. The beds which they haue are made of Gossopine cotton, and wrought artificially of diuers colours, which they carie about with them when they trauell, and making the same fast to two trees, lie therein they and their women. The people bee surely gentle and tractable, and such as desire to liue peaceablie, or else had it bene vnpossible for the Spaniards to haue conquered them as they did, and the more to liue now peacable, they being many in number, and the Spaniards so few.

From hence we departed the eight and twentie, and the next day we passed betweene the maineland and the island called Tortuga, a very lowe Island, in the yeere of our Lord God one thousand fiue hundred sixtie fiue aforesaid, and sailed along the coast vntil the first of Aprill, at which time the Captaine sayled along in the Jesus pinnace to discerne the coast, and saw many Caribes a shore, and some also in their Canowas, which made tokens vnto him of friendship, and showed him golde, meaning thereby that they would traffique for wares. Whereupon hee stayed to see the maners of them, and so for two or three trifles gaue such things as they had about them, and departed: but the Caribes were very importunate to haue them come a shore, which if it had not bene for want of wares to traffique with them, he would not haue denied them, because the Indians we sawe before were very gentle people, and such as doe no man hurt. But as God would haue it, hee wanted that thing, which if hee had had, would haue bene his confusion: for there were no kinde of people as wee tooke them to bee, but more deuelish a thousand partes, and are eaters and deuourers of any man they catche, as it was afterwards declared vnto vs at Burboroata by a Carauell comming out of Spaine with certaine souldiours and a captain generall sent by the king for those Eastuard parts of the Indians, who sailing along in his pinnace as our Captaine did to descrie the Coast, was by the Caribes called a shore with sundrie tokens made to him of friendshippe, and golde shewed as though they desired traffique, with the which the Spaniardes being moued, suspecting no deceite at all, went a Shore amongst them, who was no sooner a shore, but with 4. or 5. more was taken, the rest of his company being inuaded by them, saued themselues by flight, but they that were taken, paid their ransome with their liues, and were presently eaten. And this is their practice to toll with their golde the ignorant to their snares: they are bloudsuckers both of Spaniards, Indians, and all that light in their laps, not sparing their

The Isle of Tortuga.

The crueltie of the Caribes.

owne countrymen if they can conueniently come by them. Their pollicie in fight with the Spaniards is maruellous: for they choose for their refuge the mountaines and woods where the Spaniards with their horses cannot follow them, And if they fortune to be met in the plaine where one horseman may ouerunne 100. of them, they haue a deuise of late practised by them to pitch stakes of wood in the ground, and also small iron pikes to mischiefe their horses, wherein they show themselues politike warriours. They haue more abondance of golde then all the Spaniards haue, and liue vpon the mountains where the mines are in such number, that the Spaniards haue much adoe to get any of them from them, and yet sometimes by assembling a great number of them, which happeneth once in two yeeres, they get a piece from them, which afterwards they keepe sure inough.

Thus hauing escaped the daunger of them, wee kept our course along the coast, and came the third of Aprill to a Towne called Burboroata,[1] where his ships came to an anker, and hee himselfe went a shore to speeke with the Spaniardes, to whome he declared himselfe to be an Englishman, and came thither to trade with them by the way of merchandize, and therefore required licence for the same. Unto whom they made answere, that they were forbidden by the king to traffique with any forren nation, vpon penaltie to forfeit their goods, therefore they desired him not to molest them any further, but to depart as he came, for other comfort he might not looke for at their hands, because they were subiects, and might not goe beyond the law. But he replied that his necessitie was such he might not so doe: for being in one of the Queens Armados of England, and hauing many souldiours in them, he had neede both of some refreshing for them, and of victuals, and of money also, without the which he could not depart, and

Burboroata.

[1] Burburata, on the coast of Venezuela.

with much other talke persuaded them not to feare any dishonest part of his behalfe towards them, for neither would he commit any such thing to the dishonour of his prince, nor yet for his honest reputation and estimation, vnlesse hee were too rigorously delt withall, which he hoped not to finde at their handes, in that it should as well redounde to their profite, as his owne, and also he thought they might do it without daunger, because their princes were in amitie one with another, and for our partes wee had free trafique in Spaine and Flaunders, which are in his dominions, and therefore hee knew no reason why he should not haue the like in all his dominions. To the which the Spaniardes made answere, that it lay not in them to giue any licence, for that they had a Gouernour to whom the gouernment of those partes was committed, but if they would stay tenne dayes, they would send to their Gouernour who was three score leagues off, and would return answere within the space appointed, of his mind.

In the meane time they were contented he should bring his ships into harbour, and there they would deliuer him any victuals he would require. Whereupon, the fourth day we went in, where being one day and receiuing all things according to promise, the Captaine advised himselfe that to remain there tenne dayes idle, spending victuals and men's wages, and perhaps in the ende receiue no good answere from the Gouernour, it were meere follie, and therefore determined to make request to haue licence for the sale of certaine lean and sicke Negroes which he had in his shippe like to die upon his hands if he kept them ten dayes, hauing litle or no refreshing for them, whereas other men hauing them, they would bee recouered well inough. And this request hee was forced to make, because he had not otherwise wherewith to pay for victuals and for necessaries which he should take: which request being put in writing and presented, the officers and towne-dwellers assembled together, and finding his request so reasonable, graunted him licence for thirtie Negroes, which afterwards they caused the officers to view, to the intent they should grant to nothing but that were very reasonable, for feare of answering thereunto afterwards. This being past, our captaine according to their licence, thought to haue made sale, but the day past and none came to buy, who before made show that they had great neede of them, and therefore wist not what to surmise of them, whether they went about to prolong the time of the Governour his answere because they would keepe themselues blamelesse, or for any other pollicie he knew not, and for that purpose sent them worde, maruelling what the matter was that none came to buie them. They answered, because they had graunted licence onely to the poore to buie those Negroes of small price, and their money was not so readie as other mens of more wealth.

More then that, as soone as euer they saw the shippes, they conueyed away their money by their wiues that went into the mountaines for feare, and were not yet returned, and yet asked two dayes to seeke their wiues and fetch their money. Notwithstanding, the next day divers of them came to cheapen, but could not agree of price, because they thought the price too high. Whereupon the Captaine perceiuing they went about to bring downe the price, and meant to bie, and would not confesse if he had licence, that hee might sell at any reasonable rate, as they were woorth in other places, did send for the Principals of the Towne, and made a shew hee would depart, declaring himselfe to be very sory that hee had so much troubled them, and also that he had sent for the Gouernour to come downe, seeing now his pretence was to depart, whereat they maruelled much, and asked him what cause mooued him thereunto, seeing by their working he was in possibilitie to haue his licence. To the which he replied that it was not onely a licence that he sought, but profite, which hee perceiued was not there to be had, and therefore would seeke further, and withall shewed him his writings what he paied for his Negroes, declaring also the great charge he was at in his shipping, and men's wages, and therefore to counteruaile his charge, hee must sell his Negroes for a greater price then they offered. So they doubting his departure, put him in comfort to sell better there than in any other place. And if it fell out that he had no licence, that he should not lose his labour in tarying, for they would buie without licence. Whereupon, the Captaine, being put in comfort, promised them to stay, so that he might make sale of his leane Negroes, which they graunted vnto. And the next day did sell some of them, who hauing bought and paied for them, thinking to haue had a discharge of the Customer for the custome of the Negroes, being the King's dutie, they gaue it away to the poore for God's sake, and did refuse to giue the discharge in writing, and the poore not trusting their wordes, for feare, leaste hereafter it might bee demaunded of them, did refraine from buying any more, so that nothing els was done ontill the Gouernours comming downe, which was the fourteenth day, and then the Captaine made petition, declaring that hee was come thither in a shippe of the Queen's maiesties of England, beyng bound to Guinie, and thither driuen by winde and weather, so that being come thither, hee had neede of sundry necessaries for the reparation of the said Nauie, and also great neede of money for the paiment of his Souldiours, vnto whom he had promised paiment, and therefore although hee would, yet would not they depart without it, and for that purpose requested licence for the sale of certaine of his Negroes, declaring that although they were forbidden to traffique with straungers, yet for that there was a great amitie betweene their princes, and that the thing pertained to our Queenes highnesse, hee thought he might doe their prince great seruice, and that it would be well taken at his handes to doe it in this cause. The which allegations, with diuers others put in request, were presented vnto the Gouernour who sitting as counsell for that matter, granted vnto his request for licence. But yet there fell out another thing which was the abating of the kings custome, being vpon euery slaue 30. duckets, which would not be granted vnto.

Whereupon the captain perceiuing that they would neither come neere his price hee looked for by a great deale, nor yet would abate the kings custome of that they offered, so that either hee must bee a great looser by his wares, or els compell the officers to abate the same kings custome which was too vnreasonable, for to a higher price hee could not bring the buiers. Therefore the sixteenth of

An hundred Englishmen in armour.

Aprill hee prepared one hundred men well armed with bowes, arrowes, harquebusses and pikes, with the which hee marched to the towne wardes, and beyng perceiued by the Gouernour, hee straight with all expedition sent messengers to know his request, desiring him to marche no further forward vntill hee had answere againe, which incontinent he should haue. So our captaine declaring how vnreasonable a thing the kings custome was, requesting to haue the same abated, and to pay seuen and a halfe per centum, which is the ordinarie custome for wares thorough his dominions there, and vnto this if they would not graunt, he would displease them. And this worde beyng caried to the Gouernour, answere was returned that all things should bee to his content, and thereupon hee determined to depart, but the soldiours and mariners finding so little credite in their promises, demaunded gages for the performance of the premisses, or els they would not depart. And thus they being constrained to send gages, we departed, beginning our traffique, and ending the same without disturbance. Thus hauing made traffique in the harborough vntill the 28. our Captaine with his ships intended to goe out of the roade, and purposed to make shew of his departure, because now the common sort hauing imploied their money, the rich men were come to towne, who made no shew that they were come to buie, so that they went about to bring downe the price, and by this pollicie the captaine knew they would be made the more eger, for feare lest we departed, and they should goe without any at all.

The nine and twentie we being at anker without the roade, a French shippe called the Greene Dragon of New-hauen, whereof was captaine one Bon Temps came in, who saluted vs after the manner of the Sea, with certaine pieces of ordinaunce, and we resaluted him with the like againe: with whom hauing communication, he declared that he had bene at the Mine in Guinie, and was beaten off by the Portingals Gallies, and inforced to come thither to make sale of such wares as he had: and further that the like was happened vnto the Minion, besides the Captaine Dauie Carlet and a merchaunt with a doozen mariners betrayed by the Negroes at their first arriual thither, and remaining prisoners with the Portingals, besides other misadventures of the losse of their men, happened thorough the great lacke of fresh water, with great doubts of bringing home the ships, which was most sorowfull for vs to vnderstand.

The reports of the mishaps of the Minion in Guinie.

Thus hauing ended our traffique here the 4. of May, wee departed, leauing the French man behind us, the night before the which, the Caribes whereof I haue made mention before, being to the number of 200. came in their Canowas to Burboroata, intending by night to haue burned the towne, and taken the Spaniards, who being more vigilant because of our being there, than their custome was, perceiuing them comming, raised the towne, who in a moment being a horsebacke, by means their custome is for all doubts to keepe their horses readie sadled, in the night set vpon

May.

Horses kept ready sadled.

them, and tooke one, the rest making shift for themselues, escaped away. But this one, because he was their guide, and was the occasion that diuers times they had made inuasion upon them, had for his trauell a stake thrust through his fundement, and so out at his necke.

The sixt of May aforesayd, wee came to an Island called Curasoa,[1] where wee had thought to haue ankred, but could not find ground, and hauing let fall an anker with two cables, were faine to weie it againe, and the 7. sayling along the coast to seeke an harborow, and could finde none, came to an anker where wee rode open in the sea. In this place wee had traffique for Hides, and found great refreshing both of beefe, mutton and lambes, whereof there was such plentie, that saving the skinnes, we had the flesh giuen vs for nothing, the plentie whereof was so abundaunt, that the worst in the ship thought scorn not onely of mutton, but also of sodden lambe, which they disdained to eate vnrosted.

Exceeding plentie of cattell in Curasoa.

The increase of Cattell in this Island is maruellous, which from a doozen of each sort brought thither by the Gouernour, in 25. yeeres had 100. thousand at the least, and of other Cattell was able to kill without spoile of the increase 15. hundred yeerely, which he killeth for the skinnes, and of the flesh saueth onely the tongues, the rest he leaueth to the foule to deuour. And this I am able to affirme, not vpon the Gouernours owne report, who was the first that brought the increase thither, and so remaineth vnto this day, but also by that I sawe myselfe in one field, where an hundred oxen lay one by another all whole, sauing the skin and tongue taken away, and it is not so maruelous a thing why they doe thus cast away the flesh in all the Islands of the West Indies, seeing the land is great, and more then they are able to inhabite, the people fewe, hauing delicate

[1] Curaçoa is thirty miles long by ten. It was first settled in 1527 by order of Charles V, and was captured by the Dutch in 1632.

fruit and meates inough besides to feed vpon, which they rather desire, and the increase which passeth mans reason to beleeve, when they come to a great number: for in S. Domingo an Island called by the finders thereof, Hispaniola, is so great quantitie of Cattell, and such increase thereof, that notwithstanding the daily killing of them for their hides, it is not able to asswage the number of them, but they are deuoured by wild dogs, whose number is such by suffering them first to range the woods and mountains that they eate and destroy 60000. a yeere, and yet small lacke found of them. And no maruell, for the said Island is almost as big as all England, and being the first place that was found of all the Indies, and of long time inhabited before the rest, and therefore it ought of reason to be most populous, and to this hower the Viceroy and Counsell roiall, abideth there as in the chiefest place of all the Indies to prescribe orders to the rest for the kings behalfe, yet have they but one citie and 13. villages in all the same Island, whereby the spoile of them in respect of the increase is nothing.

The 15. of the foresaid moneth we departed from Curasoa, being not a little to the reioicing of our Captaine and vs, that we had there ended our traffique, for notwithstanding our sweetemeate we had sower sauce, for by reason of our riding so open at sea, what with blastes whereby our ankers being agrounde, then at once came home, and also with contrary windes blowing, whereby for feare of the shore we were faine to hale off to haue ankerhold, sometimes a whole day and a night turning vp and downe, and this happened not once, but halfe a doozen times in the space of our being there.

The 16. we passed by an Island called Aruba,[1] and the 17 at night ankred 6. howers at the West end of Cabo de La Vela, and in the morning being the 18. weied againe, keep-

[1] A little island fourteen leagues west of Curaçoa.

ing our course, in the which time the captaine sailing by the shore in the pinnace, came to the Rancheria, a place where the Spaniards vse to fish for pearles, and there spoke with a Spaniard, who told him how farre off he was from Rio de la Hacha,[1] which because he would not overshoote, ankered that night againe, and the 19. came thither, where hauing talke with the kings treasurer of the Indies resident there, declared his quiet traffique in Burboroata, and shewed a certificate of the same, made by the gouernour thereof, and therefore he desired to haue the like there also: but the treasurer made answer that they were forbidden by the Viceroy and counsell of S. Domingo, who hauing intelligence of our being on the coast, did send expresse commission to resist vs, with all the force they could, insomuch that they durst not traffique with vs in no case, alleaging that if they did, they should loose all that they did traffique for, besides their bodies at the magistrates commaundement. Our captaine replied, that he was in an Armado of the Queenes maiesties of England, and sent about other her affaires, but driuen besides his pretended voyage, was inforced by contrary windes to come into those partes, where he hoped to find such friendship as he should doe in Spaine, to the contrary whereof he knew no reason in that there was amitie betwixt their princes.

But seeing they would contrary to all reson goe about to withstand his traffique, he would it should not be said by him, that hauing the force he hath, to be driuen from his traffique perforce, but he would rather put it in aduenture to try whether he or they should have the better, and therefore willed them to determine either to giue him licence to trade, or else to stand to their owne harmes: so vpon this it was determined hee should have licence to trade, but

[1] So called from the first Spanish settlers having given the Indians a hatchet to show them where water might be found. The mouth of the Rio de la Hacha, in 11° 31′ 30″ N., is famous for its pearl fishery.

they would giue him such a price as was the one halfe lesse then he had sold for before, and thus they sent word they would do, and none otherwise, and if it liked him not he might do what he would, for they were not determined to deale otherwise with him. Wherevpon, the Captaine waying their vnconscionable request, wrote to them a letter that they delt too rigorously with him, to goe about to cut his throte in the price of his commodities, which were so reasonablie rated, as they could not by a great deale have the like at any other mans hands. But seeing they had sent him this to his supper, hee would in the morning bring them as good a breakfast. And therefore in the morning being the 21. of May, he shot of a whole culuer into summon the towne, and preparing one hundred men in armour went a shore, hauing in his great boate two faulcons of brasse, and in the other boates double bases in their noses, which being perceiued by the townesmen, they incontinent in battell araie with their drumme and ensigne displayed, marched from the Towne to the sands, of footemen to the number of an hundred and fiftie, making great bragges with their cries, and weauing vs a shore, whereby they make a semblans to haue fought with vs in deede. But our captaine perceauing them so bragge, commaunded the two faulcons to bee discharged at them, which put them in no small feare to see, as they afterwards declared, such great pieces in a boate. At euery shotte they fell flatte to the ground, and as we approched neere vnto them, they broke their arraie, and dispersed themselues so much for feare of the ordinaunce, that at last they went all away with their ensigne. The horsemen also being about thirtie, made as braue a shew as might be, coming vp and downe with their horses, their braue white leather Targets in the one hand, and their Jauelings in the other, as though they would haue receiued vs at our landing. But when we landed, they gaue ground, and consulted what they should

M. Haukins his letter to the treasurer of Rio de la Hacha.

doe, for litle they thought we would haue landed so boldly: and therefore as the Captaine was putting his men in aray, and marched foruard to haue encountred with them, they sent a messenger on horsebacke with a flagge of truce to the Captaine, who declared that the treasurer maruelled what he went to doe to come a shore in that order, in consideration that they had graunted to euery reasonable request that hee did demaund: but the Captaine not well contented with this messenger, marched forwards. The messenger praied him to stay his men, and said if he would come apart from his men, the treasurer would come and speake with him, whereunto he did agree to common together. The Captaine onely with his armour without weapon, and the treasurer on horseback with his Jaueling, was afraid to come neere him for feare of his armour, which he said was worse then his weapon, and so keeping aloofe communing together, graunted in fine to all his requests. Which being declared by the Captaine to the company, they desired to haue pledges for the performance of all things, doubting that otherwise, when they had made themselues stronger, they would haue bene at defiance with vs: and seeing that now they might haue what they would request, they iudged it to be more wisdome to be in assurance then to be forced to make any more labours about it. So vpon this, gages were sent, and we made our traffique quietly with them. In the meantime while we staid here, we watred a good bredth off from the shore, whereby the strẽgth of the fresh water running into the sea, the salt water was made fresh. In this riuer we saw many crocodils of sũdry bignesses, but some as big as a boat with 4. feet, a long broad mouth, and a long taile, whose skin is so hard, that a sword will not pierce it. His nature is to liue out of the water as a frog doth, but he is a great deuourer, and spareth neither fish, which is his common food, nor beasts, nor men, if he take them, as the proofe thereof was knowen by a Negroe, who as he was filling water in the riuer was by one of them caried cleane away, and neuer seene after. His nature is euer when he would haue his praie, to crie, and sobbe like a christian bodie, to prouoke them to come to him, and then he snatcheth at them, and thereupon came this prouerbe that is appleid vnto women when they weepe, Lachryma Crocodili, the meaning whereof is, that as the Crocodile when he crieth, goeth then about most to deceiue, so doth a woman most commonly when she weepeth. Of these the master of the Jesus watched one and by the bankes side stroke him with a pike of a bill in the side, and after 3. or 4. times turning in sight, he sunke downe, and was not afterwards seene. In the time of our being in the riuers of Guinie, we saw many of a monstrous bignes, amongst the which the Captaine being in one of the barks comming downe the same, shot a faulcon at one, which very narowly he missed, and with a feare plunged into the water, making a streame like the way of a boate.

Now while we were here, whether it were of a feare that the Spaniards doubted wee would haue done them some harme before wee departed, or for any treason that they pretended towards vs, I am not able to say, but there came thither a captaine from some of the other townes, with a doozen souldiers, who vpon a time that our Captaine and the treasurer cleared all things betweene them, and were in a communication of a debt of the gouernours of Burboroata, which was to be paied by the said treasurer, who would not answere the same by any meanes. Certaine words of displeasure passed betwixt the captaine and him, and parting the one from the other, the treasurer possibly doubting that our Captaine would perforce haue sought the same, did immediately commaund his men in armour both horsemen and footemen: but because the Captaine was in the Riuer on the backe side of the towne with his other boates, and all his men vnarmed and without weapons, it was to be iudged he ment him little good, hauing that aduantage of him, that comming vpon the sudden, he might haue mischieved many of his men, but the captaine hauing vnderstanding thereof, not trusting to their gentlenesse, if they might haue the aduantage, departed aboord his ships, and at night returned againe, and demanded amongst other talke, what they ment by assembling their men in that order, and they answered, that their captaine being come to towne, did muster his men according to his accustomed maner. But it is to bee iudged to bee a cloake, in that coming for the purpose he might haue done it sooner, but the trueth is, they were not of force vntil then, whereby to enterprise any matter against vs, by means of pikes and harquebusses, whereof they haue want, and were now furnished by our captaine, and also 3. faulcons, which hauing got in other places, they had secretly conueied thither, which made them the bolder and also for that they saw now a conuenient place to do such a feat, and time also seruing thereunto, by the means that our men were not only vnarmed and vnprouided, as at no time before the like but also were occupied in hewing of wood, and least thinking of any harme: there were occasions to prouoke them thereunto. And I suppose they went about to bring it to effect in that I with another gentleman being in the towne, thinking of no harme towards vs, and seeing men assembling in armour to the treasurer's house, whereof I maruelled, and reuoking to minde the former talke betweene the captaine and him, and the vnreadinesse of our men, of whom aduantage might haue bene taken, departed out of the Towne immediately to giue knowledge thereof, but before we came to our men by a slight shot, two horsemen riding a gallop were come neere vs, being sent, as we did gesse, to stay vs least we should carie newes to our captaine; but seeing vs so neere our men staied their horses, comming together, and suffering us to passe, belike because we were so neere, that if they

The author of this storie.

had gone abont the same they had been espied by some of our men which then immediately would haue departed, whereby they should haue bene frustrate of their pretence: and so the two horsemen ridde about the bushes to espy what we did, and seeing vs gone, to the intent they might shadow their comming downe in post, whereof suspicion might be had, fained a simplo excuse in asking whether he could sell any wine, but that seemed so simple to the Captaine that standing in doubt of their curtesie, he returned in the morning with his 3. boates, appointed with bases in their noses, and his men with weapons accordingly, where as before he carried none, and thus dissembling all iniuries conceiued of both partes, the captaine went a shore, leauing pledges in the boates for himselfe, and cleared all things betweene the treasurer and him, sauing for the gouernours debt, which the one by no means would answere, nor the other, because it was not his due debt, he would not molest him for it, but was content to remit it vntill another time, and therefore departed, causing the two barkes which rode near the shore to weie and goe vnder saile, which was done to the intent that the captaine demaunding a testimoniall of his good behauiour there, could not haue the same vntill he were vnder the saile readie to depart, and therefore at night went for the same againe, and receiued it at the treasurers hand, of whom very curteously he tooke his leave, and departed shooting of the bases of his boate for his farewell, and the townesmen also shot off foure faulcons and thirtie harquebusses, and this was the first time that we knew of the conueyance of theyr faulcons.

The 31. of May we departed, keeping our course to Hespaniola, and the fourth of June we had sight of an Island, which we made to be Jamaica, maruelling that by the vehement course of the seas we should be driuen so farre to leeward: for setting our course to the Westend of Hispaniola we fell with the middle of Jamaica, notwithstanding that to all mens sight it shewed a head land, but they were all deceiued by the clouds that lay vpon the land two dayes together, in such sort that we thought it to be the head land of the said Island. And a Spanyard being in the ship, who was a merchant, and inhabitant in Jamaica, hauing occasion to go to Guinie, and being by treason taken of the Negroes, and afterwards bought by the Tangomangoes, was by our Captaine brought from thence, and had his passage to go into his countrey, who perceiuing the land, made as though he knew euery place thereof, and pointed to certaine places, which he named to be such a place, and such a mans ground, and that behinde such a point was the harborow, but in the end he pointed so from one point to another, that we were a leeboord of all places, and found ourselues at the West end of Jamaica before we were aware of it, and being once to leeward, there was no getting vp againe, so that by trusting of the Spanyard's knowledge, our captaine sought not to speake with any of the inhabitants, which if he had not made himselfe sure of, he would have done, as his custom was in other places, but this man was a plague not onely to our captaine, who made him loose, by ouershooting the place, two thousand pounds of hides, which he might have gotten, but also to himselfe, who being three yeares out of his countrey, and in great miserie in Guinie, both among the Negroes and Tangomangoes, and in hope to come to his wife and friends, as he made sure account, in that at his going into the pinnesse, when he went a shoare he put on his new clothes, and for ioy flung away his olde, could not afterwards finde any habitation, neither there nor in all Cuba, which we sayled all along, but it fell out euer, by one occasion or other, that we were put beside the same, so that he was fayne to be brought into England, and it happened to him as it did to a Duke of Samaria, when the Israelites were beseiged, and were in great misery with hunger, and being tolde by the Prophet Elizæus, that a bushell of flower should be solde for a sickle,[1] would not beleeue him, but thought it vnpossible: and for that cause Elizæus prophesied he should see the same done, but he should not eate thereof:[2] so this man being absent three yeeres, and not euer thinking to haue seene his owne countrey, did see the same, went vpon it, and yet was it not his fortune to come to it, or to any habitation, whereby to remaine with his friendes according to his desire.

Thus hauing sailed along the coast two dayes, we departed the seuenth of June, being made to beleeue by the Spanyard, that it was not Jamaica, but rather Hispaniola, of which opinion the captaine also was, because that which he made Jamaica seemed to be but a piece of the land, and thereby tooke it rather to be Hispaniola, by the lying of the coast, and also for that being ignorant of the force of the currant, he could not beleeue he was so farre driuen to leeward, and therefore setting his course to Jamaica, and after certaine dayes, not finding the same perceiued then certainly that the Island which he was at before, was Jamaica, and that the clouds did deceiue him, whereof he maruelled not a little: and the mistaking of the place came to as ill a passe as the ouershooting of Jamaica: for by this did he also ouerpasse a place in Cuba, called Santa Cruz,[3] where, as he was informed, was great store of hides to be had: and thus being disappointed of two of his ports, where he thought to haue raised great profit by his traffike, and also to haue found great refreshing of victualles and water for his men, was now disappointed greatly, and such want he had of fresh water, that he was forced to seeke the shoare to obtaine the same, which he had sight of after certaine dayes ouerpassed with stormes and contrary windes, but yet not of the maine of Cuba, but of certain Islands, in number two hundred, whereof the most part was deserted of inhabitants: by the which Islands the captaine passing in his pinnesse,

June.

The deceitfull force of the currant.

Two hundred Islands, for the most part not inhabited.

[1] Shekel.

[2] II Kings, vii, 1, 2, 17.

[3] On the south coast, between Guanco and the Bay of Matanzas.

could find no fresh water vntill he came to an Island bigger than all the rest, called the Isle of Pinas, where we ankered with our shippes the sixteenth of June, and found water, which although it were neither so toothsome as running water, by the meanes it is standing, and but the water of raine, and also being neere the sea was brackish, yet did we not refuse it, but were more glad thereof, as the time then required, then we should have beene another time with fine conduct water. Thus being reasonably watred we were desirous to depart, because the place was not very conuenient for such shippes of charge as they were, because there were many shoales leeward, and also lay open to the sea for any winde that should blowe, and therefore the captaine made the more haste away, which was not vnneedful: for little sooner were there ankers weyed, and foresayle set, but there arose such a storme, that they had not much to spare for doubling out of the shoales: for one of the barks not being fully ready as the rest was faine for haste to cutte the cable in the hawse, and loose both anker and cable to saue herselfe.

Thus the seuenteenth of June we departed and the twentieth fell with the West end of Cuba, called Cape S. Anthony, where for the space of three dayes, we doubled along till we came beyond the shoales, which are 20 leagues beyond S. Anthony. And the ordinary brese taking vs, which is the Northeast winde, put us the 24 from the shoare, and therefore we went to the Northwest to fetch winde, and also to the coast of Florida to haue the help of the currant, which was iudged to haue set to the Eastward: so the 29. we found ourselues in 27 degrees, and in the soundings of Florida where we kept our selues the space of foure dayes, sailing along the coast as neere as we could, in tenne or twelue fathome water, having all the while no sight of land.

The fift of July we had sight of certaine Islandes of sand, called the Tortugas (which is lowe land) where the captaine

The Cape of S. Anthony in Cuba.

Florida.

July.

The isles of Tortugas.

went in with his pinnesse, and found such a number of birds, that in halfe an houre he loded her with them, and if they had beene tenne boates more, they might haue done the like. These Islandes beare the name of Tortels because of the number of them, which there doe breed, whose nature is to liue both in the water and vpon land also, but breed onely upon the shoare, in making a great pit wherein they lay egges to the number of three or foure hundred, and couering them with sand, are hatched by the heat of the sunne, and by this means commeth the great increase. Of these we tooke very great ones, which haue both back and belly all of bone of the thickenesse of an inch, the fish whereof we proued, eating much like veale, and finding a number of egges in them, tasted also of them, but they did eat very swelly. Heere we ankered sixe houres, and then springing a fayre gale of winde, we weyed anker, and made saile toward Cuba, whither we came the sixt day, and weathered as farre as the Table, being a hill so called, because of the forme thereof: heere we lay off and on all night, to keepe that we had gotten to windewarde, intending to haue watered in the morning, if we could haue done it, or else if the winde had come larger, to have plyed to windewarde to the Hauana, which is a harbarow wherevnto all the fleet of the Spanyards come, and doe there tarry to haue one the company of the other. This hill we thinking to haue bene the Table, made account (as it was indeed) the Hauana, to be but eight leagues to windeward, but by the persuasion of a Frenchman, who made the Captaine belieue he knew the Table very well, and had beene at the Hauana, said that it was not the Table, and that the Table was much higher, and neerer to the sea side, and that there was no plaine grounde to the Eastward, nor hilles to the Westward, but all was contrary, and that behinde the hilles to the Westward was the Hauana; to which persuasion being giuen by some, and they not of the worst,

Great store of birds.

A Hill called the Table.

The port of Hauana.

the captaine was persuaded to go to leeward, and so sailed along the seuenth and eight dayes, finding no habitation, nor no other Table, and perceiuing his folly to give eare to such praters, was not a little sorry, both because he did consider what time he should spend ere he could get so farre to windewarde againe, which would haue bene with the weathering which we had 10 or 12 dayes worke, and what it would have beene longer he knew not, and that (which was worst) he had not aboue a dayes water, and therefore knew not what shift to make: but in fine, because the want was such, that his men could not liue with it, he determined to seeke water, and to go further to leeward, to a place (as it is set in the card) called Rio de los porcos, which he was in doubt of both whether it were inhabited, and whether there were water or not, and whether for the shoales he might haue such accesse with his shippes that he might conueniently take in the same: and while we were in those troubles, and kept our way to the place aforesaid, almighty God our guide (who would not suffer vs to runne into any further danger, which we had beene like to haue incurred, if we had ranged the coast of Florida along as we did before, which is so dangerous (by reports) that no shippe escapeth which commeth thither, as the Spanyards have very well prooued the same) sent vs the eight day at night a fayre Westerly winde, whereupon the Captaine and company consulted, determining not to refuse Gods gift, but euery man was contented to pinch his owne bellie whatsoeuer had happened, and taking the said winde, the ninth day of July got to the Table, and sailing the same night, vnawares ouershot the Hauana, at the which place we thought to have watered, but the next day, not knowing that we had ouershot the same, sailed along the coast, seeking it, and the eleuenth day in the morning, by certaine knowen markes, we vnderstood that we had ouershotte it twentie leagues: in which coast ranging, we found no conuenient watering place, whereby there was no remedy but to dissemble, and to water vpon the coast of Florida: for, to go further to the Eastward, we could not for the shoales, which are very dangerous, and because the currant shooteth to the Northeast, we doubted by the force thereof to be set vpon them, and therefore durst not approach them: so making but reasonable way the day aforesaid and all night: the 12 day in the morning, we fell with the Islands vpon the cape of Florida, which we could scant double by the meanes that fearing the shoales to the Eastwards, and doubting the currant comming out of the West, which was not of that force we made account of, for we felt little or none till we fell with the cape, and then felt such a currant, that bearing all sailes against the same yet were driuen backe againe a great pace: the experience whereof we had by the Jesus pinnesse, and the Sallomons boate, which were sent the same day in the afternoone, while the shippes were becalmed, to see if they could finde any water vpon the Islands aforesaid, who spent a great part of the day in rowing thither, being farther off than they deemed it to be, and in the meane time a fayre gale of winde springing at sea, the shippes departed, making a signe to them to come away, who although they saw them depart, because they were so neere the shoare would not loose all the labour they had taken, but determined to keepe theyr way, and see if there were any water to be had, making no account but to finde the shippes well enough: but they spent so much time in filling the water which they had founde that the night was come before they could make an end, and hauing lost the sight of the shippes, rowed what they could, but were wholly ignorant which way they should seeke them againe, as in deede there was a more doubt than they knew of. For when they departed, the shippes were in no currant, and sayling but a mile further, found one so strong, that bearing all sailes, it could not preuaile against the same, but were driuen backe: where-

The state of the currant of Florida.

upon the captaine sent the Sallomon, with the other two barkes, to beare neere the shoare all night, because the currant was lesse there a great deale, and to beare light with shooting off a piece now and then, to the intent the boates might better knowe how to come to them.

The Jesus also bare a light in her toppegallant, and shot off a piece also now and then, but the night passed and the morning was come, being the thirteenth day, and no newes could be heard of them, but the shippes and barkes forsook not, but to looke still for them, yet they thought it was all in vain, by the meanes they heard not of them all the night past, and therefore determined to tarry no longer, seeking for them till noone, and if they heard no newes, then they would depart to the Jesus, who perforce (by the vehemency of the currant) was carryed almost out of sight, but as God would haue it, now time being come, and they hauing tacked about in the pinnesses top, had sight of them, and tooke them up: they in the boates, being to the number of one and twentie, hauing sight of the shippes, and seeing them tacking about, whereas before at the first sight of them did greatly reioyce, were now in a greater perplexetie than euer they were: for by this they thought themselues vtterly forsaken, whereas before they were in some hope to have found them. Truely God wrought maruellously for them, for they themselues hauing no victualles but water, and being sore oppressed with hunger, were not of opinion to bestowe any further time in seeking the shippes than that present noone time, so that if they had not at that instant espyed them, then had they gone to the shoare to haue made prouision for victualles, and with such thinges as they could have gotten, either to haue gone for that part of Florida where the Frenchmen are (which would haue beene very hard for them to haue done, because they wanted victualles to bring them thither, being one hundred and twentie leagues off) or els to haue remayned amongst the Floridians, at whose handes they were put in comfort by a French man who was with them, that had remayned in Florida at the first finding thereof, a whole yeere together, to receiue victualles sufficient and gentle intertainement, if neede were, for a yeere or two, vntil which time God might haue prouided for them. But how contrary this would haue fallen out to theyr expectations, it is hard to iudge, seeing those people of the cape of Florida, are of more sauage and fierce nature, and more valiant than any of the rest, which the Spanyards well prooued, who being fiue hundred men, who intended then to land, returned few or none of them, but were inforced to forsake the same, and of theyr cruelty mention is made in the booke of the Decades, of a fryer, who taking vpon him to persuade the people to subiection, was by them taken with his skinne cruelly pulled ouer his eares, and his flesh eaten.

In these Islands they being ashoare, found a dead man dryed in a maner whole, with other heads and bodyes of men, so that those sorte of men are eaters of the flesh of men, as well as the Canibals. But to returne to our purpose.

The fourteenth day the shippe and barks came to the Jesus, bringing them news of the recouery of the men, which was not a little to the reioicing of the captaine, and the whole company: and so then altogether they kept on theyr way along the coast of Florida, and the fifteenth day came to an anker, and so from six and twentie degrees to thirtie degrees and half, where the Frenchmen are, ranging all the coast along, seeking for fresh water, ankering euery night, because we woulde ouershoote no place of fresh water, and in the day time the captaine in the shippes pinnesse sayled along the shoare, went into euery creeke, speaking with diuers of the Floridians, because he would vnderstand where the Frenchmen inhabited, and not finding them in eight and twentie degrees as it was declared vnto him, mar-

M. Hawkins ranged all the coast of Florida.

uelled thereat, and neuer left sailing along the coast till he found them, who inhabited in a riuer, by them called the riuer of May, and standeth in thirtie degrees and better. In ranging this coast along, the captaine found it to be all an Island and therefore it is all lowe land, and very scant of fresh water, but the countery was maruellously sweet, with both marish and medow ground, and goodly woods among. There they found sorrell to growe as abundantly as grasse, and nere theyr houses were great store of mayis and mill, and grapes of great bignesse, but of taste much like our English grapes. Also deere great plenty, which came vpon the sands before them. Theyr houses are not many together, for in one house a hundred of them do lodge: they being made much like a great barne, and in strength not inferiour to ours, for it hath stanchions and rafters of whole trees, and couered with Palmito leaues, hauing no place diuided, but one small roome for their King and Queene. In the middest of this house is a hearth where they make great fyres all night, and vpon certaine pieces of wood hewen in for the bowing of their backes, and another place made high for theyr heads, they lye vpon the same which they put one by another all along the walles on both sides. In their houses they remaine onely in the nights, and in the day they desire the fieldes, where they dresse their meat, and make prouision for victualles, which they prouide onely for a meale from hand to mouth. There is one thing to be maruelled at, for the making of their fire, and not onely they but also the Negroes doe the same, which is made onely by two stickes, rubbing them one against another, and this they may doe in any place they come, where they finde sticks sufficient for the purpose. In theyr apparell the men onely vse deere skinnes, wherewith some onely couer their priuy members, other some use the same as garments to couer them before and behinde, which skinnes are painted, some yellow and red, some black and russett, and euery man

The riuer of May.

Florida found to be cut in Islands.

Sorrell.

The commodities of Florida.

The houses of Florida.

The maner of kindling of fire in Florida.

according to his owne fancy. They do not omit to paint their bodies also with curious knots, or antique worke, as euery man in his owne fancy deuiseth, which painting, to haue it continue the better, they vse with a thorne to pricke their flesh, and dent in the same, whereby the painting may haue better holde. In their warres they vse a slighter couler of painting their faces, thereby to make themselues shew the more fierce: which after their warres ended they wash away againe. In their warres they vse bowes and arrowes, whereof their bowes are made of a kinde of yew, but blacker then ours, but many passing the strength of the Negroes or Indians, for it is not greatly inferior to ours; their arrowes also of a great length, but yet of reeds like other Indians, but varying in two points both for length, and also for nocks and fethers, which the other lacke, whereby they shoot very steddy: the heads of the same are vipers teeth, bones of fishes, flint stones, piked pointes of kniues, which hauing gotten of the Frenchmen, broke the same, and put the points of them in their arrowes heads: some of them haue their heads of siluer, other some that haue want of these, put in a kinde of hard wood, notched, which perceth as farre as any of the rest. In their fight, being in the woods, they vse a maruellous pollicie for their owne safegarde, which is by clasping a tree in their armes, and yet shooting notwithstanding: this pollicy they vsed with the Frenchmen in their fight, whereby it appeareth that they are people of some pollicy: and although they are called by the Spanyards "Gentetriste",[1] that is to say, sad people, meaning thereby, that they are not men of capacity: yet haue the Frenchmen found them so witty in their answers, that by the captaines owne report, a councellour with vs could not giue a more profound reason.

The women also in their apparell vse painted skinnes, but most of them gownes of mosse, somewhat longer then our mosse, which they sowe together artificially, and make the

[1] "Gente triste", a sad people.

same surpleswise, wearing their haire downe to theyr shoulders, like the Indians.

In this riuer of May aforesaid the captain entring with his pinnesse, found a French ship of fourscore tunne, and two pinnesses of fifteen tunne a piece, by her, and speaking with the keepers thereof, they tolde him of a fort two leagues vp, which they had built, in which theyr captaine Mounsieur Laudonier was, with certaine souldiers therein. To whom our captaine sending to vnderstand of a watring place, where he might conueniently take it in, and to haue licence for the same, he straight because there was no conuenient place but vp the riuer fiue leagues, where the water was fresh, did send him a pilot for the more expedition thereof, to bring in one of his barkes, which going in with other boats prouided for the same purpose, ankered before the fort, into the which our captaine went, where he was by the general, with other captaines and souldiers, very gently intertained, and declared vnto him the time of their being there, which was 14 months, with the extremity they were driuen to for want of victuals, hauing brought very little with them, in which place they being 200. men at their first comming, had in short space eaten al the mayis they could buy of the inhabitants about them and therefore were driuen certeine of them to serue a king of the Floridians against other of his enemies for milk and other victualles, which hauing gotten, could not serue them, being so many so long a time, but want came vpon them in such sort, that they were faine to gather acornes, which being stamped small, and often washed to take away the bitterness of them, did vse the same for bread, eating withall sundry times rootes, whereof they found many good and wholesome, and such as serue rather for medicines then for meates alone. But this hardnesse not contenting some of them, who would not take the paynes so much as to fish in the riuer before theyr doores, but would haue all thinges put in theyr mouthes, did rebel agaynst the

The French fort.

Monsieur Laudonier.

Bread made of acorns.

captaine, taking away first his armour and afterward imprisoning him: and so to the number of fourscore of them, departed with a barke and a pinnesse, spoyling theyr store of victuall, and taking away a great part therof with them, and so went to the Islands of Hispaniola and Jamaica a rouing, where they spoiled, and pilled the Spanyardes, and hauing taken two caruels laden with wine and casaua, which is a bread made of roots, and much other victualles and treasure, had not the grace to depart therewith, but were of such haughtie stomacks, that they thought their force to be such that no man durst meddle with them, and so kept harborough in Jamaica, going dayly a shoare at their pleasure. But God which would not suffer such euile doers vnpunished, did indurate their hearts in such sorte, that they lingered the time so long, that a ship and galeasse being made out of S. Domingo, and came thither into the harborough, and tooke twentie of them, whereof the most part were hanged, and the rest carried into Spayne, and some (to the number of fiue and twentie) escaped in the pinnesse, and came to Florida, where at their landing they were put in prison, and incontinent foure of the chiefest being condemned, at the request of the souldiours, did passe the harquebussess, and then were hanged vpon a gibbet. This lacke of threescore men was a great discourage and weakning to the rest, for they were of the best souldiours that they had: and whereas they had now made the inhabitants weary of them by their daily crauing of mayis, hauing no wares left to content them withall, and therefore inforced to robbe them, and to take away their victuall perforce, was the occasion that the Floridians (not well contented therewith) did take certaine of theyr companie in the woods, and slew them, whereby there grew great warres betwixt them and the Frenchmen, and therefore they being but a few in nũber durst not venture abroad, but at such time as they were inforced therevnto for want of food to do the same:

The occasion of the falling out with the Floridians.

and going twentie harquebussess in a company, were set vpon by eightene kings, hauing seuen or eight hundred men, which with one of their bowes slew one of their men, and hurt a dozen, and droue them all downe to theyr boats, whose pollicy in fight was to be maruelled at, for hauing shot at diuers of their bodies, which were armed, and perceiuing that their arrowes did not preuaile against the same, they shot at their faces & legs, which were the places that the Frenchmen were hurt in. Thus the Frenchmen returned being in ill case by the hurt of their men, hauing not aboue forty souldiors left vnhurt, whereby they might ill make any more inuasions vpon the Floridians, and keepe their fort withall: which they must haue beene driuen vnto, had not God sent vs thither for their succour, for they had not aboue ten dayes victuall left before we came. In which perplexity oure captaine seeing them, spared them out of his ship twenty barrels of meale, aud four pipes of beanes, with diuers other victuals and necessaries which he might conueniently spare, and to helpe them the better homewards whither they were bound before our comming, at their request, we spared them one of our barks of fifty tunnes. Notwithstanding the great want that the Frenchmen had, the ground doth yeeld victuals sufficient, if they would haue taken paines to get the same, but they being souldiours, desired to liue by the sweat of other mens browes: for while they had peace with the Floridians, they had fish sufficient, by weares they made to catch the same: but when they grew to warres, the Floridians tooke away the same againe, and then would not the Frenchmen take the paines to make any more. The ground yeldeth naturally grapes in great store, for in the time that the Frenchmen were there, they made twenty hogsheads of wine. Also it yeeldeth roots passing good, deere maruellous store, with diuers other beasts, and fowle, seruiceable to the vse of man. These be things wherewith a man might liue, hauing corne or mayis wherewith to make

The French greatly relieued by M. Hawkins.

Twentie hogsheads of wine made in Florida like to the wine of France.

bread: for mayis maketh good sauory bread, and cakes as fine as flower. Also it maketh good meale beaten and sodden with water and eateth like pappe wherewith we feed children. It maketh also good beuerage sodden in water, and nourishable: which the Frenchmen did vse to drink of in the morning, and it assuaged their thirst, so that they had no need to drinke all the day after. And this mayis was the greatest lacke they had, because they had no laborers to sowe the same, and therefore to them that should inhabit the land it were requisit to haue laborers to till and sowe the ground. For they hauing victuals of theyr owne, whereby they neither rob nor spoile the inhabitants, may liue not onely quietly with them, who naturally are more desirous of peace then of warres, but also shall haue abundance of victuals profered them for nothing: for it is with them as it is with one of vs, when we see another man euer taking away from vs, although we haue enough besides, yet then we thinke all to little for ourselues: for surely we haue heard the Frenchmen report, and I know it by the Indians that a very little contenteth them, for the Indians with the head of mayis roasted, will trauel a whole day, and when they are at the Spanyards finding, they giue them nothing but sodden herbs and mayis, and in this order I saw three score of them feed, who were laden with wares, and came fiftie leagues off. The Floridians when they trauel haue a kinde of herbe dryed,[1] which with a cane, and an earthen cup in the end, with fire, and the dried herbs put together do sucke thoro the cane the smoke thereof, which smoke satisfieth their hunger, and therewith they liue foure or five days without meat or drinke, and this all the Frenchmen vsed for this purpose: yet do they holde opinion withall, that it causeth water and fleame to void from their stomacks. The commodities of this land are more then are yet knowne to any man: for besides the land itselfe, whereof there is more then any king Christian is able to inhabit, it flourisheth with medow, pasture ground,

Laborers necessarie to inhabit new countries.

Tabacco, and the great vertue thereof.

[1] Tobacco.

with woods of cedar and cypres, and other sorts, as better cannot be in the world, they have for apothicary herbes, trees, roots and gumme great store, as Storax liquide, Turpintine, Gumme, Myrre and Frankinsense, with many others, whereof I know not the names. Coulers both red, black, yellow, and russet, very perfect, wherewith they paint their bodies, and deere skinnes which they weare about them, that with water it neither fadeth away, nor altereth couler.

The variety of commodoties in Florida.

Coulers.

Golde and siluer.

Golde and siluer they want not: for at the Frenchmen first comming thither, they had the same offered them for little or nothing, for they receiued for a hatchet two pound weight of golde, because they knew not the estimation thereof: but the souldiours being greedy of the same, did take it from them, giuing them nothing for it: the which they perceiuing, that both the Frenchmen did greatly esteeme it, and also did rigorously deale with them, at last would not be knowen they had any more, neither durst they weare the same for feare of being taken away; so that sauing at their first comming, they could get none of them: And how they came by this golde and siluer, the Frenchmen knew not as yet, but by gesse, who hauing trauelled to the southwest of the cape, hauing found the same dangerous, by meanes of sandey banks, as we also haue found the same, and there finding masts which were wracks of Spanyard's comming from Mexico, iudged that they had gotten treasure by them. For it is most true that diuers wracks haue beene made of Spanyards, hauing much treasure. For the Frenchmen hauing trauelled to the capeward a hundred and fiftie miles, did finde the Spanyards with the Floridians, which they brought afterwards to theyr fort, wherof one being in a carauell, coming from the Indias was cast away foureteene yeeres ago, and the other twelve yeeres, whose fellows some escaped, other some were slaine by the inhabitants.

Two Spanyards liued long among the Floridians.

It seemeth they had estimation of their gold and siluer,

for it is wrought flat and grauen, which they weare about their necks, other some made round like a pancake, with a hole in the middest to bolster vp their brestes withall, because they think it a deformitie to haue great brestes. As for mines either of gold or siluer, the Frenchmen can hear of none they haue vpon the Island, but of copper, whereof as yet also they haue not made the proofe, because they were but few men: but it is not vnlike, but that, in the maine where are high hilles, may be golde and silver as well as in Mexico, because it is all one maine. The Frenchmen obtained pearles of them of great bignesse, but they were blacke by meane of roasting of them, for they do not fish for them as the Spanyards do, but for their meat: for the Spanyardes vsed to keep dayly a fishing some two or three hundred Indians, some of them that be of choyse a thousand: and their order is to go in Canoaes, or rather great pinnesses, with thirtie men in a piece, whereof the one halfe, or most part be diuers, the rest doe open the same for the pearles: for it is not suffered that they should vse dragging, for that would bring them out of estimation, and marre the beads of them. The oysters which haue the smallest sort of pearles are found in seven or eight fathome water, but the greatest in eleuen or twelue fathoms.

Pieces of golde grauen among the Floridiãs.

Florida esteemed an Island.

The copper was found perfect golde, called by the sauages, Syeroa phyra.

Pearles

The Floridians have pieces of Unicornes hornes, which they wear about their necks, whereof the Frenchmen obtayned many pieces. Of those Unicornes they haue many, for that they doe affirme it to be a beast with one horne, which coming to the riuer to drinke, putteth the same into the water before shee drinketh. Of these Unicornes there is of our company, that hauing gotten the same of the French men, brought home thereof to shewe. It is therefore to be presupposed that there are more commodities, as well as that, which for want of time, and people sufficient to inhabite the same, cannot yet come to light; but I trust God will reueale the same before it be long, to the great profite of them that shall take it in hand.

Unicorns hornes, which the inhabitãts call Souamamma.

Beastes. Of beastes in this country, besides Deere, Foxes, Hares, Pollcats, Cunnies, Ownces, Leopards, I am not able certainely to say: but it is thought that there are Lions and Tygers as well as Unicornes, Lions especially, if it bee true that it is said of the enmity betweene them and the Unicornes. For there is no beast but hath his enemy, as the Cunny the Polcat, a Sheepe the Wolfe, the Elephant the Rinoceros, aud so of other beasts the like: insomuch, that whereas the one is the other can not be missing. And seeing I haue made mention of the beastes of this Countrey, it shal not be from my purpose to speak also of the venomous beastes, as Crocodiles, whereof there is a great abundance, Adders of great bignesse, wherrof our men killed some of a yard and a halfe longe. Also I heard a miracle of one of these adders, vpou which a Faulcon seazing, the saide adder did clasp her taile about her, which the French Captaine seeing, came to the rescue of the faulcon, and tooke her slaying the adder, and this faulcon being wilde hee did reclaime her, and kept her for the space of 2. months, at which time for very want of meat he was faine to cast her off. On these adders the Frenchmen did feede to no litle admiration of vs, and affirmed the same to be a delicate meate. And the Captaine of the Frenchmen saw also a Serpent with 3. heads and 4. feete, of the bignesse of a great Spaniell, which for want of a harquebusse he durst not attempt to slay. Of the fishe also they haue in the riuer, pike, roche, salmon, troute, and diuers other small fishes, and of a great fish, some of the length of a man and longer, being of bignesse accordingly, hauing a snoute much like a sworde of a yard long. There be also of sea fishes which wee sawe comming along the coast flying, which are of the bignesse of a smelt, the biggest sorte whereof haue four winges, but the other haue but two. Of these we sawe comming out of Guinea, a hundreth in a companie, which being chased by the Gilt heads, otherwise called the Bonitoes, doe to auoide them the better

Faulcons in Florida.

Serpents.

take their flight out of the water, but yet are they not able to flie farre, because of the drying of their winges, which serue them not to flye but when they are moyste, and therefore when they can flye no further fall into the water, and hauing wette their winges take a newe flight againe. These Bonitoes be of bignesse like a carpe, and in colour like a mackarell, but it is the swiftest fish in swimming that is, and followeth her praye very fiercely not onely in the water, but also out of the water: for as the flying fish taketh her flight, so doeth this Bonitoe leape after them, and taketh them sometime aboue the water. They were some of those Bonitoes, which being galled by a fisgig did follow our ship comming out of Guinea 500. leagues.

There is a sea foule also that chaseth this flying fish as wel as the Bonito: for as the flying fish taketh her flight, so doth this foule pursue to take her, which to beholde is a greater pleasure then hauking, for both the flights are as pleasant, and also more often then 100. times: for the foule can flie no way but one or other lighteth in her pawes, the nomber of them are so abundant. There is an innumerable yonge frie of these flying fishes which commonly keepe about the shippe, and are not so big as butterflies, and yet by flying doe auoyde the vnsatiablenesse of the Bonito. Of the bigger sort of these fishes, we tooke many, which both night and day flew into the sailes of our shippe, and there was not one of them which was not worth a Bonito: for being put vpon a hooke drabling in the water, the Bonito would leape thereat, and so was taken. Also, we tooke many with a white clothe made fast to a hooke, which being tied so short in the water, that it might leape out, and in, the greedie Bonito thinking it to be a flying fish leapeth thereat, and is deceiued. Wee tooke also Dolphins, which (Dolphins.) are of very goodly colour and proportion to beholde, and no lesse delicate in taste. Foules also there be many, both vpon lande and vpon sea. But concerning them on the land I am not able to name them, because my abode was there so short. But for the foule of the fresh riuers, these two I noted to be the chiefe, whereof the Flemengo is one, hauing all redde fethers, and long redde legs like a Herne, a necke according to the bill redde, whereof the vpper nebbe haugeth an inche ouer the nether. And an Egripte[1] which is all white as the swanne, with legges like to an hearneshewe, and of bignesse accordingly, but it hath in her taile feathers of so fine a plume, that it passeth the Estridge his feather. Of sea foule aboue all other not common in Englande, I noted the Pellicane, which is faigned to be the louingest birds that is: which rather then her yong shoulde want, will spare her heart bloud out of her bellie, but for all this louingness she is very deformed to beholde, for shee is of colour russet, notwithstanding in Guinea I have seene of them as white as a swanne, hauing legges like the same, and a body like the Herne, with a long necke, and a thicke long beake, from the nether iawe whereof downe to the breast passeth a skinne of such a bignesse, asisable to receive a fishe as bigge as ones thigh, and this her bigge throat and long bill doeth make her seeme so ougly.

Flemingo.

The Egript.

The Pellicane.

Here I haue declared the estate of Florida, and the commodoties therein to this day knowen, which although it may seeme vnto some, by the meanes that the plentie of Golde and Siluer is not so abundant, as in other places, that the cost bestowed vpon the same, will not bee able to quite the charges: yet am I of the opinion that by that which I haue seene in other Islandes of the Indians, where such increase of cattell hath been that of twelue head of beasts in 25. yeeres, did in the hides of them raise 1000. pound profite yeerely, that the increase of cattell onely would raise profite sufficient for the same. For wee may consider, if so small a portion did raise so much gaines in such a short time, what would a greater doe in many yeeres. And surely I may this affirme, that the ground of the Indians for the

Measure to reape a sufficient profite in Florida and Virginia.

[1] Egret.

breed of cattell, is not in any point to be compared to this of Florida, which all the yeere long is so greene, as any time in the Sommer with vs: which surely is not to be marueiled at, seeing the Countrey standeth in so watrie a climate: for once a day withoute faile, they haue a showre of raine. Which by meanes of the Countrey it selfe, which is drie, and more feruent hot then ours, doeth make all things to flourish therein, and because there is not the thing wee all seeke for, being rather desirous of present gaines, I do therefore affirme the attempt thereof to be more requisite for a prince, who is of power able to goe thorow with the same, rather than for any subiect.

From thence we departed the 28. of July, vpon our voyage homewards, hauing there all things as might be most conuenient for our purpose, and tooke leaue of the Frenchmen that there still remained, who, with diligence determined to make great speede after, as they coulde. Thus by meanes of contrary windes oftentimes, we prolonged our voyage in such manner that victuals scanted with vs, so that wee were diuers (or rather the most part) in despaire of euer comming home, had not God of his goodnesse better prouided for vs, then our deseruing. In which state of great miserie, we were prouoked to call vpon him by feruent prayer, which mooued him to heare vs, so that we had a prosperous winde, which did set vs so farre shotte, as to be vpon the banke of Newfoundland, on S. Bartlemewes eue, and sounded, thereupon finding ground at 130. fathoms, being that day somewhat becalmed, and tooke a great nomber of fresh codde fish, which greatly relieued vs, and very glad thereof, the next day departing, by lingering little gales for the space of foure or fiue days, at the which we sawe a couple of French ships, and had so much fish as woulde serue us plentifully for all the rest of the way, the Captaine paying for the same both golde and siluer, to the iust value thereof, vnto the cheife owners of the said shippes, which they not looking for anything at all, were glad in themselues to meete with such goode intertainement at sea, as they had at our handes. After which departure from them, with a good large winde the 20. of September we came to Padstow in Cornewall God be thanked, in safetie, with the losse of 20. persons in all the voyage, and profitable to the venturers of the saide voyage, as also to the whole Realme, in bringing home both golde, siluer, pearles and other iewels great store. His name therefore be praised for euermore. Amen.

Their arriual in the moneth of September, 1565.

The names of certaine Gentlemen, that were in this voyage.

M. Iohn Hawkins.
M. Iohn Chester, Sir William Chester's sonne.[1]
M. Anthony Parkhurst.
M. Fitzwilliam.[2]
M. Thomas Woorley.
M. Edward Lacy (with diuers others).

The Register and true accompts of all herein expressed, hath bene approued by mee, John Sparke the yonger, who went vpon the same voyage, and wrote the same.

[1] Sir William Chester was a draper of London, and Lord Mayor in 1560. By his wife Elizabeth, daughter of Thomas Lovett of Astwell, in Northamptonshire, he had five sons. William, the eldest, was ancestor of a line of baronets now extinct. Thomas, the second, was Bishop of Elphin, in Ireland. John Chester, the third son, who was with Hawkins in this second voyage, died without issue.

[2] See Introduction. Fitzwilliam afterwards acted as agent for Sir John Hawkins in Spain.

The arriuall and courtesie of M. Hawkins to the distressed *Frenchmen in Florida, is elsewhere also* recorded, both in French, and English, in the history of. Laudonier, written by himselfe, and printed in Paris, Anno 1586.

And translated into English by me Richard Hakluyt, Anno 1587. And published as followeth.

As eche of vs were much tormented in minde with diuers cogitations, the third of August I descried foure sailes in the Sea, as I walked vpon a little hill, whereof I was exceeding well apayde. I sent immediately one of them that were with me, to aduertise those of the fort thereof, which were so glad of those newes, that one would haue thought them to be out of their wits, to see them laugh and leape for ioy. After these shippes had cast ancre, we descried that they sent off their shippe boates to land, whereupon I caused one of mine to be armed with diligence to sende to meete them, and to knowe who they were. In the mean while, fearing least they were Spaniards, I set my souldiours in order and readinesse, attending the returne of Captaine Vasseur, and my lieutenant, which were gone to meete them, who brought me word that they were Englishmen. And in trueth they had in their companie one whose name was Martine Attinas of Diepe, which at that time was in their seruice: which in the behalfe of M. Iohn. Haukins their Generall came to request me that I would suffer them to take fresh water, whereof they stoode in great neede, signifying vnto me that they had bene aboue 15 dayes on the coast to get some. He brought vnto me from the Generall 2. flagons of wine, and bread made of wheate, which greatly

Laudoniere and his companie.

F

refreshed mee, forasmuch as for 7. moneths space, I never tasted a drop of wine: neuerthelesse it was all diuided amongst the greatest part of my souldiers: this Martin Attinas had guided the Englishmen to our coast, wherewith he was acquainted, for in the yere 1562 he came thither with me and therfore the General sent him to me. Therfore after I had granted his request he signified the same vnto the general, which the next day folowing caused one of his small ships to enter into the riuer, and came to see me in a great shipboat, accompanied with gentlemē honorably apparelled, yet vnarmed, he sent for great store of bread and wine to distribute thereof to euery one. On my part I made him the best cheare I could possibly, and caused certaine sheepe and poultry to be killed, which vnto this present I had caused carefully to be preserued, hoping to store the coũtrey withal. Now 3 dayes passed while the English general remained with me, during which time the Indians came in from all parts to see me, and asked me whether he were my brother. I told them he was so, and signified vnto them that he was come to see me, and ayde me with so great store of victuals, that frō hence forward I should haue no need to take anything of them. The bruit hereof incontinently was spryed ouer all the countrie, in such sort, as Ambassadors came vnto me from al parts, which on the behalfe of the kings their masters, desired to make alliance with me, and euen they which before sought to make warre against me, came to offer their seruice and friendship vnto me: whereupon I receiued them, and gratified them with certaine presents. The general immediately vnderstood the desire and vrgent occasion which I had to returne into France: whereupon he offred to transport me, and al my company home: whereunto notwithstanding I would not agree, being in doubt vpon what occasion he made so large an offer. For I knew not how the case stood betwixt the French and the English: and although he promised me on his faith to put me on land in France, before he would touch in England, yet I stood in doubt least he would attempt somewhat in Florida in the name of his Mistresse: wherefore I flatly refused his offer. Whereupon there rose a great mutinie among my souldiers, which said that I sought to destroy them al, and that the Brigandine whereof I spoke before, was not sufficient to transport them, considering the season of the yeere, wherein wee were. The bruite and mutinie increased more and more: for after that the generall was returned to his ships, he told certaine gentlemen and souldiers which went to see him, partly to make good cheere with him, he declared and said vnto them, that he greatly doubted, that hardly we should be able to passe safely in those vessels which we had, and that in case we should enterprise the same, we should no doubt be in great ieopardie. Notwithstanding, if I were so cõtented, he would transport part of my men in his ships, and that he would leaue me a small ship to transport the rest.

The souldiers were no sooner come home, but they signified the offer vnto their companions, which incontinently consented together, that in case I would not accept the same, they would imbarke themselues with him, and forsake me, so that he would receiue them according to his promise. They therefore assembled themselues together, and came to seeke me in my chamber, and signified vnto me their intention. Whereunto I promised to answere them in one houre after. In which meane space I gathered together the principall members of my companie, which, after I had broken the matter with them, answered mee all with one voyce, that I ought not to refuse his offer, nor contemne the occasion which presented itselfe. And that they could not think euill of it in France, if, being forsaken as we were, wee ayded our selues with such meanes, as God hath sent to vs. After sundrie debatings of this matter, in conclusion I gaue my aduise that we ought to deliuer him the price of the shippe which he was to leaue vs, and that for my part I was content to giue him the best of my stuffe, and the siluer which I had gathered in the countrey.

Siluer in Florida.

Whereupon notwithstanding, it was determined, that I should keepe the siluer, for feare least the Queen of Englande seeing the same, shoulde the rather bee incouraged to set footing there, as before she had desired. That it was farre better to carry it into Fraunce, to giue incouragement to our Princes not to leave off such an enterprise of so great importance for our Common wealth. And that seeing wee were resolued to depart, it was farre better to giue him our Artillerie, which otherwise wee should be constrained to leaue behinde vs, or to hide in the ground, by reason of the weaknesse of our men, being not able to embarke the same. This point being thus concluded, and resolued on, I went (my selfe) vnto the English Generall, accompanied with my lieutenant, and Captaine Vasseur, Captaine Verdier, and Trenchant the pilot, and my seriant, al men of experience in such affaires, and knowing sufficiently how to driue such a bargaine. We therefore tooke a view of the ship, which the Generall would sell, whom we drew to such reason, that he was content to stand vnto mine owne mens iudgment, who esteemed it to bee worth 700. crowns, whereof we agreed very friendly. Wherefore I deliuered him in earnest of the summe, 2. bastards, 2. minions, one thousand of yron, and one thousand of pouder, this bargaine thus made, he considered the necessitie wherein we were, hauing for al our sustenance but mil[1] and water: whereupon being mooued with pitie, he offered to relieue me with 20. barrels of meale, 6. pipes of beanes, one hogshead of salt, and 100. of waxe to make candles. Moreouver for so much as he saw my souldiers goe barefoote, he offered me besides 50. paire of shoes, which I accepted, and agreed of a price with him, and gaue him a bill of my hand for the same, for which vntil this pre-

[1] Millet.

sent I am indebted to him. He did more than this, for particularly he bestowed vpon my selfe a great iarre of oyle, a iarre of vineger, a barrel of oliues, and a great quantitie of rise, and a barrel of white bisket: besides he gaue diuers presents to the principall officers of my company, according to their qualities. So that I may say, we receiued as many courtesies of the General, as it was possible to receiue of any man liuing. Wherein doutlesse, he hath wonne the reputation of a good and charitable man, deseruing to be esteemed as much of vs al, as if he had saued all our liues. Incontinent after his departure, I spared no paines to hasten my men to make biscuits of the meale which hee had left me, and to hoope my caskes to take in water needeful for the voyage.

Thus farre Laudoniere, concerning M. Haukins and his courtesie.

The 3. vnfortunate voyage made with the Iesus, the *Minion, and foure other shippes, to the partes of* Guinea, and the West Indias, in the yeere 1567. and 1568. by M. Iohn Haukins.

THE shippes departed from Plymmouth, the second day of October, Anno 1567. and had reasonable weather, vntil the seuenth day, at which time fortie leagues North from Cape Finister, there arose an extreme storme, which continued foure daies, in such sorte, that the fleete was dispersed, and all our great boates lost, and the Iesus our chiefe shippe, in such case, as not thought able to serue the voyage; whereupon in the same storme we sette our course homeward, determining to giue over the voyage: but the elevent day of the same moneth, the winde changed with faire weather, whereby we were animated to followe our enterprise, and so did, directing our course with the Islands of Grand Canaries, where according to an order before prescribed, all our shippes before dispersed, mette in one of those Islands, called Gomera, where we tooke water, and departed from thence the fourth day of Nouember, towards the coast of Guinea, and arrived at Cape Verde, the eighteenth of Nouember: where we landed 150. men, hoping to obtaine some Negroes, where we gatte but fewe, and those with great hurte and damage to our men, which chiefly proceeded from their enuenomed arrows; and although in the beginning, they seemed to be but small hurtes, yet there hardely escaped any, that had blood drawen of them, but died in strange sorte, with their mouths shutte, some ten dayes before he died, and after their woundes were whole, where I my selfe had one of the greatest wounds, yet

A storme.

Gomera.

Nouember.

Enuenomed arrowes.

thanks be to God, escaped. From thence we passed the time upon the coast of Guinea, searching with all diligence, the Rivers from Rio grande, vnto Sierra Leona, till the twelfth of Januarie, in which time wee had not gotten together a hundreth and fiftie Negroes: yet notwithstanding the sickness of our men, and the late time of the yeere commanded vs away, and thus hauing nothing wherewith to seeke the coast of the West Indies, I was with the rest of our Companie in consultation to goe to the coast of the Myne, hoping therto haue obtained some golde for our wares, and thereby to have defraied our charge. But even in that present instant, there came to vs a Negroe, sent from a King, oppressed by other Kings his neighbours, desiring our aide, with promise, that as many Negroes as by these wares might be obtained, as well of his part, as of ours, should be at our pleasure: whereupon we concluded to give aide, and sent 120. of our men, which the fifteenth of Januarie, assaulted a towne of the Negroes of our Allies aduersaries, which had in it 8000. Inhabitants, and very strongly impaled and fenced, after their manner, but it was so well defended, that our men prevailed not but lost sixe men, and 40. hurt, so that our men sent forthwith to me for more helpe: whereupon considering that the good successe of this enterprise might highly further the commodotie of our voyage, I went myselfe, and with the helpe of the King of our side, assaulted the towne both by land and sea, and very hardly with fire, (their houses being covered with dry Palme leaues) obtained the towne, and put the Inhabitants to flight, where we tooke 250. persons, men, women, and children, and by our friend the King of our side, there was taken 600. prisoners, whereof we hoped to haue had our choice: but the Negro (in which nation is seldome or never found truth) meant nothing lesse: for that night he remoued his campe, and prisoners, so that we were faine to content vs with those

December. Januarie.

A towne of 8000. Negroes taken.

No truth in Negroes.

fewe which we had gotten our selues. Now had we obtained between 4. and 500. Negroes, wherewith we thought it somewhat reasonable to seeke the coast of the West Indies, and there, for our Negroes, and other our merchandize, we hoped to obtaine, whereof to counteruaile our charges with some gaines, whereunto we proceeded with all diligence, furnished our watring, took fuell, and departed the coast of Guinea the third of Februarie, continuing at the sea with a passage more harde, then before hath beene
March. accustomed, till the 27th day of March, which day we had
Dominica. sight of an Island, called Dominica, vpon the coast of the west Indies, in 14. degrees: from thence we coasted from place to place, making our trafficke with the Spaniards, as we might, somewhat hardly, because the King had straightly commanded all his Gouernours in those partes, by no means to suffer any trade to be made with vs: notwithstanding
Aprill we had reasonable trade, and courteous entertainment, from the Isle of Margarita, vnto Cartagena, without anything greatly worth the noting, sauing at Capo de la Vela, in a
May. towne called Rio de la Hache, from whence came all the pearles: the treasurer who had the charge there, would by no means agree to any trade, or suffer vs to take water, he had fortified his towne with diuers bulwarks in all places, where it might be entred, and furnished himselfe with 100. Hargabusiers, so that he thought by famine to have enforced vs to have put a land our Negroes: of which purpose he had not greatly failed vnles we had by force entred the towne: which (after we could by no means obtaine his favour)
June. we were enforced to do, and so with 200. men brake in vpon
Rio de la Hacha taken. their bulwarkes, and entred the towne with the losse only of ii. men of our partes, and no hurte done to the Spanyards because after their volye of shott discharged they all fled.

Thus hauing the town, with some circumstance, as partly by the Spanyards desire of Negroes and partly by friendship of the Treasorer, we obtained a secrete trade: whereupon the Spanyards resorted to vs by night, and bought of vs to the number of 200. Negroes: in all other places where we traded the Spanyard inhabitants were glad of vs and traded willingly.

At Cartagena, the last towne we thought to have seene on the coast, we could by no meanes obtaine to deale with any Spanyard the gouernor was so straight, and because our trade was so neere finished we thought not good either to aduenture any landing, or to detract further time, but in peace departed from thence the 24. July, hoping to haue escaped the time of their stormes which then soone after began to raigne, the which they call Furicanos, but passing by the west end of Cuba, towards the coast of Florida there happened to vs the xii. day of August an extreme storme which continued by the space of 4. daies, which so beat the Jesus, that we cut downe all her higher buildings, her rudder also was sore shaken, and with all was in so extreame a leake that we were rather vpon the point to leave her then to keepe her any longer, yet hoping to bring all to good passe sought the coast of Florida where we found no place nor Hauen for our ships because of the shalownes of the coast: thus being in greater despaire, and taken with a new storme which continued other 3 dayes, we were inforced to take for our the Port which serueth the Citie of Mexico called St. John de Vllua which standeth in six. degrees: in seeking of which Port we took in our way iii. ships which carried passengers to the nomber of C. which passengers we hoped should be a meane to vs the better to obtaine victuals for our money, and a quiet place for the repairing of our fleete: shortly after the xvi. of September we entered the Port of St. John de Vllua and in our entrie the Spanyardes thinking vs to be the fleete of Spaine, the chief officers of the Countrey came aborde vs, which being deceived of their expectation were greatly dismayed: but

Cartegena. July. Furicanos. Storme. September. Saint Iohn de Vllua, a Port. The Spanyards deceiued.

immediately when they saw our demaund was nothing but victuals, were recomforted. I found also in the same Port xii. ships which had in them by the report 200000 li. in golde and siluer all which (being in my possession, with the Kinges Island, as also the passengers before in my way thitherwarde stayde) I set at libertie, without the taking from them the wayght of a grote: onely because I woulde not bee delayed of my dispatch, I stayed two men of estimation and sent post immediately to Mexico, which was 200. miles from vs, to the Presidentes and Counsell there, shewing them of our arriuall there by the force of weather, and the necessitie of the repaire of our shippes and victualls, which wantes wee required as friends to king Philip to be furnished of for our money: and that the Presidentes and Counselle there should with all conuenient speede take order, that at the arriuall of the Spanishe fleete which was daily looked for, there might be no cause of quarrel rise between vs and them, but for the better maintenance of amitie, their commaundment might be had in that behalfe.

Our requests.

The fleete of Spaine.

This message being sent away the sixteenth day of September at night, being the very day of our arriual, in the next morning which was the sixteenth day of the same moneth, we saw open of the Hauen xiii. great shippes, and vnderstanding them to be the fleète of Spaine, I sent immediately to aduertise the General of the fleete of my being there, doing him to vnderstand, that before I would suffer them to enter the Port, there should some other order of conditions passe betweene vs for our safe being there, and maintenance of peace: now it is to be vnderstood that this Port is a little Island of stones not three foote aboue the water in the hierst place, and but a bow shoote of length any way. This Island standeth from the maine land two bowe shootes or more, also it is to be vnderstood that there is not in all this coaste any other place for shippes to arriue in safetie, because the north wind hath there such violence

The maner of the Port S. John de Vllua.

that vnles the shippes be very safely mored with their ancres fastned vpon the Island, there is no remedie for these North windes but death: also the place of the Hauen was so little, that of necessitie the shippes must ride one aboorde the other, so that we could not giue place to them, nor they to vs: and here I began to bewaile that which after folowed, for now said I, I am in two dangers, and forced to receaue the one of them. That was, either I must haue kept out the fleete from entring the Port, that which with Gods helpe I was very well able to do, or els suffer them to enter in with their accustomed treason, which they never faile to execute, where they may haue opportunitie, or circumuent it by any meanes: if I had kept them out, then had there bin present shipwarke of al the fleete which amounted in value to sixe millions, which was in value of our money 1800000. li. which I considered I was not able to aunswere, fearing the Queens Maiesties indignation in so weighty a matter. Thus with my selfe reuoluing the doubts, thought rather better to abide the Jutt of the vncerteinty, than the certeinty. The vncerteine doubt I accompt was their treasure which by good policy I hoped might be preuented, and therefore as chusing the least mischief I proceeded to conditions.

North winds perilous.

1800. thousand pound.

Now was our first messenger come and retorned from the fleete with report of the arriual of a vice Roy,[1] so that he had auethority, both in all this Province of Mexico (otherwise called noua Hispania) and in the sea, who sent vs word that we should send our conditions, which of his part should (for the better maintenance of amity betweene the Princes) be both fauorably granted and faithfully performed, with many faire words how passing the coast of the Indies he had vnderstood of our honest behauiour towards the inhabitants

A vice Roy.

Faire wordes begiled.

[1] This was Don Martin Henriquez, Viceroy of Mexico from 1568 to 1580. In his time the Inquisition was introduced. He became Viceroy of Peru in 1581, and died at Lima in 1583.

where we had to do as wel elswhere as in the same Port, the which I let passe, thus following our demand we required victual for our mony, and licence to sel as much ware as might fornish our wants, and that there might be of either part xii. gentlemen as hostages for the maintenance of peace: and that the Island for our better safety might be in our owne possession, during our abode there, and such ordinance as was planted in the same Island, which was xi. pieces of Brasse: and that no Spanyarde might land in the Island with any kind of weapon: these conditions at the first, he somewhat misliked, chiefly the gard of the Island to be in our owne keeping, which if they had had, we had soon knowen our fare: for with the first North wind they had cut our cables and our ships had gone ashore: but in the ende he concluded to our request, bringing the xii. hostages to x. which with all speede of either part we are receaued, with a writing from the vice Roy signed with his hand and sealed with his seale of all the conditions concluded, and forthwith a trumpet blowne with comandement that none of either part should be meane to inuiolate the peace vpon paine of death: and further it was concluded that the two generals of the fleetes should meete, and give faith eche to other for the performance of the premises which was so done. Thus at the end of 3 daies all was concluded, and the fleete entred the Port, saluting one another as the maner of the sea doth require. Thus, as I said before, thursday we entred the Port, friday we sawe the fleete, and on monday at night they entred the Port: then we laboured ii. daies placing the English ships by themselues, and the Spanish ships by themselues, the captaines of each part and inferiour men of theyr partes promissing great amity of all sides: which euen with all fidelity was ment of our part, so the Spanyardes ment no thing lesse of their parts, but from the maine land had furnished themselues with a supplie of men to the nomber of 1000, and ment the next thursday, being the 23 of Septem-

Our requests.

The peace concluded.

Treason.

ber, at dinner time, to set vpon vs of all sides, the same thursday, in the morning, the treason being at hand, some appearance shewed, as shifting of weapons from ship to ship, planting and bending of ordinance from the ship to the Island where our men warded, passing to and fro of companies of men more then required for their necessary busines, and many other yll licklyhodes which caused vs to haue a vehement suspition, and therewithall sent to the vice Roy to enquire what was ment by it, which sent immediatly straight commandement to vnplant all things suspicious, and also sent word that he in the faith of a vice Roy would be our defence from all villanies. Yet we being not satisfied with this aunswere because we suspected a great nomber of men to be hid in a great ship of 900 tonnes which was mored next vnto the Minion, sent againe to the vice Roy the master of the Jesus which had the Spanish tongue and required to be satisfyed if any such thing were or not, which seeing the vice Roy that the treason must be discouered, forthwith stayed our master, blewe the trumpet, and of all sides set vpon vs; our men which warded ashore being stricken with soden feare, gaue place, fled, and sought to recouer succour of the shippes, the Spanyardes being before prouided for the purpose landed in all places in multitudes from their shippes, which they might easely doe without boates, and slewe all our men a shore without mercy, a fewe of them escaped aborde the Jesus. The great shippe which had by the estimation 300 men placed in her secretly, immediately fell aborde the Minion which by Gods apointment in the time of the suspition we had, which was only one halfe houre, the Minion was made ready to auoide and so leesing hir hedfastes, and hayling away by the stearne fastes shee was gotten out: thus with Gods helpe she defended the violence of the first brunt of these CCC. men. The Minion being paste out they came aborde the Jesus, which also with very much adoe and the losse of many of our men weare defended and kept out.

A vice Roy false of his worde.

The treason brake forth.

Sudden feare.

The Minion escaped hardly.

There were there also two other shippes that assaulted the Jesus at the same instant, so that she had hard getting loose, but yet with some time we had cut our hedfastes, and gotten out by the stearn fastes. Now when the Jesus and the Minion were gotten abroad two shippes length from the Spanish fleete, the fight beganne hot of all sides, that within one houre the Admirall of the Spanyardes was supposed to be suncke their vice Admirall burned and one other of there principall ships supposed to be sunke, so that the ships were little to annoy us.

The Jesus escaped hardly.

Sharpe warres.

3. Ships of the Spanyardes consumed.

Then it is to be vnderstood that all the ordinance vpon the Islande was in the Spanyardes handes, which did vs so great annoyance, that it cutt all the Mastes and yardes of the Jesus in such sort there was no hope to carry her away: also it sunke our small shippes, whereupon wee determined to place the Jesus on that side of the Minion that shee myght abide all the batterie from the lande, and so be a defence for the Minion till night, and then to take such reliefe of victuall and other necessaries from the Jesus as the time would suffer vs, and to leaue her. As wee were thus determining, and had placed the Minion from the shott of the lande, suddenly the Spanyardes had fired two great shippes which were comming directly with vs, and having no meanes to auoide the fire, it bread among our men a marueilous feare, so that some said, let vs depart with the Minion, other sayd, let vs see where the winde will carrie the fyre from vs.

A hard case.

Fire.

But to bee short, the Minion men which had alwayes there sayles in a readinesse, thought to make sure worke, and so without eyther consent of the Captaine or Master cutte their sayle, so that verie hardly I was receaued into the Minion.

The most part of the men that were left a lyue in the Jesus made shift and followed the Minion in a small boat, the rest, which the little boate was not able to receaue, were inforced to abide the mercy of the Spanyards (which I doubt was very little): so with the Minion onely and the Judith (a small barke of fiftie tunne) wee escaped, which barke the same night forsooke vs in our great myserie: wee were nowe remooued with the Minion from the Spanyshe shippes two bowe shootes and there roade all that nyght: the next morning wee recouered an Ilande a myle from the Spanyardes, where there tooke vs a North winde, and being left onely with two Ankers and two cables (for in this conflicte wee loste three Cables and two Ankers) wee thought alwayes vpon death which euer was present, but God preserued vs to a longer tyme.

Small hope to be had of tyrants.

A storme.

The weather waxed seasonable, and the Satturday we set sayle, and having a great nomber of men and lyttle victuals our hope of life waxed lesse and lesse: some desired to yelde to the Spanyardes, some rather desired to obtayne a place where they might giue themselues to the Infidels, and some had rather abide with a little pittance the mercie of God at Sea: so thus with manie sorrowfull hearts wee wandred in an unknowen Sea by the space of fourteene dayes, tyll hunger inforced vs to seeke the lande, for birdes were thought very good meate, rattes, cattes, mise, and dogges, none escaped that might be gotten, parrates and monkayes that were had in great prise, were thought then very profitable if they serued the tourne one dinner: thus in the ende the eyght day of October wee came to the lande in the botome of the same bay of Mexico in twenty three degrees and a halfe where wee hoped to haue founde inhabitantes of the Spanyardes, reliefe of victualles, and place for the repaire of our shippe, which was so sore beaten with shotte from our enemyes and brused with shooting of our owne ordinance, that our weary and weake armes were scarce able to defende and keepe out the water. But all things happened to the contrary, for we founde neyther people, victuall, nor hauen of reliefe, but a place where hauing faire weather with some perill we might land a boate: our people being forced with hunger desired to be set a land, whereunto I concluded.

Small hope of life.

Hard choise.

Miseries.

October.

Many miseries.

And such as were willing to land I put them apart, and such as were desirous to goe homewards, I put apart, so that they were indifferently parted a hundred of one side and a hundred of the other side: these hundred men we set a land with all diligence in this little place before said,[1] which being landed, we determined there to refresh our water, and so with our little remains of victuals to take the Sea.

The next day hauing a lande with me fiftie of our hundreth men that remained for the speedier preparing of our water aborde, there arose an extreme storme, so that in three dayes we could by no meanes repayre our shippe: the shippe also was in such perill that euery hour we looked for shipwracke.

The greatest miserie of all.

But yet God againe had mercie on vs, sent faire weather, had aborde our water, and departed the sixteene day of October, after which day wee had faire and prosperous weather till the sixteene day of Nouember, which day God be praysed wee were cleere from the coast of the Indians, and out of the Channell and Goulfe of Bahama, which is betweene the Cape of Florida, and the Islandes of Cuba. After this growing neere to the colde Countrie, our men being oppressed with Famine, died continually, and they that were left, grewe into such weaknes that wee were scantly able to manure our ship, and the wind being alwaies yll for vs to recouer England, determined to go with Galicia in Spaine, with intent there to releeue our company and other extreame wants. And being arriued the last day of December in a place near vnto Vigo called Ponte vedra, our men with excess of freshe meate grew into miserable diseases, and died a great part of them. This matter was borne out as long as it might be, but in the

The Goulfe of Bahama.

Nouember.

December.

[1] Graphic accounts of the terrible sufferings of the men who were put on shore, and of the atrocities committed on them by the Inquisition at Mexico, were given by David Ingram of Barking in Essex, and Miles Philips, two of the survivors. They are printed in Hakluyt's *Principal Navigations* (1589), pp. 557 to 560.

end although there was none of our men suffered to goe a lande, yet by accesse of the Spanyardes, our feblenes was knowen to them. Whereupon they ceased not to seeke by all meanes to betraie vs, but with all speede possible we departed to Vigo, where we had some helpe of certaine English ships and xii. fresh men wherewith we repaired our wants as we might, and departing the xx. day of Januarie 1568, ar- Januarie. riued in Mounts bay in Cornewale the xxv. of the same moneth, praised be God therefore.

If all the miseries and troublesome affaires of this sorrowfull voyage should be perfectly and thoroughly written, there should neede a paynfull man with his penne, and as great a time as hee had that wrote the liues and deathes of the martirs.

IOHN HAWKINS.

THE

OBSERVATIONS

OF

S[IR] RICHARD HAVV-KINS KNIGHT, IN HIS *VOIAGE INTO THE* *South Sea.*

Anno Domini 1593.

Per varios Casus, Artem Experientia fecit,
Exemplo monstrante viam.—MANIL. li. 1.

LONDON

Printed by *I. D.* for IOHN IAGGARD, and are to be sold at his shop at the Hand and Starre in Fleete-streete, *neere the Temple Gate. 1622.*

G 2

TO THE

MOST ILLUSTRIOUS AND MOST EXCELLENT

PRINCE CHARLES, PRINCE OF WALES,

DUKE OF CORNEWALL, EARLE OF CHESTER, ETC.

AMONGST other neglects prejudiciall to this state, I have observed, that many the worthy and heroyque acts of our nation, have been buried and forgotten: the actors themselves being desirous to shunne emulation in publishing them, and those which overlived them, fearefull to adde, or to diminish from the actors worth, judgement, and valour, have forborne to write them; by which succeeding ages have been deprived of the fruits which might have beene gathered out of their experience, had they beene committed to record. To avoyd this neglect, and for the good of my country, I have thought it my duty to publish the observations of my South Sea Voyage; and for that unto your highnesse, your heires, and successors, it is most likely to be advantagious (having brought on me nothing but losse and misery), I am bold to use your name, a protection unto it, and to offer it with all humblenes and duty to your highnesse approbation, which if it purchase, I have attained my desire, which shall ever ayme to performe dutie.

Your Highnesse humble

And devoted servant,

RICHARD HAWKINS.

TO THE READER.

HAD *that worthie knight, the author, lived to have seen this his Treatise published, he would perhaps himselfe have given the account thereof: for by his owne directions it was put to the presse, though it pleased God to take him to his mercy during the time of the impression. His purpose was to have recommended both it and himselfe unto our most excellent Prince Charles, and himselfe wrote the Dedication, which being imparted unto me, I conceited that it stood not with my dutie to suppresse it.*

Touching the discourse it selfe, as it is out of my element to judge, so it is out of my purpose to say much of it. This onely I may boldly promise, that you shall heere find an expert seaman, in his owne dialect, deliver a true relation of an unfortunat voyage; which howsoever it proved lamentable and fatall to the actors, may yet prove pleasing to the readers: it being an itch in our natures to delight in newnes and varietie, be the subject never so grievous. This (if there were no more) were yet worthy your perusall; and is as much as others have with good acceptance afforded in relations of this nature. Howbeit besides the bare series and context of the storie, you shall heere finde interweaved, sundry exact descriptions of Countries, Townes, Capes, Pro-

montories, Rivers, Creeks, Harbours, and the like, not unprofitable for navigators; besides many notable observations, the fruites of a long experience, that may give light touching marine accidents, even to the best captaines and commaunders: who if they desire to learn by precepts, shall here find store: but if examples prevaile more with them, here are also aliena pericula. *If you believe mee not, reade and judge.* Farewell.

THE OBSERVATIONS

OF

SIR RICHARD HAWKINS, KNIGHT,

IN HIS

VOYAGE INTO THE SOUTH SEA.

SECTION I.

WITH the counsels consent, and helpe of my father, Sir John Hawkins,[1] knight, I resolved a voyage to be made for the Ilands of Japan, of the Phillippinas, and Molucas, the kingdomes of China, and East Indies, by the way of the Straites of Magelan, and the South Sea.

The principall end of our designements, was, to make a perfect discovery of all those parts where I should arrive, as well knowne as unknowne, with their longitudes and latitudes; the lying of their coasts; their head lands; their ports, and bayes; their cities, townes, and peoplings; their manner of government; with the commodities which the countries yielded, and of which they have want, and are in necessitie.

The necessary use of discoveries.

Of travaile.

For this purpose, in the end of anno 1588, returning from the journey against the Spanish Armado, I caused a ship to be builded in the river of Thames, betwixt three and foure hundred tunnes, which was finished in that perfection as could be required; for she was pleasing to the eye, profitable for stowage, good of sayle, and well conditioned.

Of shipping.

[1] See Introduction.

Sect. I.

The day of her launching been appoynted, the Lady Hawkins (my mother-in-law[1]) craved the naming of the ship, which was easily granted her: who knowing what voyage was pretended to be undertaken, named her the *Repentance:* what her thoughts were, was kept secret to her selfe; and although many times I expostulated with her, to declare the reason for giving her that uncouth name, I could never have any other satisfaction, than that repentance was the safest ship we could sayle in, to purchase the haven of Heaven. Well, I know, shee was no prophetess, though a religious and most vertuous lady, and of a very good understanding.

Yet too propheticall it fell out by Gods secrete judgements, which in his wisdome was pleased to reveale unto us by so unknowne a way, and was sufficient for the present, to cause me to desist from the enterprise, and to leave the ship to my father, who willingly took her, and paid the entire charge of the building and furnishing of her, which I had concorted or paid. And this I did not for any superstition I have in names, or for that I thinke them able to further or hinder any thing; for that all immediately dependeth upon the Providence of Almightie God, and is disposed by him alone.

Improper names for shipping.

Yet advise I all persons ever (as neere as they can) by all meanes, and in all occasions, to presage unto themselves the good they can, and in giving names to terestriall workes (especially to ships), not to give such as meerly represent the celestial character: for few have I knowne, or seen, come to a good end, which have had such attri-

[1] Second wife of his father, Sir John Hawkins. She was Margaret, daughter of Charles Vaughan, Esq., of Hergest Court, co. Hereford. Lady Hawkins was a bed-chamber woman to the Queen. She survived her husband twenty-six years, dying in 1621. Her Will was dated April 23rd, 1619. Her mother was Elizabeth, daughter of Sir F. Baskerville, of Eardisley Castle, co. Hereford.

Sect. I.

The *Revenge*.

butes. As was plainely seene in the *Revenge*, which was ever the unfortunatist ship the late queenes majestie had during her raigne; for coming out of Ireland, with Sir John Parrot,[1] shee was like to be cast away upon the Kentish coast. After, in the voyage of Sir John Hawkins, my father, anno 1586, shee strucke aground coming into Plimouth, before her going to sea. Upon the coast of Spaine, shee left her fleete, readie to sinke with a great leake: at her returne into the harbour of Plimouth, shee beate upon Winter stone; and after, in the same voyage, going out at Portsmouth haven, shee ranne twice aground; and in the latter of them, lay twentie-two houres beating upon the shore: and at length, with eight foote of water in hold, shee was forced off, and presently ranne upon the Oose: and was cause that shee remained there (with other three ships of her majesties) six months, till the spring of the yeare; when coming about to bee decked,[2] entring the river of Thames, her old leake breaking upon her, had liked to have drowned all those which were in her. In anno 1591, with a storme of wind and weather, riding at her moorings in the river of Rochester, nothing but her bare masts over head, shee was turned topsie-turvie, her kele uppermost: and the cost and losse shee wrought, I have too good cause to remember, in her last voyage, in which shee was lost, when shee gave England and Spain just cause to remember her. For the Spaniards, themselves confesse, that three of their ships sunke by her side, and was the death of above 1500 of their men, with the losse

See Master Hacluits Relations.

[1] Sir John Perrot, an experienced soldier, was appointed President of Munster in 1571. In 1584 he became Lord Deputy of Ireland. Froude describes him (xii, p. 201) "as a straightforward soldier, vain, passionate, but anxious to do what was right". Sir John Chichester, who was afterwards Lord Deputy, married his daughter Letitia. Perrot was superseded, at his own request, in 1588; false accusations were brought against him, and he died of a broken heart in the Tower.

[2] Docked?

Sect. I.

of a great part of their fleete, by a storme which suddainly tooke them the next day. What English died in her, many living are witnesses: among which was Sir Richard Greenfield, a noble and valiant gentleman, vice-admirall in her of her majesties fleete. So that, well considered, she was even a ship loaden, and full fraught with ill successe.

The *Thunderbolt* of London.

The like wee might behold in the *Thunderbolt*, of London, who, in one voyage (as I remember), had her mast cleft with a thunderbolt, upon the coast of Barbary. After in Dartmouth, going for admirall of the Whaftage,[1] and guard of the fleete for the river of Bourdieux, had also her poope blown up with fire sodainly, and unto this day, never could be knowne the cause, or manner how: and lastly, shee was burned with her whole companie in the river of Bourdieux, and Master Edward Wilson, generall in her, slaine by his enemies, having escaped the fire.

The *Jesus* of Lubeck.

The successe of the *Jesus* of Lubecke, in St. John de Vlua, in the Nova Spania, infamous to the Spaniardes,[2] with my *Repentance*, in the South Sea, taken by force, hath utterly impoverished, and overthrowne our house.

The *Repentance*.

The *Journey* of Spaine.

The *Journey* of Spaine, pretended for England, anno 1587, called the *Journey of Revenge*, left the principall of their men and ships on the rocks of Cape Finister, and the rest made a lamentable end, for the most part in the Groyne.[3] No more for this poynt, but to our purpose.

[1] Convoy? Whafter. A term applied to ships of war,—probably from their carrying flags or whafts.

[2] This alludes to a base attack made on Sir John Hawkins, after he had entered into a friendly agreement with the Viceroy. See page 77.

[3] Cerogne (F.) Coruña (S.).

SECTION II.

The *Repentance* being put in perfection, and riding at Detford, the queens majestie passing by her, to her pallace at Greenwych, commanded her bargemen to row round about her, and viewing her from post to stemme, disliked nothing but her name, and said that shee would christen her anew, and that henceforth shee should be called the *Daintie;* which name she brooked as well for her proportion and grace, as for the many happie voyages she made in her majesties service; having taken (for her majestie) a great Bysten,[1] of five hundred tunnes, loaden with iron and other commodities, under the conduct of Sir Martin Furbusher; a caracke bound for the East Indies, under my fathers charge, and the principall cause of taking the great caracke, brought to Dartmouth by Sir John Borrow, and the Earl of Cumberlands shippes, anno 1592, with others of moment in other voyages.[2] To us, shee never brought but cost, trouble, and care. Therefore my father resolved to sell

[1] Probably an abbreviation or misprint for Biscayan. Lediard relates, that in 1592, an expedition, fitted out against the Spaniards, "took a great Biscayan shipp of six hundred tunnes, laden with all sorts of small iron-work".

[2] This great caracke was taken, after a sharp engagement, by six ships; which were dispatched expressly to the Azores, to lie in wait for the East India carackes. The expedition left under the command of Sir Walter Raleigh and Sir John Borrough. Sir Walter was, however, superseded by Sir Martin Frobisher. She was called the "*Madre de Dios*", a seven-decked ship of one hundred and sixty-five feet from stem to stern, manned with six hundred men. The burthen of this caracke was sixteen hundred tons, and she carried thirty-two brass guns. Her cargo, besides jewels, *which never came to light*, was as follows: spices, drugs, silks, and calicoes, besides other wares, many in number, but less in value, as elephants' teeth, china, cocoa-nuts, hides, ebony, and cloth made from rinds of trees. All which being appraised, was reckoned to amount to at least one hundred and fifty thousand pounds. The carracke, or Carraca, was a large vessel of two masts, used in the India and Brazilian trade.

Sect. II. her, though with some losse, which he imparted with me: and for that I had ever a particular love unto her, and a desire shee should continue ours, I offered to ease him of the charge and care of her, and to take her with all her furniture at the price he had before taken her of me; with resolution to put in execution the voyage for which shee was first builded; although it lay six months and more in suspence, partly, upon the pretended voyage for Nombre de Dios and Panama, which then was fresh a foote; and partly, upon the caracke at Dartmouth, in which I was imployed as a commissioner; but this businesse being ended, and the other pretence waxing colde, the fift of March I resolved, and beganne to goe forward with the journey, so often talked of, and so much desired.

Considerations for pretended voyages.

And having made an estimate of the charge of victualls, munition, imprests,[1] sea-shore, and necessaries for the sayd ship: consorting another of a hundred tunnes which I waited for daily from the Straites of Giberalter, with a pynace of sixtie tunes, all mine owne: and for a competent number of men for them; as also of all sorts of merchandises for trade and traffique in all places where wee should come; I began to wage men, to buy all manner of victualls and provisions, and to lade her with them, and with all sorts of commodities (which I could call to minde) fitting; and dispatched order to my servant in Plimouth, to put in a readinesse my pynace;[2] as also to take up certaine provisions, which are better cheape in those parts than in London, as beefe, porke, bisket, and sider. And with the diligence I used, and my father's furtherance, at the end of one moneth, I was ready to set sayle for Plimouth, to joyne with the rest of my shippes and provisions. But the expecting of the coming of the lord high admirall, Sir Robert Cecill, principall secretary to her majestie, and Sir

Provisions better provided at Plimouth, then at London.

[1] Bounty? or perhaps wages paid in advance.

[2] A small vessel fitted with sails and oars.

Walter Rawley, with others, to honour my shippe and me with their presence and farewell, detayned me some dayes: and the rayne and untemperate weather deprived me of the favour, which I was in hope to have received at their hands. Whereupon being loath to loose more time, and the winde serving according to my wish, the eight of April, 1593, I caused the pilot to set sayle from Blackwall, and to vayle[1] down to Gravesend, whither that night I purposed to come.

Having taken my unhappy last leave of my father Sir John Hawkins, I tooke my barge, and rowed down the river, and coming to Barking, wee might see my ship at an anchor in the midst of the channell, where ships are not wont to more themselves: this bred in me some alteration. And coming aboord her, one and other began to recount the perill they had past of losse of ship and goods, which was not little; for the winde being at east northeast, when they set sayle, and vered out southerly, it forced them for the doubling of a point to bring their tacke aboard, and looffing up; the winde freshing sodenly the shipp began to make a little hele; and for that shee was very deep loaden, and her ports open, the water began to enter in at them, which no bodie having regard unto, thinking themselves safe in the river, it augmented in such manner as the waight of the water began to presse downe the side, more than the winde: at length when it was seene and the shete flowne, shee could hardly be brought upright. But God was pleased that with the diligence and travell of the company, she was freed of that danger; which may be a gentle warning to all such as take charge of shipping, even before they set sayle, eyther in river or harbour, or other part, to have an eye to their ports, and to see those shut and callked, which may cause danger; for avoyding the many mishaps which dayly chance for the neglect

[1] Drop down.

Sect. II. thereof, and have beene most lamentable spectacles and examples unto us: experiments in the *Great Harry*,[1] admirall of England, which was overset and suncke at Portsmouth, with her captaine, Carew, and the most part of his company drowned in a goodly summers day, with a little flawe of winde; for that her ports were all open, and making a small hele, by them entred their destruction; where if they had beene shut, no wind could have hurt her, especially in that place.

In the river of Thames, Master Thomas Candish had a small ship over-set through the same negligence. And one of the fleete of Syr Francis Drake, in Santo Domingo harbour, turned her keele upward likewise, upon the same occasion: with many others, which we never have knowledge of.

And when this cometh to passe, many times negligence is cloaked with the fury of the winde: which is a double fault; for the truth being knowne, others would bee warned to shun the like neglects; for it is a very bad ship whose masts crackt not asunder, whose sayles and tackling flie not in pieces, before she over-set, especially if she be English built. And that which over-setteth the ship is the waight of the water that presseth down the side, which as it entreth more and more, increaseth the waight, and the impossibilitie of the remedie: for, the water not entring, with easing of the sheate, or striking the sayles or putting the ship before the winde or sea, or other diligences, as occasion is offered (and all expert mariners know) remedie is easily found.

[1] The *Great Harry* was built in the reign of Henry VII, and was accidentally burnt at Woolwich in 1553. She was the first two-decker. Sir Richard Hawkins forgot that it was the *Mary Rose* that sunk at Spithead, as Sir W. Monson tells us, on the very day that King Henry had dined on board. The *Great Harry* was once nearly sunk at Spithead, on the day the French fleet appeared at St. Helen's, "by a little sway in casting the ship about, the ports being sixteen inches from the water".

With this mischaunce the mariners were so daunted, that they would not proceede with the ship any further, except shee was lighted, which indeede was needelesse, for many reasons which I gave: but mariners are like to a stiffe necked horse, which taking the bridle betwixt his teeth, forceth his rider to what him list, mauger his will; so they having once concluded, and resolved, are with great difficultie brought to yeelde to the raynes of reason; and to colour their negligence, they added cost, trouble, and delay. In fine, seeing no other remedie, I dispatched that night a servant of mine to give account to my father of that which had past, and to bring mee presently some barke of London, to goe along with me to Plimouth; which not finding, he brought me a hoye, in which I loaded some sixe or eight tunnes, to give content to the company; and so set sayle the 13th of Aprill, and the next day wee put in at Harwich, for that the winde was contrary, and from thence departed the 18th of the sayd moneth in the morning.

When wee were cleere of the sands, the winde veered to the south-west, and so we were forced to put into Margat Roade, whither came presently after us a fleete of Hollanders of above an hundreth sayle, bound for Rochell, to loade salt; and in their companie a dozen shippes of warre; their wafters very good ships and well appointed in all respects. All which came alongst by our ship, and saluted us, as is the custome of the sea, some with three, others with five, others with more peeces of ordinance.

The next morning the winde vering easterly, I set sayle, and the Hollanders with me, and they with the flood in hand, went out at the North-sands-head, and I through the Gulls to shorten my way, and to set my pilote ashore.

Comming neere the South-fore-land, the winde began to vere to the south-east and by south, so as we could not double the point of the land, and being close abourd the shoure, and puting our ship to stay, what with the chapping

Sect. III. sea, and what with the tide upon the bowe, she mist staying, and put us in some danger, before we could flatt about; therefore for doubling the point of any land better is ever a short bourd, then to put all in perill.[1]

Being tacked about, wee thought to anchor in the Downes, but the sayles set, we made a small bourd, and after casting aboute agayne, doubled the foreland, and ran alongst the coast till we came to the Isle of Wight: where being becalmed, wee sent ashore Master Thomson, of Harwich, our pilot, not being able before to set him on shore for the perversnes of the winde.

Being cleere of the Wight, the wind vered southerly, and before we came to Port-land, to the west, south-west, but with the helpe of the ebbe wee recovered Port-land-roade, where we anchored all that night; and the next morning with the ebbe, wee set sayle againe, the winde at west south-west; purposing to beare it up, all the ebbe, and to stop the flood being under sayle.

SECTION III.

The providence of the Dutch.

The fleete of Flemings which had beene in our company before, came towring into the road, which certainly was a thing worth the noting, to behold the good order the masters observed in guard of their fleete.

The admirall headmost, and the rest of the men of warre, spread alongst to wind-ward, all saving the vice-admirall and her consort, which were lee-most and stern-most of all; and except the admirall, which was the first, that came to an anchor, none of the other men of warre anchored, before

[1] This is sound advice and good seamanship. In turning to windward, it is wise to keep in the fair way, so that in case of missing stays, you have not a danger under your lee.

all the fleete was in safetie; and then they placed themselves round about the fleete; the vice-admirall sea-most and lee-most; which we have taught unto most nations, and they observe it now a dayes better then we, to our shame, that being the authors and reformers of the best discipline and lawes in sea causes, are become those which doe now worst execute them.

The English authors of sea discipline.

And I cannot gather whence this contempt hath growne, except of the neglect of displicine, or rather in giving commands for favour to those which want experience of what is committed to their charge: or that there hath bene little curiositie in our countrey in writing of the discipline of the sea; which is not lesse necessary for us, then that of the law; and I am of opinion, that the want of experience is much more tollerable in a generall by land, than in a governour by sea: for in the field, the lieutenant generall, the sergeant major, and the coronels supply what is wanting in the generall, for that they all command, and ever there is place for counsell, which in the sea by many accidents is denied; and the head is he that manageth all, in whom alone if there be defect, all is badly governed, for, by ignorance how can errors be judged or reformed? And therefore I wish all to take upon them that which they understand, and refuse the contrary.

By them againe neglected.

As Sir Henry Palmer, a wise and valiant gentleman, a great commander, and of much experience in sea causes, being appoynted by the queens majesties counsell, to goe for generall of a fleete for the coast of Spaine, anno 1583, submitting himselfe to their lordships pleasure, excused the charge, saying, that his trayning up had beene in the narrow seas; and that of the other he had little experience: and therefore was in dutie bound to intreate their honours to make choice of some other person, that was better acquainted and experimented in those seas; that her majestie and their lordships might be the better served. His modestie

The modesty of Sir Henry Palmer.

Sect. IV.

and discretion is doubtlesse to be had in remembrance and great estimation; for the ambition of many which covet the command of fleetes, and places of government (not knowing their compasse, nor how, nor what to command) doe purchase to themselves shame; and losse to those that employ them: being required in a commander at sea, a sharpe wit, a good understanding, experience in shipping, practise in management of sea business, knowledge in navigation, and in command. I hold it much better to deserve it, and not to have it, then to have it not deserving it.

Parts required in a commander at sea.

SECTION IV.

THE fruits and inconveniences of the latter we daily partake of, to our losse and dishonor. As in the fleete that went for Burdieux, anno 1592, which had six gallant ships for wafters. At their going out of Plimouth, the vice-admirall, that should have been starnmost of all, was the headmost, and the admirall the last, and he that did execute the office of the vice-admirall, lanching off into the sea, drew after him the greater parte of the fleete, and night comming on, and both bearing lights, caused a separation: so that the head had a quarter of the bodie, and the fleete three quarters, and he that should goe before, came behinde. Whereof ensued, that the three parts meeting with few Spanish men of warre, wanting their head, were a prey unto them. For the vice-admirall, and other wafters, that should be the shepheards to guard and keepe their flocke, and to carry them in safetie before them, were headmost, and they the men who made most hast to flie from the wolfe. Whereas, if they had done as they ought, in place of losse and infamie, they had gained honor and reward.

The losse of the Burdieux fleete anno 1592.

The cause.

This I have beene enformed of by the Spanish and English,

Sect. IV.

which were present in the occasion. And a ship of mine, being one of the starnmost, freed her selfe, for that shee was in warlike manner, with her false netting, many pendents and streamers, and at least sixteen or eighteen peeces of artillery; the enemie thinking her to be a wafter, or ship of warre, not one of them durst lay her aboord: and this the master and company vaunted of at their returne.

In the same voyage, in the river of Burdieux (as is credibly reported), if the six wafters had kept together, they had not onely not received damage, but gotten much honour and reputation. For the admirall of the Spanish armado, was a Flemish shippe of not above 130 tunnes, and the rest flie-boates and small shipping, for the most part. The weakness of the enemy.

And although there were twenty-two sayle in all, what manner of ships they were, and how furnished and appoynted, is well knowne, with the difference.

In the fleete of her majestie, under the charge of my father Sir John Hawkins, anno 1590, upon the coast of Spaine, the vice-admirall being a head one morning, where his place was to be a sterne, lost us the taking of eight men of warre loaden with munition, victuals, and provisions, for the supplie of the souldiers in Brittaine:[1] and although they were seven or eight leagues from the shore, when our vice-admirall began to fight with them, yet for that the rest of our fleete were some four, some five leagues, and some more distant from them, when we beganne to give chase, the Spaniards recovered into the harbour of Monge,[2] before our admiral could come up to give direction; yet well beaten, with losse of above two hundreth men, as they themselves confessed to me after. The voyage of Sir John Hawkins, anno 1590.

[1] The Spaniards sent assistance of troops and stores to the Duc de Mercœur in Brittany, in his war against Henry IV, which was not concluded until 1598.

[2] Mugia, a harbour on the coast of Galicia, fourteen miles north of Cape Finisterre. Sir Wm. Monson calls it Mongia.

Sect. IV.

And doubtlesse, if the wind had not over-blowne, and that to follow them I was forced to shut all my lower ports, the ship I undertooke doubtles had never endured to come to the port; but being double fli-boates, and all of good sayle, they bare for their lives, and we what we could to follow and fetch them up.

Sir Richard Greenfield at Flores.

In this poynt, at the Isle of Flores, Sir Richard Greenfield got eternall honour and reputation of great valour, and of an experimented souldier, chusing rather to sacrifice his life, and to passe all danger whatsoever, then to fayle in his obligation, by gathering together those which had remained a shore in that place, though with the hazard of his ship and companie; and rather we ought to imbrace an honourable death, then to live with infamie and dishonour, by fayling in dutie; and I account, that he and his country got much honor in that occasion; for one ship, and of the second sort of her majesties, sustained the force of all the fleete of Spain, and gave them to understand, that they be impregnible, for having bought deerely the boording of her, divers and sundry times, and with many joyntly, and with a continuall fight of fourteen or sixteen houres, at length leaving her without any mast standing, and like a logge in the seas, shee made, notwithstanding, a most honourable composition of life and libertie for above two hundreth and sixtie men, as by the pay-booke appeareth: which her majestie of her free grace, commanded, in recompence of their service, to be given to every one his six moneths wages. All which may worthily be written in our chronicles in letters of gold, in memory for all posterities, some to beware, and others, by their example in the like occasions, to imitate the true valour of our nation in these ages.[1]

[1] The first account of the famous fight of Sir Richard Grenville, in the *Revenge*, against fifty-three Spanish ships, was written by Sir Walter Raleigh, and appeared in the same year, 1591.—*A Report of the truth of the fight about the Iles of Azores this last summer, betwixt the "Revenge",*

Sect. IV.

Captaine Vavisor.

In poynt of Providence, which captaine Vavisor, in the *Foresight*,[1] gave also good proofe of his valour, in casting about upon the whole fleete, notwithstanding the greatnesse and multitude of the Spanish armado, to yeeld that succour which he was able; although some doe say, and I consent with them, that the best valour is to obey, and to follow the head, seeme that good or bad which is commanded. For

one of Her Majesties shippes, and an Armada of the King of Spaine (London, 1591). This Report was reprinted in Hakluyt's Voyages (ii, p. 169), and in the second edition of 1812 (ii, p. 662). The next account is contained in the poem written by Gervase Markham, brother of my ancestor Sir Robert Markham of Cotham, which was published in 1595. The title is—"*The Most Honorable* Tragedie of Sir Richard Grinuile, Knight (*Brama assai, poco spero, nulla chieggio*) (London, 1595), 4to. There is a third account of the voyage, written by the Dutch traveller Jan Huygen van Linschoten, which will be found in his *Itinerario* (Amsterdam, 1595), translated into English in 1598 (1 vol., folio). All three accounts were published in one small volume, in Mr. Arber's series of *English Reprints*, in 1871. The poem gives the most detailed history of this glorious naval fight, and appears to be based mainly on Sir Walter Raleigh's Report.

Mr. Tennyson had Arber's little volume of reprints before him when he wrote that noble ballad—*The Revenge: A Ballad of the Fleet*—published in No. xiii of the *Nineteenth Century*, for March 1878. He takes some points from all three accounts of Raleigh, Markham, and Linschoten. The further remarks of Sir Richard Hawkins in the text are extremely interesting.—C. R. M.

[1] In the list of seven ships composing Lord Thomas Howard's fleet, we find the *Foresight*, Captain Vavasour. He deserves great credit for attempting to yield what succour he was able to the gallant Sir R. Grenville. One other vessel followed, or perhaps set, the example: the *George Noble*, of London, falling under the lee of the *Revenge*, asked Sir Richard if he had anything to command him; but as he was one of the victuallers and but of small force, Sir Richard bid him shift for himself, and leave him to his fortune. Lediard adds in a note, that it is more than probable had all the other vessels behaved with the same vigour and resolution as Sir Richard and his company, they might have given a good account of the Spanish fleet. It is to be regretted the name of the commander of the *George Noble* is not recorded. We know not which to admire most, his bravery in fully acting up to the principle of "succouring a known friend in view", or the magnanimity of Sir Richard in dismissing him from an unequal contest.

Sect. V. God himselfe telleth us, that obedience is better than sacrifice. Yet in some occasions, where there is difficultie or impossibilitie to know what is commanded, many times it is great discretion and obligation, judiciously to take hold of the occasion to yeelde succour to his associats, without putting himselfe in manifest danger. But to our voyage.

SECTION V.

Being cleare of the race of Portland, the wind began to suffle[1] with fogge and misling rayne, and forced us to a short sayle, which continued with us three dayes; the wind never veering one poynt, nor the fogge suffering us to see the coast.

The third day in the fogge, we met with a barke of Dartmouth, which came from Rochell, and demanding of them if they had made any lande, answered, that they had onely seene the Edie stone that morning, which lyeth thwart of the sound of Plimouth, and that Dartmouth (as they thought) bare off us north north-east: which seemed strange unto us; for we made account that we were thwart of Exmouth. Within two houres after, the weather beganne to cleare up, and we found ourselves thwart of the Berry,[2] and might see the small barke bearing into Torbay, having over-shot her port; which error often happeneth to those that make the land in foggie weather, and use not good diligence by sound, by lying off the land, and other circumstances, to search the truth; and is cause of the losse of many a ship, and the sweet lives of multitudes of men.[3]

That evening we anchored in the range of Dartmouth, till the floud was spent; and the ebbe come, wee set sayle again.

[1] *Souffler*—to blow.

[2] Berry Head, the west point of Tor Bay.

[3] It is still unfortunately too much the custom to risk the loss of ship and "sweet lives", by neglecting the use of the lead.

Sect. VI.

And the next morning early, being the 26th of Aprill, wee harboured our selves in Plimouth.

My ship at an anchor, and I ashore, I presently dispatched a messenger to London, to advise my father, Sir John Hawkins, what had past: which not onely to him, but to all others, that understood what it was, seemed strange; that the wind contrary, and the weather such as it had beene, wee could be able to gaine Plimouth; but doubtlesse, the *Daintie* was a very good sea ship, and excellent by the winde; which with the neap streames, and our diligence to benefit our selves of all advantages, made fezible that which almost was not to be beleeved.

Parts requisite in a good mariner.

And in this occasion, I found by experience, that one of the principall parts required in a mariner that frequenteth our coastes of England, is to cast his tydes, and to know how they set from poynt to poynt, with the difference of those in the Channell from those of the shore.[1]

SECTION VI.

Now presently I began to prepare for my dispatch, and to hasten my departure; and finding that my ship which I expected from the Straites came not, and that shee was to goe to London to discharge, and uncertaine how long shee might stay, I resolved to take another of mine owne in her place, though lesser, called the *Hawke*, onely for a victualler; purposing in the coast of Brazil, or in the Straites,[2] to take out her men and victualls, and to cast her off.

[1] The tide runs two or three hours later in the offing than in shore; by attending to this, a vessel working down channel may gain great advantage.

[2] Of Magellan.

SECTION VII.

Sect. VII. WITH my continuall travell, the helpe of my good friends, and excessive charge (which none can easily beleeve, but those which have proved it), towardes the end of May, I was readie to set sayle with my three ships, drawne out into the sound, and began to gather my company aboord.

The 28th of May (as I remember) began a storme of winde, westerly; the two lesser shippes presently harboured themselves, and I gave order to the master of the *Daintie* (called Hugh Cornish), one of the most sufficientest men of his coate, to bring her also into Catt-water, which he laboured to doe; but being neere the mouth of the harbour, and doubting least the anchor being weighed, the ship might cast the contrary way, and so run on some perill, entertained himselfe a while in laying out a warpe, and in the meane time, the wind freshing, and the ship riding by one anchor, brake the flooke of it, and so forced them to let fall another; by which, and by the warpe they had layd out, they rydd. The storme was such, as being within hearing of those upon the shore, we were not able by any meanes to send them succour, and the second day of the storme, desiring much to goe aboord, there joined with me captaine William Anthony, captaine John Ellis, and master Henry Courton, in a light horsman,[1] which I had: all men exercised in charge, and of valour and sufficiencie, and from their youth bred up in businesse of the sea: which notwithstanding, and that wee laboured what we could, for the space of two houres against waves and wind, we could find no possibilitie to accomplish our desire; which seene, we went aboord the other shippes, and put them in the best securitie we could. Thus busied, we might see come driving by us the mayne mast of the *Daintie*, which made

A cruell storme.

And therein the effects of courage and advice.

[1] Probably what is now called a "gig"; a fast-pulling boat.

me to feare the worst, and so hasted a shore, to satisfie my longing. Sect. VII.

And comming upon Catt-downe, wee might see the ship heave and sett, which manifestly shewed the losse of the mast onely, which was well imployed; for it saved the ship, men, and goods. For had shee driven a ships length more, shee had (no doubt) beene cast away; and the men in that place could not chuse but run into danger.

The losse of the pynace.

Comming to my house to shift me (for that we were all wette to the skinne), I had not well changed my clothes, when a servant of mine, who was in the pynace at my comming ashore, enters almost out of breath, with newes, that she was beating upon the rocks, which though I knew to be remedilesse, I put my selfe in place where I might see her, and in a little time after she sunk downe right. These losses and mischances troubled and grieved, but nothing daunted me; for common experience taught me, that all honourable enterprises are accompanied with difficulties and dangers; *Si fortuna me tormenta; Esperança me contenta:*[1] of hard beginnings, many times come prosperous and happy events. And although, a well-willing friend wisely foretold me them to be presages of future bad successe, and so disswaded me what lay in him with effectual reasons, from my pretence, yet the hazard of my credite, and danger of disreputation, to take in hand that which I should not prosecute by all meanes possible, was more powerfull to cause me to goe forwardes, then his grave good counsell to make me desist. And so the storme ceasing, I beganne to get in the *Daintie*, to mast her a-new, and to recover the *Fancy*, my pynace, which, with the helpe and furtherance of my wives father, who supplyed all my wants, together with my credit (which I thanke God was

[1] Obviously a phrase of the period. Ancient Pistol is made to say "Si fortuna me tormenta, spero me contenta".—*Henry IV*, 2nd Part, Act v, Scene 5.)

Sect. VII.

unspotted) in ten dayes put all in his former estate, or better. And so once againe, in Gods name, I brought my shippes out into the sound, the wind being easterly, and beganne to take my leave of my friends, and of my dearest friend, my second selfe, whose unfeyned tears had wrought me into irresolution, and sent some other in my roome, had I not considered that he that is in the daunce, must needs daunce on, though he doe but hopp, except he will be a laughing stocke to all the lookers on: so remembering that many had their eyes set upon me, with diverse affections, as also the hope of good successe (my intention being honest and good), I shut the doore to all impediments, and mine eare to all contrary counsell, and gave place to voluntary banishment from all that I loved and esteemed in this life, with hope thereby better to serve my God, my prince and countrie, then to encrease my tallent any way.[1]

Abuses of some sea-faring men.

And so began to gather my companie aboord, which occupied my good friends and the justices of the towne two dayes, and forced us to search all lodgings, tavernes, and ale-houses. (For some would be ever taking their leave and never depart: some drinke themselves so drunke, that except they were carried aboord, they of themselves were not able to goe one steppe: others, knowing the necessity of the time, fayned themselves sicke: others, to be indebted to their hostes, and forced me to ransome them; one, his chest; another, his sword: another, his shirts; another, his carde and instruments for sea: and others, to benefit themselves of the imprest given them, absented themselves, making a lewd living in deceiving all whose money they could lay hold of: which is a scandall too rife amongst our sea-men: by it they committing

[1] Familiar as we are with the present resources of the dockyard at Plymouth, we can hardly estimate the firmness that could bear up against such mischances; of this stuff were the founders of the British naval power composed.

three great offences: 1, Robbery of the goods of another person; 2, breach of their faith and promise; 3, and hinderance (with losse of time) unto the voyage; all being a common injury to the owners, victuallers, and company; which many times hath beene an utter overthrow and undoing to all in generall. An abuse in our common-wealth necessarily to be reformed; and as a person that hath both seene, and felt by experience, these inconveniences, I wish it to be remedied; for, I can but wonder, that the late lord high admiral of England, the late Earle of Cumberland;[1] and the Lord Thomas Howard,[2] now Earle of Suffolke, being of so great authoritie, having to their cost and losse so often made experience of the inconveniences of these lewd proceedings, have not united their goodnesses and wisdomes to redress this dis-loyall and base absurditie of the vulgar.

[1] George Clifford, third Earl of Cumberland, was born in 1558. He first sent forth a fleet of three ships, for discovery, in 1586, which returned without accomplishing anything. In 1588 he himself commanded the *Elizabeth Bonaventure* in the fleet against the Spanish Armada. In the same year he fitted out a second fleet; and in 1589 he sailed in the *Victory*, with two other ships, for the West Indies. He took the town of Fayal, and captured twenty-eight prizes worth £20,000; but suffered great hardships, and was severely wounded. In 1591 he again sailed with five ships for the Mediterranean, and in 1592 his fleet was at the Azores. In 1593 he sailed, with Monson as his second in command, for the West Indies; and in 1594 annoyed the Spaniards at the Azores. He then built a fine ship at Deptford, named by Queen Elizabeth the *Malice Scourge*. He sailed in it, with nineteen other ships, in 1598, and harassed the Spanish settlements in the West Indies. He sold this ship to the East India Campany. The Earl of Cumberland died in 1605, and was buried at Skipton.

[2] Lord Thomas Howard was the eldest son of the fourth Duke of Norfolk, by his second wife Margaret, daughter of Lord Audley of Walden. He was born in 1561, and commanded a ship in the fleet of 1588, when he was knighted. In 1591 he was off the Azores, retiring on the approach of a superior Spanish force. He also served in the expedition to Cadiz, under Essex, in 1596. In 1597 he was created Lord Howard of Walden, and in 1603 James created him Earl of Suffolk. He died in 1626. One of his daughters was the notorious Countess of Somerset, the other was Countess of Salisbury, and he had eight sons.

Sect. VII.

Master Thomas Candish.

Master Thomas Candish, in his last voyage, in the sound of Plimouth, being readie to set sayle, complained unto me, that persons which had absented themselves in imprests, had cost him above a thousand and five hundred pounds: these varlets within a few dayes after his departure, I saw walking the streets of Plimouth, whom the justice had before sought for with great diligence; and without punishment. And therefore it is no wonder that others presume to do the like. *Impunitas peccandi illecebra.*

Master George Reymond.

The like complaint made master George Reymond;[1] and in what sort they deal with me is notorious, and was such, that if I had not beene provident to have had a third part more of men then I had need of, I had beene forced to goe to the sea unmanned; or to give over my voyage. And many of my company, at sea, vaunted how they had cosoned the Earle of Cumberland, master Candish, master Reymond, and others; some of five pounds, some of ten, some of more, and some of lesse. And truely, I thinke, my voyage prospered the worse, for theirs and other lewd persons company, which were in my ship; which, I thinke, might be redressed by some extraordinary, severe, and present justice, to be executed on the offenders by the justice in that place where they should be found. And for finding them, it were good that all captaines, and masters of shippes, at their departure out of the port, should give unto the head justice, the names and signes of all their runnawayes, and they presently to dispatch to the nigher ports the advise agreeable, where meeting with them, without further delay or processe, to use martial law upon them. Without doubt, seeing the law once put in execution, they and all others would be terrified from such villanies.

[1] Captain George Raymond commanded the expedition of three ships which undertook the first voyage to the East Indies in 1591. He was in the *Penelope*, and his second, James Lancaster, was in the *Edward Bonaventure.* But the two ships parted company after rounding the Cape of Good Hope, and Raymond was never heard of again.

It might be remedied also by utter taking away of all imprests, which is a thing lately crept into our commonwealth, and in my opinion, of much more hurt than good unto all; and although my opinion seeme harsh, it being a deed of charitie to help the needy (which I wish ever to be exercised, and by no meanes will contradict), yet for that such as goe to the sea (for the most part) consume that money lewdly before they depart (as common experience teacheth us): and when they come from sea, many times come more beggerly home then when they went forth, having received and spent their portion before they imbarked themselves; and having neither rent nor maintenance more then their travell, to sustaine themselves, are forced to theeve, to cozen, or to runne away in debt. Besides, many times it is an occasion to some to lye upon a voyage a long time; whereas, if they had not that imprest, they might perhaps have gayned more in another imployment, and have beene at home agayne, to save that which they waite for. For these, and many more weightie reasons, I am still bold to maintaine my former assertions.

The inconvenience of imprests.

Those onely used in his majesties shippes I comprehend not in this my opinion: neither the imprests made to married men, which would be given to their wives monethly in their absence, for their reliefe. For that is well knowne, that all which goe to the sea now-a-dayes, are provided of foode, and house-roome, and all things necessary, during the time of their voyage; and, in all long voyages, of apparell also: so that nothing is to be spent during the voyage. That money which is wont to be cast away in imprestes, might be imployed in apparell, and necessaries at the sea, and given to those that have need, at the price it was bought, to be deducted out of their shares or wages at their returne, which is reasonable and charitable. This course taken, if any would runne away, in Gods name fare him well.

The true use of imprests.

Sect. VIII. Some have a more colourable kinde of cunning to abuse men, and to sustaine themselves. Such will goe to sea with all men, and goe never from the shore. For as long as boord wages last, they are of the company, but those taking end, or the ship in readinesse, they have one excuse or other, and thinke themselves no longer bound, but whilst they receive money, and then plucke their heads out of the coller. An abuse also worthie to be reformed.

SECTION VIII.

The greater part of my companie gathered aboord, I set sayle the 12th of June 1593, about three of the clocke in the afternoon, and made a bourd or two off and in, wayting the returne of my boat, which I had sent a-shore, for dispatch of some businesse; which being come aboord, and all put in order, I looft[1] near the shore, to give my farewell to all the inhabitants of the towne, whereof the most part were gathered together upon the Howe, to shew their gratefull correspondency, to the love and zeale which I, my father, and predecessors, have ever borne to that place, as to our naturall and mother towne. And first with my noyse of trumpets, after with my waytes,[2] and then with my other musicke, and lastly, with the artillery of my shippes, I made the best signification I could of a kinde farewell. This they answered with the waytes of the towne, and the ordinance on the shore, and with shouting of voyces; which with the fayre evening and silence of the night, were heard a great distance off. All which taking end, I sent instructions and directions to my other ships.

The consequence of instructions at departure.

[1] From the Dutch word *loeven*, to ply to windward.

[2] The "waytes" seem to have been either music played during the setting of the watch, or occasionally, to show that a look-out was kept.

Which is a poynt of speciall importance; for that I have seene commanders of great name and reputation, by neglect and omission of such solemnities, to have runne into many inconveniences, and thereby have learnt the necessitie of it. Whereby I cannot but advise all such as shall have charge committed unto them, ever before they depart out of the port, to give unto their whole fleete, not onely directions for civill government, but also where, when, and how to meete, if they should chance to loose company, and the signes how to know one another a-far off, with other poynts and circumstances, as the occasions shall minister matter different, at the discretion of the wise commander.

But some may say unto me, that in all occasions it is not convenient to give directions: for that if the enemy happen upon any of the fleete, or that there be any treacherous person in the company, their designments may be discovered, and so prevented.

To this I answere, that the prudent governour, by good consideration may avoyde this, by publication of that which is good and necessarie for the guide of his fleete and people; by all secret instructions, to give them sealed, and not to be opened, but comming to a place appoynted (after the manner of the Turkish direction to the Bashawes, who are their generalls); and in any eminent perill to cast them by the boord, or otherwise to make away with them, for he that setteth sayle, not giving directions in writing to his fleete, knoweth not, if the night or day following, he may be separated from his company: which happeneth sometimes: and then, if a place of meeting be not knowne, he runneth in danger not to joyne them together agayne.

And for places of meeting, when seperation happeneth, I am of opinion, to appoynt the place of meeting in such a height, twentie, or thirtie, or fortie leagues off the land or iland. East or west is not so fitting, if the place afford it, as some sound betwixt ilands, or some iland, or harbour.

Sect. IX.

Objections against meeting in harbours.

It may be alleged in contradiction, and with probable reason, that it is not fit for a fleete to stay in a harbour for one ship, nor at an anchor at an iland, for being discovered, or for hinderance of their voyage.

Answered.

Yet it is the best; for when the want is but for one or two ships, a pynace or ship may wayte the time appoynted and remaine with direction for them. But commonly one ship, though but a bad sayler, maketh more haste then a whole fleete, and is at the meeting place first, if the accident be not very important.

The place of meeting, if it might be, would be able to give, at the least, refreshing of water and wood.

SECTION IX.

LANCHING out into the channell, the wind being at east and by south, and east south-east, which blowing hard, and a flood in hand, caused a chapping sea, and my vice-admirall bearing a good sayle made some water, and shooting off a peece of ordinance, I edged towardes her to know the cause; who answered me, that they had sprung a great leake, and that of force they must returne into the sound; which seeing to be necessary, I cast about, where anchoring, and going aboord, presently found, that betwixt wind and water, the calkers had left a seame uncalked, which being filled up with pitch only, the sea labouring that out, had been sufficient to have sunk her in short space, if it had not beene discovered in time.

False calking.

And truely there is little care used now adaies amongst our countrimen in this profession, in respect of that which was used in times past, and is accustomed in France, in Spaine, and in other parts. Which necessitie will cause to be reformed in time, by assigning the portion that every

Sect. x.

workeman is to calke; that if there be damage through his default, he may be forced to contribute towards the losse occasioned through his negligence.

For prevention thereof.

And for more securitie I hold it for a good custome used in some parts, in making an end of calking and pitching the ship, the next tide to fill her with water, which will undoubtedly discover the defect, for no pitcht place without calking, can suffer the force and peaze[1] of the water. In neglect whereof, I have seene great damage and danger to ensue. The *Arke Royall* of his majesties, may serve for an example: which put all in danger at her first going to the sea, by a trivuell hole left open in the post,[2] and covered only with pitch. In this point no man can be too circumspect, for it is the security of ship, men and goods.[3]

Example.

SECTION X.

THIS being remedied, I set sayle in the morning, and ran south-west, till we were cleere of Ushent; and then south south-west, till we were some hundred leagues off, where wee met with a great hulke, of some five or six hundred tunnes, well appointed, the which my company (as is naturall to all mariners), presently would make a prize, and loaden with Spaniard's goods; and without speaking to her, wished that the gunner might shoote at her, to cause her to amaine.[4] Which is a bad custome received and used of many ignorant persons, presently to gun at all whatsoever they discover, before they speake with them; being con-

Advise for shooting at sea.

[1] Weight—*peso.* (Spanish.)

[2] Stern-post.

[3] A trivial hole left open, or a treenail not driven by a careless workman, may cause the failure of an important expedition; or at least cause great mischief and discomfort: which neglect still occasionally happens.

[4] *Amener le pavillon*—to haul down the ensign.

Sect. x.

trary to all discipline, and many time is cause of dissention betwixt friends, and the breach of amitie betwixt princes; the death of many, and sometimes losse of shippes and all, making many obstinate, if not desperate; whereas in using common courtesie, they would better bethinke themselves, and so with ordinarie proceeding (justified by reason, and the custome of all well disciplined people) might perhaps many times breede an increase of amitie, a succour to necessity, and excuse divers inconveniencies and sutes which have impoverished many: for it hath chanced by this errour, that two English ships, neither carrying flag for their particular respects, to change each with other a dozen payre of shott, with hurt to both, being after too late to repent their follie. Yea a person of credit hath told mee, that two English men of warre in the night, have layed each other aboord willingly, with losse of many men and dammage to both, onely for the fault of not speaking one to the other; which might seem to carrie with it some excuse, if they had beene neere the shore, or that the one had beene a hull,[1] and the other under sayle, in feare shee should have escaped, not knowing what shee was (though in the night it is no wisedome to bourd with any ship), but in the maine sea, and both desiring to joyne, was a sufficient declaration that both were seekers; and therefore by day or night, he that can speake with the ship hee seeth, is bound, upon payne to be reputed voyd of good government, to hayle her before hee shoote at her. Some man may say, that in the meanetime, shee might gaine the winde: in such causes, and many others, necessity giveth exception to all lawes; and experience teacheth what is fit to be done.

Sundry mischances for neglect thereof.

Object.

Answer.

Master Thomas Hampton.

Master Thomas Hampton,[2] once generall of a fleete of

[1] Under bare poles.

[2] Captain Thomas Hampton served with his father, Sir John Hawkins. See page 6 and page 7 (n.).

wafters, sent to Rochell, anno 1585, with secret instructions, considering (and as a man of experience), wisely understanding his place and affaires, in like case shut his eare to the investigations and provocations of the common sort, preferring the publique good of both kingdomes before his owne reputation with the vulgar people: and as another Fabius Maximus, *cunctando restituit rem, non ponendo rumores ante salutem.* The French kings fleete comming where he was, and to winde-ward of him, all his company were in an uproare; for that hee would not shoote presently at them, before they saw their intention: wherein had beene committed three great faults: the first and principall, the breach of amitie betwixt the princes and kingdomes: the second, the neglect of common courtesie, in shooting before hee had spoken with them: and the third, in shooting first, being to lee-wards of the other.

Sect. x.

The French and English fleete salute one another.

Besides, there was no losse of reputation, because the French kings fleete was in his owne sea; and therefore for it to come to winde-ward, or the other to go to lee-ward, was but that which in reason was required, the kingdomes being in peace and amitie. For every prince is to be acknowledged and respected in his jurisdiction, and where hee pretendeth it to be his.

The French generall likewise seemed well to understand what he had in hand; for though he were farre superiour in forces, yet used hee the termes which were required; and comming within speech, hayled them, and asked if there were peace or warre betwixt England and France: whereunto answere being made that they knew of no other but peace, they saluted each other after the manner of the sea, and then came to an anchor all together, and as friends visited each other in their ships.

One thing the French suffered (upon what occasion or ground I know not), that the English alwayes carried their flag displayed; which in all other partes and kingdomes is

The English carry up their flag in the French seas.

Sect. x.

not permitted: at least, in our seas, if a stranger fleete meete with any of his majesties ships, the forraigners are bound to take in their flags, or his majesties ships to force them to it, though thereof follow the breach of peace or whatsoever discommodity. And whosoever should not be jealous in this point, hee is not worthy to have the commaund of a cock-boat committed unto him: yea no stranger ought to open his flag in any port of England, where there is any shipp or fort of his majesties, upon penaltie to loose his flagg, and to pay for the powder and shott spend upon him. Yea, such is the respect to his majesties shippes in all places of his dominions, that no English ship displayeth the flagge in their presence, but runneth the like daunger, except they be in his majesties service: and then they are in predicament of the kings ships. Which good discipline in other kingdomes is not in that regard as it ought, but sometimes through ignorance, sometimes of malice, neglect is made of that dutie and acknowledgement which is required, to the cost and shame of the ignorant and malicious.

The honour of his majesties ships.

In queen Maries raigne, king Philip of Spaine, comming to marry with the queene, and meeting with the royall navie of England, the lord William Howard, high admirall of England, would not consent, that the king in the narrow seas should carrie his flagge displayed, untill he came into the harbour of Plimouth.

Practised at the comming in of King Philip into England.

I being of tender yeares, there came a fleete of Spaniards of above fiftie sayle of shippes, bound for Flaunders, to fetch the queen, Donna Anna de Austria,[1] last wife to Philip the second of Spaine, which entred betwixt the iland and the maine, without vayling their top-sayles, or taking in of their flags: which my father, Sir John Hawkins, (admirall

And in the passage of Dona Anna de Austria.

[1] Anne, daughter of the Emperor Maximilian and of Maria, sister of Philip II, was born in 1549. She married her uncle, Philip II, as his fourth wife, in 1570, and was mother of Philip III. She died in 1580.

of a fleete of her majesties shippes, then ryding in Catt-water), perceiving, commanded his gunner to shoote at the flagge of the admirall, that they might thereby see their error: which, notwithstanding, they persevered arrogantly to keepe displayed; whereupon the gunner at the next shott, lact[1] the admirall through and through, whereby the Spaniards finding that the matter beganne to grow to earnest, tooke in their flags and top-sayles, and so ranne to an anchor. Sect. x.

The generall presently sent his boat, with a principall personage to expostulate the cause and reason of that proceeding; but my father would not permit him to come into his ship, nor to heare his message; but by another gentleman commanded him to returne, and to tell his generall, that in as much as in the queenes port and chamber, he had neglected to doe the acknowledgment and reverence which all owe unto her majestie (especially her ships being present), and comming with so great a navie, he could not but give suspition by such proceeding of malicious intention, and therefore required him, that within twelve houres he should depart the port, upon paine to be held as a common enemy, and to proceed against him with force.

Which answere the generall understanding, presently imbarked himselfe in the same boat, and came to the *Jesus of Lubecke*, and craved licence to speake with my father; which at the first was denyed him, but upon the second intreatie was admitted to enter the ship, and to parley. The Spanish generall began to demand if there were warres betwixt England and Spaine: who was answered, that his arrogant manner of proceeding, usurping the queene his mistresses right, as much as in him lay, had given sufficient cause for breach of the peace, and that he purposed presently to give notice thereof to the queene and her counsell, and in the meane time, that he might depart.

[1] Probably derived from *lâcher un coup:* to fire a shot.

Sect. x. Whereunto the Spanish generall replyed, that he knew not any offence he had committed, and that he would be glad to know wherein he had misbehaved himselfe. My father seeing he pretended to escape by ignorance, beganne to put him in mind of the custome of Spaine and Fraunce, and many other parts, and that he could by no meanes be ignorant of that, which was common right to all princes in their kingdomes; demanding, if a fleete of England should come into any port of Spaine (the kings majesties ships being present), if the English should carry their flags in the toppe, whether the Spanish would not shoote them downe; and if they persevered, if they would not beate them out of their port. The Spanish generall confessed his fault, pleaded ignorance not malice, and submitted himselfe to the penaltie my father would impose: but intreated, that their princes (through them) might not come to have any jarre. My father a while (as though offended), made himselfe hard to be intreated, but in the end, all was shut up by his acknowledgement, and the auncient amitie renewed, by feasting each other aboord and ashore.

As also in her repassage. The self same fleete, at their returne from Flaunders, meeting with her majesties shippes in the Channell, though sent to accompany the aforesaid queene, was constrained during the time that they were with the English, to vayle their flagges, and to acknowledge that which all must doe that passe through the English seas.[1] But to our voyage.

[1] In those days the principle of "mare clausum" was acted upon; now it is "mare liberum" everywhere.

SECTION XI.

COMMING within the hayling of the hulke, wee demanded whence shee was? Whether shee was bound? And what her loading? Shee answered, that shee was of Denmarke, comming from Spaine, loaden with salt; we willed her to strike her top-sayles, which shee did, and shewed us her charter-parties, and billes of loading, and then saluted us, as in the manner of the sea, and so departed. Sect. XII.

SECTION XII.

THE next day the wind became southerly, and somewhat too much, and my shipps being all deepe loaden, beganne to feel the tempest, so that wee not able to lye by it, neither a hull nor a try, and so with an easie sayle bare up before the wind, with intent to put into Falmouth; but God was pleased that comming within tenne leagues of Sylly, the wind vered to the north-east, and so we went on in our voyage.

Thwart of the Flees of Bayon,[1] wee met with a small ship of master Wattes,[2] of London, called the *Elizabeth*, which came out of Plimouth some eyght dayes after us; of whom wee enformed ourselves of some particularities, and wrote certaine letters to our friends, making relation of what had past till that day, and so tooke our farewell each of the other. The like we did with a small carvell[3] of

[1] The islands that lie off Bayona, near Vigo.

[2] Probably Alderman Sir John Watts, Governor of the East India Company in 1601, and Lord Mayor 1606. In 1594 he was one of those who fitted out the fleet under Lancaster, for the Pernambuco voyage.

[3] *Carabela* (Spanish), a small vessel so called.

Sect. XII. Plimouth, which wee mett in the height of the rocke in Portingall.[1]

From thence wee directed our course to the ilands of Madera; and about the end of June, in the sight of the ilands, we descryed a sayle some three leagues to the east-wards, and a league to windward of us, which by her manner of working, and making, gave us to understand, that shee was one of the kings frigatts; for shee was long and snugg, and spread a large clewe, and standing to the west-wards, and wee to the east-wards to recover her wake, when we cast about, shee beganne to vere shete, and to goe away lasking;[2] and within two glasses, it was plainely seene that shee went from us, and so we followed on our course, and shee seeing that, presently stroke her top-sayles, which our pynace perceiving, and being within shot continued the chase, till I shot off a peece and called her away; which fault many runne into, thinking to get thereby, and sometimes loose themselves by being too bold to venture from their fleete; for it was impossible for us, being too leeward, to take her, or to succour our owne, shee being a ship of about two hundred tunnes.

The dutie of pynaces. And pynaces to meddle with ships, is to buy repentance at too deare a rate. For their office is, to wayte upon their fleete, in calmes (with their oares) to follow a chase, and in occasions to anchor neere the shore, when the greater ships cannot, without perill; above all, to be readie and obedient at every call. Yet will I not, that any wrest my meaning; neither say I, that a pynace, or small ship armed, may not take a great ship unarmed; for daily experience teacheth us the contrary.

The Madera Ilands. The Madera Ilands are two: the greater, called La Madera, and the other, Port Santo; of great fertilitie, and rich in sugar, conserves, wine, and sweet wood, whereof

[1] Still well known as the rock of Lisbon.

[2] With the wind abeam.

they take their name. Other commodities they yeeld, but these are the principall. The chiefe towne and port is on the souther side of the Madera, well fortified; they are subject to the kingdome of Portingall; the inhabitants and garrison all Portingalles. Sect. XII.

The third of July, we past along the Ilands of Canaria, which have the name of a kingdome, and containe these seaven ilands: Grand Canaria, Tenerifa, Palma, Gomera, Lancerota, Forteventura, and Fierro. These ilands have abundance of wine, sugar, conserves, orcall,[1] pitch, iron, and other commodities, and store of cattell, and corne, but that a certaine worme, called *gorgosho,* breedeth in it, which eateth out the substance, leaving the husk in manner whole. The head iland, where the justice, which they call *Audiencia,* is resident, and whither all sutes have their appealation and finall sentence, is the grand Canaria, although the Tenerifa is held for the better and richer iland, and to have the best sugar; and the wine of the Palma is reputed for the best. The pitch of these ilands melteth not with the sunne, and therefore is proper for the higher works of shipping. Betwixt Forteventura and Lancerota is a goodly sound, fit for a meeting place for any fleete; where is good anchoring and aboundance of many sorts of fish. There is water to be had in most of these ilands, but with great vigilance. For the naturalls of them are venturous and hardie, and many times clime up and downe the steepe rockes and broken hills, which seeme impossible, which I would hardly have beleeved, had I not seene it, and that with the greatest art and agilitie that may be. Their armes, for the most part, are launces of nine or ten foote, with a head of a foote and halfe long, like unto bore-spears, save that the head is somewhat more broad.

Canarie Ilands.

Gorgosho.

Two things are famous in these ilands, the Pike of Tene-

[1] *Orchilla*—a lichen yielding a purple dye.

Sect. XII.

The description of Tenerifa.

rifa, which is the highest land in my judgement that I have seene, and men of credit have told they have seene it more than fortie leagues off.[1] It is like unto a sugar loafe, and continually covered with snow, and placed in the middest of a goodly vallie, most fertile, and temperate round about it. Out of which, going up to the Pike, the colde is so great, that it is insufferable, and going downe to the townes of the iland, the heate seemeth most extreame, till they approach neere the coast. The other is a tree in the iland of Fierro, which some write and affirme, with the dropping of his leaves, to give water for the sustenance of the whole iland, which I have not seene, although I have beene on shoare on the iland; but those which have seene it, have recounted this mysterie differently to that which is written; in this manner: that this tree is placed in the bottome of a valley, ever florishing with broad leaves, and that round about it are a multitude of goodly high pynes, which over-top it, and as it seemeth were planted by the divine providence to preserve it from sunne and wind. Out of this valley ordinarily rise every day great vapours and exhalations, which by reason that the sunne is hindered to worke his operation, with the heighte of the mountaines towards the south-east, convert themselves into moysture, and so bedewe all the trees of the valley, and from those which over-top this tree, drops down the dewe upon his leaves, and so from his leaves into a round well of stone, which the naturalls of the land have made to receive the water, of which the people and cattle have great reliefe; but sometimes it raineth, and then the inhabitants doe reserve water for many days to come, in their cisternes and tynaxes,[2] which is that they drinke of, and wherewith they principally sustaine themselves.

Of a tree in Fierro.

The citty of the Grand Canaria, and chiefe port, is on the

[1] Captain Vidal, R.N., made the height of the Peak 12,370 feet.

[2] *Tinaja* (Sp.), a large wide-mouthed jar for catching rain.

west side of the island; the head town and port of Tenerifa is towards the south part, and the port and towne of the Palma and Gomera, on the east side. Sect. XIII.

In Gomera, some three leagues south-ward from the towne, is a great river of water, but all these ilands are perilous to land in, for the seege[1] caused by the ocean sea, which always is forcible, and requireth great circumspection; whosoever hath not urgent cause, is either to goe to the east-wards, or the west-wards of all these ilands, as well to avoyd the calmes, which hinder sometimes eight or ten dayes sayling, as the contagion which their distemperature is wont to cause, and with it to breed calenturas, which wee call burning fevers. These ilands are sayd to be first discovered by a Frenchman, called John de Betancourt, about the year 1405.[2] They are now a kingdome subject to Spaine.

The first discoverers of these Ilands.

SECTION XIII.

Being cleare of the ilands, wee directed our course for Cape Black,[3] and two howres before sunne set, we had sight of a carvell some league in the winde of us, which seemed to come from Gynea, or the ilands of Cape de Verde, and for that hee, which had the sery-watch,[4] neglected to look out, being to lee-ward of the ilands, and so out of hope of sight of any shipp, for the little trade and contrariety of the winde, that though a man will, from few places hee can recover the ilands. Comming from the south-wards, wee had

[1] Further on written "sedge", surf (?).

[2] *The Canarian, or Book of the Conquest and Conversion of the Canarians in the Year* 1402, *by Messire Jean de Bethencourt;* was translated and edited for the Hakluyt Society by Mr. Major in 1872.

[3] Cape Blanco.

[4] Probably the evening watch.

Sect. XIII. the winde of her, and perhaps the possession also, whereof men of warre are to have particular care; for in an houre and place unlookt for, many times chance accidents contrary to the ordinary course and custome; and to have younkers in the top continually, is most convenient and necessary, not onely for descrying of sayles and land, but also for any sudden gust or occasion that may be offered.

Note.

Exercises upon the southwards of the countries.

Seeing my selfe past hope of returning backe, without some extraordinary accident, I beganne to set in order my companie and victuals. And for that to the south-wards of the Canaries is for the most part an idle navigation, I devised to keepe my people occupied, as well to continue them in health (for that too much ease in hott countries is neither profitable nor healthfull), as also to divert them from remembrance of their home, and from play, which breedeth many inconveniences, and other bad thoughts and workes which idleness is cause of; and so shifting my companie, as the custome is, into starboord and larboord men, the halfe to watch and worke whilest the others slept and take rest; I limited the three dayes of the weeke, which appertayned to each, to be imploied in this manner; the one for the use and clensing of their armes, the other for roomeging, making of sayles, nettings, decking, and defences for our shippes; and the third, for clensing their bodies, mending and making their apparell, and necessaries, which though it came to be practised but once in seaven dayes, for that the Sabboth is ever to be reserved for God alone, with the ordinary obligation which each person had besides, was many times of force to be omitted. And thus wee entertained our time with a fayre wind, and in few dayes had sight of the land of Barbary, some dozen leagues to the northwards of Cape Black.

Before wee came to the Cape, wee tooke in our sayles, and made preparation of hookes and lines to fish. For in all that coast is great abundance of sundry kinds of fish, but especially of porgus, which we call breames; many Portingalls and Spaniards goe yearely thither to fish, as our country-men to the New-found-land, and within Cape Black have good harbour for reasonable shipping, where they dry their fish, paying a certaine easie tribute to the kings collector. In two houres wee tooke store of fish for that day and the next, but longer it would not keepe goode: and with this refreshing set sayle again, and directed our course betwixt the ilands of Cape de Verd and the Maine. These ilands are held to be scituate in one of the most unhealthiest climates of the world, and therefore it is wisedome to shunne the sight of them, how much more to make abode in them.

Cape de Verd.

The un-wholsom-nesse there of.

In two times that I have beene in them, either cost us the one halfe of our people, with fevers and fluxes of sundry kinds; some shaking, some burning, some partaking of both: some possesst with frensie, others with sloath, and in one of them it cost me six moneths sicknesse, with no small hazard of life; which I attribute to the distemperature of the ayre, for being within fourteene degrees of the equinoctiall lyne, the sunne hath great force all the yeare, and the more for that often they passe, two, three, and four yeares without rayne; and many times the earth burneth in that manner as a man well shodd, cannot endure to goe where the sunne shineth.

The heate.

The breze.

With which extreame heate the bodie fatigated, greedily desireth refreshing, and longeth the comming of the breze, which is the north-east winde, that seldome fayleth in the after-noone at foure of the clocke, or sooner; which comming cold and fresh, and finding the poores of the body open, and (for the most part) naked, penetrateth the very bones, and so causeth sudden distemperature, and sundry manners of sicknesse, as the subjects are divers whereupon they worke.

Departing out of the calmes of the ilands, and comming

Sect. XIII. into the fresh breeze, it causeth the like, and I have seene within two dayes after that we have partaked of the fresh ayre, of two thousand men, above a hundred and fiftie have beene crazed in their health.

The remedie. The inhabitants of these ilands use a remedie for this, which at my first being amongst them, seemed unto me ridiculous; but since, time and experience hath taught to be grounded upon reason. And is, that upon their heads they weare a night-capp, upon it a montero,[1] and a hat over that, and on their bodies a sute of thicke cloth, and upon it a gowne, furred or lyned with cotton, or bayes, to defend them from the heate in that manner, as the inhabitants of cold countries, to guard themselves from the extreamitie of the colde. Which doubtlesse, is the best diligence that any man can use, and whosoever prooveth it, shall find himselfe lesse annoyed with the heate, then if he were thinly cloathed, for that where the cold ayre commeth, it peirceth not so subtilly.

The influence of the moone in hot countries. The moone also in this climate, as in the coast of Guyne, and in all hott countries, hath forcible operation in the body of man; and therefore, as the plannet most prejudiciall to his health, is to be shunned; as also not to sleepe in the open ayre, or with any scuttle or window open, whereby the one or the other may enter to hurt.

For a person of credit told me, that one night, in a river of Guyne, leaving his window open in the side of the cabin, the moone shining upon his shoulder, left him with such an extraordinary paine and furious burning in it, as in above twentie houres, he was like to runne madde, but in fine, with force of medicines and cures, after long torment, he was eased.

Some I have heard say, and others write, that there is a starre which never seperateth it self from the moone, but a small distance; which is of all starres the most beneficiall

[1] *Montera*—a species of hat worn in Spain.

to man. For where this starre entreth with the moone, it maketh voyde her hurtfull enfluence, and where not, it is most perilous. Which, if it be so, is a notable secret of the divine Providence, and a speciall cause amongst infinite others, to move us to continuall thanksgiving: for that he hath so extraordinarily compassed and fenced us from infinite miseries, his most unworthie and ungratefull creatures. Sect. XIII.

Of these ilands are two pyles:[1] the one of them lyeth out of the way of trade, more westerly, and so little frequented; the other lyeth some fourscore leagues from the mayne, and containeth six in number, to wit: Saint Iago, Fuego, Mayo, Bonavisto, Sal, and Bravo.[2]

They are belonging to the kingdome of Portingall, and inhabited by people of that nation, and are of great trade, by reason of the neighbour-hood they have with Guyne and Bynne;[3] but the principall is the buying and selling of negroes. They have store of sugar, salt, rice, cotton wool, and cotton-cloth, amber-greece, cyvit, oliphants teeth, brimstone, pummy stone, spunge, and some gold, but little, and that from the mayne.

Saint Iago is the head iland, and hath one citie and two townes, with their ports. The cittie called Sant Iago, whereof the iland hath his name, hath a garrison, and two fortes, scituated in the bottome of a pleasant valley, with a running streame of water passing through the middest of it, whither the rest of the ilands come for justice, being the seat of the Audiencia, with his bishop. Saint Iago.

[1] Groups.

[2] The Cape Verde Islands are Sant' Antao, Sao Vicente, Santa Luzia, Sao Nicolao, Sal, Boa Vista, Maio, San Thiago, and Brava. They are between 14° 20′ and 17° 20′ N. and 22° 25′ and 35° 30′ W. Boa Vista, the nearest, is two hundred miles from the coast of Africa. The group was discovered in 1446 by an expedition sent by Prince Henry, but it was known to the ancients under the name of Insulæ Gorgones.

[3] Coast of Guinea and Bight of Benin.

Sect. XIII. The other townes are Playa,[1] some three leagues to the eastwards of Saint Iago, placed on high, with a goodly bay, whereof it hath his name; and Saint Domingo, a small towne within the land. They are on the souther part of the iland, and have beene sacked sundry times in anno 1582, by Manuel Serades, a Portingall, with a fleete of French-men; in anno 1585, they were both burnt to the ground by the English, Sir Francis Drake being generall;[2] and in anno 1596, Saint Iago was taken and sacked by the English, Sir Anthony Shyrley being generall.[3]

Sacked by Manuel Serades, Sir Francis Drake, and Sir Anthony Shyrley.

Fuego. The second iland is Fuego; so called, for that day and night there burneth in it a vulcan, whose flames in the night are seene twentie leagues off in the sea. It is by nature fortified in that sort, as but by one way is any accesse, or entrance into it, and there cannot goe up above two men a brest. The bread which they spend in these ilands, is brought from Portingall and Spaine, saving that which they make of rice, or of mayes, which wee call Guynne-wheate.

[1] Porto Praya.

[2] Sir Francis Drake sailed, in 1585, with a fleet of twenty sail to make reprisals on the Spaniards in the West Indies. His captains were Fenner, Frobisher, Knollis, and Carlisle to command the troops. They left Plymouth in September, took Porto Praya, and then proceeded to the West Indies.

[3] Anthony Shirley was one of the famous three brothers, sons of Sir Thomas Shirley of Wiston in Sussex. He was born in 1568, and first served under the Earl of Essex in Brittany, but was recalled in 1593 for receiving an order of knighthood from Henry IV. An account of the expedition to the West Indies, in the course of which he sacked Santiago, is given by Hakluyt. In 1598 he left England, served in the Low Countries with Sir Francis Vere, and then went by Venice to Persia, where he was well received by Shah Abbas the Great. There are accounts of his travels by W. Parry, printed in 1601, by A. Nixon, 1607, and by Sir Anthony himself, 1613. Abbas sent Sir Anthony Shirley as ambassador to the Princes of Europe, which employment took him to Moscow, Prague, Rome, Lisbon, Madrid, and Morocco. He eventually took service under the King of Spain, and was living in Spain as late as 1636. See *The Sherley Brothers*.

The best watering is in the ile of Bravo, on the west part of the iland, where is a great river, but foule anchoring, as is in all these ilands, for the most part. The fruits are few, but substantiall, as palmitos, plantanos, patatos, and coco-nutts. Bravo.

The palmito is like to the date tree, and as I thinke a kinde of it, but wilde. In all parts of Afrique and America they are found, and in some parts of Europe, and in divers parts different. In Afrique, and in the West Indies they are small, that a man may cut them with a knife, and the lesser the better: but in Brazill, they are so great, that with difficultie a man can fell them with an axe, and the greater the better; one foote within the top is profitable, the rest is of no value; and that which is to be eaten is the pith, which in some is better, in some worse. The Palmito.

The plantane is a tree found in most parts of Afrique and America, of which two leaves are sufficient to cover a man from top to toe. It beareth fruit but once, and then dryeth away, and out of his roote sprouteth up others, new. In the top of the tree is his fruit, which groweth in a great bunch, in the forme and fashion of puddings, in some more, in some lesse. I have seene in one bunch above foure hundred plantanes, which have weighed above fourescore pound weight. They are of divers proportions, some great, some lesser, some round, some square, some triangle, most ordinarily of a spanne long, with a thicke skinne, that peeleth easily from the meate; which is either white or yellow, and very tender like butter, but no conserve is better, nor of a more pleasing taste. For I never have seene any man to whom they have bred mis-like, or done hurt with eating much of them, as of other fruites. The plantane.

The best are those which ripen naturally on the tree, but in most partes they cut them off in braunches, and hange them up in their houses, and eate them as they ripe. For the birds and vermine presently in ripning on the tree, are

Sect. XIII.

Placentia. feeding on them. The best that I have seene are in Brasill, in an iland called Placentia, which are small, and round, and greene when they are ripe; whereas the others in ripning become yellow. Those of the West Indies and Guynne are great, and one of them sufficient to satisfie a man; the onely fault they have is, that they are windie. In some places they eate them in stead of bread, as in Panama, and other parts of Tierra Firme. They grow and prosper best when their rootes are ever covered with water; they are excellent in conserve, and good sodden in different manners, and dried on the tree, not inferior to suckett.[1]

The cocos, and their kindes. The coco nutt is a fruit of the fashion of a hassell nutt, but that it is as bigge as an ordinary bowle, and some are greater. It hath two shells, the uttermost framed (as it were) of a multitude of threeds, one layd upon another, with a greene skinne over-lapping them, which is soft and thicke; the innermost is like to the shell of a hassell nutt in all proportion, saving that it is greater and thicker, and some more blacker. In the toppe of it is the forme of a munkies face, with two eyes, his nose, and a mouth. It containeth in it both meate and drinke; the meate white as milke, and like to that of the kernell of a nutt, and as good as almonds blancht, and of great quantitie: the water is cleare, as of the fountaine, and pleasing in taste, and somewhat answereth that of the water distilled of milke. Some say it hath a singular propertie in nature for conserving the smoothnesse of the skinne; and therefore in Spaine and Portingall, the curious dames doe ordinarily wash their faces and necks with it. If the holes of the shell be kept close, they keepe foure or six moneths good, and more; but if it be opened, and the water kept in the shell, in few dayes it turneth to vineger.

They grow upon high trees, which have no boughes; onely in the top they have a great cap of leaues, and under

[1] *Succade*—preserved citron.

them groweth the fruite upon certaine twigs. And some affirme that they beare not fruite before they be above fortie yeares old, they are in all things like to the palme trees, and grow in many parts of Asia, Afrique, and America. The shels of these nuts are much esteemed for drinking cups, and much cost and labour is bestowed upon them in carving, graving, and garnishing them, with silver, gold, and precious stones. Sect. XIV.

In the kingdome of Chile, and in Brasill, is another kinde of these, which they call coquillos (as wee may interpret, little cocos) and are as big as wal-nuts; but round and smooth, and grow in great clusters; the trees in forme are all one, and the meate in the nut better, but they have no water.

Another kinde of great cocos groweth in the Andes of Peru, which have not the delicate meate nor drinke which the others have, but within are full of almonds, which are placed as the graines in the pomegrannet, being three times bigger then those of Europe, and are much like them in tast.

In these ilands are cyvet-cats, which are also found in parts of Asia and Afrique; esteemed for the cyvet they yeelde, and carry about them in a cod in their hinder parts, which is taken from them by force. Cyvet catts.

In them also are store of monkies, and the best proportioned that I have seene; and parrots, but of colour different to those of the West Indies, for they are of a russet or gray colour, and great speakers. Munkeyes. Parrots.

SECTION XIV.

With a faire and large winde, we continued our course, till we came within five degrees of the equinoctiall lyne, where the winde tooke us contrary by the south-west, about the

Sect. xiv. twentie of Julie, but a fayre gale of wind and a smooth sea, so that wee might beare all a taunt;[1] and to advantage ourselves what wee might, wee stoode to the east-wards, being able to lye south-east and by south. The next day about nine of the clocke, my companie being gathered together to serve God, which wee accustomed to doe every morning and evening, it seemed unto me that the coulour of the sea was different to that of the daies past, and which is ordinarily where is deepe water; and so calling the captaine, and master of my ship, I told them that to my seeming the water was become very whitish, and that it made shewe of sholde water. Whereunto they made answere, that all the lynes in our shippes could not fetch ground: for wee could not be lesse than threescore and tenne leagues off the coast, which all that kept reckoning in the ship agreed upon, and my selfe was of the same opinion. And so wee applyed ourselves to serve God, but all the time that the service endured, my heart could not be at rest, and still me thought the water beganne to waxe whiter and whiter. Our prayers ended, I commanded a lead and a lyne to be brought, and heaving the lead in fourteene fathoms, wee had ground, which put us all into a maze, and sending men into the toppe, presently discovered the land of Guynne, some five leagues from us, very low land. I commanded a peece to be shott, and lay by the lee, till my other shippes came up. Which hayling us, wee demanded of them how farre they found themselves off the land; who answered, some threescore and tenne, or fourescore leagues: when wee told them wee had sounded and found but fourteene fathomes, and that we were in sight of land, they began to wonder. But having consulted what was best to be done, I caused my shalop to be manned, which I towed at the sterne of my ship continually, and sent her and my pynace

[1] *All sail set*—at present its signification is confined to a vessel rigged and ready for sea.

a head to sound, and followed them with an easie sayle, till we came in seaven and six fathome water, and some two leagues from the shore anchored, in hope by the sea, or by the land to find some refreshing. The sea we found to be barren of fish, and my boates could not discover any landing place, though a whole day they had rowed alongst the coast, with great desire to set foote on shore, for that the sedge[1] was exceeding great and dangerous. Which experienced, wee set sayle, notwithstanding the contrarietie of the winde, sometimes standing to the west-wards, sometime to the east-wards, according to the shifting of the wind. Sect. xv.

SECTION XV.

Here is to be noted, that the error which we fell into in our accompts, was such as all men fall into where are currants that set east or west, and are not knowne; for that there is no certaine rule yet practised for triall of the longitude, as there is of the latitude, though some curious and experimented of our nation, with whom I have had conference about this poynt, have shewed me two or three manner of wayes how to know it.[2] Note.

This, some years before, was the losse of the *Edward Cotton*, bound for the coast of Brasill, which taken with the winde contrary neere the lyne, standing to the east-wards, and making accompt to be fiftie or sixtie leagues off the coast, with all her sayles standing, came suddenly a ground upon the sholes of Madre-bomba, and so was cast away, The losse of the *Edward Cotton*.

[1] Surf.

[2] It is still the custom to attribute all similar discordancies to the effect of current. This is a simple if not very philosophical mode of making the reckoning agree with observation. In this case, probably both the reckoning of the ship and the position of the land on the chart were faulty.

Sect. xv. though the most part of their company saved themselves upon raffes; but with the contagion of the countrie, and bad entreatie which the negros gave them, they died; so that there returned not to their country above three or foure of them.

But God Almightie dealt more mercifully with us, in shewing us our error in the day, and in time that wee might remedie it; to him be evermore glory for all.

This currant from the line equinoctiall, to twentie degrees northerly, hath great force, and setteth next of anything east, directly upon the shore; which we found by this meanes: standing to the westwards, the wind southerly, when we lay with our ships head west, and by south, we gayned in our heith[1] more then if wee had made our way good west south-west; for that, the currant tooke us under the bow: but lying west, or west and by north, we lost more in twelve houres then the other way we could get in foure and twentie. By which plainly we saw, that the currant did set east next of any thing. Whether this currant runneth over one way, or doth alter, and how, we could by no meanes understand, but tract of time and observation will discover this, as it hath done of many others in sundry seas.

The currant that setteth betwixt New-found-land and Spaine, runneth also east and west, and long time deceived many, and made some to count the way longer, and others shorter, according as the passage was speedie or slowe; not knowing that the furtherance or hinderance of the currant was cause of the speeding or flowing of the way. And in sea cardes I have seene difference of above thirtie leagues betwixt the iland Tercera and the mayne. And others have recounted unto me, that comming from the Indias, and looking out for the ilands of Azores, they have had

[1] The term height is used for latitude; probably because the pole star was the principal object used to determine position.

sight of Spaine. And some have looked out for Spaine, and have discovered the ilands. Sect. xv.

The selfe same currant is in the Levant sea, but runneth trade betwixt the maynes, and changeable sometimes to the east-wards, sometimes to the west-wards.

In Brasill and the South sea, the currant likewise is changeable, but it runneth ever alongst the coast, accompanying the winde, and it is an infallible rule, that twelve or twentie foure houres before the wind alters, the currant begins to change.

In the West Indies onely the currant runneth continually one way, and setteth alongst the coast from the equinoctiall lyne towards the north. No man hath yet found that these courrants keepe any certaine time, or run so many dayes, or moneths, one way as another, as doth the course of ebbing and flowing, well known in all seas; only neere the shore they have small force; partly, because of the reflux which the coast causeth, and partly for the ebbing and flowing, which more or lesse is generall in most seas.[1]

When the currant runneth north or south, it is easily discovered by augmenting or diminishing the height; but how to know the setting of the currant from east to west in the mayne sea, is difficult; and as yet I have not knowne any man, or read any authour, that hath prescribed any certaine meane or way to discover it. But experience teacheth that in the mayne sea, for the most part, it is variable; and therefore the best and safest rule to prevent the danger (which the uncertainty and ignorance heereof may cause), is carefull and continuall watch by day and night, and upon the east and west course ever to bee before the shipp, and to use the meanes possible to know the errour, by the rules which newe authours may teach; beat-

[1] The current in the West Indies, known as the Gulf stream, runs to the northward through the Gulf of Florida, and then trending to the eastward, expends its force in the Atlantic.

Sect. xvi. ing off and on, sometimes to the west-wards, sometimes to the east-wards, with a fayre gayle of winde.

SECTION XVI.

The scurvey. BEING betwixt three or foure degrees of the equinoctiall line, my company within a few dayes began to fall sicke, of a disease which sea-men are wont to call the scurvey: and seemeth to bee a kind of dropsie, and raigneth most in this climate of any that I have heard or read of in the world; though in all seas it is wont to helpe and increase the miserie of man; it possesseth all those of which it taketh hold, with a loathesome sloathfulnesse, even to eate; they would be content to change their sleepe and rest, which is the most pernicious enemie in this sicknesse, that is knowne. It bringeth with it a great desire to drinke, and causeth a generall swelling of all parts of the body, especially of the legs and gums, and many times the teeth fall out of the jawes without paine.

The signes. The signes to know this disease in the beginning are divers: by the swelling of the gummes, by denting of the flesh of the leggs with a mans finger, the pit remayning without filling up in a good space. Others show it with their lasinesse: others complaine of the cricke of the backe, etc., all which are, for the most part, certaine tokens of infection.

The cause. The cause of this sicknes some attribute to sloath; some to conceite; and divers men speake diversly: that which I have observed is, that our nation is more subject unto it than any other; because being bred in a temperate clymate, where the naturall heate restrayned, giveth strength to the stomacke, sustayning it with meates of good nourishment, and that in a wholesome ayre; whereas comming into the

Sect. xvi.

hot countries (where that naturall heate is dispersed through the whole body, which was wont to be proper to the stomache; and the meates for the most part preserved with salt, and its substance thereby diminished, and many times corrupted), greater force for digestion is now required than in times past; but the stomache finding less virtue to doe his office, in reparting to each member his due proportion in perfection, which either giveth it rawe, or remayneth with it indigested by his hardnes or cruditie, infeebleth the body, and maketh it unlusty and unfit for any thing; for the stomache being strong (though all parts els be weake), there is ever a desire to feede, and aptnes to perform what soever can be required of a man; but though all other members be strong and sound, if the stomache be opprest, or squemish, all the body is unlustie, and unfit for any thing, and yeeldeth to nothing so readily as sloathfulnes, which is confirmed by the common answere to all questions: as, will you eate? will you sleepe? will you walke? will you play? The answere is, I have no stomache: which is as much as to say, no, not willingly: thereby confirming, that without a sound and whole stomache, nothing can bee well accomplished, nor any sustenance well digested.[1]

Seething of meat in salt water.

The seething of the meate in salt water, helpeth to cause this infirmitie, which in long voyages can hardly be avoyded: but if it may be, it is to be shunned; for the water of the sea to man's body is very unwholesome. The corruption of the victuals, and especially of the bread, is very pernicious; the vapours and ayre of the sea also is nothing profitable, especially in these hot countries, where are many

Corruption of victuall.

Vapours of the sea.

[1] The cause of scurvy is now known to be the absence of fresh food, especially fresh vegetable food. Since greater attention has been paid to diet, and also to the cleanliness and ventilation of the vessel, and since long voyages have become of rare occurrence, this disease has nearly disappeared.

Sect. XVI. calmes. And were it not for the moving of the sea by the force of windes, tydes, and currants, it would corrupt all the world.

The experience I saw in anno 1590, lying with a fleete of her majesties ships about the ilands of the Azores, almost six moneths; the greatest part of the time we were becalmed: with which all the sea became so replenished with several sorts of gellyes, and formes of serpents, adders, and snakes, as seemed wonderfull: some greene, some blacke, some yellow, some white, some of divers coulours; and many of them had life, and some there were a yard and halfe, and two yards long; which had I not seene, I could hardly have beleeved. And hereof are witnesses all the companies of the ships which were then present; so that hardly a man could draw a buckett of water cleere of some corruption. In which voyage, towards the end thereof, many of every ship (saving of the *Nonpereil*, which was under my charge, and had onely one man sicke in all the voyage), fell sicke of this disease, and began to die apace, but that the speedie passage into our country was remedie to the crazed, and a preservative for those that were not touched. The best prevention for this disease (in my judgement) is to keepe cleane the shippe; to besprinkle her ordinarily with vineger, or to burne tarre, and some sweet savours; to feed upon as few salt meats in the hot country as may be; and especially to shunne all kindes of salt fish, and to reserve them for the cold climates; and not to dresse any meate with salt water, nor to suffer the companie to wash their shirts nor cloathes in it, nor to sleepe in their cloaths when they are wett. For this cause it is necessarily required, that provision be made of apparell for the company, that they may have wherewith to shift themselves; being a common calamitie amongst the ordinary sort of mariners, to spend their thrift on the shore, and to bring to sea no more cloaths then they have backes. For the

Azores.

The remedies.

By dyet.

By shift.

bodie of man is not refreshed with any thing more than with shifting cleane cloaths; a great preservative of health in hott countries.

The second antidote is, to keepe the companie occupied in some bodily exercise of worke, of agilitie, of pastimes, of dauncing, of use of armes; these helpeth much to banish this infirmitie. Thirdly, in the morning, at discharge of the watch, to give every man a bit of bread, and a draught of drinke, either beere or wine mingled with water (at the least, the one halfe), or a quantitie mingled with beere, that the pores of the bodie may be full, when the vapours of the sea ascend up.

By labour.

By early eating and drinking.

The morning draught should be ever of the best and choysest of that in the ship. Pure wine I hold to be more hurtfull then the other is profitable. In this, others will be of a contrary opinion, but I thinke partiall. If not, then leave I the remedies thereof to those physitions and surgeons who have experience; and I wish that some learned man would write of it, for it is the plague of the sea, and the spoyle of mariners. Doubtlesse, it would be a meritorious worke with God and man, and most beneficiall for our countrie; for in twentie yeares, since that I have used the sea, I dare take upon me to give accompt of ten thousand men consumed with this disease.

That which I have seene most fruitfull for this sicknesse, is sower oranges and lemmons, and a water which amongst others (for my particular provision) I carryed to the sea, called Dr. Stevens his water, of which, for that his vertue was not then well knowne unto me, I carryed but little, and it tooke end quickly, but gave health to those that used it.

By sower orranges and lemons.

By Doctor Stevens water.

The oyle of vitry[1] is beneficiall for this disease; taking two drops of it, and mingled in a draught of water, with a little sugar. It taketh away the thirst, and helpeth to

By oyle of vitry.

[1] Oil of vitriol or sulphuric acid.

Sect. XVI.

By the ayre of the land.

clense and comfort the stomache. But the principall of all, is the ayre of the land; for the sea is naturall for fishes, and the land for men. And the oftener a man can have his people to land, not hindering his voyage, the better it is, and the profitablest course that he can take to refresh them.[1]

[1] These are very interesting remarks on the scurvy. Sir Richard Hawkins takes a broader and more scientific view of the question than do the bigoted "lime-juicers" of the present day. The cause of scurvy is the absence of fresh food. The preventives, as Sir Richard truly says, are fresh food, good ventilation, cleanliness, and bodily exercise with amusements. Medicines, such as lime-juice, "Dr. Stevens his water", and "oyle of vitry", take a secondary place. They may help both as cures and preventives, but with other circumstances tending to produce the disease, lime-juice alone will neither prevent nor cure. The "Scurvy Committee", which recently reported on the outbreak in the Arctic Expedition of 1875-76 came to conclusions directly opposed to the evidence. None of the extended travelling parties of former Arctic expeditions took lime-juice except on one occasion, and on that one occasion alone was there an outbreak of scurvy. During the late expedition itself scurvy broke out in eight cases, when men were taking lime-juice regularly. The whole mass of evidence confirmed all former Arctic experience, and showed that the absence of lime-juice on some of the sledges was not the cause of the outbreak of scurvy. In the cases where lime-juice was not taken on sledges, the reason was that it could not have been used in the intense cold. The evidence also proved that lime-juice alone, without fresh food, will not cure the scurvy. Lime-juice, as Sir James Lancaster and Sir Richard Hawkins discovered three centuries ago, is an excellent medicine in helping to arrest the disease; but without the aid of good ventilation, cleanliness, and fresh food, lime-juice alone will neither prevent nor cure. The opposite conclusion of the "Scurvy Committee" is opposed to all the evidence they took, and to all experience. Of course every precaution should be taken against scurvy, and, as soon as fresh vegetable food is absent, daily rations of lime-juice must be taken when it is possible. In sledge travelling in the Arctic Regions, during April and May, it is not possible to take lime-juice in the form in which it is supplied to ships; and Sir George Nares was quite right not to send it.

For some further notices of outbreaks of scurvy in these early voyages, see the *Voyages of Sir James Lancaster*, etc., a volume issued by the Hakluyt Society in 1878, pages 4, 61, 62, 113, 222.

SECTION XVII.

Sect. XVII.

The company sicke and dismayed.

HAVING stood to the westwards some hundreth leagues and more, and the wind continuing with us contrarie, and the sicknesse so fervent, that every day there dyed more or lesse,—my companie in generall began to dismay, and to desire to returne homewards, which I laboured to hinder by good reasons and perswasions; as that to the West Indies we had not above eight hundreth leagues, to the ilands of Azores little lesse, and before we came to the ilands of Cape de Verde, that we should meete with the breze; for every night we might see the reach goe contrary to the winde which wee sayled by; verifying the old proverbe amongst mariners,—that he hath need of a long mast, that will sayle by the reach: and that the neerest land and speediest refreshing we could look for, was the coast of Brasill: and that standing towards it with the wind we had, we shortned our way for the Indies; and that to put all the sicke men together in one shippe, and to send her home was to make her their grave. For we could spare but few sound men, who were also subject to fall sicke, and the misery, notwithstanding, remedilesse. With which they were convinced, and remayned satisfied. So leaving all to their choyse, with the consideration of what I perswaded, they resolved, with me, to continue our course, till that God was pleased to looke upon us with his Fatherly eyes of mercie.

Brasill.

As we approached neerer and neerer the coast of Brasill, the wind began to veer to the east-wardes; and about the middle of October, to be large and good for us; and about the 18th of October, we were thwart of Cape Saint Augustine,[1] which lyeth in sixe degrees to the southwards of the

Cape S. Augustine.

[1] Cape St. Agostinhos, in 8° 20′ S.

Sect. XVII.

lyne; and the twenty-one in the height of Farnambuca,[1] but some fourscore leagues from the coast; the twentie foure in the height of Bayea de Todos Santos;[2] neere the end of October, betwixt seventeen and eighteen degrees, we were in sixteen fathomes, sounding of the great sholes, which lye alongst the coast, betwixt the Bay of Todos Santos, and the port of Santos, alias Pura Senora de Vitoria;[3] which are very perilous.[4]

Farnambuca. Todos Santos. Pura de Vitoria.

But the divine Providence hath ordayned great flockes of small birds, like snytes,[5] to live upon the rockes and broken lands of these sholes, and are met with ordinarily twentie leagues before a man come in danger of them.

It shall not be amisse here to recount the accidents which befell us during this contrary winde, and the curiosities to be observed in all this time. Day and night we had continually a fayre gale of winde, and a smooth sea, without any alteration; one day, the carpenters having calked the decke of our shippe, which the sunne with his extreame heate had opened, craved licence to heate a little pitch in the cook-roome; which I would not consent unto by any meanes; for that my cook-roomes were under the decke, knowing the danger; until the master undertooke that no danger should come thereof. But he recommended the charge to another, who had a better name then experience. He suffered the pitch to rise, and to runne into the fire, which caused so furious a flame as amazed him, and forced all to flie his heate. One of my company, with a double payre of gloves, tooke off the pitch-pot, but the fire forced him to let slip his hold-fast, before he could set it on the hearth, and so overturned it, and as the pitch began to runne, so the fire to enlarge it selfe, that in a moment a great part of the shippe was on a light fire. I

Dangers of fire. By beating of pitch.

[1] Pernambuco is north of Cape St. Agostinhos.

[2] Bahia is in 12° 58′ 3″ S.

[3] Victoria is in 20° 19′ 2″ S.

[4] Shoals called the Abrolhos.

[5] Snyte for snipe.

being in my cabin, presently imagined what the matter was, and for all the hast I could make, before I came the fire was above the decke: for remedie whereof, I commanded all my companie to cast their rugge-gownes into the sea, and ropes fastened unto them. These I had provided for my people to watch in; for in many hott countries the nights are fresh and colde; and devided one gowne to two men, a starboord and a larboord man; so that he which watched had ever the gowne: for they which watched not, were either in their cabins, or under the decke, and so needed them not. The gownes being well soked, every man that could, tooke one, and assaulted the fire; and although some were singed, others scalded, and many burned, God was pleased that the fire was quenched, which I thought impossible; and doubtlesse, I never saw my selfe in greater perill in all the dayes of my life. Let all men take example by us, not to suffer, in any case, pitch to be heate in the ship, except it be with a shotte heate in the fire, which cannot breed daunger; nor to permit fire to be kindled, but upon meere necessitie; for the inconvenience thereof is for the most part remedilesse.[1]

By taking tobacco.

With drinking of tobacco it is said, that the *Roebucke* was burned in the range of Dartmouth.

The *Primrose*, of London, was fired with a candle, at Tilbery-hope, and nothing saved but her kele.

And another ship bound for Barbary, at Wapping.

The *Jesus of Lubecke* had her gunner-roome set on fire with a match, and had beene burnt without redemption, if that my father, Sir John Hawkins, knight, then generall in her, had not commaunded her sloppers[2] to be stopt, and

[1] Heating pitch, and drawing off spirits in the hold, using a light, are the most common causes that lead to fire. Excluding the air is the best remedy, and no better device could have been hit upon than wetting the rug gowns.

[2] Holes in the ship's side to carry off the water. The term now in use is *scupper*: slopper appears to be as good a word.

Sect. XVII.

By hooping and scutling of caske.

the men to come to the pumpes, wherof shee had two which went with chaynes; and plying them, in a moment there was three or foure inches of water upon the decke, which with scoopes, swabbles,[1] and platters, they threw upon the fire, and so quenched it, and delivered both ship and men out of no small danger.

Great care is to be had also in cleaving of wood, in hooping or scuttling[2] of caske, and in any businesse where violence is to be used with instruments of iron, steele, or stone: and especially in opening of powder, these are not to be used, but mallets of wood; for many mischances happen beyond all expectation.

I have been credibly enformed by divers persons, that comming out of the Indies, with scuttling a butt of water, the water hath taken fire, and flamed up, and put all in hazard. And a servant of mine, Thomas Grey, told me, that in the shippe wherein he came out of the Indies, anno 1600, there happened the like; and that if with mantles they had not smothered the fire, they had bin all burned with a pipe of water, which in scutling took fire.

Master John Hazlelocke reported, that in the arsenall of Venice happened the like, he being present. For mine

By nature of waters.

own part, I am of opinion, that some waters have this propertie, and especially such as have their passage by mines of brimstone, or other mineralls, which, as all men know, give extraordinary properties unto the waters by which they runne. Or it may be that the water being in wine caske, and kept close, may retayne an extraordinary propertie of the wine.[3] Yea, I have drunke fountaine and

[1] Swabs are a species of mop, made of a collection of rope yarns, used to dry the deck. *Swebban*—(Anglo-Saxon) to sweep.

[2] *To scuttle*—to make openings. *Escotilla* (Spanish), is applied to the openings in the deck, called by us hatch-ways. The term scuttle is also applied to the small openings made in the ship's side to admit light and air.

[3] If impure water be confined in a close cask, gas will be generated, and the effect described happen.

river waters many times, which have had a savour as that of brimstone. Sect. XVIII.

Three leagues from Bayon, in France, I have proved of a fountaine that hath this savour, and is medicinable for many diseases. In the South sea, in a river some five leagues from Cape Saint Francisco, in one degree and a halfe to the northwardes of the lyne, in the bay of Atacames, is a river of fresh water, which hath the like savour. Of this I shall have occasion to speake in another place, treating of the divers properties of fountaines and rivers; and therefore to our purpose.

SECTION XVIII.

We had no small cause to give God thankes and prayse for our deliverance; and so, all our ships once come together, wee magnified his glorious name for his mercie towards us, and tooke an occasion hereby to banish swearing out of our shippes, which amongst the common sort of mariners and sea-faring men is too ordinarily abused. So with a generall consent of all our companie, it was ordayned that in every ship there should be a palmer or ferula, which should be in the keeping of him who was taken with an oath; and that he who had the palmer should give to every other that he tooke swearing, in the palme of the hand, a palmada with it, and the ferula. And whosoever at the time of evening, or morning prayer, was found to have the palmer, should have three blowes given him by the captaine or master; and that he should be still bound to free himselfe, by taking another, or else to runne in daunger of continuing the penaltie: which executed, few dayes reformed the vice; so that in three dayes together, was not one oath heard to By swearing.

Sect. XIX.

be sworne. This brought both ferulas and swearing out of use.[1]

And certainly, in vices, custome is the principall sustenance; and for their reformation, it little availeth to give good counsell, or to make good lawes and ordenances except they be executed.

SECTION XIX.

In this time of contrary wind, those of my company which were in health, recreated themselves with fishing, and beholding the hunting and hawking of the sea, and the battell betwixt the whale and his enemies, which truly are of no small pleasure. And therefore for the curious, I will spend some time in declaration of them.

Ordinarily such ships as navigate betweene the tropiques, are accompanied with three sorts of fish: the dolphin, which the Spaniards call *dozado;* the *bonito,* or Spanish makerell; and the sharke, alias *tiberune.*

The dolphin.

The dolphin I hold to be one of the swiftest fishes in the sea. He is like unto a breame, but that he is longer and thinner, and his scales very small. He is of the colour of the rayn-bow, and his head different to other fishes; for, from his mouth halfe a spanne, it goeth straight upright, as the head of a wherry, or the cut-water of a ship. He is very good meate if he be in season, but the best part of him is his head, which is great. They are some bigger, some

[1] In the instructions given by the Lords Generals, the Earl of Essex and Charles Lord Howard, Lord High Admiral of England, to the captains of the ships composing the expedition to Cadiz, in 1596, the second article runs thus: "Item—You shall forbid swearing, brawling, dicing, and such like disorders, as may breed contention and disorder in your ship, wherein you shall also avoid God's displeasure and win his favour."

Sect. XIX.

lesser; the greatest that I have seene, might be some foure foote long.

I hold it not without some ground, that the auncient philosophers write, that they be enamoured of a man; for in meeting with shipping, they accompany them till they approach to colde climates; this I have noted divers times. For disembarking out of the West Indies, anno 1583, within three or foure dayes after, we met a scole[1] of them, which left us not till we came to the ilands of Azores, nere a thousand leagues. At other times I have noted the like.

But some may say, that in the sea are many scoles of this kinde of fish, and how can a man know if they were the same?

Who may be thus satisfied, that every day in the morning, which is the time that they approach neerest the ship, we should see foure, five, and more, which had, as it were, our eare-marke; one hurt upon the backe, another neere the tayle, another about the fynnes; which is a sufficient proofe that they were the same: for if those which had received so bad entertainment of us would not forsake us, much less those which we had not hurt. Yet that which makes them most in love with ships and men, are the scrappes and refreshing they gather from them.

The bonito, or Spanish makerell, is altogether like unto a makerell, but that it is somewhat more growne; he is reasonable foode, but dryer than a makerell. Of them there are two sorts: the one is this which I have described; the other, so great as hardly one man can lift him. At such times as wee have taken of these, one sufficed for a meale for all my company. These, from the fynne of the tayle forwards, have upon the chyne seven small yellow hillocks, close one to another. The bonito.

[1] A shoal or scull of fish; that is, separated from the main body. This is Horne Tooke's derivation. We think the term is more commonly applied to the main body itself.

Sect. XIX. The dolphins and bonitos are taken with certaine instruments of iron which we call vysgeis,[1] in forme of an eel speare, but that the blades are round, and the poynts like unto the head of a broad arrow: these are fastened to long staves of ten or twelve foote long, with lynes tied unto them, and so shott to the fish from the beake-head, the poope, or other parts of the shippe, as occasion is ministered. They are also caught with hooks and lynes, the hooke being bayted with a redd cloth, or with a white cloth made into the forme of a fish, and sowed upon the hooke.

The sharke. The shark, or tiberune, is a fish like unto those which wee call dogge-fishes, but that he is farre greater. I have seene of them eight or nine foote long; his head is flatt and broad, and his mouth in the middle, underneath, as that of the scate; and he cannot byte of the bayte before him, but by making a halfe turne; and then he helpeth himselfe with his tayle, which serveth him in stead of a rudder. His skinne is rough (like to the fish which we call a rough hound), and russet, with reddish spottes, saving that under the belly he is all white: he is much hated of sea-faring men, who have a certaine foolish superstition with them, and say, that the ship hath seldome good successe, that is much accompanied with them.

It is the most ravenous fish knowne in the sea; for he swalloweth all that he findeth. In the puch[2] of them hath beene found hatts, cappes, shooes, shirts, leggs and armes of men, ends of ropes, and many other things; whatsoever is hanged by the shippes side, hee sheereth it, as though it were with a razor; for he hath three rowes of teeth on either side, as sharpe as nailes; some say they are good for pick-tooths. It hath chanced that a yonker casting himselfe into the sea to swimme, hath had his legge bitten off above the knee by one of them. And I have beene en-

[1] *Fisgig* or *grains*—a small trident used for striking fish. From the Spanish *fisga*.

[2] Pouch or stomach.

formed, that in the *Tyger*, when Sir Richard Greenfield[1] went to people Virginia, a sharke cut off the legge of one of the companie, sitting in the chaines and washing himselfe. They spawne not as the greatest part of fishes doe, but whelpe, as the dogge or wolfe; and for many dayes after that shee hath whelped, every night, and towards any storme, or any danger which may threaten them hurt, the damme receiveth her whelpes in at her mouth, and preserveth them, till they be able to shift for themselves. I have seene them goe in and out, being more than a foote and halfe long: and after taking the damme, we have found her young ones in her belly.[2] Sect. XIX.

Every day my company tooke more or lesse of them, not for that they did eat of them (for they are not held wholesome; although the Spaniards, as I have seene, doe eate them), but to recreate themselves, and in revenge of the injuries received by them; for they live long, and suffer much after they bee taken, before they dye.

At the tayle of one they tyed a great logge of wood, at another, an empty batizia,[3] well stopped; one they yoaked like a hogge; from another, they plucked out his eyes, and so threw them into the sea. In catching two together, they bound them tayle to tayle, and so set them swimming; another with his belly slit and his bowels hanging out, which his fellowes every one would have a snatch at; with other infinite inventions to entertayne the time, and to avenge themselves; for that they deprived them of swimming, and fed on their flesh being dead. They are taken with harping irons, and with great hookes made of purpose, with swyvels and chaines; for no lyne nor small rope can hold them, which they share not asunder.

There doth accompany this fish divers little fishes, which

[1] Grenville.

[2] One species produces its young alive: others in a hard membraneous pouch.

[3] Probably a small cask.

Sect. XIX. are callet pilats fishes, and are ever upon his fynnes, his head, or his backe, and feed of the scraps and superfluities of his prayes. They are in forme of a trought, and streked like a makerell, but that the strekes are white and blacke, and the blacke greater then the white.

The manner of hunting and hawking representeth that which we reasonable creatures use, saving onely in the disposing of the game. For by our industry and abilitie the hound and hawke is brought to that obedience, that whatever they seize is for their master: but here it is otherwise: for the game is for him that seizeth it. The dolphins and bonitoes are the houndes, and the alcatraces the hawkes, and the flying fishes the game; whose wonderfull making magnifieth the Creator, who for their safetie and helpe, hath given them extraordinary manner of fynnes, which serve in stead of wings, like those of the batt or rere-mouse; of such a delicate skinne, interlaced with small bones so curiously, as may well cause admiration in the beholders. They are like unto pilchards in colour, and making; saving that they are somewhat rounder, and (for the most part) bigger. They flie best with a side wind, but longer then their wings be wett they cannot sustaine the waight of their bodies; and so the greatest flight that I have seene them make, hath not beene above a quarter of a myle. They commonly goe in scoles, and serve for food for the greater fishes, or for the foules. The dolphins and bonitos doe continually hunt after them, and the alcatraces lye soaring in the ayre, to see when they spring, or take their flight; and ordinarily, he that escapeth the mouth of the dolphin or bonito, helping himselfe by his wings, falleth prisoner into the hands of the alcatrace, and helpeth to fill his gorge.

Flying fishes.

Alcatrace. The alcatrace[1] is a sea-fowle, different to all that I have seene, either on the land or in the sea. His head like unto

[1] The man-of-war bird, or cormorant—*Pelecanidæ*. On the coast of Brazil, in latitude twenty-four, are the Alcatrasse islands.

the head of a gull, but his bill like unto a snytes bill, somewhat shorter, and in all places alike. He is almost like tó a heronshaw; his leggs a good spanne long, his wings very long, and sharpe towards the poynts, with a long tayle like to a pheasant, but with three or foure feathers onely, and these narrower. He is all blacke, of the colour of a crow, and of little flesh; for he is almost all skinne and bones. He soareth the highest of any fowle that I have seene, and I have not heard of any, that hath seene them rest in the sea.

Now of the fight betwixt the whale and his contraries; which are the sword-fish and the thresher. The whale is of the greatest fishes in the sea; and to count but the truth, unlesse dayly experience did witnesse the relation, it might seeme incredible; hee is a huge unwildlie fish, and to those which have not seene of them, it might seeme strange, that other fishes should master him; but certaine it is, that many times the thresher and sword-fish, meeting him joyntly, doe make an end of him.

The fight of the whale,

The sword-fish[1] is not great, but strongly made; and in the top of his chine, as a man may say, betwixt the necke and shoulders, he hath a manner of sword, in substance like unto a bone, of four or five inches broad, and above three foote long, full of prickles of either side: it is but thin, for the greatest that I have seene hath not beene above a finger thicke.

with the sword fish

The thresher is a greater fish, whose tayle is very broad and thicke, and very waightie. They fight in this maner; the sword fish placeth himselfe under the belly of the whale, and the thresher upon the ryme[2] of the water, and with his tayle thresheth upon the head of the whale, till hee force

and thresher.

[1] *Xiphias*—the sword or snout is about three-tenths of his whole length.

[2] *The surface*—from cream or ream, what rises to the surface—or perhaps from rim, brim.

Sect. XIX. him to give way; which the sword fish perceiving, receiveth him upon his sword, and wounding him in the belly forceth him to mount up againe (besides that he cannot abide long under water, but must of force rise upp to breath): and when in such manner they torment him, that the fight is sometimes heard above three leagues distance, and I dare affirme, that I have heard the blowes of the thresher two leagues off, as the report of a peece of ordinance; the whales roaring being heard much further. It also happeneth sundry times that a great part of the water of the sea round about them, with the blood of the whale, changeth his colour. The best remedy the whale hath in this extremitie to helpe himselfe, is to get him to land, which hee procureth as soone as hee discovereth his adversaries; and getting the shore, there can fight but one with him, and for either of them, hand to hand, he is too good. The whale is a fish not good to be eaten, hee is almost all fat, but esteemed for his trayne; and many goe to the New-found-land, Greene-land, and other parts onely to fish for them; which is in this maner; when they which seeke the whale discover him, they compasse him round about with pynaces or shalops. In the head of every boat is placed a man, with a harping iron, and a long lyne, the one end of it fastned to the harping iron, and the other end to the head of the boat, in which it lyeth finely coiled; and for that he cannot keepe long under water, he sheweth which way he goeth, when rising neere any of the boates, within reach, he that is neerest, darteth his harping iron at him. The whale finding himself to be wounded, swimmeth to the bottome, and draweth the pynace after him; which the fisher-men presently forsake, casting themselves into the sea; for that many times he draweth the boat under water: those that are next, procure to take them up. For this cause all such as goe for that kind of fishing, are experimented in swimming. When one harping iron is fastned in the whale, it

The taking of the whale.

is easily discerned which way he directeth his course: and so ere long they fasten another, and another in him. When he hath three or foure boates dragging after him, with their waight, his bleeding, and fury, he becommeth so over-mastred, that the rest of the pynaces with their presence and terror, drive him to the place where they would have him, nature instigating him to covet the shore. Sect. XIX.

Being once hurt, there is little need to force him to land. Once on the shore, they presently cut great peeces of him, and in great cauldrons seeth them.[1] The uppermost in the cauldrons is the fatt, which they skimme off, and put it into hogsheads and pipes. This is that they call whales oyle, or traine oyle, accompted the best sort of traine oyle. It is hard to be beleeved, what quantitie is gathered of one whale; of the tongue, I have beene enformed, have many pipes beene filled. The fynnes are also esteemed for many and sundry uses; as is his spawne for divers purposes: this wee corruptly call *parmacittie;* of the Latine word, *sperma-ceti.*[2]

Amber-greece.

And the precious amber-greece some thinke also to be found in his bowells, or voyded by him: but not in all seas: yea, they maintaine for certaine, that the same is ingendred by eating an hearbe which groweth in the sea. This hearbe is not in all seas, say they, and therefore, where it wanteth, the whales give not this fruit. In the coast of the East Indies in many partes is great quantitie. In the coastes of Guyne, of Barbary, of the Florida, in the islands of Cape de Verde, and the Canaries, amber-greece hath beene many times found, and sometimes on the coast

[1] In the early days of the whale fishery, when the fish were plentiful, the oil was boiled out on shore, near the place of capture.

[2] "And telling me the sovereign'st thing on earth
Was parmaceti for an inward bruise."—*Henry IV*, Part I.

Spermaceti is obtained from the brain of the sperm whale,—*physeter macrocephalus*—not from the spawn.

Sect. XIX. of Spaine and England. Whereupon it is presumed, that all these seas have not the hearbe growing in them. The cause why the whale should eate this hearbe, I have not heard, nor read. It may be surmised, that it is as that of the becunia,[1] and other beasts, which breed the beazer stone;[2] who feeding in the valleyes and mountaines, where are many venemous serpents, and herbes, when they find themselves touched with any poyson, forthwith they runne for remedie to an hearbe, which the Spaniards call *contra-yerva*, that is to say, contrary to poyson: which having eaten, they are presently cured: but the substance of the hearbe converteth it selfe into a medicinal stone; so it may be, that the whale feeding of many sortes of fishes, and some of them, as is knowne, venemous, when he findeth himselfe touched, with this hearbe he cureth himselfe; and not being able to digest it, nature converteth it into this substance, provoketh it out, or dyeth with it in his belly; and being light, the sea bringeth it to the coast.

All these are imaginations, yet instruments to moove us to the glorifying of the great and universal Creatour of all whose secret wisedome, and wonderfull workes, are incomprehensible.

Amber-greece. But the more approved generation of the amber-greece, and which carrieth likliest probabilitie is, that it is a liquor which issueth out of certaine fountaines, in sundry seas, and being of a light and thicke substance, participating of the ayre, suddenly becommeth hard, as the yellow amber, of which they make beads;[3] which is also a liquor of a

[1] Vicuña; the wild species of llama, in the Peruvian Andes.

[2] Acosta devotes a chapter to the bezoar stones, which, he says, are found in all the animals of the llama tribe. Those taken out of the stomachs of vicuñas are larger than the bezoars of llamas and alpacas. Acosta explains the cause of this concretion, and its medicinal virtues. (*Hist. natural y moral de las Indias*, lib. IV, cap. 42.)

[3] Ambergris is known to be a morbid secretion formed in the intestines of the sperm whale (*Physeter macrocephalus*), and is found float-

fountayne in the Germayne sea. In the bottom it is soft and white, and partaking of the ayre becommeth hard and stonie: also the corrall in the sea is soft, but comming into the ayre, becommeth a stone.

Those who are of this former opinion, thinke the reason why the amber greece is sometimes found in the whale, to be, for that he swalloweth it, as other things which he findeth swimming upon the water; and not able to digest it, it remaineth with him till his death.

By the Indians.

Another manner of fishing and catching the whale I cannot omit, used by the Indians, in Florida; worthy to be considered, in as much as the barbarous people have found out so great a secret, by the industry and diligence of one man, to kill so large and huge a monster: it is in this manner.

The Indian discovering a whale, procureth two round billets of wood, sharpneth both at one end, and so binding them together with a cord, casteth himselfe with them into the sea, and swimmeth towards the whale: if he come to him, the whale escapeth not; for he placeth himselfe upon his necke, and although the whale goeth to the bottome, he must of force rise presently to breath (for which nature hath given him two great holes in the toppe of his head, by which, every time that he breatheth, he spouteth out a great quantitie of water); the Indian forsaketh not his holde, but riseth with him, and thrusteth in a logg into one of his spowters, and with the other knocketh it in so fast, that by no meanes the whale can get it out. That fastned, at another opportunitie, he thrusteth in the second logg into the other spowter, and with all the force he can, keepeth it in.

The whale not being able to breath, swimmeth presently ashore, and the Indian a cock-horse upon him, which his

ing on the sea, on the sea coast, or in the sand near the sea coast. Its use is now entirely confined to perfumery. *Ambre-gris* (grey amber).

Sect. xx. fellowes discovering, approach to helpe him, and to make an end of him: it serveth them for their foode many dayes after.

Since the Spaniards have taught them the estimation of amber greece, they seeke curiously for it, sell it to them, and others, for such things as they best fancie, and most esteeme; which are, as I have been enformed, all sortes of edge tooles, copper, glasses, glasse-beads, red caps, shirts, and pedlery ware. Upon this subject, divers Spaniards have discoursed unto mee, who have beene eye witnesses thereof, declaring them to be valorous, ventrous, and industrious: otherwise they durst not undertake an enterprise so difficult and full of danger.

SECTION XX.

Best times to passe the lyne from the north-wards to the southward.

From the tropike of Cancer to three or foure degrees of the equinoctiall, the breze, which is the north-east winde, doth raigne in our ocean sea the most part of the yeare, except it be neere the shore, and then the wind is variable. In three or foure degrees of eyther side the line, the winde hangeth southerly, in the moneths of July, August, September, and October; all the rest of the yeare, from the Cape Bona Esperança to the ilands of Azores, the breze raygneth continually; and some yeares in the other moneths also, or calmes; but he that purposeth to crosse the lyne from the north-wards to the south-wards, the best and surest passage is, in the moneths of January, February, and March. In the moneths of September, October, and November, is also good passage, but not so sure as in the former.[1]

[1] According to Horsburgh, the least favourable season for getting to the southward, is the period from June to September inclusive.

SECTION XXI.

Sect. xxi.

Betwixt nineteene and twenty degrees to the south-wards of the lyne, the winde tooke us contrary, which together with the sicknes of my people made mee to seeke the shore; and about the end of October, we had sight of the land, which presently by our height and the making of it, discovered it selfe to be the port of Santos,[1] alias Nostra Senora de Victoria, and is easie to be knowne, for it hath a great high hill over the port, which (howsoever a man commeth with the land) riseth like a bell, and comming neere the shore, presently is discovered a white tower or fort, which standeth upon the top of a hill over the harbour, and upon the seamost land. It is the first land a man must compasse before he enter the port. Comming within two leagues of the shore, we anchored; and the captaynes and masters of my other ships being come aboord, it was thought convenient (the weaknes of our men considered, for wee had not in our three ships twenty foure men sound), and the winde uncertaine when it might change, we thought with pollicie to procure that which wee could not by force; and so to offer traffique to the people of the shore; by that meanes to prove if wee could attayne some refreshing for our sicke company.

In execution whereof, I wrote a letter to the governour in Latine, and sent him with it a piece of crymson velvet, a bolt of fine holland, with divers other things, as a present; and with it, the captaine of my ship, who spake a little broken Spanish, giving the governour to understand that I was bound to the East Indies, to traffique in those parts, and that contrary windes had forced me upon that coast: if that hee were pleased to like of it, for the commodities

[1] Victoria, a Brazilian port in the Bay of Espirito Santo, in 20° 19′ 2″ S.

Sect. XXI. the country yeelded in aboundance, I would exchange that which they wanted. With these instructions my captaine departed about nine of the clocke in the morning, carrying a flagge of truce in the head of the boate, and sixteene men well armed, and provided; guided by one of my company which two yeares before had beene captaine in that place, and so was a reasonable pilot.

Entering the port, within a quarter of a mile is a small village, and three leagues higher up is the chief towne; where they have two forts, one on eyther side of the harbour, and within them ride the ships which come thither to discharge, or loade. In the small village is ever a garrison of one hundreth souldiers, whereof part assist there continually, and in the white tower upon the top of the hill, which commaundeth it.

Heere my captaine had good entertainment, and those of the shore received his message and letter, dispatching it presently to the governour, who was some three leagues off in another place: at least they beare us so in hand. In the time that they expected the post, my captaine with one other entertained himselfe with the souldiers a shore, who after the common custome of their profession (except when they be *besonios*[1]), sought to pleasure him, and finding that he craved but oranges, lemmons, and matters of smal moment for refreshing for his generall, they suffered the women and children to bring him what hee would, which hee gratified with double pistolets,[2] that I had given him for that purpose. So got hee us two or three hundreth oranges and lemmons, and some fewe hennes.

All that day and night, and the next day, till nine of the

[1] Bisoño—(Spanish) raw, undisciplined:—

Pistol. Under which king, Bezonian? speak or die.

Henry IV, Part II.

[2] The double pistole was a coin of about the value of thirty or thirty-five shillings.

clocke, wee waited the returne of our boate; which not appearing, bred in me some suspition; and for my satisfaction, I manned a light horseman which I had, and the *Fancie*, the best I could, shewing strength where was weaknesse and infirmity, and so set sayle towardes the port; our gunner taking upon him to bee pilot, for that he had beene there some yeares before. Sect. XXI.

Thus, with them we entred the harbour. My captaine having notice of our being within the barre, came aboord with the boat, which was no small joy to me; and more, to see him bring us store of oranges and lemmons, which was that we principally sought for, as the remedie of our diseased company. He made relation of that had past, and how they expected present answere from the governour. We anchored right against the village; and within two houres, by a flagge of truce, which they on the shore shewed us, we understood that the messenger was come: our boat went for the answere of the governour, who said, he was sorry that he could not accomplish our desire, being so reasonable and good; for that in consideration of the warre betwixt Spaine and England, he had expresse order from his king, not to suffer any English to trade within his jurisdiction, no, nor to land, or to take any refreshing upon the shore. And therefore craved pardon, and that wee should take this for a resolute answere: and further required us to depart the port within three dayes, which he said he gave us for our courteous manner of proceeding. If any of my people from that time forwards, should approach to the shore, that he would doe his best to hinder and annoy them. With this answere wee resolved to depart; and before it came, with the first faire wind we determined to be packing: but the wind suffered us not all that night, nor the next day. In which time, I lived in a great perplexitie, for that I knew our own weaknesse, and what they might doe unto us, if that they had knowne so much. For any

Sect. XXI. man that putteth himselfe into the enemies port, had need of Argus eyes, and the wind in a bagge,[1] especially where the enemie is strong, and the tydes of any force. For with either ebbe or flood, those who are on the shore may thrust upon him inventions of fire: and with swimming or other devises, may cut his cables. A common practise in all hot countries. The like may be effected with raffes, cannoas, boates, or pynaces, to annoy and assault him: and if this had beene practised against us, or taken effect, our shippes must of force have yeelded themselves; for they had no other people in them but sicke men; but many times opinion and feare preserveth the shippes, and not the people in them.

For prevention of annoyances, etc., in harbours.

Wherefore it is the part of a provident governour, to consider well the daungers that may befall him, before he put himselfe into such places; so shall he ever be provided for prevention.

In Saint John de Vlua, in the New Spaine, when the Spanyards dishonoured their nation with that foule act of perjury, and breach of faith, given to my father, Sir John Hawkins (notorious to the whole world),[2] the Spanyards fired two great shippes, with intention to burne my fathers *Admirall*, which he prevented by towing them with his boates another way.

The great armado of Spaine, sent to conquer England, anno 1588, was with that selfe same industry overthrowne; for the setting on fire of six or seaven shippes (whereof two were mine), and letting them drive with the flood, forced them to cut their cables, and to put to sea, to seeke a new way to Spaine.[3] In which the greatest part of their best shippes and men were lost and perished.

[1] So that he may get away when it pleases him.

[2] See page 77.

[3] Alluding to the attempt the fleet made to return northabout. In the British Museum is preserved a curious old pack of playing cards, on

For that my people should not be dismayed, I dispatched presently my light horsman, with onely foure men, and part of the refreshing, advising them that with the first calme or slent[1] of wind, they should come off. Sect. xxi.

The next night, the wind comming off the shore, wee set sayle, and with our boates and barkes sounded as we went.

It flowed upon the barre not above foure foote water, and once in foure and twentie houres, as in some parts of the West Indies; at full sea, there is not upon the barre above seventeen or eighteen foote water. The harbour runneth to the south-westwards. He that will come into it, is to open the harbour's mouth a good quarter of a league before he beare with it, and be bolder of the wester side; for of the easterland[2] lyeth a great ledge of rocks, for the most part, under water, which sometimes break not; but with small shipping, a man may goe betwixt them and the poynt.

The vertue of oranges.

Comming aboord of our shippes, there was great joy amongst my company; and many, with the sight of the oranges and lemmons, seemed to recover heart. This is a wonderfull secret of the power and wisedome of God, that hath hidden so great and unknowne vertue in this fruit, to be a certaine remedie for this infirmitie; I presently caused them all to be reparted[3] amongst our sicke men, which were so many, that there came not above three or foure to a share: but God was pleased to send us a prosperous winde the next day, so much to our comfort, that not any one dyed before we came to the ilands, where we pretended to refresh ourselves; and although our fresh water had

which are depicted subjects relating to the defeat of the "Spanish Armada". On the ten of spades is shewn a consultation about returning by the North Ocean.

[1] Such a wind as would enable them to lie aslant or obliquely near the desired course. It is commonly said that "a calm is half a fair wind"; it is more than this, as out of thirty-two points, twenty would be fair.

[2] Easterhand?

[3] *Répartir*—(French) to divide.

Sect. XXII. fayled us many dayes before we saw the shore, by reason of our long navigation, without touching any land, and the excessive drinking of the sicke and diseased, which could not be excused, yet with an invention I had in my shippe, I easily drew out of the water of the sea, sufficient quantitie of fresh water to sustaine my people with little expence of fewell; for with foure billets I stilled a hogshead of water, and therewith dressed the meat for the sicke and whole. The water so distilled, we found to be wholesome and nourishing.

Distilling of salt water.

SECTION XXII.

The coast from Santos to Cape Frio, lyeth west and by south, southerly. So we directed our course west southwest. The night comming on, and directions given to our other shippes, we sett the watch, having a fayre fresh gale of wind and large. My selfe with the master of our ship, having watched the night past, thought now to give nature that which shee had beene deprived of, and so recommended the care of steeridge to one of his mates; who with the like travell past being drowsie, or with the confidence which he had of him at the helme, had not that watchfull care which was required; he at the helme steered west, and west and by south, and brought us in a little time close upon the shore;[1] doubtlesse he had cast us all away, had not God extraordinarily delivered us; for the master being in his dead sleepe, was suddenly awaked, and with such a fright that he could not be in quiet: whereupon waking his youth, which ordinarily slept in his cabin by him, asked

Unskilfulnesse of the masters mate.

Providence of God, and the care of the master.

[1] The coast lies nearer south and by west, than west and by south, so they would certainly have run on shore without any blame attaching to the helmsman.

him how the watch went on; who answered, that it could not be above an houre since he layd himselfe to rest. He replyed, that his heart was so unquiet that he could not by any meanes sleepe, and so taking his gowne, came forth upon the deck, and presently discovered the land hard by us. And for that it was sandie and low, those who had their eyes continually fixed on it, were dazeled with the reflection of the starres, being a fayre night, and so were hindered from the true discovery thereof. But he comming out of the darke, had his sight more forcible, to discerne the difference of the sea, and the shore. So that forthwith he commaunded him at the helme, to put it close a starbourd, and tacking our ship, wee edged off; and sounding, found scant three fathome water, whereby we saw evidently the miraculous mercie of our God; that if he had not watched over us, as hee doth continually over his, doubtlesse we had perished without remedie. To whom be all glory, and prayse everlastingly, world without end. Sect. XXII.

Immediatly we shot off a peece, to give warning to our other shippes; who having kept their direct course, and far to wind-wards and sea-wards, because we carried no light, for that we were within sight of the shore, could not heare the report; and the next morning were out of sight.

SECTION XXIII.

In this poynt of steeridge, the Spaniards and Portingalls doe exceede all that I haue seene, I mean for their care, which is chiefest in navigation. And I wish in this, and in all their workes of discipline, wee should follow their examples; as also those of any other nation. Care of steeridge,

In every ship of moment, upon the halfe decke, or quar- exquisit in the Spanyards and Portingalls.

Sect. xxiv. ter decke,[1] they have a chayre or seat; out of which whilst they navigate, the pilot, or his adjutants[2] (which are the same officers which in our shippes we terme the master and his mates), never depart, day nor night, from the sight of the compasse; and have another before them, whereby they see what they doe, and are ever witnesses of the good or bad steeridge of all men that take the helme. This I have seene neglected in our best shippes, yet nothing more necessary to be reformed. For a good helme-man may be overcome with an imagination, and so mis-take one poynt for another;[3] or the compasse may erre, which by another is discerned. The inconveniences which hereof may ensue, all experimented sea-men may easily conceive, and by us take warning to avoyd the like.

SECTION XXIV.

Cape Blanco.

THE next day about tenne of the clocke, wee were thwart of Cape Blanco,[4] which is low sandie land, and perilous; for foure leagues into the sea (thwart it), lye banks of sand, which have little water on them; on a sudden we

[1] The quarter deck may be defined as the space betwixt the mainmast and the after-hatchway; it seems also to have been called the half deck. Both terms refer to the fact that before the mainmast, the skids or beams were not planked. We still speak of being *on* the quarter deck, but *under* the half deck. The quarter deck is set apart for purposes of parade, and there the officer of the watch should always be sought.

[2] *Adjutare*—(Latin) to assist.

[3] On a still night, unless the attention of the helmsman be continually excited, it is quite possible that he get into a dreamy state, and, if at the same time, the officer of the watch is thinking of "those far away", the ship may be run for a time some points off her course. In the preceding section, Sir Richard well describes the difficulty of distinguishing betwixt a sandy shore and the water, on a calm bright night.

[4] Cape Saint Thomé, in 22° 2′ S.

found our selves amongst them, in lesse then three fathome water; but with our boat and shalope we went sounding, and so got cleare of them. Sect. XXIV.

The next day following, we discovered the ilands where wee purposed to refresh ourselves. They are two, and some call them Saint James, his ilands, and others, Saint Annes.[1] They lie in two and twenty degrees and a halfe to the south-wards of the lyne; and towards the evening (being the fifth of November) we anchored betwixt them and the mayne, in six fathome water, where wee found our other shippes. Saint James ilands, alias Saint Annes.

All which being well moored, we presently began to set up tents and booths for our sicke men, to carry them a shore, and to use our best diligence to cure them. For which intent our three surgeons, with their servants and adherents, had two boates to wayte continually upon them, to fetch whatsoever was needfull from the shippes, to procure refreshing, and to fish, either with netts, or hookes and lynes. Of these implements wee had in aboundance, and it yeelded us some refreshing. For the first dayes, the most of those which had health, occupied themselves in romeging our ship; in bringing ashore of emptie casks; in filling of them, and in felling and in cutting of wood: which being many workes, and few hands, went slowly forwards.

Neere these ilands, are two great rockes, or small ilands adjoyning. In them we found great store of young gannetts in their nests, which we reserved for the sicke, and being boyled with pickled porke well watered,[2] and mingled with oatmeale, made reasonable pottage, and was good refreshing and sustenance for them. This provision fayled us not, till our departure from them. Gannets.

Upon one of these rocks also, we found great store of

[1] Now called Santa Anna, between Cape Saint Thomé and Cape Frio.

[2] Well soaked in water to remove the salt.

Sect. XXIV. Purslane. the hearbe purslane,[1] which boyled and made into sallets, with oyle and vinegar, refreshed the sicke stomaches, and gave appetite.

With the ayre of the shore, and good cherishing, many recovered speedily. Some died away quickly, and others continued at a stand. We found here some store of fruits; Cherries. a kind of cherry that groweth upon a tree like a plum-tree, red of colour, with a stone in it, but different in making to ours, for it is not altogether round, and dented about: they have a pleasing taste.

Palmitos. In one of the ilands, we found palmito trees, great and high, and in the toppe a certain fruit like cocos, but no bigger then a wall-nut. We found also a fruit growing upon trees in codds, like beanes, both in the codd and the fruit. Some of my company proved of them,[2] and they Purgatives. caused vomits and purging, as any medicine taken out of the apothecaries shop, according to the quantitie received. They have hudds, as our beanes, which shaled off; the kernell parteth itselfe in two, and in the middle is a thin skinne, like that of an onion, said to be hurtfull, and to cause exceeding vomits, and therefore to be cast away.

Monardus writing of the nature and propertie of this fruit, as of others of the Indies, for that it is found in other The use of *kavas purgativas.* parts, also calleth them *kavas purgativas*, and sayth, that they are to be prepared by peeling them first, and then taking away the skinne in the middle, and after beaten into powder, to take the quantitie of five or six, either with wine or sugar. Thus they are good against fevers, and to purge grosse humors; against the colicke, and payne of the joynts; in taking them a man may not sleepe, but is to use the dyet usuall, as in a day of purging.

[1] *Portulaca sativa*—a fleshy-leaved plant, much esteemed in hot countries for its cooling properties.

[2] Great caution should be used in tasting unknown fruits; perhaps this tree was the *croton tiglium*, every part of which possesses powerful drastic properties.

Sect. xxiv.

One other fruit we found, very pleasant in taste, in fashion of an artechoque, but lesse; on the outside of colour redd, within white, and compassed about with prickles; our people called them pricke-pears;[1] no conserve is better. They grow upon the leaves of a certaine roote, that is like unto that which we call *semper viva* and many are wont to hang them up in their houses; but their leaves are longer and narrower, and full of prickes on either side. The fruit groweth upon the side of the leafe, and is one of the best fruites that I have eaten in the Indies. In ripening, presently the birds or vermine are feeding on them; a generall rule to know what fruit is wholesome and good in the Indies, and other parts. Finding them to be eaten of the beastes or fowles, a man may boldly eate of them.

Arte-choques or prick-peares.

A good note to take or refuse unknowne fruits.

The water of these ilands is not good: the one, for being a standing water, and full of venemous wormes and serpents, which is neare a butt-shott from the sea shore; where we found a great tree fallen, and in the roote of it the names of sundry Portingalls, Frenchmen, and others, and amongst them, Abraham Cockes; with the time of their being in this island.

The other, though a running water, yet passing by the rootes of certaine trees, which have a smell as that of garlique, taketh a certaine contagious sent of them. Here two of our men dyed with swelling of their bellies. The accident we could not attribute to any other cause, then to this suspitious water. It is little, and falleth into the sand, and soketh through it into the sea; and therefore we made a well of a pipe, and placeth it under the rocke from which it falleth, and out of it filled our caske: but we could not fill above two tunnes in a night and day.

Contagious water.

[1] A species of cactus; the fruit is eaten in Sicily and elsewhere. We cannot join Sir Richard in its praise: perhaps as he had been long at sea, he found it grateful. The cochineal insect feeds on one species of this plant.

SECTION XXV.

Sect. xxvi. So after our people began to gather their strength, wee manned our boates, and went over to the mayne, where presently we found a great ryver of fresh and sweete water, and a mightie marish countrie; which in the winter[1] seemeth to be continually over-flowne with this river, and others, which fall from the mountaynous country adjacent.

We rowed some leagues up the ryver, and found that the further up we went, the deeper was the river, but no fruit, more then the sweate of our bodies, for the labour of our handes.

At our returne, wee loaded our boate with water, and afterwardes from hence wee made our store.

SECTION XXVI.

Wast and losse of men.

THE sicknesse having wasted more than the one halfe of my people, we determined to take out the victualls of the *Hawke*, and to burne her; which wee put in execution. And being occupied in this worke, we saw a shippe turning to windwards, to succour her selfe of the ilands;[2] but having discryed us, put off to sea-wards.

Two dayes after, the wind changing, we saw her againe running alongst the coast, and the *Daintie* not being in case to goe after her, for many reasons, we manned the *Fancie*, and sent her after her; who about the setting of the sunne fetched her up, and spake with her; when finding her to be a great fly-boat, of at least three or foure hundreth tunnes, with eighteen peeces of artillery, would

[1] This river is now called the Maccahé; probably it floods in the rainy season.

[2] By working up under their lee.

have returned, but the wind freshing in, put her to leewards; and standing in to succour her selfe of the land, had sight of another small barke, which after a short chase shee tooke, but had nothing of moment in her, for that she had bin upon the great sholes of Abreoios,[1] in eighteen degrees, and there throwne all they had by the board, to save their lives.

This and the other chase were the cause that the *Fancie* could not beat it up in many dayes: but before we had put all in a readinesse, the wind changing, shee came unto us, and made relation of that which had past; and how they had given the small barke to the Portingalls, and brought with them onely her pilot, and a marchant called Pedro de Escalante of Potosi.

SECTION XXVII.

Industry of the Indians. They surprise the French.

In this coast, the Portingalls, by industrie of the Indians, have wrought many feats. At Cape Frio they tooke a great French ship in the night, the most of her company being on the shore, with cannoas, which they have in this coast so great, that they carry seventie and eightie men in one of them. And in Isla Grand,[2] I saw one that was above threescore foote long, of one tree, as are all that I have seen in Brasill, with provisions in them for twentie or thirtie days. At the iland of San Sebastian,[3] neere Saint Vincent, the Indians killed about eightie of Master Can-

San Sebastian.

[1] These shoals, already alluded to at page 144, are now called the Abrolhos: there is a channel betwixt the islets and the main: the soundings extend to the eastward eighty or ninety miles.

[2] Ilha Grande, on the coast, to the west of Rio de Janeiro.

[3] On the coast of Brazil, between Rio and Santos.

Sect. XXVII. dish his men, and tooke his boate, which was the overthrow of his voyage.[1]

Kill the English,

There commeth not any ship upon this coast, whereof these cannoas give not notice presently to every place. And wee were certified in Isla Grand, that they had sent an Indian from the river of Ienero,[2] through all the mountaines and marishes, to take a view of us, and accordingly made a relation of our shippes, boates, and the number of men which we might have. But to prevent the like danger that might come upon us being carelesse and negligent, I determined one night, in the darkest and quietest of it, to see what watch our company kept on the shore; manned our light horsman, and boat, armed them with bowes and targetts, and got a shore some good distance from the places where were our boothes, and sought to come upon them undiscovered: we used all our best endevours to take them at unawares, yet comming within fortie paces, we were discovered: the whole and the sicke came forth to oppose themselves against us. Which we seeing, gave them the hubbub, after the manner of the Indians, and assaulted them, and they us; but being a close darke night, they could not discerne us presently upon the hubbub.[3]

and discover us.

From our shippe the gunner shott a peece of ordinance over our heads, according to the order given him, and thereof we tooke occasion to retyre unto our boates, and within a little space came to the boothes and landing places,

[1] This was the second voyage of Thomas Cavendish, after he had been round the world. Cavendish was in the *Leicester*, and John Davis, the great Arctic Navigator, commanded the *Desire*. They sailed from Plymouth in August 1591. They attacked the towns of San Vicente and Santos and then sailed towards the Straits of Magellan. The voyage was a failure, and Cavendish died on the passage home.

[2] Rio de Janeiro.

[3] Whoop! whoop! Cotgrave gives us the meaning of *hootings* and *whoopings*: noises wherewith swine are scared, or infamous old women disgraced.

as though wee came from our shippes to ayd them. They began to recount unto us, how that at the wester poynt of the iland, out of certaine cannoas, had landed a multitude of Indians, which with a great out-cry came upon them, and assaulted them fiercely; but finding better resistance than they looked for, and seeing themselves discovered by the shippes, tooke themselves to their heeles and returned to their cannoas, in which they imbarked themselves, and departed. One affirmed, he saw the cannoas; another, their long hayre; a third, their bowes; a fourth, that it could not be, but that some of them had their payments. And it was worth the sight, to behold those which had not moved out of their beds in many moneths, unlesse by the helpe of others, gotten some a bow-shoot off into the woods, others into the toppes of trees, and those which had any strength, joyned together to fight for their lives. In fine, the boothes and tents were left desolate.[1]

Sect. XXVII.

The events of a good watch.

To colour our businesse the better, after we had spent some houres in seeking out and joyning the companie together, in comforting, animating, and commending them, I left them an extraordinary guard for that night, and so departed to our shippes, with such an opinion of the assault given by the Indians, that many so possessed, through all the voyage, would not be perswaded to the contrary. Which impression wrought such effect in most of my companie, that in all places where the Indians might annoy us, they were ever after most carefull and vigilant, as was convenient.

In these ilands it heigheth and falleth some five or six

[1] A sudden sensation, be it from fear or otherwise, has a surprising effect upon persons sick or bed-ridden. Lediard relates that in a sharp engagement with a combined squadron of French and Dutch ships, off St. Christopher, in 1667, Sir John Harman, the English commander, who had been lame and in great pain from the gout, upon discovering the enemy's fleet, got up, walked about, and gave orders as well as ever, till the fight was over, and then became as lame as before.

Sect. XXVII. foot water, and but once in two and twentie houres; as in all this coast, and in many parts of the West Indies; as also in the coast of Perew and Chely, saving where are great bayes or indraughts, and there the tydes keep their ordinary course of twice in foure and twentie houres.

Palmito iland. In the lesser of these ilands, is a cove for a small ship to ryde in, land-lockt, and shee may moore her sele to the trees of either side. This we called Palmito iland, for the aboundance it hath of the greater sort of palmito trees; the other hath none at all. A man may goe betwixt the ilands with his ship, but the better course is out at one end.

In these ilands are many scorpions, snakes, and adders, with other venomous vermine. They have parrots, and a certaine kinde of fowle like unto pheasants, somewhat bigger, and seeme to be of their nature. Here we spent above a moneth in curing of our sicke men, supplying our wants of wood and water, and in other necessary workes. And the tenth of December, all things put in order, we set sayle for Cape Frio, having onely six men sicke, with purpose there to set ashore our two prisoners before named: and anchoring under the Cape, we sent our boat a shore, but they could not finde any convenient place to land them in, and so returned.[1] The wind being southerly, and not good to goe on our voyage, we succoured our selves within Isla Grand, which lyeth some dozen or fourteene leagués from the cape, betwixt the west, and by south and west south-west; the rather to set our prisoners a shore.

Ienero. In the mid-way betwixt the Cape and this iland, lyeth the river Ienero, a very good harbour, fortified with a gar-

[1] Cape Frio has since become remarkable as the point on which H.M.S. *Thetis* was wrecked in December 1830, the night after she had left Rio Janeiro. A landing was effected, and nearly the whole crew saved. A snug cove north of the cape, with a boat entrance to the southward, was much used during the operations afterwards carried on to attempt to recover the treasure embarked in her.

rison, and a place well peopled. The Isla Grand is some eight or ten leagues long, and causeth a goodly harbour for shipping. It is full of great sandie bayes, and in the most of them is store of good water; within this iland are many other smaller ilands, which cause divers sounds and creekes; and amongst these little ilands, one, for the pleasant scituation and fertilitie thereof, called Placentia. This is peopled, all the rest desert: on this island our prisoners desired to be put a shore, and promised to send us some refreshing. Whereto we condescended, and sent them ashore, with two boates well man'd and armed, who found few inhabitants in the iland; for our people saw not above foure or five houses, notwithstanding our boats returned loaden with plantynes, pinias,[1] potatoes, sugar-canes, and some hennes. Amongst which they brought a kind of little plantyne, greene, and round, which were the best of any that I have seene.

Sect. XXVII.

Little iland.

With our people came a Portingall, who said, that the island was his; he seemed to be a Mistecho,[2] who are those that are of a Spanish and an Indian brood, poorely apparalled and miserable; we feasted him, and gave him some trifles, and he, according to his abilitie, answered our courtesie with such as he had.

The wind continuing contrary, we emptied all the water wee could come by, which we had filled in Saint James his iland, and filled our caske with the water of this Isla Grand. It is a wildernesse, covered with trees and shrubs so thicke, as it hath no passage through, except a man make it by force. And it was strange to heare the howling and cryes of wild beastes in these woods day and night, which we could not come at to see by any meanes; some like lyons, others like beares, others like hoggs, and of such and so many diversities, as was admirable.

Isla Grand.

Heere our nets profited us much; for in the sandy bayes

[1] Pine apples, *Ananassa sativa*.

[2] Mestizo.

Sect. xxvii.

Shells of mother of pearle.

they tooke us store of fish. Upon the shore, a full sea-mark, we found in many places certaine shels, like those of mother of pearles, which are brought out of the East Indies, to make standing cups, called *caracoles;* of so great curiositie as might move all the beholders to magnifie the maker of them: and were it not for the brittlenes of them, by reason of their exceeding thinnes, doubtles they were to bee esteemed farre above the others; for, more excellent workemanship I have not seene in shels.[1]

The eigteenth of December, we set sayle, the wind at north-east, and directed our course for the Straites of Magalianes. The twenty two of this moneth, at the going too of the sunne, we descryed a Portingall ship, and gave her chase, and comming within hayling of her, shee rendred her selfe without any resistance; shee was of an hundred tuns, bound for Angola, to load negroes, to be carried and sold in the river of Plate. It is a trade of great profit, and much used, for that the negroes are carried from the head of the river of Plate, to Potosi, to labour in the mynes. It is a bad negro, who is not worth there five or six hundreth peeces, every peece of tenne ryals, which they receive in ryals of plate,[2] for there is no other marchandize in those partes. Some have told me, that of late they have found out the trade and benefit of cochanilia, but the river suffereth not vessels of burthen; for if they drawe above eight or seaven foote water, they cannot goe further then the mouth of the river, and the first habitation is above a hundred and twenty leagues up, whereunto many barkes trade yearely, and carry all kinde of marchandize serving for Potosi and Paraquay; the money which is thence returned, is distributed in all the coast of Brasill.

Price of negroes.

Cassavi meale.

The loading of this ship was meale of cassavi, which the

[1] Probably a species of nautilus.

[2] The ryal of silver, of which ten went to a "piece", is in value about fivepence of our money.

Portingals call *Farina de Paw*.[1] It serveth for marchandize in Angola, for the Portingals foode in the ship, and to nourish the negroes which they should carry to the river of Plate. This meale is made of a certaine roote which the Indians call *yuca*, much like unto potatoes. Of it are two kindes: the one sweete and good to be eaten (either rosted or sodden) as potatoes, and the other of which they make their bread, called *cassavi*; deadly poyson, if the liquor or juyce bee not thoroughly pressed out. So prepared it is the bread of Brazill, and many parts of the Indies, which they make in this maner: first they pare the roote, and then upon a rough stone they grate it as small as they can, and after that it is grated small, they put it into a bag or poke, and betwixt two stones, with great waight, they presse out the juyce or poyson, and after keepe it in some bag, till it hath no juyce nor moysture left.[2] Of this they make two sorts of bread, the one finer and the other courser, but bake them after one maner. They place a great broad smooth stone upon other foure which serve in steede of a trevet, and make a quicke fire under it, and so strawe the flower or meale a foote long, and halfe a foot broad. To make it to incorporate, they sprinkle now and then a little water, and then another rowe of meale, and another sprinkling, till it be to their minde; that which is to be spent presently, they make a finger thicke, and sometimes more thicke; but that which they make for store, is not above halfe a finger thicke, but so hard, that if it fall on the ground it will not breake easily. Being newly baked, it is reasonable good, but after fewe dayes it is not to be eaten, except it be soaked in water. In some partes they suffer the meale to become fenoed,[3] before they make

Sect. XXVII.

The preparing thereof for food.

[1] *Farina do pao*—flour of wood.

[2] Cassava or manioc is of the natural order *Euphorbiaceæ*. The root abounds with a poisonous juice, but this after maceration is driven off by heat, and the fecula is obtained in an edible state. Tapioca is a preparation of cassava.

[3] *Vinewed*—mouldy.

Sect. XXVII. it into bread, and hold it for the best, saying that it giveth it a better tast; but I am not of that opinion. In other parts they mingle it with a fruite called agnanapes, which are round, and being ripe are grey, and as big as an hazell nut, and grow in a cod like pease, but that it is all curiously wrought: first they parch them upon a stone, and after beate them into powder, and then mingle them with the fine flower of cassavi, and bake them into bread, these are their spice-cakes, which they call *xauxaw*.

Agnanapes. The agnanapes are pleasant, give the bread a yellowish coulour, and an aromaticall savour in taste.[1] The finer of this bread, being well baked, keepeth long time, three or foure yeares. In Brazill, since the Portingalls taught the Indians the use of sugar, they eate this meale mingled with remels[2] of sugar, or molasses; and in this manner the Portingalls themselves feed of it.

But we found a better manner of dressing this farina, in making pancakes, and frying them with butter or oyle, and sometimes with *manteca de puerco;* when strewing a little sugar upon them, it was meate that our company desired above any that was in the shippe.

And for beverage. The Indians also accustome to make their drinke of this meale, and in three severall manners.

First in chewing it in their mouths, and after mingling it with water after a loathsome manner, yet the commonest drinke that they have; and that held best which is chewed by an old woman.

The second manner of their drinke, is baking it till it be halfe burned, then they beate it into powder; and when they will drinke, they mingle a small quantitie of it with water, which giveth a reasonable good taste.

The third, and best, is baking it, as aforesaid, and when

[1] Probably cacao (*theobroma cacao*), well known from the beverage of the same name, and from which chocolate is manufactured.

[2] In the Devonshire dialect, *remlet* means a remnant.

it is beaten into powder, to seeth it in water; after that it is well boyled, they let it stand some three or foure dayes, and then drinke it. So, it is much like the ale which is used in England, and of that colour and taste. Sect. XXVII.

The Indians are very curious in planting and manuring of this *yuca*. It is a little shrubb, and carryeth branches like hazell wands; being growne as bigge as a mans finger, they breake them off in the middest, and so pricke them into the ground: it needeth no other art or husbandry, for out of each branch grow two, three, or foure rootes, some bigger, some lesser: but first they burne and manure the ground, the which labour, and whatsoever els is requisite, the men doe not so much as helpe with a finger, but all lyeth upon their poore women, who are worse than slaves; for they labour the ground, they plant, they digge and delve, they bake, they brew, and dresse their meate, fetch their water, and doe all drudgerie whatsoever: yea, though they nurse a childe, they are not exempted from any labour; their childe they carry in a wallet about their necke, ordinarily under one arme, because it may sucke when it will. The manner of planting *yuca*. With the labour of the women.

The men have care for nothing but for their cannoas, to passe from place to place, and of their bowes and arrowes to hunt, and their armes for the warre, which is a sword of heavie blacke wood, some foure fingers broad, an inch thicke, and an ell long, something broader towards the toppe then at the handle. They call it *macana*, and it is carved and wrought with inlayd works very curiously, but his edges are blunt. If any kill any game in hunting, he bringeth it not with him, but from the next tree to the game, he breaketh a bough (for the trees in the Indies have leaves for the most part all the yeare), and all the way as he goeth streweth little peeces of it, here and there, and comming home giveth a peece to his woman, and so sends her for it.

Sect. XXVIII. If they goe to the warre, or in any journey, where it is necessary to carry provision or marchandize, the women serve to carry all, and the men never succour nor ease them; wherein they shew greater barbarisme then in any thing, in my opinion, that I have noted amongst them, except in eating one another.

Polygamy of the Indians. In Brasill, and in the West Indies, the Indian may have as many wives as he can get, either bought or given by her friends: the men and women, for the most part, goe Their attire. naked, and those which have come to know their shame, cover onely their privie parts with a peece of cloth, the rest of their body is naked. Their houses resemble great barnes, covered over or thatched with plantyne leaves, which reach to the ground, and at either end is the doore.

Their manner of housing. In one house are sometimes ten or twentie households: they have little household stuffe, besides their beds, which they call *hamacas*,[1] and are made of cotton, and stayned with divers colours and workes. Some I have seene white, of great curiositie. They are as a sheete laced at both ends, and at either end of them long strappes, with which they fasten them to two posts, as high as a mans middle, and so sit rocking themselves in them. Sometimes they And sleeping. use them for seates, and sometimes to sleepe in at their pleasures. In one of them I have seene sleepe the man, his wife, and a childe.

SECTION XXVIII.

We tooke out of this prize, for our provision, some good quantitie of this meale, and the sugar shee had, being not

[1] The hammock now in general use at sea, takes its name from this term.

above three or four chestes: after three dayes we gave the ship to the Portingalls, and to them libertie. In her was a Portingall knight, which went for governour of Angola, of the habit of Christ, with fiftie souldiers, and armes for a hundreth and fiftie, with his wife and daughter. He was old, and complained that after many yeares service for his king, with sundry mishapps, he was brought to that poore estate, as for the relief of his wife, his daughter and himselfe, he had no other substance, but that he had in the ship. It moved compassion, so as nothing of his was diminished, which though to us was of no great moment, in Angola it was worth good crownes. Onely we disarmed them all, and let them depart, saying that they would returne to St. Vincents. Sect. xxix.

We continued our course for the Straites, my people much animated with this unlookt for refreshing, and praised God for his bounty, providence, and grace extended towards us. Here it will not be out of the way to speake a word of the particularities of the countrie.

SECTION XXIX.

Brasill is accounted to be that part of America which lyeth towards our north sea, betwixt the river of the Amazons, neere the lyne to the northwards, untill a man come to the river of Plate in thirty-six degrees to the southwards of the lyne. The description of Brasill.

This coast generally lyeth next of any thing south and by west; it is a temperate countrie, though in some parts it exceedeth in heat; it is full of good succors for shipping, and plentifull for rivers and fresh waters; the principal habitations are, Farnambuca,[1] the Bay De todos los Santos,[2] Its havens.

[1] Pernambuco.

[2] Bahia.

Sect. xxix. Nostra Senora de Victoria, alias Santos,[1] the river Ienero,[2] Saint Vincents, and Placentia; every of them provided of a good port. The winds are variable, but for the most part trade[3] along the coast.

Its commodities. The commodities this country yeeldeth, are the wood called Brasill,[4] whereof the best is that of Farnambuc (so also called, being used in most rich colours); good cotton-wooll, great store of sugar, balsamon, and liquid amber.

Its wants. They have want of all maner of cloth, lynnen, and woollen, of iron, and edge-tools, of copper, and principally in some places, of wax, of wine, of oyle, and meale (for the country beareth no corn), and of all maner of haberdashery-wares, for the Indians.

The bestiall thereof. The beasts that naturally breed in this country are tygers, lyons, hoggs, dogges, deere, monkeyes, mycos, and conies (like unto ratts, but bigger, and of a tawney colour), armadilloes, alagartoes, and store of venemous wormes and serpents, as scorpions, adders, which they call vinoras; and of them, one kind, which the divine Providence hath created with a bell upon his head, that wheresoever he goeth, the sound of it might be heard, and so the serpent shunned; for his stinging is without remedie. This they call the vynora with the bell; of them there are many, and great stores of snakes, them of that greatnesse, as to write the truth, might seeme fabulous.

The discommodities. Another worm there is in this country, which killed many of the first inhabitants, before God was pleased to

[1] Victoria. [2] Rio de Janeiro.

[3] Blow steadily—in one direction.

[4] Before the discovery of America, dye woods were known by this denomination; and Brazil owes its name to the quantity of wood of this nature found among its forests. See a very full discussion of the origin of the name Brazil, both for the dye wood and for the country, in a foot note at page 22 of the *Narrative of a Voyage to the West Indies and Mexico by Samuel Champlain*, edited by Alice Wilmere for the Hakluyt Society in 1859.

discover a remedie for it, unto a religious person; it is like a magot, but more slender, and longer, and of a greene colour, with a red head; this worme creepeth in at the hinder parts, where is the evacuation of our superfluities, and there, as it were, gleweth himselfe to the gutt, there feedeth of the bloud and humors, and becommeth so great, that stopping the naturall passage, he forceth the princi-pall wheele of the clocke of our bodie to stand still, and with it the accompt of the houres of life to take end, with most cruell torment and paine, which is such, that he who hath beene throughly punished with the collique can quickly decipher or demonstrate. The antidote for this pernicious worme is garlique; and this was discovered by a physitian to a religious person.

Sect. xxx.

SECTION XXX.

Betwixt twenty-six and twenty-seven degrees neere the coast lyeth an iland; the Portingalls call it Santa Catalina, which is a reasonable harbour, and hath good refreshing of wood, water, and fruit. It is desolate, and serveth for those who trade from Brasill to the river of Plate, or from the river to Brasill, as an inne, or bayting place.[1] Santa Catalina.

In our navigation towards the Straites, by our observa-tion wee found that our compass varyed a poynt and better to the eastwards. And for that divers have written curiously and largely of the variation thereof, I referre them that desire the understanding of it, to the *Discourse* of Master William Aborrawh,[2] and others; for it is a secret, Variation of the compasse.

[1] Saint Catherine's now ranks as a port after Rio Janeiro and Bahia.

[2] A misprint for Borough. Mr. Borough, Comptroller of the Navy, found the variation of the compass at Limehouse to be 11° 19′ E. in 1580. He published a discourse on the variation of the compass (Lon-

Sect. xxx. whose causes well understood are of greatest moment in all navigations.

In the height of the river of Plate, we being some fiftie leagues off the coast, a storme took us southerly, which endured fortie-eight houres.[1] In the first day, about the going downe of the sunne, Robert Tharlton, master of the *Fancie*, bare up before the wind, without giving us any token or signe that shee was in distresse. We seeing her to continue her course, bare up after her, and the night comming on, we carried our light; but shee never answered us; for they kept their course directly for England, which was the overthrow of the voyage, as well for that we had no pynace to goe before us, to discover any danger, to seeke out roades and anchoring, to helpe our watering and refreshing; as also for the victuals, necessaries, and men which they carryed away with them: which though they were not many, yet with their helpe in our fight, we had taken the Vice-Admirall, the first time she bourded with us, as shall be hereafter manifested. For once we cleered her decke, and had wee beene able to have spared but a dozen men, doubtlesse wee had done with her what we would; for shee had no close fights.[2]

The overthrow of the voyage.

don, 1581). But the first observer of the variation in London was Robert Norman, the Hydrographer, who made it 11° 15′ E. He published *A Newe Attractive contaigninge a Shorte Discourse of the Magnet or Loadestone, whereunto are anexed other Necessarie Rules for the Arte of Navigation, by Robert Norman, Hydrographer* (1581, Richard Ballard, London). Norman also discovered the dip or inclination of the needle in 1576. In 1657 there was no variation in London. In 1723 it was 14° 17′ W. In 1815 it was 24° 27′ W. The compasses constructed on Mr. Norman's pattern, were sold by Dr. Hood near the Minories, the author of *A Regiment of the Sea* (1596). The twenty-third chapter is devoted to the subject of the variation of the compass.

[1] Sudden squalls are generated on the Pampas or plains lying round Buenos Ayres, called thence Pamperos; which do great damage. See the account of one in the Voyages of the *Adventure* and *Beagle*.

[2] Probably barricades to retire behind in case of being boarded. The

Moreover, if shee had beene with me, I had not beene discovered upon the coast of Perew. But I was worthy to be deceived, that trusted my ship in the hands of an hypocrite, and a man which had left his generall before in the like occasion, and in the selfe-same place; for being with Master Thomas Candish, master of a small ship in the voyage wherein he dyed, this captaine being aboord the Admirall, in the night time forsooke his fleet, his generall and captaine, and returned home.

Sect. xxx.

The cause.

Infidelitie.

This bad custome is too much used amongst sea-men, and worthy to be severely punished; for doubtless the not punishing of those offenders hath beene the prime cause of many lamentable events, losses, and overthrowes, to the dishonour of our nation, and frustrating of many good and honourable enterprises.

In this poynt of discipline, the Spaniards doe farre surpasse us; for whosoever forsaketh his fleete, or commander, is not onely severely punished, but deprived also of all charge or government for ever after. This in our countrie is many times neglected; for that there is none to follow the cause, the principalls being either dead with griefe, or drowned in the gulfe of povertie, and so not able to wade through with the burthen of that suite, which in Spaine is prosecuted by the kings atturney, or fiscall; or at least, a judge appoynted for determining that cause purposely.

Discipline of the Spanish.

Yea, I cannot attribute the good successe the Spaniard hath had in his voyages and peoplings, to any extraordinary vertue more in him then in any other man, were not discipline, patience, and justice far superior. For in valour, experience, and travell, he surpasseth us not; in shipping, preparation, and plentie of vituals, hee commeth not neere us; in paying and rewarding our people, no nation did goe beyond us: but God, who is a just and bountifull rewarder,

The only cause of their prosperities.

piratical prahus of the Indian Archipelago are fitted with a similar defence.

Sect. xxx. regarding obedience farre above sacrifice, doubtlesse, in recompence of their indurance, resolution, and subjection to commandment, bestoweth upon them the blessing due unto it. And this, not for that the Spaniard is of a more tractable disposition, or more docible nature than wee, but that justice halteth with us, and so the old proverbe is verified, *Pittie marreth the whole cittie.*

Thus come we to be deprived of the sweet fruit, which the rod of discipline bringeth with it, represented unto us in auncient verses, which as a relique of experience I have heard in my youth recorded by a wise man, and a great captaine, thus:

The rod by power divine, and earthly regall law,
Makes good men live in peace, and bad to stand in awe:
For with a severe stroke the bad corrected be,
Which makes the good to joy such justice for to see;
The rod of discipline breeds feare in every part,
Reward by due desert doth joy and glad the heart.

The cunning of runnawayes.

These absentings and escapes are made most times onely to pilfer and steale, as well by taking of some prise when they are alone, and without commaund, to hinder or order their bad proceedings, as to appropriate that which is in their trusted ship; casting the fault, if they be called to account, upon some poore and unknowne mariners, whom they suffer with a little pillage to absent themselves, the cunninglier to colour their greatest disorders and robberies.

And ignoble captaines.

For doubtlesse, if he would, hee might have come unto us with great facilitie; because within sixteen houres the storme ceased, and the winde became fayre, which brought us to the Straites, and dured many days after with us at north-east. This was good for them, though naught for us: if he had perished any mast or yard, sprung any leake, wanted victuals, or instruments for finding us, or had had any other impediment of importance, hee might have had some colour to cloake his lewdnes:[1] but his masts and yards being sound, his shippe staunch and loaden with victuales for two yeares at the least, and having order from place to place, where to find us, his intention is easily seene to bee bad, and his fault such, as worthily deserved to bee made exemplary unto others. Which he manifested at his returne, by his manner of proceeding, making a spoyle of the prise hee tooke in the way homewards, as also of that which was in the ship, putting it into a port fit for his purpose, where he might have time and commodity to doe what hee would.

Sect. xxx.

Verified at their returne.

Wee made account that they had beene swallowed up of the sea, for we never suspected that anything could make them forsake us; so, we much lamented them. The storme ceasing, and being out of all hope, we set sayle and went on our course. During this storme, certaine great fowles, as big as swannes, soared about us, and the winde calming, setled themselves in the sea, and fed upon the sweepings of our ship; which I perceiving, and desirous to see of them, because they seemed farre greater then in truth they were, I caused a hooke and lyne to be brought me; and with a peece of a pilchard I bayted the hook, and a foot from it, tyed a peece of corke, that it might not sinke deepe, and threw it into the sea, which, our ship driving with the sea, in a little time was a good space from us, and one of the fowles being hungry, presently seized upon it, and the hooke in his upper beake. It is like to a faulcons bill, but that the poynt is more crooked, in that maner, as by no meanes he could cleare himselfe, except that the lyne brake, or the hooke righted: plucking him towards the ship, with the waving of his wings he eased the waight of his body; and being brought to the sterne of our ship, two of our company went downe by the ladder of the poope, and seized

Birds like swans.

Caught with line and hooke.

[1] Misbehaviour. Tooke derives *lewd* from the Anglo-Saxon *læwan*—to delude or mislead.

Sect. xxx.

on his necke and wings; but such were the blowes he gave them with his pinnions, as both left their hand-fast, being beaten blacke and blewe; we cast a snare about his necke, and so tryced him into the ship.

Prove good refreshment.

By the same manner of fishing, we caught so many of them, as refreshed and recreated all my people for that day. Their bodies were great, but of little flesh and tender; in taste answerable to the food whereon they feed.[1]

They were of two colours, some white, some grey; they had three joynts in each wing; and from the poynt of one wing to the poynt of the other, both stretched out, was about two fathomes.

Care of the Pentagones.

The wind continued good with us, till we came to forty-nine degrees and thirty minutes, where it tooke us westerly, being, as we made our accompt, some fiftie degrees from the shore. Betwixt forty-nine and forty-eight degrees, is Port Saint Julian, a good harbour, and in which a man may grave his ship, though shee draw fifteene or sixteene foote water: but care is to be had of the people called Pentagones.[2] They are treacherous, and of great stature, so the most give them the name of gyants.[3]

The second of February, about nine of the clocke in the morning, we discryed land, which bare south-west of us, which wee looked not for so timely; and comming neerer and neerer unto it, by the lying, wee could not conjecture what land it should be; for we were next of anything in forty-eight degrees, and no platt nor sea-card which we had made mention of any land which lay in that manner, neere about that height; in fine, wee brought our lar-borde tacke aboord, and stood to the north-east-wardes all that day and

[1] This fowl was doubtless the albatross (Diomedea), which seems to be a corruption of the Portuguese word *alcatraz*. The practice of fishing for them still continues, though more for recreation than for refreshment.

[2] Patagonians.

[3] Magalhaens reported them as giants; and Fitzroy states them to average nearly six feet.

Sect. xxx.

night, and the winde continuing westerly and a fayre gale, wee continued our course alongst the coast the day and night following. In which time wee made accompt we discoverd well neere threescore leagues of the coast. It is bold, and made small shew of dangers.

A description of the unknowne land.

The land is a goodly champion country, and peopled: we saw many fires, but could not come to speake with the people; for the time of the yeare was farre spent, to shoot the Straites, and the want of our pynace disabled us for finding a port or roade; not being discretion with a ship of charge, and in an unknowne coast, to come neere the shore before it was sounded; which were causes, together with the change of winde (good for us to passe the Straite), that hindered the further discovery of this land, with its secrets: this I have sorrowed for many times since, for that it had likelihood to be an excellent country. It hath great rivers of fresh waters; for the out-shoot of them colours the sea in many places, as we ran alongst it. It is not mountaynous, but much of the disposition of England, and as temperate. The things we noted principally on the coast, are these following; the westermost poynt of the land, with which we first fell, is the end of the land to the west-wardes, as we found afterwards. If a man bring this poynt south-west, it riseth in three mounts, or round hillockes: bringing it more westerly, they shoot themselves all into one; and bringing it easterly, it riseth in two hillocks. This we call poynt Tremountaine. Some twelve or foureteene leagues from this poynt to the east-wardes, fayre by the shore, lyeth a low flat iland of some two leagues long; we named it Fayre Iland; for it was all over as greene and smooth as any meddow in the spring of the yeare.

A caveat for comming suddenly too neere an unknowne land.

Poynt Tremountaine.

Fayre Iland.

Some three or four leagues easterly from this iland, is a goodly opening, as of a great river, or an arme of the sea, with a goodlie low countrie adjacent. And eight or

Sect. xxx.

tenne leagues from this opening, some three leagues from the shore, lyeth a bigge rocke, which at the first wee had thought to be a shippe under all her sayles: but after, as we came neere, it discovered it selfe to be a rocke, which we called *Condite-head;* for that howsoever a man commeth with it, it is like to the condite heads about the cittie of London.

Condite head.

All this coast, so farre as wee discovered, lyeth next of any thing east and by north, and west and by south. The land, for that it was discovered in the raigne of Queene Elizabeth, my soveraigne lady and mistres, and a maiden Queene, and at my cost and adventure, in a perpetuall memory of her chastitie, and remembrance of my endeavours, I gave it the name of HAWKINS *maiden-land.*[1]

Hawkins maiden-land.

Before a man fall with this land, some twentie or thirtie leagues, he shall meete with bedds of oreweed, driving to and fro in that sea, with white flowers growing upon them, and sometimes farther off; which is a good show and signe the land is neere, whereof the westermost part lyeth some threescore leagues from the neerest land of America.

Bedds of oreweed with white flowers.

With our fayre and large wind, we shaped our course for the Straites; and the tenth of February we had sight of land, and it was the head land of the Straites to the north-wards, which agreed with our height, wherein we found our selves to be, which was in fifty-two degrees and fortie minutes.

Our comming to the Straites.

Within a few houres we had the mouth of the Straites open, which lyeth in fifty-two degrees, and fifty minutes. It riseth like the North Foreland in Kent,

[1] It is generally supposed that this land was the Falkland Islands; but as they lie betwixt 51° and 53°, this cannot be reconciled with being "next of anything in 48°". In this parallel, the main land projects to the eastward; and this perhaps was the land he descried. The rock like a sail might be the Bellaco rock.

The Falkland Islands were really discovered by Captain John Davis in 1591.

Sect. xxx.

and is much like the land of Margates. It is not good to borrow neere the shore, but to give it a fayre birth; within a few houres we entred the mouth of the Straites, which is some six leagues broad, and lyeth in fifty-two degrees, and fifty minutes: doubling the poynt on the star-board, which is also flat, of a good birth, we opened a fayre bay, in which we might discry the hull of a ship beaten upon the beach. It was of the Spanish fleete, that went to inhabite there, in anno 1582, under the charge of Pedro Sarmiento,[1] who at his returne was taken prisoner, and brought into England.

Pedro Sarmiento buildeth San-Philip.

In this bay the Spaniards made their principall habitation, and called it the cittie of Saint Philip, and left it peopled; but the cold barrennes of the countrie, and the malice of the Indians, with whom they badly agreed, made speedie end of them, as also of those whom they left in the middle of the Straites, three leagues from Cape Froward[2] to the east-wards, in another habitation.

We continued our course alongst this reach (for all the Straites is as a river altering his course, sometimes upon one poynt, sometimes upon another) which is some eight leagues long, and lyeth west north-west. From this we

[1] The expedition of Drake having excited considerable alarm in Peru, the viceroy despatched Don Pedro Sarmiento with orders to take him dead or alive. Proceeding to the Strait of Magellan in pursuit, he complied with the portion of his instructions which directed him to make a careful survey. On his arrival in Spain he pointed out to the King of Spain, Philip II, the importance of fortifying the Straits, to prevent the passage of strangers. Accordingly an expedition was fitted out, which, after some accidents, founded the two settlements of Jesus and San Felipe. The site of the last is now known as Port Famine: so named from the disasters which befell the unhappy colonists, who perished from want. Sarmiento himself having been blown off the coast, appears to have used every effort to obtain and forward supplies from Brazil to his friends, but, proceeding to Europe for further assistance, he was captured and taken to England.

[2] Cape Froward is the southern extremity of South America, in 53° 53′ 43″ S., and in the middle of Magellan Strait.

Sect. xxx. entred into a goodly bay, which runneth up into the land northerly many leagues; and at first entrance a man may see no other thing, but as it were a maine sea. From the end of this first reach, you must direct your course west south-west, and some fourteene or fifteene leagues lyeth one of the narrowest places of all the Straites; this leadeth unto another reach, that lyeth west and by north some six leagues.

Here, in the middle of the reach, the winde tooke us by the north-west, and so we were forced to anchor some two or three dayes. In which time, we went a shore with our boates, and found neere the middle of this reach, on the star-boord side, a reasonable good place to ground and trimme a small ship, where it higheth some nine or ten foote water. Here we saw certaine hogges, but they were so farre from us, that wee could not discerne if they were of those of the countrie, or brought by the Spaniards; these were all the beasts which we saw in all the time we were in the Straites.

In two tydes we turned through this reach, and so recovered the ilands of Pengwins; they lie from this reach foure leagues southwest and by west. Till you come to this place, care is to be taken of not comming too neere to any poynt of the land; for being, for the most part, sandie, they have sholding off them, and are somewhat dangerous. These ilands have beene set forth by some to be three; we could discover but two: and they are no more, except that part of the mayne, which lyeth over against them, be an iland, which carrieth little likelihood, and I cannot determine it. A man may sayle betwixt the two ilands, or betwixt them and the land on the larboord side; from which land to the bigger iland, as it were, a bridge or ledge, on which is foure or five fathome water; and to him that commeth neere it, not knowing thereof, may justly cause

Note.

The ilands of Pengwins.

feare: for it showeth to be shold water with his rypling, like unto a race.[1] Sect. xxx.

Betwixt the former reach, and these ilands, runneth up a goodly bay into the country to the north-wards. It causeth a great indraught, and above these ilands runneth a great tide from the mouth of the Straites to these ilands; the land on the larboord side is low land and sandy, for the most part, and without doubt, ilands, for it hath many openings into the sea, and forcible indraughts by them, and that on the starboord side, is all high mountaynous land from end to end; but no wood on eyther side. Before wee passed these ilands, under the lee of the bigger iland, we anchored, the wind being at north-east, with intent to refresh ourselves with the fowles of these ilands. They are of divers sorts, and in great plentie, as pengwins, wilde duckes, gulles, and gannets; of the principall we purposed to make provisions, and those were the pengwins; which in Welsh, as I have beene enformed, signifieth a white head. From which derivation, and many other Welsh denominations given by the Indians, or their predecessors, some doe inferre that America was first peopled with Welsh-men; and Motezanna,[2] king, or rather emperour of Mexico, did recount unto the Spaniards, at their first comming, that his auncestors came from a farre countrie, and were white people. Which, conferred with an auncient cronicle, that I have read many yeares since, may be conjectured to bee a prince of Wales, who many hundredth yeares since, with certain shippes, sayled to the westwards, with intent to make new discoveries. Hee was never after heard of.[3]

Good provision in the Straites.

[1] The tides run with great velocity in some parts of the Straits. The rippling might justly cause fear, ignorant as the parties were of the extent of the rise and fall of tide. Fitz Roy relates that an American captain hardly recovered being told that it amounted to six or seven fathoms.

[2] Montezuma.

[3] The story of Madoc is told by Southey, and much curious lore connected with it may be gathered from the foot-notes to his poem.

Sect. xxx.

The description of the pengwin.

The pengwin is in all proportion like unto a goose, and hath no feathers, but a certaine doune upon all parts of his body, and therefore cannot fly, but avayleth himselfe in all occasions with his feete, running as fast as most men. He liveth in the sea, and on the land; feedeth on fish in the sea, and as a goose on the shore upon grasse. They harbour themselves under the ground in burrowes, as the connies, and in them hatch their young. All parts of the iland where they haunted were undermined, save onely one valley, which it seemeth they reserved for their foode; for it was as greene as any medowe in the moneth of Aprill, with a most fine short grasse. The flesh of these pengwins is much of the savour of a certaine fowle taken in the ilands of Lundey and Silley, which wee call puffins: by the tast it is easily discerned that they feede on fish. They are very fatt, and in dressing must be flead[1] as the bytern; they are reasonable meate, rosted, baked, or sodden, but best rosted. We salted some dozen or sixteen hogsheads, which served us, whilest they lasted, in steede of powdred beefe.

Hunting the pengwin.

The hunting of them, as we may well terme it, was a great recreation to my company, and worth the sight, for in determining to catch them, necessarily was required good store of people, every one with a cudgell in his hand, to compasse them round about, to bring them, as it were, into a ring; if they chanced to break out, then was the sport; for the ground being undermined, at unawares it fayled, and as they ran after them, one fell here, another there; another, offering to strike at one, lifting up his hand, sunke upp to the arme-pits in the earth; another, leaping to avoyd one hole, fell into another. And after the first slaughter, in seeing us on the shore, they shunned us, and procured to recover the sea; yea, many times seeing

[1] Birds which are strong-flavoured are rendered edible by stripping off their skin.

themselves persecuted, they would tumble downe from such high rocks and mountaines, as it seemed impossible to escape with life. Yet as soone as they came to the beach, presently wee should see them runne into the sea, as though they had no hurt. Where one goeth, the other followeth, like sheepe after the bel-wether: but in getting them once within the ring, close together, few escaped, save such as by chance hid themselves in the borrowes; and ordinarily there was no drove which yeeldeth us not a thousand or more: the manner of killing them which the hunters used, being in a cluster together, was with their cudgels to knocke them on the head; for though a man gave them many blowes on the body, they died not; besides, the flesh bruised is not good to keepe. The massaker ended, presently they cut off their heads, that they might bleed well: such as wee determined to keepe for store, wee saved in this maner. First, we split them, and then washed them well in sea water, then salted them; having layne some sixe howres in salt, wee put them in presse eight howres, and the blood being soaked out, we salted them againe in our other caske, as is the custome to salte beefe; after this maner they continued good some two moneths, and served us in stead of beefe.

Sect. xxx.

The keeping for store.

The gulls and gannets were not in so great quantitie, yet we wanted not young gulles to eate all the time of our stay about these ilands. It was one of the delicatest foodes that I have eaten in all my life.

The gulls.

The ducks are different to ours, and nothing so good meate; yet they may serve for necessitie. They were many, and had a part of the iland to themselves severall, which was the highest hill, and more than a musket shot over.

Ducks.

In all the dayes of my life, I have not seene greater art and curiositie in creatures voyd of reason, then in the placing and making of their nestes; all the hill being so

Sect. xxxi. full of them, that the greatest mathematician of the world could not devise how to place one more then there was upon the hill, leaving onely one path-way for a fowle to passe betwixt.

The hill was all levell, as if it had beene smoothed by art; the nestes made onely of earth, and seeming to be of the selfe same mould; for the nests and the soyle is all one, which, with water that they bring in their beakes, they make into clay, or a certaine daube, and after fashion them round, as with a compasse. In the bottome they containe the measure of a foote; in the height about eight inches; and in the toppe, the same quantitie over; there they are hollowed in, somewhat deepe, wherein they lay their eggs, without other prevention. And I am of opinion that the sunne helpeth them to hatch their young: their nests are for many yeares, and of one proportion, not one exceeding another in bignesse, in height, nor circumference: and in proportionable distance one from another. In all this hill, nor in any of their nestes, was to be found a blade of grasse, a straw, a sticke, a feather, a moate, no, nor the filing of any fowle, but all the nestes and passages betwixt them, were so smooth and cleane, as if they had beene newly swept and washed.

All of which are motives to prayse and magnifie the universall Creator, who so wonderfully manifesteth his wisedome, bountie, and providence in all his creatures, and especially for his particular love to ingratefull mankinde, for whose contemplation and service he hath made them all.

SECTION XXXI.

Of seales, or sea-wolves. One day, having ended our hunting of pengwins, one of our mariners walking about the iland, discovered a great company of seales, or sea-wolves (so called for that they are in the sea, as the wolves on the land), advising us that he left them sleeping, with their bellies tosting against the sunne. Wee provided ourselves with staves, and other weapons, and sought to steale upon them at unawares, to surprise some of them; and comming down the side of a hill, wee were not discovered till we were close upon them: notwithstanding, their sentinell, before we could approach, with a great howle waked them: wee got betwixt the sea and some of them, but they shunned us not; for they came directly upon us; and though we dealt here and there a blow, yet not a man that withstood them, escaped the overthrow. They reckon not of a musket shott, a sword peirceth not their skinne, and to give a blow with a staffe, is as to smite upon a stone: onely in giving the blow upon his snowt, presently he falleth downe dead. Sect. XXXI.

After they had recovered the water, they did, as it were, scorne us, defie us, and daunced before us, untill we had shot some musket shott through them, and so they appeared no more.

This fish is like unto a calfe, with four leggs, but not above a spanne long: his skinne is hayrie like a calfe; but these were different to all that ever I have seene, yet I have seene of them in many parts; for these were greater, and in their former parts like unto lyons, with shagge hayre, and mostaches.

They live in the sea, and come to sleepe on the land, and they ever have one that watcheth, who adviseth them of any accident.

They are beneficiall to man in their skinnes for many purposes; in their mostaches for pick-tooths, and in their fatt to make traine-oyle. This may suffice for the seale, for that he is well knowne.

SECTION XXXII.

Sect. xxxii.

Devises in sudden accidents.

One day, our boates being loaden with pengwins, and comming aboord, a sudden storme tooke them, which together with the fury of the tyde, put them in such great danger, that although they threw all their loading into the sea, yet were they forced to goe before the wind and sea, to save their lives. Which we seeing, and considering that our welfare depended upon their safetie, being impossible to weigh our anchor, fastned an emptie barrell well pitched to the end of our cable, in stead of a boy, and letting it slip, set sayle to succour our boates, which in short space wee recovered, and after returned to the place where we ryd before.

The storme ceasing, we used our diligence by all meanes to seeke our cable and anchor; but the tyde being forcible, and the weeds (as in many parts of the Straites), so long, that riding in fourteene fathome water, many times they streamed three and four fathomes upon the ryme of the water; these did so inrole our cable, that we could never set eye of our boy; and to sweepe for him was but lost labour, because of the weeds, which put us out of hope to recover it.[1]

And so our forcible businesse being ended, leaving instructions for the *Fancie* our pynace, according to appointment, where to find us, we inroled them in many folds of paper, put them into a barrell of an old musket, and stopped it in such a manner as no wett could enter; then placing it an end upon one of the highest hills, and the most frequented of all the iland, wee imbarked our selves, and set sayle with the wind at north-west, which could serve us but

[1] *Fucus giganteus.*—In the voyage of the *Adventure* and *Beagle* it was found firmly rooted in twenty fathome, yet streaming fifty feet upon the surface.

to the end of that reach, some dozen leagues long, and some three or four leagues broad. It lyeth next of any thing, till you come to Cape Agreda, south-west; from this Cape to Cape Froward, the coast lyeth west south-west. Sect. XXXII.

Some foure leagues betwixt them, was the second peopling of the Spaniards: and this Cape lyeth in fiftie five degrees and better. The second peopling of the Spaniards.

Thwart Cape Froward, the wind larged with us, and we continued our course towards the iland of Elizabeth; which lyeth from Cape Froward some foureteene leagues west and by south. This reach is foure or five leagues broad, and in it are many channells or openings into the sea; for all the land on the souther part of the Straites are ilands and broken land; and from the beginning of this reach to the end of the Straites, high mountaynous land on both sides, in most parts covered with snow all the yeare long.

Betwixt the iland Elizabeth and the mayne, is the narrowest passage of all the Straites; it may be some two musket shott from side to side.[1] From this straite to Elizabeth bay is some four leagues, and the course lyeth north-west and by west. Elizabeth bay.

This bay is all sandie and cleane ground on the easter part; but before you come at it, there lyeth a poynt of the shore a good byrth off, which is dangerous. And in this reach, as in many parts of the Straites, runneth a quick and forcible tyde. In the bay it higheth eight or nine foote water. The norther part of the bay hath foule ground, and rockes under water: and therefore it is not wholesome borrowing of the mayne. One of master Thomas Candish his pynaces, as I have been enformed, came a-ground upon one of them, and he was in hazard to have left her there.

From Elizabeth bay to the river of Ieronimo, is some five leagues. The course lyeth west and by north, and west. The river of Ieronimo.

[1] The narrowest part is in Crooked Reach, a little to the westward of St. Jerome point: here the strait is about one mile across.

Sect. xxxii. Here the wind scanted, and forced us to seek a place to anchor in. Our boates going alongst the shore, found a reasonable harbour, which is right against that which they call river Ieronimo; but it is another channell, by which a man may disemboake the straite, as by the other which is accustomed; for with a storme, which took us one night, suddenly we were forced into that opening unwittingly; but in the morning, seeing our error, and the wind larging, with two or three bourds wee turned out into the old channell, not daring for want of our pynace to attempt any new discoverie.[1]

Blanches bay.

This harbour we called Blanches bay: for that it was found by William Blanch, one of our masters mates. Here having moored our shippe, we began to make our provision of wood and water, whereof was plentie in this bay, and in all other places from Pengwin ilands, till within a dozen leagues of the mouth of the Straites.

Now finding our deckes open, with the long lying under the lyne and on the coast of Brasill, the sunne having beene in our zenith many times, we calked our ship within bourd and without, above the decks. And such was the diligence we used, that at foure dayes end, we had above threescore pipes of water, and twentie boats of wood stowed in our ship; no man was idle, nor otherwise busied but in necessary workes: some in felling and cleaving of wood: some in carrying of water; some in romaging; some in washing; others in baking; one in heating of pitch; another in gathering of mussells; no man was exempted, but knew at evening whereunto he was to betake himselfe the morning following.

Objection of waste.

Some man might aske me how we came to have so many emptie caske in less then two moneths; for it seemeth

[1] This was probably the opening into Otway water, leading to Skyring water, but not disemboguing into the Pacific.

much that so few men in such short time, and in so long a voyage, should waste so much? Sect. XXXII.

Whereto I answere, that it came not of excessive expence; for in health we never exceeded our ordinary; but of a mischance which befell us unknowne in the iland of Saint James, or Saint Anne, in the coast of Brasill, where we refreshed our selves, and according to the custome layd our caske a shore, to trimme it, and after to fill it, the place being commodious for us. But with the water a certaine worm, called *broma* by the Spaniard, and by us *arters*, entred also, which eat it so full of holes that all the water soaked out, and made much of our caske of small use. This we remedied the best wee could, and discovered it long before we came to this place. Answere.

Hereof let others take warning, in no place to have caske on the shore where it may be avoyded; for it is one of the provisions which are with greatest care to be preserved in long voyages, and hardest to be supplyed. These *arters* or *broma*, in all hott countries, enter into the plankes of shippes, and especially where are rivers of fresh water; for the common opinion is that they are bred in fresh water, and with the current of the rivers are brought into the sea; but experience teacheth that they breed in the great seas in all hott clymates, especially neere the equinoctiall lyne; for lying so long under and neere the lyne, and towing a shalop at our sterne, comming to clense her in Brasill, we found her all under water covered with these wormes, as bigge as the little finger of a man, on the outside of the planke, not fully covered, but halfe the thicknesse of their bodie, like to a gelly, wrought into the planke as with a gowdge. And naturall reason, in my judgement, confirmeth this; for creatures bred and nourished in the sea, comming into fresh water die; as those actually bred in ponds or fresh rivers, die presently, if they come into salt water. Warning against wormes.

Sect. XXXII.

But some man may say, this fayleth in some fishes and beasts. Which I must confesse to be true; but these eyther are part terrestryall, and part aquatile, as the mare-maide, sea-horse, and other of that kind, or have their breeding in the fresh, and growth or continuall nourishment in the salt water, as the salmond, and others of that kinde.

Sheathing of shippes.

In little time, if the shippe be not sheathed, they put all in hazard; for they enter in no bigger then a small Spanish needle, and by little and little their holes become ordinarily greater then a mans finger. The thicker the planke is, the greater he groweth; yea, I have seene many shippes so eaten, that the most of their plankes under water have beene like honey combes, and especially those betwixt wind and water. If they had not been sheathed, it had bin impossible that they could have swomme. The entring of them is hardly to be discerned, the most of them being small as the head of a pinne.[1] Which, all such as purpose long voyages, are to prevent by sheathing their shippes.

And for that I have seene divers manners of sheathing, for the ignorant I will set them downe which by experience I have found best.

In Spaine and Portingall.

In Spaine and Portingall, some sheathe their shippes with lead; which, besides the cost and waight, although they use the thinnest sheet-lead that I have seene in any place, yet it is nothing durable, but subject to many casualties.

With double plankes.

Another manner is used with double plankes, as thicke without as within, after the manner of furring: which is little better then that with lead; for, besides his waight,

[1] The *teredo navalis* is very destructive. Nothing but metal is proof against its ravages. It is not clear what may be its purpose in boring into any wood that comes in its way, for it is thought not to be nourished by what it destroys.

it dureth little, because the worme in small time passeth through the one and the other. Sect. XXXII.

A third manner of sheathing hath beene used amongst some with fine canvas; which is of small continuance, and so not to be regarded. With canvas.

The fourth prevention, which now is most accompted of, is to burne the utter planke till it come to be in every place like a cole, and after to pitch it; this is not bad. With burnt plankes.

In China, as I have been enformed, they use a certaine betane or varnish, in manner of an artificiall pitch, wherewith they trim the outside of their shippes. It is said to be durable, and of that vertue, as neither worme nor water peirceth it; neither hath the sunne power against it. In China with varnish.

Some have devised a certaine pitch, mingled with glasse and other ingredients, beaten into powder, with which if the shippe be pitched, it is said, the worme that toucheth it dyeth; but I have not heard that it hath beene useful.

But the most approved of all, is the manner of sheathing used now adayes in England, with thin bourds, halfe inche thicke; the thinner the better; and elme better than oake; for it ryveth not, it indureth better under water, and yeeldeth better to the shippes side. In England.

The invention of the materialles incorporated betwixt the planke and the sheathing, is that indeed which avayleth; for without it many plankes were not sufficient to hinder the entrance of this worme; this manner is thus:

Before the sheathing board is nayled on, upon the inner side of it they smere it over with tarre halfe a finger thicke and upon the tarre another halfe finger thicke of hayre, such as the whitelymers use, and so nayle it on, the nayles not above a spanne distance one from another; the thicker they are driven, the better. Best manner of sheathing.

Some hold opinion that the tarre killeth the worme; others, that the worme passing the sheathing, and seeking a way through, the hayre and the tarre so involve him that

Sect. xxxiii he is choked therewith; which me thinkes is most probable; this manner of sheathing was invented by my father, and experience hath taught it to be the best and of least cost.[1]

SECTION XXXIII.

SUCH was the diligence we used for our dispatch to shoot the Straites, that at foure dayes ende, wee had our water and wood stowed in our shippe, all our copper-worke finished, and our shippe calked from post to stemme; the first day in the morning, the winde being fayre, we brought our selves into the channell, and sayled towards the mouth of the Straites, praising God; and beginning our course with little winde, we descryed a fire upon the shore, made by the Indians for a signe to call us; which scene, I caused a boat to be man'de, and we rowed ashore, to see what their meaning was, and approaching neere the shore, wee saw a cannoa, made fast under a rock with a wyth, most artificially made with the rindes of trees, and sowed together with the finnes of whales; at both ends sharpe, and turning up, with a greene bough in either end, and ribbes for strengthening it. After a little while, we might discerne on the fall of the mountaine (which was full of trees and shrubbes), two or three Indians naked, which came out of certaine caves or coates. They spake unto us, and made divers signes; now poynting to the harbour, out of which we were come, and then to the mouth of the Straites; but we understood nothing of their meaning. Yet left they

[1] These inventions have been improved upon by the use of copper and other metals; of these, copper is the best; and an approved method of applying it, is over a coating of *felt*. Truly there is nothing new under the sun.

us with many imaginations, suspecting it might be to advise us of our pynace, or some other thing of moment; but for that they were under covert, and might worke us some treacherie (for all the people of the Straites, and the land nere them, use all the villany they can towards white people, taking them for Spaniards, in revenge of the deceit that nation hath used towards them upon sundry occasions; as also for that by our stay we could reap nothing but hinderance of our navigation), wee hasted to our shippe, and sayled on our course. Sect. xxxiii

From Blanches Bay to long reach, which is some foure leagues, the course lyeth west south-west entring into the long reach, which is the last of the Straits, and longest. For it is some thirty-two leagues, and the course lyeth next of any thing north-west. Long Reach.

Before the setting of the sunne, wee had the mouth of the straits open, and were in great hope the next day to be in the South sea; but about seaven of the clocke that night, we saw a great cloud rise out of the north-east, which began to cast forth great flashes of lightnings, and sodainely sayling with a fresh gale of wind at north-east, another more forcible tooke us astayes;[1] which put us in danger; for all our sayles being a taut, it had like to overset our ship, before we could take in our sayles. And therefore in all such semblances it is great wisedome to carry a short sayle, or to take in all sayles.

Heere we found what the Indians forewarned[2] us of; for they have great insight in the change of weather, and besides have secret dealings with the prince of darknesse, who many times declareth unto them things to come. By Note.

[1] *Taken astayes*—another term for taken aback.

[2] It is possible that the natives may have been aware of the coming change. The suspicion entertained of them is an instance of the mistakes often fallen into by misconceiving the motives of those whose language cannot be understood.

Sect. XXXIII this meanes and other witch-crafts, which he teacheth them, hee possesseth them, and causeth them to doe what pleaseth him.

Within halfe an houre it began to thunder and raine, with so much winde as wee were forced to lye a hull, and so darke, that we saw nothing but when the lightning came. This being one of the narrowest reaches of all the straites, wee were forced, every glasse, to open a little of our fore-sayle, to cast about our ships head: any man may conceive if the night seemed long unto us, what desire we had to see the day. In fine, Phœbus with his beautiful face lightned our hemisphere, and rejoyced our heartes (having driven above twenty-foure leagues in twelve houres, lying a hull: whereby is to be imagined the force of the winde and current).

We set our fore-sayle, and returned to our former harbour, from whence, within three or foure dayes, we set sayle againe, with a faire winde, which continued with us till we came within a league of the mouth of the straite; here the winde tooke us againe contrary, and forced us to returne againe to our former port; where being ready to anchor, the wind scanted with us in such maner, as wee were forced to make a bourd. In which time, the winde and tide put us so farre to lee-wards, that we could by no meanes seize it: so we determined to goe to Elizabeth bay, but before we came at it, the night overtooke us; and this reach being dangerous and narrow, wee durst neither hull, nor trye,[1] or turne to and againe with a short sayle, and therefore bare alongst in the middest of the channell, till we were come into the broad reach, then lay a hull till the morning.

When we set sayle and ran alongst the coast, seeking

[1] To hull, is to lie without sail set; to try, with only low sail; whence we have now special storm sails, called try sails. We believe the correct expression is "to try" either a *hull* or *under sail*.

with our boate some place to anchor in. Some foure leagues to the west-wards of Cape Froward, we found a goodly bay, which wee named English bay; where anchored, we presently went a shore, and found a goodly river of fresh water, and an old cannoa broken to peeces, and some two or three of the houses of the Indians, with peeces of seale stinking ripe. These houses are made in fashion of an oven seven or eight foote broad, with boughes of trees, and covered with other boughes, as our summer houses; and doubtless do serve them but for the summer time, when they come to fish, and profit themselves of the sea. For they retyre themselves in the winter into the country, where it is more temperate, and yeeldeth better sustenance: for on the mayne of the Straits, wee neyther saw beast nor fowle, sea fowle excepted, and a kind of blacke-bird, and two hoggs towards the beginning of the straites.

Sect. XXXIII

English bay.

Here our ship being well moored, we began to supply our wood and water that we had spent. Which being a dayes worke, and the winde during many dayes contrary, I endevoured to keepe my people occupied, to divert them from the imagination which some had conceived, that it behooved we should returne to Brasill, and winter there, and so shoot the straites in the spring of the yeare.

Sloth cause of imagination.

So one day, we rowed up the river, with our boat and light horseman, to discover it and the in-land: where having spent a good part of the day, and finding shold water, and many trees fallen thwart it, and little fruite of our labour, nor any thing worth the noting, we returned.

Another day we trayned our people a-shore, being a goodly sandie bay; another, we had a hurling of batchelers against married men. This day we were busied in wrestling, the other in shooting; so we were never idle, neyther thought we the time long.

SECTION XXXIV.

Sect. xxxiv. AFTER we had past here some seven or eight dayes, one evening, with a flawe from the shore, our ship drove off into the channell, and before we could get up our anchor, and set our sayles, we were driven so farre to lee-wards, that we could not recover into the bay: that night comming on, with a short sayle, we beate off and on till the morning. At the break of the day, conferring with the captaine and master of my ship what was best to be done, we resolved to seeke out Tobias Cove, which lyeth over against Cape Fryo, on the southern part of the straites, because in all the reaches of the straites, for the most part, the wind bloweth trade, and therefore little profit to be made by turning to winde-wards. And from the ilands of the Pengwins to the ende of the straites towards the South sea, there is no anchoring in the channell; and if we should be put to lee-wards of this cove, we had no succour till we came to the ilands of Pengwins: and some of our company which had bin with master Thomas Candish in the voyage in which he died,[1] and in the same cove many weekes, undertooke to be our pilots thither. Whereupon we bare up, being some two leagues thither, having so much winde as we could scarce lye by it with our course and bonnet of each; and bearing up before the winde, wee put out our topsayles and spritsayle, and within a little while the winde began to fayle us, and immediately our ship gave a mightie blow upon a rocke, and stucke fast upon it. And had we had but the fourth part of the wind which we had in all the night past, but a moment before we strucke the rocke, our shippe, doubtlesse, with the blow had broken her selfe all to peeces. But our provident and most gracious God, which commaundeth wind and sea, watched over us, and delivered us with his powerfull hand from the unknowne

Tobias Cove.

Setting of the ship upon a rock.

[1] See note at page 172.

danger and hidden destruction, that so we might prayse him for his fatherly bountie and protection, and with the prophet David say, *Except the Lord keepe the cittie, the watch-men watch in vaine;* for if our God had not kept our shippe, we had bin all swallowed up alive without helpe or redemption; and therefore he for his mercies sake grant that the memoriall of his benefits doe never depart from before our eyes, and that we may evermore prayse him for our wonderfull deliverance, and his continuall providence by day and by night. Sect. XXXIV.

My company with this accident were much amazed, and not without just cause. Immediately we used our endevour to free our selves, and with our boates sounded round about our shippe, in the mean time assaying[1] our pumpe to know if our shippe made more water then her ordinary; we found nothing increased, and round about our shippe deepe water, saving under the mid-shippe, for shee was a floate a head and a sterne: and bearing some fathome before the mayne mast, and in no other part, was like to be our destruction; for being ebbing water, the waight in the head and sterne by fayling of the water, began to open her plankes in the middest; and upon the upper decke, they were gone one from another some two fingers, some more; which we sought to ease and remedie by lightning of her burden, and throwing into the sea all that came to hand; and laying out an anchor, we sought to wend her off;[2] and such was the will and force we put to the capsten and tackles fastned upon the cable, that we plucked the ring of the anchor out of the eye, but after recovered it, though not serviceable.

The company dismayed.

Diligence to free it.

All our labour was fruitlesse, till God was pleased that the flood came, and then we had her off with great joy and comfort, when finding the current favourable with us, we

To the laborious God propitious.

[1] *To assay*—to prove. Ancient mode of writing essay.

[2] *To move her off.*—To wind a ship now means to turn her. The term is probably derived from to wend.

Sect. xxxiv. stood over to English bay, and fetching it, we anchored there, having been some three houres upon the rocke, and with the blow, as after we saw when our ship was brought aground in Perico (which is the port of Panama), a great part of her sheathing was beaten off on both sides in her bulges,[1] and some foure foote long and a foote square of her false stemme, joyning to the keele, wrested a crosse, like unto a hogges yoake, which hindered her sayling very much.

and therefore praysed. Here we gave God prayse for our deliverance, and afterward procured to supply our wood and water, which we had throwne overbourd to ease our shippe, which was not much: that supplyed, it pleased God (who is not ever angry), to looke upon us with comfort, and to send us a fayre and large wind, and so we set sayle once againe, in hope to disemboke the straite; but some dozen leagues before we came to the mouth of it, the wind changed, and forced us to seeke out some cove or bay, with our boates to ride in neere at hand, that we might not be forced to returne farre backe into the straites.

Crabby cove. They sounded a cove some sixteene leagues from the mouth of the straite, which after we called Crabby cove. It brooked its name well for two causes; the one for that all the water was full of a small kinde of redd crabbes; the other, for the crabbed mountaines which overtopped it; a third, we might adde, for the crabbed entertainement it gave us. In this cove we anchored, but the wind freshing in, and three or foure hilles over-topping, like sugar-loaves, altered and straightned the passage of the wind in such manner, as forced it downe with such violence in flawes and furious blusterings, as was like to over-set our shippe at an anchor, and caused her to drive, and us to weigh; but before we could weigh it, shee was so neere the rockes, and

[1] Now called bilge — that part of the ship's bottom that bulges or swells out. When a ship takes the ground and heels over, the bilge bears all the strain, and consequently suffers damage.

the puffes and gusts of wind so sodaine and uncertaine, sometimes scant, sometimes large, that it forced us to cut our cable, and yet dangerous if our shippe did not cast the right way. Here necessitie, not being subject to any law, forced us to put our selves into the hands of him that was able to deliver us. We cut our cable and sayle all in one instant; and God, to shew his power and gratious bountie towardes us, was pleased that our shippe cast the contrary way towardes the shore, seeming that he with his own hand did wend her about; for in lesse then her length shee flatted,[1] and in all the voyage but at that instant, shee flatted with difficultie, for that shee was long, the worst propertie shee had. On either side we might see the rockes under us, and were not halfe a shippes length from the shore, and if she had once touched, it had beene impossible to have escaped. Sect. xxxv.

Magnified ever be our Lord God, which delivered Ionas out of the whales belly; and his apostle Peter from being overwhelmed in the waves; and us from so certaine perishing.

SECTION XXXV.

From hence we returned to Blanches bay, and there anchored, expecting Gods good will and pleasure. Here beganne the bitternesse of the time to increase, with blustering and sharpe winds, accompanied with rayne and

[1] *To flat in*, means so to adjust the sails as to cause them to act with the greatest effect to turn the ship's head from the wind; this is done when the ship is nearly taken aback, either by a sudden flaw or by carelessness at the helm. As applied here, it means that the vessel came round on her heel. The time vessels take in performing a similar evolution, bears a certain ratio to their length; long ships requiring more time than short ones.

Sect. xxxv. sleeting snow, and my people to be dismayde againe, in manifesting a desire to returne to Brasill, which I would never consent unto, no, nor so much as to heare of.

Voyages over-throwne by pretences.

And all men are to take care that they go not one foote backe, more than is of mere force; for I have not seene that any who have yeelded thereunto, but presently they have returned home. As in the voyage of master Edward Fenton, which the Earle of Cumberland set forth, to his great charge. As also in that of master Thomas Candish, in which he dyed. Both which pretended to shoote the Straites of Magelan, and by perswasion of some ignorant persons, being in good possibilitie, were brought to consent to returne to Brasill, to winter, and after in the spring to attempt the passing of the straite againe. None of them made any abode in Brazill; for presently as soone as they looked homeward, one with a little blustering wind taketh occasion to loose company; another complaineth that he wanteth victuals; another, that his ship is leake; another, that his masts, sayles, or cordidge fayleth him. So the willing never want probable reasons to further their pretences. As I saw once (being but young, and more bold than experimented), in anno 1582, in a voyage, under the charge of my uncle, William Hawkins, of Plimouth, Esquire, in the Indies, at the wester end of the iland of San Iuan de Portorico. One of the shippes, called the barke *Bonner*, being somewhat leake, the captaine complained that she was not able to endure to England; whereupon a counsell was called, and his reasons heard and allowed. So it was concluded that the victuall, munition, and what was serviceable, should be taken out of her, and her men divided amongst our other shippes; the hull remaining to be sunke or burned.

Edward Fenton and master Thomas Candish.

Master William Hawkins.

To which I never spake word till I saw it resolved; being my part rather to learne than to advise. But seeing the fatall sentence given, and suspecting that the captaine made the matter worse then it was, rather upon pollicy to come into another ship, which was better of sayle, then for any danger they might runne into; with as much reason as my capacitie could reach unto, I disswaded my unkle privately; and urged, that seeing wee had profited the adventurers nothing, wee should endevour to preserve our principall, especially having men and victualls. But seeing I prevayled not, I went further, and offered to finde out in the same shippe and others, so many men, as with me would be content to carry her home, giving us the third part of the value of the ship, as shee should be valued at, at her returne, by foure indifferent persons; and to leave the vice-admirall which I had under my charge, and to make her vice-admirall. Sect. xxxv.

Whereupon, it was condescended that we should all goe aboard the shippe, and that there it should be determined. The captaine thought himselfe somewhat touched in reputation, and so would not that further triall should be made of the matter: saying, that if another man was able to carry the shippe into England, he would in no case leave her; neither would he forsake her till shee sunke under him.

The generall commended him for his resolution, and thanked me for my offer, tending to the generall good; my intention being to force those who for gaine could undertake to carry her home, should also do it gratis, according to their obligation. Thus, this the leake-ship went well into England; where after shee made many a good voyage in nine yeares, wherein shee was imployed to and fro; and no doubt would have served many more, had shee not beene laid up and not used, falling into the hands of those which knew not the use of shipping. It were large to recount the voyages and worthy enterprises overthrowne by this pollicie, with the shippes which have thereby gone to wracke.

SECTION XXXVI.

Sect. xxxvi.

Danger to hearken unto reasons of returne.

By this and the like experiences, remembring and knowing that if once I consented to turne but one foote backe, I should overthrow my voyage, and loose my reputation, I resolved rather to loose my life, than to give eare to such prejudiciall counsell. And so as the weather gave leave, we entertained our selves the first dayes in necessary workes, and after in making of coale (for wood was plentifull, and no man would commence an action of wast against us), with intent, the wind continuing long contrary, to see if wee could remedie any of our broken anchors; a forge I had in my shippe, and of five anchors which we brought out of England, there remained but one that was serviceable.

In the ilands of Pengwins we lost one; in Crabbe cove, another; of a third, upon another occasion we broke an arme; and the fourth, on the rocke had the eye of his ring broken. This, one day devising with my selfe, I made to serve, without working him a new. Which when I tooke first in hand, all men thought it ridiculous; but in fine, we made it in that manner so serviceable, as till our ship came to Callao, which is the port of Lima, shee scarce used any other anchor; and when I came from Lyma to Panama, which was three yeares after, I saw it serve the admirall in which I came (a ship of above five hundredth tunnes), without other art or addition, then what my owne invention contrived.

The mending of an unserviceable anchor.

And for that in the like necessitie or occasion, others may profit themselves of the industrie, I will recount the manner of the forging our eye without fire or iron. It was in this sort.

From the eye of the shanke about the head of the crosse, we gave two turnes with a new strong halser, betwixt three and foure inches, giving a reasonable allowance for that which should be the eye, and served in stead of the ring; then we fastned the two ends of the halser, so as in that part it was as strong as in any other, and with our capsten stretched the two byghtes, that every part might bear proportionably; then armed we all the halser round about with six yarne synnets, and likewise the shank of the anchor, and the head with a smooth matt made of the same synnet: this done, with an inch rope, wee woolled the two byghtes to the shanke, from the crosse to the eye, and that also which was to serve for the ring, and fitted the stocke accordingly. This done, those who before derided the invention, were of opinion, that it would serve for a need; onely they put one difficultie, that with the fall or pitch of the anchor in hard ground, with his waight he would cut the halser in sunder on the head; for prevention whereof, we placed a panch, as the mariners terme it, upon the head of the anchor, with whose softnesse this danger was prevented, and the anchor past for serviceable.[1]

Entertainement of time to avoyd idlenesse.

Some of our idle time we spent in gathering the barke and fruite of a certaine tree, which we found in all places of the straites where we found trees. This tree carrieth his fruite in clusters like a hawthorne, but that it is greene, each berry of the bignesse of a pepper corne, and every of them containing within four or five graynes, twise as bigge as a mustard-seed, which broken, are white within, as the good pepper, and bite much like it, but hotter. The barke of this tree hath the savour of all kinde of spices together, most comfortable to the stomache, and held to be better than any spice whatsoever. And for that a learned country-man of ours, Doctor Turner, hath written of it, by the name of *Winters barke*, which I have said may suffice. The

In gathering of Winters barke.

[1] Synnet is plait made from rope yarns. Wooling or woolding is performed by passing turns of rope round a spar or rope, either for strength, or, as in this case, to prevent chafe; if spun yarn is used, it is called serving.

Sect. xxxvi. leafe of this tree is of a whitish greene, and is not unlike to the aspen leafe.[1]

Other whiles we entertained our selves in gathering of pearles out of mussels, whereof there are aboundance in all places, from Cape Froward to the end of the straites.

Of pearles. The pearles are but of a bad colour, and small; but it may be that in the great mussels, in deeper water, the pearles are bigger, and of greater value; of the small seed pearle, there are great quantitie, and the mussels were a great refreshing unto us; for they are exceeding good, and in great plentie. And here let me crave pardon if I erre, seeing I disclaime from being a naturalist, by delivering my opinion touching the breeding of these pearles, which I thinke to be of a farre different nature and qualitie to those found in the East and West Indies, which are found in oysters; growing in the shell, under the ruff of the oyster, some say of the dewe, which I hold to be some old philosophers conceit, for that it cannot bee made probable how the dew should come into the oyster; and if this were true, then questionlesse, wee should have them in our oysters as in those of the East and West Indies; but those oysters were, by the Creator, made to bring foorth this rare fruite, all their shels being, to looke to, pearle itselfe. And the other pearles found in our oysters and mussels, in divers partes, are ingendred out of the fatnesse of the fish, in the very substance of the fish; so that in some mussels have beene found twenty, and thirty, in severall partes of the fish, and these not perfect in colour, nor clearenes, as those found in the pearle-oysters, which are ever perfect in colour and cleareues, like the sunne in his rising, and therefore called orientall, and not as is supposed, because out

[1] The tree called Winter's bark, *Drimys Winteri*, was discovered by Captain Winter, one of Drake's officers. The bark is agreeably aromatic, and was found useful in cases of scurvy. See also Darwin's *Naturalist's Voyage* (Murray, ed. 1852), pp. 235, 281.

of the East, for they are as well found in the West, and no way inferior to those of the East Indies. Sect. XXXVI.

Other fish, besides seales and crabbes, like shrimpes, and one whale, with two or three porpusses, wee saw not in all the straites. Heere we made also a survay of our victuals; and opening certaine barrels of oaten meale, wee found a great part of some of them, as also of our pipes and fatts[1] of bread, eaten and consumed by the ratts; doubtlesse, a fifth part of my company did not eate so much as these devoured, as wee found dayly in comming to spend any of our provisions.

Prevention of ratts.

When I came to the sea, it was not suspected that I had a ratt in my shippe; but with the bread in caske, which we transported out of the *Hawke*, and the going to and againe of our boates unto our prise, though we had diverse catts and used other preventions, in a small time they multiplyed in such a maner as is incredible. It is one of the generall calamities of all long voyages, and would bee carefully prevented as much as may bee. For besides that which they consume of the best victuals, they eate the sayles; and neither packe nor chest is free from their surprises. I have knowne them to make a hole in a pipe of water, and saying the pumpe, have put all in feare, doubting least some leake had beene sprung upon the ship.

The calamities they bring to a ship.

Moreover, I have heard credible persons report, that shippes have beene put in danger by them to be sunke, by a hole made in the bulge.[2] All which is easily remedied at the first, but if once they be somewhat increased, with difficulty they are to be destroyed. And although I propounded a reward for every ratt which was taken, and sought meanes

[1] Used for vats.

[2] The devastation caused by rats is very great. We have, however, never heard of their gnawing through the bottom. Indeed, if there be any truth in the old sailor's superstition that rats always leave a vessel when in a dangerous state, they must be too clever to try so dangerous an experiment.

Sect. xxxvii

by poyson and other inventions to consume them; yet their increase being so ordinary and many, wee were not able to cleare our selves from them.

SECTION XXXVII.

At the end of fourteene dayes, one evening, being calme, and a goodly cleare in the easter-boord, I willed our anchor to be weyed,[1] and determined to goe into the channell, whereof ensued a murmuring amongst my company, who were desirous to see the winde setled before we put out of the harbour: and in part they had reason, considering how wee had beene canvassed from place to place; yet on the other side, if wee went not out before night, wee should loose the whole nights sayling, and all the time which we should spend in warping out; which would be, doubtles, a great part of the fore-noone. And although the master signified unto mee the disposition of my people, and master Henry Courton (a discreete and vertuous gentleman, and my good friend, who in all the voyage was ever an especial furtherer of all that ever I ordained or proposed), in this occasion sought to divert me, that all but my selfe were contrarily inclined to that which I thought fit: and though the common saying be, that it is better to erre with many, then, all contradicting, a one to hit the right way, yet truth tolde mee this proverbe to bee falsely founded; for that it was not to bee understood, that for erring it is better, but because it is supposed that by hitting a man shall get emulation of the contradictors: I encountered it with another, that sayeth, better to be envied than pittied; and well con-

Backwardness in the company.

and the consequences thereof.

[1] Much discussion has arisen as to whether this should be written *way*, or *weigh*. We think the correct phraseology is this: when the anchor is *weighed*, the ship is under *way*.

sidering, that being out of the harbour, if the winde took us contrary, to goe to Elizabeth bay was better then to bee in the port; for a man must of force warpe in and out of it, and in the time that the shippe could be brought foorth into the channell, the winde being good, a man might come from Elizabeth bay to the port, and that there we should have the wind first, being more to the east-wardes, and in an open bay, and moreover might set sayle in the night, if the wind should rise in the evening or in the night; whereas, in the port, of force, we must waite the light of the day. I made my selfe deafe to all murmurings, and caused my commaund to be put in execution, and, doubtlesse, it was Gods gracious inspiration, as by the event was seene; for being gotten into the channell, within an houre, the winde came good, and we sayled merrily on our voyage; and by the breake of the day, wee had the mouth of the straites open, and about foure of the clocke in the afternoone, wee were thwart of Cape Desire;[1] which is the westermost part of the land on the southern side of the straites.

Sec. xxxviii

SECTION XXXVIII.

Advertisements for commanders.

Here such as have command may behold the many miseries that befall them, not onely by unexpected accidents and mischances, but also by contradictions and murmurs of their owne people, of all calamities the greatest which can befall a man of discretion and valour, and as difficult to be overcome; for, to require reason of the common sort, is, as the philosopher sayth, to seeke counsell of a madd man. Herein, as I sayd before, they resemble a stiff necked

[1] Now called Cape Pillar—on the modern charts Cape Deseado lies to the south of it. Cape Pillar is in 52° 42′ 53″ S.

Sect. xxxix. horse, who taking the bridle in his teeth, carrieth the rider whether he pleaseth; so once possessed with any imagination, no reason is able to convince them. The best remedie I can propound, is to wish our nation in this poynt to be well advised, and in especiall, all those that follow the sea, ever having before their eyes the auncient discipline of our predecessors; who in conformitie and obedience to their chiefes and commanders, have beene a mirror to all other nations, with patience, silence, and suffering, putting in execution what they have beene commanded, and thereby gained the blessings due to such vertues, and leaving to posteritie perpetuall memories of their glorious victories. A just recompence for all such as conquer themselves, and subject their most specious willes to the will of their superiors.

The advantage of obedience.

SECTION XXXIX.

In apprehension whereof at land, I cannot forebeare the discipline thereof, as at this day, and in the dayes of late memory, it hath beene practised in the states of Flaunders, Fraunce, and Brittayne; whereas the Spaniards, Wallons, Switzers, and other nations, are daily full of murmurings and mutenies, upon every sleight occasion.

The like I also wish should be imitated by those who follow the sea; that is, that those who are subject to command, presume no further then to that which belongeth unto them: *Qui nescit parere, nescit imperare.* I speake this, for that I have sometimes seene unexpert and ignorant persons, yea, unable to judge of any poynt appertaining to government, or the guide of a shippe, or company of men, presuming upon their fine witts, and enamoured of their owne conceits, contradict and dispute against grave, wise, and experimented governours: many forward fellowes,

Sect. xxxix.

Advertisements for young servitors.

thinking themselves better worthie to command, than to be commanded. Such persons I advise not to goe, but where they may command; or els looking before they leape, to consider well under whom they place themselves, seeing, for the most part, it is in their choyce to choose a governour from whom they may expect satisfaction; but choyce being once made, to resolve with the patient wife in history, that, that day wherein shee married herselfe to an husband, that very day shee had no longer any will more then the will of her husband: and so he that by sea or land placeth himselfe to serve in any action, must make reckoning that the time the journey endureth, he hath no other will, nor dispose of himselfe, than that of his commander; for in the governors hand is all power, to recompence and reward, to punish or forgive.

Likewise those who have charge and command, must sometimes with patience or sufferance overcome their fury and misconceits, according to occasions, for it is a great poynt of wisedome, especially in a generall murmuring, where the cause is just, or that, as often times it happeneth, any probable accident may divert the minds of the discontented, and give hope of remedie, or future event may produce repentance, to turne, as they say, the deafe eare, and to winke at that a man seeth. As it is sayde of Charles the fifth, emperour of Germany, and king of Spaine; who rounding his campe, one night, disguised, heard some souldiers rayle and speak evil of him: those which accompanied him were of opinion, that he should use some exemplary punishment upon them; not so, sayth he, for these, now vexed with the miseries they suffer, ease their hearts with their tongues; but if occasion present it selfe, they will not sticke to sacrifice their lives for my safetie. A resolution worthy so prudent a commander, and so magnanimous a prince.

The like is written of Fabius Maximus, the famous

Sect. xxxix. Romayne, who endured the attribute of coward, with many other infamies, rather then he would hazard the safetie of his countrie by rash and uncertaine provocations.

The patience of the Earle of Nottingham.

No lesse worthy of perpetuall memory was the prudent pollicie and government of our English navie, in anno 1588, by the worthy Earle of Nottingham,[1] lord high admirall of England; who, in like case, with mature and experimented knowledge, patiently withstood the instigations of many couragious and noble captaines, who would have perswaded him to have laid them aboord; but well he foresaw that the enemy had an armie aboord, he none; that they exceeded him in number of shipping, and those greater in bulke, stronger built, and higher molded, so that they who with such advantage fought from above, might easily distresse all opposition below; the slaughter, peradventure, prooving more fatall then the victory profitable: by being overthrowne, he might have hazzarded the kingdome; whereas by the conquest, at most, he could have boasted of nothing but glorie, and an enemy defeated. But by sufferance, he alwayes advantaged himselfe of winde and tide; which was the freedome of our countrey, and securitie of our navie, with the destruction of theirs, which in the eye of the ignorant, who judge all things by the externall appearance, seemed invincible; but truly considered, was much inferior to ours in all things of substance, as the event prooved; for we sunke, spoyled, and tooke of them many, and they diminished of ours but one small pynace, nor any man of name, save onely captaine Cooke, who dyed with honour amidst his company. The greatest dammage, that, as I remember, they caused to any of our shippes, was to the *Swallow* of her majestie, which I had in that action under my charge, with an arrow of fire shott into her beake-head, which we saw not, because of the

[1] After the defeat of the Spanish Armada, Lord Charles Howard of Effingham, was created Earl of Nottingham.

sayle, till it had burned a hole in the nose as bigge as a mans head; the arrow falling out, and driving alongst by the shippes side, made us doubt of it, which after we discovered. Sect. XLI.

SECTION XL.

In many occasions, notwithstanding, it is most prejudiciall to dissemble the reprehension and punishment of murmurings and mutterings, when they carry a likelihood to grow to a mutinie, seeme to leane to a faction, or that a person of regard or merite favoureth the intention, or contradicteth the justice, etc., and others of like qualitie. The prudent governour is to cut off this hydra's head in the beginning, and by prevention to provide remedie with expedition; and this sometimes with absolute authoritie, although the best be ever to proceed by counsell, if necessitie and occasion require not the contrary; for passion many times overruleth, but that which is sentenced and executed by consent, is justified, although sometimes erronious.[1] March 29, 1594.

Mutenies not alwayes to be winked at.

SECTION XLI.

From Cape Desire, some foure leagues north-west lye foure ilands, which are very small, and the middlemost of them is of the fashion of a sugar-loafe. We were no sooner cleare of Cape Desire, and his ledge of rockes, which

[1] The above observations appear to have occurred to our author in consequence of what had taken place during the voyages of Magalhaens and Drake. Both these great commanders, while lying at Port Saint Julian, tried for mutiny, and executed, some of their chief officers.

Sect. XLI.

lie a great way off into the sea, but the wind took us contrary by the north-west; and so we stood off into the sea two dayes and two nights to the west-wards.

In all the straites it ebbeth and floweth more or lesse, and in many places it higheth very little water; but in some bayes, where are great indraughts, it higheth eight or ten foote, and doubtlesse further in, more. If a man be furnished with wood and water, and the winde good, he may keepe the mayne sea, and goe round about the straites to the southwards, and it is the shorter way; for besides the experience which we made, that all the south part of the straites is but ilands, many times having the sea open, I remember that Sir Francis Drake told me, that having shott the straites, a storme first tooke him at north-west, and after vered about to the south-west, which continued with him many dayes, with that extremitie, that he could not open any sayle, and that at the end of the storme, he found himselfe in fiftie degrees;[1] which was sufficient testimony and proofe, that he was beaten round about the straites: for the least height of the straites is in fifty two degrees and fiftie minutes; in which stands the two entrances or mouths.

South part of the Straites ilands.

And moreover, he said, that standing about, when the winde changed, he was not well able to double the southermost iland, and so anchored under the lee of it; and going a-shore, carried a compasse with him, and seeking out the southermost part of the iland, caste himselfe downe upon the uttermost poynt, grovelling, and so reached out his bodie over it. Presently he imbarked, and then recounted unto his people that he had beene upon the southermost knowne land in the world, and more further to the southwards upon it then any of them, yea, or any man as yet knowne. These testimonies may suffice for this truth unto all, but such as are incredulous, and will beleeve nothing

Sir Francis Drake embraceth the southermost point of the world.

[1] This must be a misprint; it should be perhaps 56°.

but what they see: for my part, I am of opinion, that the straite is navigable all the yeare long, although the best time be in November, December, and January, and then the winds more favourable, which other times are variable, as in all narrow seas.[1] Sect. XLI.

Being some fiftie leagues a sea-boord the straites, the winde vering to the west-wards, we cast about to the north-wards, and lying the coast along, shaped our course for the iland Mocha. About the fifteenth of April, we were thwart of Baldivia, which was then in the hands of the Spaniards, but since, the Indians, in anno 1599, dispossessed them of it, and the Conception; which are two of the most principall places they had in that kingdome, and both ports. Mocha. Baldivia.

Baldivia had its name of a Spanish captaine so called, whom afterwards the Indians tooke prisoner, and it is said, they required of him the reason why he came to molest them and to take their country from them, having no title nor right thereunto; he answered, to get gold; which the barbarians understanding, caused gold to be molten, and poured down his throat, saying, gold was thy desire, glut thee with it.[2]

[1] Much interesting information respecting these straits will be found in the voyages of the *Adventure* and *Beagle*. Now that the labours of King and Fitz Roy, and more recently of Mayne, have provided correct charts, the road is well known.

[2] Pedro de Valdivia was the first Governor of Chile, after the transitory invasion of Almagro. He overran the whole country, and founded seven cities: Coquimbo, Santiago, Angol, Penco, Imperial, Villarica, and Lago. He founded Santiago on February 24th, 1541. Then the Araucanians rose in arms, and Valdivia seems to have carelessly underrated the danger. The mode of his death related by Hawkins, is fabulous. For the true account, see *Araucana*, Part I, Canto III; and G. de la Vega, *Comm. Real.*, Part I, Lib. VII, cap. 23. The rising took place in 1553, and continued for many years. The most fierce outbreak was in 1599. The city of Valdivia was surprised on November 24th of that year, and entirely destroyed.

Sect. XLI. It standeth in fortie degrees, hath a pleasant river and navigable, for a ship of good burden may goe as high up as the cittie; and is a goodly woody country.

Here our beefe beganne to take end, and was then as good as the day wee departeth from England; it was preserved in pickell, which, though it be more chargeable, yet the profit payeth the charge, in that it is made more durable, contrary to the opinion of many, which hold it impossible that beefe should be kept good passing the equinoctiall lyne. And of our porke I eate in the house of Don Beltran de Castro, in Lyma, neere foure yeares old, very good, preserved after the same manner, notwithstanding it had lost his pickell long before.

Some degrees before a man comes to Baldivia to the southwards, as Spaniards have told me, lyeth the iland Chule,[1] not easily to be discerned from the mayne; for he that passeth by it, cannot but thinke it to be the mayne. It is said to be inhabited by the Spaniards, but badly, yet rich of gold.

The 19th of April, being Easter-even, we anchored under the iland Mocha.[2] It lyeth in thirty-nine degrees, it may be some foure leagues over, and is a high mountainous hill, but round about the foote thereof, some half league from the sea-shore, it is champion ground, well inhabited, and manured.

From the straites to this iland, we found that either the coast is set out more westerly then it is, or that we had a great current, which put us to the west-wards: for we had not sight of land in three dayes after. Our reckoning was to see it, but for that we coasted not the land, I cannot de-

[1] Chiloe.

[2] A lofty island on the coast of Chile. Its summit is 1250 feet above the sea. Previous to the eighteenth century it was inhabited by Araucanian Indians, but they are driven out by the Spaniards. The anchorages were indifferent, and the landing bad. Mocha is about seven miles long by three broad, between 38° 20′ and 38° 26′ S.

termine, whether it was caused by the current, or lying of the land. But Spaniards which have sayled alongst it, have told me that it is a bold and safe coast, and reasonable sounding off it.

In this iland of Mocha we had communication and contratation[1] with the inhabitants, but with great vigilancie and care; for they and all the people of Chily are mortall enemies to the Spaniards, and held us to be of them; and so esteemed Sir Francis Drake when he was in this iland, which was the first land also that he touched on this coast. They used him with so fine a trechery, that they possessed themselves of all the oares in his boate, saving two, and in striving to get them also, they slew and hurt all his men: himselfe, who had fewest wounds, had three, and two of them in the head. Two of his company which lived long after, had, the one seaventeene (his name was John Bruer, who afterward was pilot with master Candish), and the other about twentie, a negroe-servant to Sir Francis Drake.

Trechery of the Indians.

And with me they used a pollicie, which amongst barbarous people was not to be imagined, although I wrought sure; for I suffered none to treate with me nor with my people with armes. We were armed, and met upon a rock compassed with water, whether they came to parley and negotiate. Being in communication with the caciques and others, many of the Indians came to the heads of our boates, and some went into them. Certaine of my people standing to defend the boates with their oares, for that there went a bad sege, were forced to lay downe their musketts; which the Indians perceiving, endevoured to fill the barrells with water, taking it out of the sea in the hollow of their hands. By chance casting mine eye aside, I discovered their slynesse, and with a truncheon, which I had in mine hand, gave the Indians three or foure good

[1] *Contractation*—commerce or dealings with them.

Sect. XLI. lamskinnes;[1] the caciques seeing it, began to give me satisfaction by using rigor towardes those which had beene in the boates; but I having gotten the refreshing I desired, and all I could hope from them, would have no further conversation with them. At our first comming, two of their caciques, who are their lords or kings, came aboord our shippe (we leaving one of our company ashore as a pledge), whom we feasted in good manner; they eat well of all that was set before them, and dranke better of our wine: one of them became a little giddie headed, and marvayled much at our artillery: I caused a peece to be primed, and after to be shott off, whereat the one started, but the other made no shew of alteration. After putting them ashore, loaden with toyes and trifles, which to them seemed great riches; from all parts of the iland the people came unto us, bringing all such things as they had, to wit, sheepe, cockes, etc. (from hennes they would not part), and divers sorts of fruits and rootes, which they exchanged with us for knives, glasses, combes, belles, beades, counters, pinnes, and other trifles. We saw little demonstration of gold or silver amongst them, though some they had; and for that we saw they made estimation of it, we would not make reckoning of it: but they gave us to understand that they had it from the mayne.

Exchanges of trifles.

Of sheepe. The sheepe of this iland are great, good, and fatt; I have not tasted better mutton any where. They were as ours, and doubtlesse of the breed of those which the Spaniards brought into the country. Of the sheepe of the country we could by no means procure any one, although we saw of them, and used meanes to have had of them; for they esteem them much, as reason willeth, serving them for many uses; as in another place, God willing, I shall declare more at large. They have small store of fish.

[1] *To lamm* is used by Beaumont and Fletcher in the sense of *beat—bruise*.

This iland is scituate in the province of Arawca,[1] and is held to be peopled with the most valiant nation in all Chily, though generally the inhabitants of that kingdome are very couragious. Sect. XLI.

They are clothed after the manner of antiquitie, all of woollen; their cassockes made like a sacke, square, with two holes for the two armes, and one for the head, all open below, without lining or other art: but of them some are most curiously wooven, and in colours, and on both sides alike. Their apparell,

Their houses are made round, in fashion like unto our pigeon houses, with a laver[2] in the toppe, to evacuate the smoake when they made fire. and housing.

They brought us a strange kinde of tobacco, made into little cakes, like pitch, of a bad smell, with holes through the middle, and so laced many upon a string. They presented us also with two Spanish letters, thinking us to be Spaniards, which were written by a captaine of a frigate, that some dayes before had received courtesie at their hands, and signified the same to the governour; wishing that the people of the iland would become good subjects to the king, and that therefore he would receive them into his favour and protection, and send them some person as governour; but none of them spake Spanish, and so we dealt with them by signes. The people of this iland, as of all Chily,[3] are of good stature, and well made, and of better countenance then those Indians which I have seene in many parts. They are of good understanding, and agilitie, and of great strength. Their weapons are bowes and arrowes, and macanas: their bowes short and strong, and their ar- People of Chily. Their weapons.

[1] The Araucans have been immortalised in the *Araucana*, a poem written by Don Alonzo de Ercilla. The first part was printed in 1569, the second in 1578. The best edition is that of Sancha (Madrid, 1776).

[2] This word is perhaps derived from *lave, to draw out, to exhaust.*

[3] Chile.

Sect. XLII. rowes of a short reed or cane, three quarters of a yard long, with two feathers, and headed with a flint stone, which is loose and hurting, the head remaining in the wound; some are headed with bone, and some with hard wood, halfe burnt in the fire. Wee came betwixt the iland and the mayne. On the south-west part of the iland lyeth a great ledge of rockes, which are dangerous; and it is good to be carefull how to come too neere the iland on all parts.

Their hate to the Spaniards.

Immediately when they discovered us, both upon the iland and the maine, wee might see them make sundry great fires, which were to give advise to the rest of the people to be in a readinesse: for they have continuall and mortall warre with the Spaniards, and the shippes they see they beleeve to be their enemies.[1] The citie imperiall lyeth over against this iland, but eight or tenne leagues into the countrey: for all the sea coast from Baldivia till thirty-six degrees, the Indians have now, in a manner, in their hands free from any Spaniards.

SECTION XLII.

Having refreshed our selves well in this iland, for that little time wee stayed, which was some three dayes, wee set sayle with great joy, and with a fayre winde sayled alongst the coast; and some eight leagues to the northwards, we anchored againe in a goodly bay, and sent our boates ashore, with desire to speake with some of the Indians of Arawca, and to see if they would be content to entertaine amitie, or to chop and change with us. But all that night and the next morning appeared not one person,

[1] In 1604, the Araucans entirely destroyed the Spanish towns of Valdivia, Imperial, Angol, Santa Cruz, Chillan, and Conception.

and so wee set sayle againe; and towardes the evening the winde began to change, and to blowe contrary, and that so much, and the sea to rise so sodainely, that we could not take in our boates without spoyling of them. This storme continued with us tenne dayes, beyond expectation, for that wee thought our selves out of the climate of fowle weather; but truely it was one of the sharpest stormes that ever I felt to endure so long.

Sect. XLII.

A cruel. storme.

In this storme, one night haling up our boates to free the water out of them, one of our younkers that went into them for that purpose, had not that regard, which reason required, unto our light horseman: for with haling her up to step into her out of the boate, he split her asunder, and so we were forced to cut her off; which was no small heartes grief unto me, for that I knew, and all my company felt, and many times lamented, the losse of her.

The import-ant losse of a small vessell.

The storme tooke end, and wee shaped our course for the iland of Saint Maries,[1] which lyeth in thirty seaven degrees and forty minuts; and before you come unto the iland some two leagues, in the trade way lyeth a rocke, which, a farre off, seemeth to be a shippe under sayle. This iland is little and low, but fertile and well peopled, with Indians and some few Spaniards in it. Some ten leagues to the north-wards of this iland, lyeth the citty Conception, with a good port; from this we coasted alongst till wee came in thirty-three degrees and forty minutes. In which height lay the ilands of Iuan Fernandes, betwixt threescore and fourscore leagues from the shore, plentiful of fish, and good for refreshing. I purposed for many reasons not to discover my selfe upon this coast, till we were past Lyma (otherwise called Cividad de Los Reyes, for that it was entered by the Spaniard the day of the three kings);[2] but

Saint Maries.

Citty of Conception.

Iuan Fernandes.

Good to avoid discovery.

[1] Santa Maria Island, off the coast of Chile, is comparatively low and dangerous, on account of numerous outlying rocks.

[2] Lima was *founded* by Pizarro on Epiphany, January 18th, 1535, and hence called the City of the Kings.

Sect. XLII. my company urged me so farre, that except I should seem in all things to over-beare them, in not condescending to that which in the opinion of all, but my selfe, seemed profitable and best, I could not but yeelde unto, though it carried a false colour, as the ende prooved, for it was our perdition. This all my company knoweth to be true, whereof some are yet living and can give testimonie.

Wilfulnesse of mariners. But the mariner is ordinarily so carried away with the desire of pillage, as sometimes for very appearances of small moment hee looseth his voyage, and many times himselfe. And so the greedines of spoyle, onely hoped for in shippes of trade, which goe too and fro in this coast, blinded them from forecasting the perill whereinto wee exposed our voyage, in discovering our selves before we past the coast of Callao, which is the port of Lyma. To be short, wee haled the coast aboord, and that evening we discovered the port of Balparizo,[1] which serveth the citty of Saint Iago, standing some twenty leagues into the countrey: when presently we descried foure shippes at an anchor: whereupon wee manned and armed our boate, which rowed towards the shippes: they seeing us turning in, and fearing that which was, ran a shore with that little they could save, and leaft us the rest; whereof we were masters in a moment, and had the rifling of all the storehouses on the shoare.

They seize upon four ships.

This night I set a good guard in all the shippes, longing to see the light of the next morning to put all things in order; which appearing, I began to survay them, and found nothing of moment, saving five hundred botozios[2] of

[1] Valparaiso, the chief port of Chile, received its name from Juan de Saavedra, a follower of Almagro, after his own native village of Valparaiso near Cuenca, in Spain. On September 3rd, 1544, Valdivia confirmed the name given by Saavedra.

[2] *Bota* is Spanish for a wine-skin or vessel: *botija*, a jar used for the same purpose.

wine, two or three thousand of hennes, and some refreshing of bread, bacon, dried beefe, waxe, candles, and other necessaries. The rest of their lading was plankes, spares, and timber, for Lyma, and the valleyes, which is a rich trade; for it hath no timber but that which is brought to it from other places. They had also many packes of Indian mantles, but of no value unto us, with much tallow, and manteca de puerco,[1] and aboundance of great new chests, in which wee had thought to be some great masse of wealth, but opening them, found nothing but apples therein; all which was good marchandize in Lyma, but to us of small accompt. The marchandize on shore in their store-houses was the like, and therefore in the same predicament. The owners of the shippes gave us to understand that at a reasonable price they would redeeme their shippes and loading, which I hearkened unto; and so admitted certaine persons which might treat of the matter, and concluded with them for a small price rather then to burne them, saving for the greatest, which I carryed with me, more to give satisfaction to my people then for any other respect; because they would not be perswaded but that there was much gold hidden in her; otherwise shee would have yeelded us more then the other three.

Sect. XLII.

And the ware-houses.

Being in this treatie, one morning at the breake of day came another shippe touring into the harbour, and standing into the shore, but was becalmed. Against her wee manned a couple of boates, and tooke her before many houres. In this shippe we had some good quantitie of gold, which shee had gathered in Baldivia, and the Conception, from whence shee came. Of this shippe was pilot and part owner, Alonso Perezbueno, whom we kept for our pilot on this coast; till moved with compassion (for that he was a man charged with wife and children), we set him ashore betwixt Santa and Truxillo.[2] Out of this shippe

They seize upon another ship,

and some gold.

[1] Lard.

[2] On the coast of Peru, north of Lima.

Sect. XLII. we had also store of good bacon, and some provision of bread, hennes, and other victuall. And for that shee had brought us so good a portion, and her owner continued with us, the better to animate him to play the honest man (though we trusted him no further then we saw him, for we presently discovered him to be a cunning fellow), and for that his other partner had lost the greatest part of gold, and seemed to be an honest man, as after he proved by his thankfulnesse in Lyma, we gave them the ship and the greatest part of her loading freely.

Light anchors brought from the North sea.

Here we supplied our want of anchors, though not according to that which was requisite in regard of the burden of our shippe; for in the South sea, the greatest anchor for a shippe of sixe or eight hundreth tunnes, is not a thousand waight; partly, because it is little subject to stormes, and partly, because those they had till our comming, were all brought out of the North sea by land; for they make no anchors in those countries. And the first artillerie they had was also brought over land, which was small; the carriage and passage from Nombre de Dios, or Porto Velo, to Panama, being most difficult and steepe, up hill and downe hill, they are all carried upon negroes backes.

And the first artillerie.

But some years before my imprisonment, they fell to making of artillery, and, since, they forge anchors also.

Sayles of cotton cloth.

Wee furnished our shippe also with a shift of sayles of cotton cloth, which are farre better in that sea then any of our double sayles; for that in all the navigation of that sea they have little rayne and few stormes; but where rayne and stormes are ordinary, they are not good; for with the wett they grow so stiffe they cannot be handled.

SECTION XLIII.

I CONCLUDED the ransome of the shippes with an auncient captaine, and of noble blood, who had his daughter there, ready to be imbarked to go to Lyma, to serve Donia Tereza de Castro, the viceroyes wife,[1] and sister to Don Beltran de Castro. Her apparell and his, with divers other things which they had imbarked in the greatest shippe, we restored, for the good office he did us, and the confidence he had of us, comming and going onely upon my word; for which he was after ever thankefull, and deserved much more. Sect. XLIII.

Another that treated with me was Captaine Iuan Contreres, owner of one of the shippes, and of the iland Santa Maria, in thirty-seaven degrees and fortie minutes. In treating of the ransomes, and transporting and lading the provisions we made choyce of, wee spent some sixe or eight dayes; at the end whereof, with reputation amongst our enemies, and a good portion towards our charges, and our shippe as well stored and victualled as the day we departed from England, we set sayle.

The time wee were in this port, I tooke small rest, and so did the master of our shippe, Hugh Cornish, a most carefull, orderly, and sufficient man, because we knew our owne weaknesse; for entring into the harbour, we had but seaventie five men and boyes, five shippes to guard, and every one moored by himselfe; which, no doubt, if our enemies had knowne, they would have wrought some stratagem upon us; for the governour of Chily was there on shore in view of us, an auncient Flanders soldier, and of experience, wisedome, and valour, called Don Alonso de

They depart from Lyma,

and conceale their weaknes.

[1] Teresa, daughter of the Count of Lemos, and wife of Don Garcia Hurtado de Mendoza, Marquis of Cañete, and Viceroy of Peru from 1590 to 1599.

Sect. XLIII.

Soto Mayor, of the habit of Saint Iago, who was after captaine generall in Terra Firme, and wrought all the inventions upon the river of Chagres, and on the shore, when Sir Francis Drake proposed to goe to Panama, in the voyage wherein he died; as also, at my comming into Spaine, he was president in Panama, and there, and in Lyma, used me with great courtesie, like a noble souldier and liberall gentleman. He confessed to me after, that he lay in ambush with three hundred horse and foote, to see if at any time wee had landed or neglected our watch, with balsas, (which is a certaine raffe made of mastes or trees fastened together), to have attempted something against us. But the enemy I feared not so much as the wine; which, notwithstanding all the dilligence and prevention I could use day and night overthrew many of my people. A foule fault, because too common amongst sea-men, and deserveth some rigorous punishment, with severitie to be executed; for it hath beene, and is daily, the destruction of many good enterprises, amidst their best hopes. And besides the ordinary fruites it bringeth forth, of beggery, shame, and sicknesse, it is a most deadly sinne. A drunkard is unfit for any government, and if I might be hired with many thousands, I would not carry with me a man known to put his felicitie in that vice, instiling it with the name of good fellowship; which in most well governed commonwealths, hath beene a sufficient blemish to deprive a man of office, of honour, and estimation. It wasteth our kingdome more then is well understood, as well by the infirmities it causeth, as by the consumption of wealth, to the impoverishing of us, and the enriching of other kingdomes.

The noblenees of Alonso de Soto.

The enemy less dangerous then the wine.

And though I am not old, in comparison of other auncient men, I can remember Spanish wine rarely to be found in this kingdome. Then hot burning feavers were not knowne in England, and men lived many more yeares. But since

Spanish wines and burning feavers unknowne in England.

the Spanish sacks have beene common in our tavernes, which, for conservation, is mingled with lyme[1] in its making, our nation complaineth of calenturas, of the stone, the dropsie, and infinite other diseases, not heard of before this wine came in frequent use, or but very seldome. To confirme which my beliefe, I have heard one of our learnedst physitians affirme, that he thought there died more persons in England of drinking wine and using hot spices in their meats and drinkes, then of all other diseases. Besides there is no yeare in which it wasteth not two millions of crownes of our substance, by convayance into forraine countries; which in so well a governed commonwealth as ours is acknowledged to be through the whole world, in all other constitutions, in this onely remaineth to be looked into and remedied. Doubtlesse, whosoever should be the author of this reformation, would gaine with God an everlasting reward, and of his country a statua of gold, for a perpetuall memory of so meritorious a worke.

Sect. XLIV.

And consumeth treasure.

SECTION XLIV.

A LEAGUE or better before a man discover this baye to the south-wards, lyeth a great rocke, or small iland, neere the shore; under which, for a need, a man may ride with his shippe. It is a good marke, and sure signe of the port, and discovering the bay a man must give a good birth to

Description of the bay.

[1] Lime was added to sack, not to preserve it, apparently, but for the same purpose that drugs are mixed in beer and spirits by brewers, publicans, and rectifiers, at the present day.

Falstaff. Villain, there's lime in this sack.—*Hen. IV.*

Host. I have spoke; let him follow; let me see thee
Froth and lime.— *Merry Wives of Windsor.*

Sect. XLIV. the poynt of the harbour; for it hath perilous rockes lying a good distance off. It neither ebbeth nor floweth in this port, nor from this till a man come to Guayaquill, which is three degrees from the equinoctiall lyne to the southwards. Let this be considered. It is a good harbour for all windes that partake not of the north; for it runneth up south and by west, and south south-west, but it hath much fowle ground.

A new devise for stopping a leake without board.

In one of these shippes we found a new devise for the stopping of a sodaine leake in a shippe under water, without board, when a man cannot come to it within board; which eased us of one that we had from the day we departed from Detford, caused by the touching a-ground of our shippe at low water, being loaden and in the neap streames, comming a-ground in the sterne, the force of the tyde caused to cast thwart, wrested her slegg, and that in such sort, as it made a continuall leake, though not much. And for that others may profit themselves of the like, I thinke it good to set downe the manner of it: which was, taking a round wicker basket, and to fill it with peeces of a junke or rope, chopped very small, and of an inch long, and after tozed all as oacombe;[1] then the basket is to be covered with a nett, the meshes of it being at the least two inches square, and after to be tied to a long pike or pole, which is to goe across the baskets mouth; and putting it under water, care is to be had to keepe the baskets mouth towardes the shippes side. If the leake be any thing great, the oacombe may be somewhat longer, and it carrieth likelihood to doe good, and seemeth to be better than the stitching of a bonnet, or any other diligence which as yet I have seene.

Spare rudders.

Another thing I noted of these shippes, which would be also used by us; that every shippe carrieth with her a spare

[1] *Teased*, pulled, or unravelled. Oakum is made from rope yarns teased or untwisted.

rudder, and they have them to hange and unhange with great facilitie; and besides, in some parts of the shippe they have the length, breadth, and proportion of the rudder marked out, for any mischance that may befall them; which is a very good prevention.[1] Sect. XLIV.

Ten leagues to the north-wards of this harbour, is the bay of Quintera,[2] where is good anchoring, but an open bay; where master Thomas Candish (for the good he had done to a Spaniard, in bringing him out of the Straits of Magellan, where, otherwise, he had perished with his company),[3] was by him betrayed, and a dozen of his men taken and slaine. But the judgement of God left not his ingratitude unpunished; for in the fight with us, in the vice-admirall, he was wounded and maymed in that manner, as, three yeares after, I saw him begge with crutches, and in that miserable estate, as he had been better dead than alive. Bay of Quintera. *Nota verum hispanum.*

From Balparizo wee sailed directly to Coquinbo, which is in thirtie degrees; and comming thwart the place, wee were becalmed, and had sight of a shippe: but for that shee was farre off, and night at hand, shee got from us, and wee having winde, entered the port, thinking to have had some shipping in it; but we lost our labour: and for that the towne was halfe a league upp in the countrey, and wee not manned for any matter of attempt, worthy prosecution, we made no abode on the shore, but presently set sayle for the Peru. This is the best harbour that I have seene in the South sea, it is land-locked for all winds, and capeable of many shippes; but the ordinary place where the shippes lade and unlade, and accommodate themselves, is betwixt a rocke and the mayne on the wester Coquinbo.

[1] We owe many good hints to Spanish seamen: this among others is used to this day.

[2] Quintero Bay, near Valparaiso.

[3] This was one of Sarmiento's unfortunate colonists.

Sect. XLIV. side, some halfe a league up within the entrance of the port, which lyeth south and south, and by east and north, and by west.

In the in-country, directly over the port, is a round piked hill, like a sugar-loafe, and before the entrance on the southern poynt of the port, comming in out of the sea, is a great rocke, a good birth from the shore; and these are the markes of the port as I remember.

Arica in Chily much commended.

Being cleere of this port, wee shaped our course for Arica, and leaft the kingdomes of Chily, one of the best countries that the sunne shineth on; for it is of a temperate clymate, and abounding in all things necessary for the use of man, with infinite rich mines of gold, copper, and sundry other mettals.

The poorest houses in it, by report of their inhabitants, have of their owne store, bread, wine, flesh, and fruite; which is so plentifull, that of their superfluitie they supply other partes. Sundry kindes of cattell, as horses, goates, and oxen, brought thither by the Spaniards, are found in heardes of thousands, wilde and without owner; besides those of the countrey, which are common to most partes of America: in some of which are found the bezar stones, and those very good and great.

Amongst others, they have little beastes like unto a squirrell, but that hee is gray; his skinne is the most delicate, soft, and curious furre that I have seene, and of much estimation (as is of reason) in the Peru; few of them come into Spaine, because difficult to be come by; for that the princes and nobles laie waite for them. They call this beast *chinchilla*, and of them they have great abundance.

For all sorts of fruits.

All fruites of Spaine they have in great plentie, saving stone fruite and almonds; for in no part of the Indies have I knowne that plumbes, cherries, or almondes have borne fruit: but they have certaine little round cocos, as those of Brasill, of the bignesse of a wall-nut, which is as good as an almond; besides it hath most of the fruites naturall to America, of which in another place I shall, God willing, speake particularly. Sect. XLIV.

The gold they gather is in two manners: the one is washing the earth in great trayes of wood in many waters; as the earth washeth away, the gold in the bottome remaineth. The other is, by force of art to draw it out of the mynes in which they finde it. In most partes of the countrie, the earth is mingled with gold; for the butizias,[1] in which the wine was, which wee found in Balparizo, had many sparkes of gold shining in them. Of it the goldsmiths I carryed with me, for like purposes, made experience. And plenty of gold.

When Baldivia and Arawca were peaceable, they yeelded greatest plentie, and the best: but now, their greatest mynes are in Coquinbo, as also the mines of copper, which they carry to the Peru, and sell it better cheape than it is ordinarily sold in Spaine.

The Indians knowing the end of the Spaniards molestation to be principally the desire of their riches, have enacted, that no man, upon paine of death, doe gather any gold. The Indians forbid the search of gold.

In Coquinbo it rayneth seldome, but every shower of rayne is a shower of gold unto them; for with the violence of the water falling from the mountaines, it bringeth from them the gold; and besides, gives them water to wash it out, as also for their ingenious to worke; so that ordinarily every weeke they have processions for rayne. Every showre a showre of gold.

In this kingdome they make much linnen and woollen cloth, and great store of Indian mantles; with which they furnish other partes; but all is course stuffe. It hath no silke, nor iron, except in mynes, and those as yet not discovered. Pewter is well esteemed, and so are fine linnen, woollen cloth, haberdashers wares, edge tooles, and armes, or munition. Linnen and woollen cloth made in Coquinbo.

[1] *Botijas*—jars.

Sect. XLIV.

It hath its governour, and *audiencia*, with two bishoppes: the one of Saint Iago, the other of the Imperiall; all under the vice-roy, *audiencia*, and primate of Lyma. Saint Iago is the metropolitan and head of the kingdome, and the seate of justice, which hath its appellation[1] to Lyma.

The valour of the Arawcans.

The people are industrious and ingenious, of great strength, and invincible courage; as in the warres, which they have susteyned above fortie yeares continually against the Spaniards, hath beene experienced. For confirmation whereof, I will alledge onely two proofes of many; the one was of an Indian captaine taken prisoner by the Spaniards; and for that he was of name, and knowne to have done his devoire against them, they cut off his hands, thereby intending to disenable him to fight any more against them: but he returning home, desirous to revenge this injury, to maintaine his libertie, with the reputation of his nation, and to helpe to banish the Spaniard, with his tongue intreated and incited them to persevere in their accustomed valour and reputation; abasing the enemy, and advancing his nation; condemning their contraries of cowardlinesse, and confirming it by the crueltie used with him, and others his companions in their mishaps; shewing them his armes without hands, and naming his brethren whose halfe feete they had cut off, because they might be unable to sit on horsebacke: with force arguing, that if they feared them not, they would not have used so great inhumanitie; for feare produceth crueltie, the companion of cowardize. Thus incouraged he them to fight for their lives, limbes, and libertie, choosing rather to die an honourable death fighting, then to live in servitude, as fruitlesse members in their common-wealth. Thus, using the office of a sergeant major, and having loaden his two stumpes with bundles of arrowes, succoured those who in the succeeding battaile had their store wasted, and changing himselfe from place

[1] Appeal.

to place, animated and encouraged his contri-men with such comfortable perswasions, as it is reported, and credibly beleeved, that he did much more good with his words and presence, without striking a strouke, then a great part of the armie did with fighting to the utmost. Sect. XLV.

The other proofe is, that such of them as fight on horsebacke, are but slightly armed, for that their armour is a beasts hide, fitted to their bodie greene, and after worne till it be dry and hard. He that is best armed, hath him double; yet any one of them with these armes, and with his launce, will fight hand to hand with any Spaniard armed from head to foote. And it is credibly reported that an Indian being wounded through the body by a Spaniards launce, with his owne hands hath crept on upon the launce, and come to grapple with his adversary, and both fallen to the ground together. By which is seene their resolution and invincible courage, and the desire they have to maintaine their reputation and libertie.

SECTION XLV.

Leaving the coast of Chily, and running towards that of Peru, my company required the third of the gold we had gotten, which of right belonged unto them; wherein I desired to give them satisfaction of my just intention, but not to devide it till we came home, and so perswaded them with the best reasons I could; alledging the difficultie to devide the barres, and being parted, how easie it was to be robbed of them, and that many would play away their portions and come home as beggarly as they came out; and that the shares could not be well made before our returne to England, because every mans merites could not be discerned nor rewarded till the end of the voyage. In conclusion, it was resolved, and agreed, that the things of price,

Sect. XLV. as gold and silver, should be put into chests with three keyes, whereof I should have the one, the master another, and the third, some other person whom they should name. This they yeelded unto with great difficultie, and not without reason; for the bad correspondence used by many captaines and owners with their companies upon their returne, defrauding them, or diminishing their rights, hath hatched many jealousies, and produced many disorders, with the overthrow of all good discipline and government, as experience teacheth; for where the souldier and mariner is unpaide, or defrauded, what service or obedience can be required at his hands?

Most men unwilling to follow covetous commanders.

The covetous captaine or commander looseth the love of those under his charge: yea, though he have all the parts besides required in a perfect commander, yet if he preferre his private profite before justice, hardly will any man follow such a leader, especially in our kingdome, where more absolute authoritie and trust is committed to those who have charge, than in many other countries.

And therefore in election of chieftaines, care would be had in examination of this poynt. The shamefull fruites whereof (found by experience of many yeares, wherein I have wandred the world), I leave to touch in particular; because I will not diminish the reputation of any. But this let me manifest, that there have been, and are, certaine persons, who, before they goe to sea, either robbe part of the provisions, or in the buying, make penurious, unholsome, and avaritious penny-worths; and the last I hold to be the least: for they robbe onely the victuallers and owners: but the others steale from owners, victuallers, and companie, and are many times the onely overthrowers of the voyage; for the company thinking themselves to be stored with foure or sixe moneths victualls, upon survay, they finde their bread, beefe, or drinke short, yea, perhaps all, and so are forced to seeke home in time of best hopes

The mischiefs of corrupt or scantie provisions.

Sect. XLV.

and imployment. This mischiefe is most ordinary in great actions.

Lastly, some are so cunning, that they not onely make their voyage by robbing before they goe to sea, but of that also which commeth home. Such gamsters, a wise man of our nation resembled to the mill on the river of Thames, for grinding both with flood and ebbe: so these at their going out, and comming home, will be sure to robbe all others of their shares. Although this be a great abuse amongst us, and but of late dayes practised, and by me spoken unto by way of animadversion, either in hope of redresse, or for infliction of punishment; yet I would have the world know, that in other countries the fault is farre more insufferable. And the principall cause which I can finde for it, is that our country imployeth her nobles, or men of credite, in all actions of moment, who rather chuse to spend wealth and gaine honor, then to gaine riches without reputation: whereas in Spaine, and other partes, the advancement of poore men and meane persons by favour and interest, produceth no other end, but private and particular respects to enrich themselves; yet the nobilitie themselves, for the most part, in all occasions pretend rewards for any small service whatsoever, which with us as yet is not in use.

Of detayning and defrauding of wages.

But the greatest and most principall robbery of all, in my opinion, is the defrauding or detaining of the companies thirdes[1] or wages, accursed by the just God, who forbiddeth the hyre of the labourer to sleepe with us. To such I speake as either abuse themselves in detayning it; or else to such as force the poore man to sell it at vile and low prices; and lastly, to such as upon fained cavils and sutes, doe deterre the simple and ignorant sort from their due

[1] "Going by thirds" means that the crew have a certain percentage on the profits of the voyage, in lieu of wages; thus their remuneration partly depends on their own exertions.

Sect. XLV. prosecutions; which being too much in use amongst us, hath bred in those that follow the sea a jealousie in all imployments, and many times causeth mutenies and infinite inconveniences. A poynt deserving consideration and reformation, and which with great facilitie may be remedied, if upright justice would put it selfe as stickler betwixt the owners and company.

Of mariners by challenge of pillage.

No less worthie of reformation are the generall abuses of mariners and souldiers, who robbe all they can, under the colour of pillage, and after make ordinance, cables, sayles, anchors, and all above deckes, to belong unto them of right, whether they goe by thirdes or wages: this proceedeth from those pilfering warres, wherein every gallant that can arme out a shippe, taketh upon him the name and office of a captaine, not knowing what to command, nor what to execute. Such commanders, for the most part, consort and joyne unto themselves disorderly persons, pyrates, and ruffians, under the title of men of valour and experience: they meeting with any prise make all upon the deckes theirs of dutie; viz.—the best peece of ordinance for the captaine; the second, for the gunner; the third, for his mate; the best cable and anchor for the master; the maine topsayle for the botesman;[1] the bonnets for the quarter masters; and the rest of the sayles for the company. The cardes and instruments of the master, for the master; the surgeans instruments and chest for the surgean; the carpenters tooles and chest for the carpenter; and so conquently of each officer, that answereth the other in the two shippes.

If one happen upon a bag of gold, silver, pearle, or precious stones, it is held well gotten, provided it be cleanly stolne, though the shippe and all her loading besides be not worth so much; little considering the common injury in defrauding the owners, victuallers, and whole companie:

[1] Boatswain?

and forgetting, that if himselfe were a jury-man upon another in like case, he would adjudge him to the gallows. But I would advise such novices to know, that our true and auncient discipline of warre is farre different, and being understood, is much more better for the generall. Besides it is grounded on Gods law (from whence all lawes should be derived), and true justice, which distributeth to every one that which belongeth to him of right, and that in due season. Sect. XLV.

The lawes of Oleron, concerning pillage.

In the time of warre in our country, as also in others by the laws of Oleron, which to our auncient sea-men were fundamental, nothing is allowed for pillage but apparell, armes, instruments, and other necessaries belonging to the persons in that shippe which is taken; and these too when the shippe is gained by dint of sword; with a proviso, that if any particular pillage exceed the valew of sixe crownes, it may be redeemed for that valew by the generall stocke, and sould for the common benefit.

If the prise render it selfe without forcible entry, all in generall ought to be preserved and sould in masse, and so equally devided; yea though the shippe be wonne by force and entry, yet whatsoever belongeth to her of tackling, sayles, or ordinance, is to bee preserved for the generalitie: saving a peece of artillery for the captaine, another for the gunner, and a cable and anchor the master; which are the rights due unto them: and these to be delivered when the shippe is in safety, and in harbour, eyther unloaden or sould. Which law or custome, well considered, will rise to be more beneficiall for the owners, victuallers, and company, then the disorders newly crept in and before remembred.

For the sayles, cables, anchors, and hull, being sould every one a part, yeeld not the one halfe which they would doe if they were sould altogether; besides the excusing of charges and robberies in the unloading and parting.

In the warres of Fraunce, in the time of queen Mary,

Sect. XLV. and in other warres, as I have heard of many auncient captaines, the companie had but the fourth part, and every man bound to bring with him the armes with which hee would fight; which in our time I have knowne also used in Fraunce: and if the company victualed themselves, they had then the one halfe, and the owners the other halfe for the shippe, powder, shott, and munition. If any prise were taken, it was sould by the tunne, shippe and goods, so as the loading permitted it; that the marchant having bought the goods, hee might presently transport them whethersoever he would. By this manner of proceeding, all rested contented, all being truely paid; for this was just dealing: if any deserved reward, he was recompensed out of the generall stocke; if any one had filched or stolne, or committed offence, hee had likewise his desert. And who once was knowne to be a disordered person, or a theefe, no man would receive him into his shippe; whereas, now a dayes many vaunt themselves of their theftes and disorders: yea I have seene the common sort of mariners, under the name of pillage, maintaine and justify their robberies most insolently, before the queens majesties commissioners, with arrogant and unseemly termes, for that they would not condiscend to their unreasonable challenges. The demaunds being better worth then five hundreth poundes, which some one pretended to be his: and that of the choysest marchandize, and most of it robbed out of that part of the shippe, which they themselves, and all the world, cannot but confesse to be marchandize.

My opinion is, that such malaperts deserve most justly to have their spoyle taken from them, or some worse consideration, and afterwards to be severely punished, in prevention of greater prejudices, then can by paper be well declared.

But I must tell you withall, such hath beene the partialitie of some commissioners in former times, that upon

Sect. XLV.

information, in lieu of punishment, opinion hath held them for tall fellowes, when, in truth, they never prove the best men in difficult occasions. For their mindes are all set on spoyle, and can bee well contented to suffer their associates to beare the brunt, whillest they are prowling after pillage, the better to gaine and mainetaine the aforesaid attributes in tavernes and disorderly places.

For the orderly and quiet men I have ever found in all occasions to bee of best use, most valiant, and of greatest sufficiency. Yet I condemne none, but those who will be reputed valiant, and are not: examine the accusation.

What ought to be reputed pillage.

All whatsoever is found upon the decke going for marchandize, is exempted out of the censure of pillage: silks, linnen, or woollen cloth in whole peeces, apparell, that goeth to be sold, or other goods whatsoever, though they be in remnants, manifestly knowne to be carryed for that end; or being comprehended in the register, or bills of lading, are not to bee contayned under the name of pillage.

Against the disloyalties of captaines.

But as I have sayd of the consort, so can I not but complaine of many captaines and governours, who, overcome with like greedie desire of gaine, condiscend to the smoothering and suppressing of this auncient discipline, the clenlier to smother their owne disloyalties, in suffering these breakebulks to escape and absent themselves, till the heate be past and partition made.

Concealment of much more value then the trading.

Some of these cause the bils of lading to be cast into the sea, or so to bee hidden that they never appeare. Others send away their prisoners, who sometimes are more worth then the shippe and her lading, because they should not discover their secret stolne treasure; for many times that which is leaft out of the register or bils of lading, with purpose to defraud the prince of his customes (in their conceits held to be excessive), is of much more value then that which the shippe and lading is worth. Yea I have knowne shippes worth two hundreth thousand pounds, and

Sect. XLV. better, cleane swept of their principall riches, nothing but the bare bulke being left unsacked. The like may be spoken of that which the disorderly mariner and the souldier termeth pillage; yet all winked at and unpunished, although such prizes have beene rendred without stroake stricken.

This, doubtlesse, cannot but be a hearts griefe and discouragement to all those who vertuously and truely desire to observe the auncient discipline of our nation, their owne honours, and the service of their soveraigne.

The prevention of undue pillagings.

But to prevent these unknowne mischiefes, and for his better discharge, I remember that my father, Sir John Hawkins, in his instructions, in actions under his charge, had this particular article: that whosoever rendred or tooke any shippe, should be bound to exhibite the bils of lading: to keepe the captaine, master, marchants, and persons of account, and to bring them to him to be examined, or into England. If they should bee by any accident seperated from him, whatsoever was found wanting (the prisoners being examined), was to bee made good by the captaine and company which tooke the shippe, and this upon great punishments. I am witness, and avow that this course did redownd much to the benefitte of the generall stocke; to the satisfactione of her majestie and counsell, the justification of his government, and the content of his followers.

Thus much have I set downe concerning these abuses and the reformation thereof, for that I have neither seene them divulged by any with whom I have gone to sea, neither yet recorded in writing by any mans pen. Let consideration present them to the eares of the powerfull. But now to our voyage.

SECTION XLVI.

RUNNING alongst the coast till wee came within a few leagues of Arica, nothing happened unto us of extraordinary noveltie or moment, for we had the brese favourable, which seldome happeneth in this climate; finding ourselves in nineteene degrees, wee haled the shore close abourd, purposing to see if there were any shipping in the road of Arica.[1] It standeth in a great large bay, in eighteene degrees: and before you come to it, a league to the southwards of the roade and towne, is a great round hill, higher then the rest of the land of the bay, neere about the towne; which wee having discovered, had sight presently of a small barke, close abourd the shore, becalmed. Manning our boate, wee tooke her, being loaden with fish, from Moromereno;[2] which is a goodly headland, very high, and lyeth betwixt twenty-foure and twenty-five degrees, and whether ordinarily some barkes use to goe a fishing every yeare.

Sect. XLVI.

Arica.

In her was a Spaniard and sixe Indians. The Spaniard, for that hee was neere the shore, swam unto the rockes; and though wee offered to returne him his barke and fish (as was our meaning), yet hee refused to accept it, and made us answere, that hee durst not, for feare least the justice should punish him. In so great subjection are the poore unto those who had the administration of justice in those partes, and in most partes of the kingdomes and countries subject to Spaine. Insomuch, that to heare the justice to enter into their doores, is to them destruction and desolation: for this cause wee carried her alongst with us.

The severity of Spaine.

In this meane while wee had sight of another tall shippe, comming out of the sea, which wee gave chase unto, but

[1] A Peruvian seaport, in 18° 27′ S.

[2] Monte Morena.

Sect. XLVI. could not fetch upp, beeing too good of sayle for us. Our small prize and boate standing off unto us, descryed another shippe, which they chased and tooke also, loaden with fish, comming from the ilands of Iuan Fernandes.

After wee opened the bay and port of Arica; but seeing it cleane without shipping, wee haled the coast alongst, and going aboord to visit the bigger prize, my company saluted me with a volley of small shot. Amongst them, one musket brake, and carryed away the hand of him that shot it, through his owne default, which for that I have seene to happen many times, I think it necessary to note in this place, that others may take warning by his harme.

Over-charging of artilleries.

The cause of the muskets breaking, was the charging with two bullets, the powder being ordayned to carry but the waight of one, and the musket not to suffer two charges of powder or shott. By this oversight, the fire is restrayned with the overplus of the waight of shott, and not being able to force both of them out, breaketh all to peeces, so to find a way to its owne center.

And I am of opinion, that it is a great errour to prove great ordinance, or small shot, with double charges of powder or shot; my reason is, for that ordinarily the mettall is proportioned to the waight of the shot which the peece is to beare, and the powder correspondent to the waight of the bullet; and this being graunted, I see no reason why any man should require to prove his peece with more then is belonging to it of right: for I have seene many goodly peeces broken with such tryals, being cleane without hony combes, cracke, flawe, or other perceavable blemish, which no doubt, with their ordinary allowance, would have served many yeares. Yea, I have beene certified by men of credit, that some gunners have taken a glory for breaking many peeces in the tryall; which is easie to be done by sundry slights and meanes not fitt to bee published, much lesse to bee exercised, being prejudiciall to the seller, and chargeable to the conscience of the practiser; therefore it were good, this excessive tryall by double charges were cleane abolished. If I should make choyce for my selfe, I would not willingly, that any peece should come into fort or shippe, under my charge, which had borne at any time more then his ordinary allowance, misdoubting, least, through the violence of the double charge, the peece may be crased within, or so forced, as at another occasion with his ordinary allowance, he might breake in peeces: how many men so many mindes: for to others this may seem harsh, for that the contrary custome hath so long time beene received, and therefore I submit to better experience, and contradict not but that in a demy culvering, a man may put two saker or minion shots, or many of smaller waight: and so in a muskett, two calever shott, or many smaller, so they exceede not the ordinary waight prescribed by proportion, arte, and experience.[1] These experiments I hold convenient upon many occasions, yea, and most necessary; but the vaine custome of double charges, to cause their peeces thereby to give a better report, I affirme can produce no other effect but danger, losse, and harme.

SECTION XLVII.

Having visited our prises, and finding nothing in them but fish, we tooke a small portion for our victualling, and gave the bigger shippe to the Spaniards againe, and the lesser wee kept, with purpose to make her our pinnas. The Indians which wee tooke in her, would by no meanes depart from us, but desired to goe with us to England, saying that the Indian and English were brothers; and in

[1] The demy-culverin was about equivalent to the nine-pounder; a saker to the six-pounder; and the minion to the four-pounder.

Sect. XLVIII.

The amity of the Indians.

all places where wee came, they shewed themselves much affectionated unto us: these were natives of Moremoreno, and the most brutish of all that ever I had seene; and except it were in forme of men and speech, they seemed altogether voyde of that which appertained to reasonable men. They were expert swimmers; but after the manner of spaniels, they dive and abide under water a long time, and swallow the water of the sea as if it were of a fresh river. Except a man see them, he would hardly beleeve how they continue in the sea, as if they were mer-maides, and the water their naturall element.

Their countrey is most barren, and poore of foode. If they take a fish alive out of the sea, or meete with a peece of salted fish, they will devoure it without any dressing, as savourely as if had beene most curiously sodden or dressed, all which makes me beleeve that they sustaine themselves of that which they catch in the sea.

The Spaniards profit themselves of their labour and travell, and recompense them badly: they are in worse condition then their slaves, for to those they give sustenance, house-roome, and clothing, and teach them the knowledge of God; but the other they use as beastes, to doe their labour without wages, or care of their bodies or soules.

SECTION XLVIII.

Thwart of Ariquipa,[1] the shippe we brought with us from Balparizo being very leake, and my companie satisfied that their hope to find any thing of worth in her was vaine, having searched her from post to stemme, condiscended to

[1] Arequipa is ninety miles inland. In those days Quilca was the port of Arequipa.

fire her; and the rather to keepe our company together, which could not well suffer any devision more then of meere necessity: so by generall accord we eased ourselves of her, and continued our course alongst the coast, till we came thwart the bay of Pisco, which lyeth within fifteene degrees and fifteene minutes. Sect. XLVIII.

Presently after wee were cleare of Cape Saugalean,[1] and his ilands, wee ranged this bay with our boate and pinnace. It hath two small ilands[2] in it, but without fruite; and being becalmed, we anchored two dayes thwart of Chilca.

By sea and by land, those of Chyly had given advise to Don Garcia Hurtado de Mendoça marquis of Cañete,[3] viceroy of Peru, resident in Lima, of our being on the coast. Hee presently with all possible diligence, put out sixe shippes in warlike order, with well neere two thousand Advise given by sea and land.

[1] Sangallan is an island off the shore with a bold cliffy outline.

[2] Afterwards so famous as the Guano Islands of Chincha. But there are three of them.

[3] Son of Don Andres Hurtado de Mendoza, Marquis of Cañete, who served under Charles V in Germany and Flanders, at Tunis and Algiers, and then went out as Viceroy of Peru in 1555, dying at Lima in 1560. The mother of Don Garcia was Maria Manrique, daughter of the Count of Osorno, President of the Council of the Indies. Garcia was the second but eldest surviving son, and was born in his father's castle at Cuenca. He succeeded his brother Diego as fourth Marquis of Cañete. After distinguishing himself in the wars of Charles V in Europe, he went out to Peru with his father, who appointed him Captain-General of Chile. He was the first ruler in Chile who defeated the Araucans, and forced them to a truce, thus giving an interval of peace to the country. Returning to Europe, he was employed on diplomatic missions in Italy and Portugal. In 1590 he went out again as Viceroy of Peru, returning in 1599. His first wife was Teresa de Castro, daughter of Don Pedro Fernandez de Castro, fifth Count of Lemos, by whom he had a son and successor, Juan Hurtado de Mendoza, fifth Marquis of Cañete. His second wife was Ana Florencia de la Cerda, sister of the Duke of Medina Celi. An account of the life and acts of the fourth Marquis of Cañete was written by Dr. Christoval Suarez de Figueroa, and his victories in Chile were celebrated by Pedro de Oña, in his poem entitled *Arauco Domado*.

Sect. XLVIII. men, and dispatched them to seeke us, and to fight with us, under the conduct of Don Beltrian de Castro Ydelaluca,[1] his wives brother; who departing out of the port of Callao, turned to wind-ward in sight over the shore, from whence they had dayly intelligence where wee had beene discovered. And the next day after our departure out of Chilca,[2] about the middle of May, at breake of day, wee had sight of each other, thwart of Cañete,[3] wee being to windwards of the Spanish armado some two leagues, and all with little or no winde. Our pinnace or prise being furnished with oares came unto us, out of which we thought to have taken our men, and so to leave her; but being able to come unto us at all times, it was held for better to keepe her till necessity forced us to leave her: and so it was determined that if we came to likelihood of boording, shee should lay our boate aboord, and enter all her men, and from thence to enter our shippe, and so to forsake her. Although, by the event in that occasion this proved good, notwithstanding I hold it to bee reproved where the enemie is farre superiour in multitude and force, and able to come and bourd if hee list; and that the surest course is to fortifie the principall the best that may bee, and to cut of all impediments, where a man is forced to defence: for that no man is assured to have time answerable to his purpose and will; and upon doubt whether the others, in hope to save themselves, will not leave him in greatest extremitie.

[1] Don Beltran de Castro was the second son of Don Pedro Fernandez de Castro Andrada, fifth Count of Lemos, by Leonora de la Cueva, daughter of Don Beltran de la Cueva, third Duke of Albuquerque. His sister Teresa married the Marquis of Cañete. The name "Ydelaluca" in the text is some wild typographical jumble.

[2] Chilca is a little coast valley surrounded by desert, north of Cañete.

[3] Cañete is a fertile valley on the Peruvian coast, between Pisco and Lima; so named after the Marquis. The native name is Huarcu.

SECTION XLIX.

WEE presently put ourselves in the best order wee could to fight and to defend ourselves: our prayers we made unto the Lord God of battails, for his helpe and our deliverance, putting our selves wholy into his hands. About nine of the clocke, the brese began to blow, and wee to stand off into the sea, the Spaniards cheeke by jole with us, ever getting to the wind-wards upon us; for that the shipping of the South sea is ever moulded sharpe under water, and long; all their voyages depending upon turning to windwardes, and the brese blowing ever southerly. Sect. XLIX.

As the sunne began to mount aloft, the wind began to fresh; which together with the rowling sea that ever beateth upon this coast, comming out of the westerne-bourd, caused a chapping sea, wherewith the admirall of the Spaniards snapt his maine mast asunder, and so began to lagge a sterne, and with him other two shippes. The vice-admirall split her maine-sayle, being come within shott of us upon our broad side, but to leewards: the reare-admirall cracked her maine-yard asunder in the middest, being a head of us. One of the armado, which had gotten upon the broad side of us, to wind-wards, durst not assault us.

With these disgraces[1] upon them, and the hand of God helping and delivering us, night comming, we began to consult what course was best to be taken to free our selves; wherein were divers opinions: some sayd it was best to stand off to the sea close by all the night; others to lye it a hull; others to cast about to the shoare-wards two glasses, and after all the night to stand off to sea close by. The admirall of the Spaniards, with the other two, were a sterne of us some four leagues; the vice-admirall a mile

[1] Used in the sense of misfortunes.

Sect. XLIX. right to le-wards of us; the reare-admirall in a manner right a head, some culvering shott; and one upon our loofe, within shott also. The moon was to rise within two houres. After much debating, it was concluded that wee should beare up before the winde, and seeke to escape betwixt the admirall and the vice-admirall, which wee put in execution, not knowing of any other disgrace befallen them, but that of the reare-admirall, till after our surrender, when they recounted unto us all that had past. In the morning at breake of day, wee were cleare of all our enemies, and so shaped our course alongst the coast, for the bay of Atacames, where we purposed to trim our pinnace, and to renue our wood and water, and so to depart upon our voyage with all possible speede.

The Spanish armado returned presently to Callao, which is the port of Lyma, or of the Citty of the Kings. It was first named Lyma, and retayneth also that name of the river, which passeth by the citty called Lyma. The Spanish armado being entred the port, the people began to goe ashore, where they were so mocked and scorned by the women, as scarce any one by day would shew his face: they reviled them with the name of cowards and golnias, and craved licence of the vice-roy to bee admitted in their roomes, and to undertake the surrendry of the English shippe. I have beene certified for truth, that some of them affronted their souldiers with daggers and pistols by their sides.

This wrought such effects in the hearts of the disgraced, as they vowed eyther to recover their reputation lost, or to follow us into England; and so with expedition, the vice-roy commaunded two shippes and a pinnace to be put in order, and in them placed the chiefe souldiers and marriners of the rest, and furnished them with victuals and munition.

The foresayd generall is once againe dispatched to seeke

us; who ranged the coastes and ports, enforming himselfe what hee could. Some fiftie leagues to the northwards of Lyma, in sight of Mongon,[1] wee tooke a shippe halfe loaden with wheate, sugar, miell de canas, and cordovan skins: which for that shee was leake, and sayled badly, and tackled in such maner as the marriners would not willingly put themselves into her, wee tooke what was necessary for our provision, and fired her.

Thwart of Truxillo,[2] we set the companie of her a shore, with the pilot which we had taken in Balparizo, reserving the pilot of the burnt shippe, and a Greeke, who chose rather to continue with us, then to hazard their lives in going a shore; for that they had departed out of the port of Santa,[3] which is in eight degrees, being required by the justice not to weigh anchor before the coast was knewne to be cleere.

It is a thing worthy to be noted, and almost incredible, with how few men they use to sayle a shippe in the South sea; for in this prise, which was above an hundred tuns, were but eight persons: and in a shippe of three hundreth tuns, they use not to put above fourteene or fifteene persons; yea, I have beene credibly enformed, that with foureteene persons, a shippe of five hundreth tuns hath beene carried from Guayaquil to Lyma, deepe loaden (which is above two hundreth leagues): and are forced ever to gaine their voyage by turning to wind-wards, which is the greatest toyle and labour that the marriners have; and slow sometimes in this voyage foure or five moneths, which is generall in all the navigations of this coast.[4] But the security from

[1] Cerro Mongon, a high point on the Peruvian coast, north of Lima, between Guarmey and Casma.

[2] Truxillo is some miles inland. Its port is Huanchaco, in 8° 6′ S.

[3] A small but good anchorage, south of Truxillo.

[4] The plan pursued at that day was to beat to windward in shore; now, by standing out boldly to the westward, the voyage to the southward, against the prevailing wind, is much shortened.

Sect. L. stormes, and certainty of the breze, with the desire to make their gaine the greater, is the cause that every man forceth himselfe to the uttermost, to doe the labour of two men.

SECTION L.

The ilands of Salomon. In the height of this port of Santa, some seven hundreth and fiftie leagues to the west-wardes, lie the ilands of Salomon, of late yeares discovered.[1] At my being in Lyma, a fleete of foure sayle was sent from thence to people them; which through the emulation and discord that arose amongst them, being landed and setled in the countrie, was utterly overthrowne; onely one shippe, with some few of the people, after much misery, got to the Philippines.[2] This I

[1] The Solomon Islands are between 7° and 11° S. latitude. Santa is in 9° S.

[2] The first expedition to the Solomon Islands was fitted out by the Viceroy Castro, and sailed from Callao in 1567, under command of the gallant young Alvaro Mendaña de Meyra, then only twenty-six years of age. After a voyage of eighty days they reached one of the Solomon Islands, named by Mendaña the Island of Santa Isabella de Estrella. Mendaña returned to Peru, but he had to wait a quarter of a century before he could induce another Viceroy to fit out an expedition. At last, the Marquis of Cañete despatched him again, and he sailed from Payta on the 16th of June, 1595. This must be the expedition referred to by Sir Richard Hawkins. The object was to attempt the colonisation of the Solomon Islands, and Mendaña had Pedro Fernandez de Quiros as chief pilot. The expedition consisted, as Sir Richard says, of four vessels. After discovering the Marquesas, named after the Marquis of Cañete, they sighted an island on the 7th September, which they named Santa Cruz; and here Mendaña resolved to form his colony. But he fell ill and died on the 17th of October, and his wife Doña Isabel took command of the expedition. Sickness broke out, and she bore up for Manilla, but only two out of the four vessels arrived there in safety. Here Doña Isabel found a second husband, with whom she went to Mexico. The best account of the expeditions of Mendaña will be found in the *Hechos de Don Garcia de Mendoza, Marques de Cañete*, by Dr.

came to the knowledge of by a large relation written from a person of credit, and sent from the Philippines to Panama. I saw it at my being there, in my voyage towards Spaine. Sect. L.

Having edged neere the coast to put the Spaniards on shore, a thicke fogge tooke us, so that wee could not see the land; but recovering our pinnace and boate, we sayled on our course, till we came thwart of the port called Malabrigo: it lyeth in seaven degrees.

In all this coast the current runneth with great force, but never keepeth any certaine course, saving that it runneth along the coast, sometimes to the south-wards, sometimes to the north-wards; which, now running to the north-wards, forced us so far into the bay, which a point of the land causeth, that they call Punta de Augussa,[1] as thinking to cleere ourselves by roving north-west, wee could not double this point, making our way north north-west. Therefore speciall care is ever to bee had of the current: and doubtlesse, if the providence of Almighty God had not freede us, wee had runne ashore upon the land, without seeing or suspecting any such danger. His name bee ever exalted and magnified for delivering us from the unknowne daunger, by calming the winde all night; the sunnes rising manifested unto us our errour and perill, by discovering unto us the land within two leagues, right a head. The current had carried us without any wind, at the least foure leagues; which seene, and the winde beginning to blow, wee brought our tackes abourd, and in short time cleared our selves. Punta de Augussa.

Thwart of this point of Augussa, lie two desert ilandes;

Christoval Suarez de Figueroa (Madrid, 1613), lib. vi. There is also a narrative of the events of the second voyage in a letter from the Pilot Quiros to Don Antonio de Morga, Governor of the Philippines. Sir Richard probably saw this letter from Quiros.

[1] Punta de Aguja, a long and level point, terminating in a bluff 150 feet high; in 5° 55′ S.

Sect. L. they call them Illas de Lobos,[1] for the multitude of seales which accustome to haunt the shore. In the bigger is very good harbour, and secure: they lie in sixe degrees thirtie minutes.

The next day after, wee lost sight of these ilands, being thwart of Payta,[2] which lyeth in five degrees; and having manned our pinnace and boate to search the port, wee had sight of a tall shippe, which having knowledge of our being on the coast, and thinking her selfe to be more safe at sea then in the harbour, put her selfe then under sayle: to her wee gave chase all that night and the next day, but in fine she being of better sayle than wee, shee freed her selfe. Thus being too lee-ward of the harbour and discovered, we continued our course alongst the shore. That evening wee were thwart of the river of Guayaquill, which hath in the mouth of it two ilands: the souther-most and biggest, called Puma,[3] in three degrees; and the other, to the northwards, Santa Clara.[4]

Puma. Puma is inhabited, and is the place where they build their principall shipping; from this river, Lyma and all the valleys are furnished with timber, for they have none but that which is brought from hence, or from the kingdome of Chile. By this river passeth the principall trade of the kingdome of Quito; it is navigable some leagues into the land, and hath great abundance of timber.

Those of the Peru, use to ground and trim their shippes in Puma, or in Panama, and in all other partes they are forced to carene their shippes. In Puma, it higheth and falleth fifteene or sixteene foote water, and from this iland till a man come to Panama, in all the coast it ebbeth and floweth more or lesse, keeping the ordinary course which the tides doe in all seas. The water of this river, by ex-

[1] Lobos de Afuera and Lobos de Tierra are two guano islands off the coast of Peru. [2] In 5° 3′ S. [3] Puna.

[4] Also called the Isla del Muerto.

perience, is medicinable, for all aches of the bones, for the stone, and strangurie: the reason which is given is, because all the bankes and low lands adjoining to this river, are replenished with salsaperillia;[1] which lying for the most part soaking in the water, it participateth of this vertue, and giveth it this force.

In this river, and all the rivers of this coast, are great abundance of *alagartoes*;[2] and it is sayd that this exceedeth the rest; for persons of credit have certified mee, that as small fishes in other rivers abound in scoales, so the alagartoes in this. They doe much hurt to the Indians and Spaniards, and are dreadfull to all whom they catch within their clutches.

SECTION LI.

Sect. LI.

SOME five or sixe leagues to the north-wards of Puna, is la Punta de Santa Elena; under which is good anchoring, cleane ground, and reasonable succour. Being thwart of this point, wee had sight of a shippe, which wee chased; but being of better saile then wee, and the night comming on, we lost sight of her, and so anchored under the Isla de Plata, to recover our pinnace and boate, which had gone about the other point of the iland, which lyeth in two degrees and fortie minutes.

[1] Speaking of Puna and Guayaquil, Cieza de Leon says—"An herb grows in abundance on this island, and in the province of Guayaquil, which is called sarsaparilla because it grows like a bramble from its birth, and small leaves grow out of the suckers and other parts of the branches." *Sarsa* (Sp.) means a bramble, and *parilla*, a vine. It is the *Smilax officinalis* H. B. K. The root was brought to Europe in about 1530. Acosta tells the same story as Sir Richard, that the water flowing past the sarsaparilla roots has healing virtues (*Nat. Hist.*, iii, cap. 17). Cieza de Leon describes the virtues of sarsaparilla and the method of using it. See my translation of Cieza de Leon, being the Hakluyt Society's volume for 1864, p. 200.

[2] Alligators.

Sect. LI.

Puerto Viejo.

The next day we past in sight of Puerto Viejo, in two degrees and ten minutes; which lying without shipping, wee directed our course for Cape Passaos.[1] It lyeth directly under the equinoctiall lyne; some fourescore leagues to the west-wards of this cape, lyeth a heape of ilands, the Spaniards call Illas de Los Galapagos: they are desert and bear no fruite. From Cape Passaos, wee directed our course to Cape Saint Francisco,[2] which lyeth in one degree to the north-wardes of the lyne; and being thwart of it, wee descried a small ship, which wee chased all that day and night; and the next morning our pinnace came to bourd her; and being a shippe of advise, and full of passengers, and our shippe not able to fetch her up, they entreated our people badly, and freed themselves; though the feare they conceived, caused them to cast all the dispatches of the king, as also of particulars, into the sea, with a great part of their loading, to bee lighter and better of sayle; for the shippes of the South sea loade themselves like lighters, or sand barges, presuming upon the securitie from stormes.

[1] Cape Passado; so called from being the first promontory after crossing the Line, coming from the north.

[2] Cape San Francisco is a high cliff, clothed with tall trees, and backed by the lofty chain of the Andes in full view from the sea. The cliffs are white. It is forty miles north of the equator. It was off Cape San Francisco that Sir Francis Drake captured his rich prize the *Cacafuego*, on the 1st of March, 1579. Cook and Dampier were off this cape on Christmas Day, 1685, and, in his narrative, Dampier says—"The country inland is high and mountainous, and appears to be woody; by the sea it is full of small points, making as many little sandy bays between them. It is of indifferent height, covered with trees, so that sailing by this coast, you see nothing but a vast grove or wood, which is so much the more pleasant because the trees are of several forms, both in respect of their youth and colour." Seemann testifies to the accuracy of this description, and adds that the cliffs in many parts are white, somewhat resembling those of Sussex and Kent. See *Narrative of the Voyage of H.M.S. "Herald"*, i, p. 63.

SECTION LII.

BEING out of hope to fetch up this shippe, wee stood in with the cape, where the land beginneth to trend about to the east-wards. The cape is high land, and all covered over with trees, and so is the land over the cape; and all the coast, from this cape to Panama, is full of wood, from the Straites of Magelan to this Cape of San Francisco.[1] In all the coast from head-land to head-land, the courses lye betwixt the north, and north and by west, and sometimes more westerly, and that but seldome. It is a bold coast, and subject to little foule weather or alteration of windes, for the brese, which is the sowtherly wind, bloweth continually from Balparizo to Cape San Francisco, except it be a great chance. Sect. LII.

Trending about the cape, wee haled in east north-east, to fetch the bay of Atacames,[2] which lyeth some seaven leagues from the cape. In the mid-way, some three leagues from the shore, lyeth a banke of sand, whereof a man must

1 Here some words must have been omitted. From the Straits to Cape San Francisco there are two regions. The more southern one, embracing Patagonia and southern Chile, is wooded; while the coasts of Bolivia and Peru are arid and for the most part treeless.

2 Atacames is in 0° 57′ 30″ N. latitude, twelve miles east of Point Galera, which is twelve miles from Cape San Francisco; and fourteen miles south-east of the entrance of the river Esmeraldas. The village of Atacames is on the sea shore at the mouth of a small river, a miserable place, consisting of a few huts, frequented by a few coasting vessels. Woodes Rogers, the buccaneer, anchored in the Bay of Atacames on the 24th of August, 1709, with his two ships, the *Duke* and *Duchess*, of Bristol. He watered at Atacames, and then proceeded to the Galapagos. Very good anchorage is found in the Bay of Atacames, and, as it seldom or never blows, vessels can anchor almost anywhere. H.M.S. *Herald*, in January 1846, anchored off the river Sua, within a walk of the village of Atacames. It was here that Mr. Edmonston, the naturalist of the *Herald* and predecessor of Dr. Seemann, was accidentally shot while getting into a boat. He was buried on shore. (See Seemann's *H.M.S. "Herald"*, i, p. 67.)

Sect. LII. have a care; for in some parts of it, there is but little water.

The tenth of June, wee came to an anchor in the bay of Atacames, which on the wester part hath a round hummock. It seemeth an iland, and in high springes I judge that the sea goeth round about it. To the east-wards it hath a high sandie cliffe, and in the middest of the bay, a faire birth from the shore, lyeth a bigge black rocke above water: from this rocke to the sandie cliffe, is a drowned marsh ground, caused by his lownesse; and a great river, which is broad, but of no depth.

Manning our boate, and running to the shore, we found presently, in the westerne bight of the bay, a deepe river, whose indraught was so great that we could not benefit our selves of it, being brackish, except at low water, which hindred our dispatch; yet in five dayes, wee filled all our emptie caske, supplied our want of wood, and grounded and put in order our pinnace.

They dismisse their Indians.

Here, for that our Indians served us to no other use but to consume our victuals, we eased our selves of them; gave them hookes and lines which they craved, and some bread for a few dayes, and replanted them in a farre better countrey then their owne, which fell out luckely for the Spaniards of the shippe which wee chased thwart of Cape San Francisco; for victuals growing short with her, having many mouthes, shee was forced to put a shore fiftie of her passengers neere the cape; whereof more than the one halfe dyed with famine and continual wading through rivers and waters: the rest, by chance, meeting with the Indians which wee had put a shore, with their fishing, guide, and industry, were refreshed, susteyned, and brought to habitation.

SECTION LIII.

OUR necessary business being ended, wee purposed the fifteenth day of May, in the morning, to set sayle; but the foureteenth in the evening, wee had sight of a shippe, some three leagues to sea-wards; and through the importunitie of my captaine and companie, I condiscended that our pinnas should give her chase; which I should not have done, for it was our destruction. I gave them precise order, that if they stood not in againe at night, they should seeke mee at Cape San Francisco, for the next morning I purposed to set sayle without delay. And so seeing that our pinnas slowed her comming, at nine of the clocke in the morning wee weyed our anchors, and stood for the cape, where wee beate off and on two dayes; and our pinnas not appearing, wee stood againe into the bay, where wee descried her turning in without a maine mast, which standing off to the sea close by, with much winde, and a chapping sea, bearing a taunt-sayle, where a little was too much (being to small purpose), sodainly they bare it by the bourd; and standing in with the shore, the winde, or rather God blinding them for our punishment, they knewe not the land; and making themselves to bee to wind-wards of the bay, bare up, and were put into the bay of San Mathew.[1] It is a goodly harbour, and hath a great Sect. LIII.

[1] The Bay of San Mateo is that part of the coast of the province of Quito (modern Republic of Ecuador), which lies east of the mouth of the river Esmeraldas. This country, between the Andes and the sea, formed, in Spanish times, the government of Atacames, bordered inland by those of Quito and Ibarra, northwards by Barbacoas, in the province of Popayan, and south by Guayaquil. Along the coast Atacames extends from 0° 34′ S. to 1° 30′ N. latitude. After its conquest by Sebastian de Belalcazar, it remained for a long time unexplored, a wild region of dense forest, traversed only by one considerable river, that of Esmeraldas. But the advantage was always understood, that would be derived from opening a port on this coast for the city of Quito, thus saving the much longer journey to Guayaquil. Sir Richard Hawkins

Sect. LIII. fresh river, which higheth fifteene or sixteene foote water, and is a good countrey, and well peopled with Indians: they have store of gold and emeralds. Heere the Spaniards from Guayaquill made an habitation, whilst I was prisoner in Lyma, by the Indians consent; but after, not able to suffer the insolencies of their guests, and being a people of stomacke and presumption, they suffered themselves to bee perswaded and led by a Molato. This leader many yeares before had fled unto them from the Spaniards: him they had long time held in reputation of their captaine generall, and was admitted also unto a chiefe office by the Spaniardes, to gaine him unto them.

The Indians led by a Molato.

But now the Indians uniting themselves together, presuming that by the helpe of this Molato, they should force

relates one attempt to settle Atacames, in the text. The Viceroy, Marquis of Montes Claros, made a second attempt in 1621, when he appointed Pablo Durango Delgadillo to be Governor of Atacames and Esmeraldas, with a contract to make a road from the town of Ibarra to the river of Santiago de Esmeraldas. On his failure in 1626, the government was conferred upon Francisco Perez Manacho, who also failed. Then followed Juan Vicencio Justiniani, who was also unable to make a road through the forests; and failure also attended the efforts of Hernando de Soto Calderon, who was appointed in 1713. Don Pedro Vicente Maldonado, however, did succeed in opening direct communication from Quito to the river Esmeraldas in 1741, and in 1746 he was appointed Governor. The distance from Quito to the mouth of the Esmeraldas is thirty-one leagues direct; but by the route there are forty-six leagues: twenty-one through the forests and twenty-five by the river. Maldonado did much to improve the country, forming five seaports, called Tumaco, Tola, San Mateo de Esmeraldas, Atacames, and La Canoa. The region is now comprised, under the Ecuadorian Government, in the province of Esmeraldas; the chief place of which is the town of Esmeraldas, in 0° 56′ N., which is several leagues nearer the mouth of the river than the old town of the same name, and consists of a few huts, with a population under five hundred.

The *Herald* anchored off the Esmeraldas river on January 27th, 1846. Seemann describes it as rising near the volcano of Pichincha, and having a course of 350 miles. Next to the Guayaquil, it is the largest river on the coast, but it is extraordinarily rapid, and will never be of great value for commercial purposes. The town of Esmeraldas is situated on the left bank.

the Spaniards out of the countrey, put their resolution into execution, drove their enemies into the woods, and slue as many as they could lay hands on; some they killed, few escaped with life; and those who had that good happe, suffered extreame misery before they came to Quito, the place of neerest habitation of Spaniards. Sect. LIII.

To this bay, assoone as our people in the pinnas saw their errour, they brought their tackes abourd, and turned and tyded it up, as they could. Assoone as we came to anchor, I procured to remedie that was amisse; in two daies wee dispatched all we had to doe, and the next morning wee resolved to set sayle, and to leave the coast of Peru and Quito.

The day appearing, we began to weigh our anchors, and being a pike, ready to cut sayle, one out of the toppe descryed the Spanish armado, comming about the cape; Spanish Armado. which by the course it kept, presently gave us to understand who they were: though my company, as is the custome of seamen, made them to be the fleete bound for Panama, loaden with treasure, and importuned that in all hast we should cut sayle and stand with them; which I contradicted, for that I was assured, that no shipping would stirre upon the coast till they had securitie of our departure (except some armado that might be sent to seeke us), and that it was not the time of the yeare to carry the treasure to Panama. And besides, in riding still at an anchor, they ever came neerer unto us; for they stood directly with us and wee kept the weather gage; where if we had put our selves under sayle, the ebbe in hand, wee should have given them the advantage, which we had in our power, by reason of the point of the bay. And being the armado, as it was, we gained time to fit ourselves, the better to fight. And truly (as before, to a stiffe-necked horse), so now againe I cannot but resemble the condition of the mariner, to any thing better, then to the current of a furious river

Sect. LIII.

repressed by force or art, which neverthelesse ceaseth not to seeke a way to overthrow both fence and banke: even so the common sort of sea-men, apprehending a conceite in their imaginations, neither experiment, knowledge, examples, reasons, nor authority, can alter and remoove them from their conceited opinions. In this extremitie, with reason I laboured to convince them, and to contradict their pretences: but they altogether without reason, or against reason, breake out, some into vaunting and bragging, some into reproaches of want of courage, others into wishings that they had never come out of their countrey, if we should refuse to fight with two shippes whatsoever. And to mend the matter, the gunner, for his part, assured me that with the first tire[1] of shott, he would lay the one of them in the sods; and our pinnace, that she would take the other to taske. One promised that he would cut downe the mayne yard; another that he would take their flagge; and all in generall shewed a great desire to come to tryall with the enemy. To some I turned the deafe eare, with others I dissembled, and armed myselfe with patience (having no other defence nor remedie for that occasion), soothing and animating them to the execution of what they promised, and perswaded them to have a little sufferance, seeing they gained time and advantage by it.

The unadvised courage of the multitude.

And to give them better satisfaction, I condiscended that our captaine, with a competent number of men, should with our pinnace goe to discover them; with order that they should not engage themselves in that manner as they might not be able to come unto us, or we to succour them. In all these divisions and opinions, our master, Hugh Dormish,[2] who was a most sufficient man for government and valour, and well saw the errors of the multitude, used his office as became him; and so did all those of best understanding.

[1] The first broadside—*tirer* (French).

[2] Cornish? See page 106.

Sect. LIII.

In short space our pinnace discovered what they were, and casting about to returne unto us, the vice-admirall, being next her, began with her chace to salute her with three or foure peeces of artillery, and so continued chasing her and gunning at her. My company seeing this, now began to change humour; and I then to encourage and perswade them to performe the execution of their promises and vaunts of valour, which they had but even now protested, and given assurance of by their proferres and forwardnesse.

And that we might have sea-roome to fight, we presently weighed anchor, and stood off to sea with all our sayles, in hope to get the weather gage of our contraries. But the winde scanting with us, and larging with them, we were forced to lee-ward. And the admirall weathering us, came rome[1] upon us: which being within musket shott, we hayled first with our noise of trumpets, then with our waytes, and after with our artilery; which they answered with artilery two for one. For they had double the ordinance we had, and almost tenne men for one. Immediately they came shoring[2] abourd of us, upon our lee quarter, contrary to our expectation, and the custome of men of warre. And doubtlesse, had our gunner been the man he was reputed to be, and as the world sould him to me, shee had received great hurt by that manner of bourding. But contrary to all expectation, our stearne peeces were unprimed, and so were all those which we had to lee-ward, save halfe one in the quarter, which discharged, wrought that effect in our contraries as that they had five or sixe foote water in hold, before they suspected it.

The beginning of the fight.

The inexperience of the Spaniards.

And carelesnesse of the English.

Hereby all men are to take warning by me, not to trust

How farre a commander is to trust his officers.

[1] Down?

[2] To sheer, or shore, means to *separate*—we use the term "sheer to", but "sheer off" appears to be the only sense in which it should be applied.

Sect. LIII.

any man in such extremities, when he himselfe may see it done: and comming to fight, let the chieftaine himselfe be sure to have all his artilery in a readinesse upon all occasions. This was my oversight, this my overthrow. For I and all my company had that satisfaction of the sufficiencie and the care of our gunner, as not any one of us ever imagined there would be any defect found in him. For my part, I with the rest of my officers, occupied our selves in cleering our deckes, laceing our nettings, making of bulwarkes, arming our toppes, fitting our wast-cloathes, tallowing our pikes, slinging our yards, doubling our sheetes, and tackes, placing and ordering our people, and procuring that they should be well fitted and provided of all things; leaving the artilery, and other instruments of fire, to the gunners dispose and order, with the rest of his mates and adherents; which, as I said was part of our perdition. For bearing me ever in hand, that he had five hundred cartreges in a readinesse, within one houres fight we were forced to occupie three persons onely in making and filling cartreges; and of five hundred elles of canvas and other cloth given him for that purpose, at sundry times, not one yard was to be found. For this we have no excuse, and therefore could not avoyd the danger, to charge and discharge with the ladell, especially in so hotte a fight.[1] And comming now to put in execution the sinking of the shippe, as he promised, he seemed a man without life or soule. So the admirall comming close unto us, I myselfe, and the master of our shippe, were forced to play the gunners.

Deceit of the gunner, and his extreme carelessnesse, and suspitious disloyalty.

The instruments of fire wherein he made me to spend immensely, before our going to sea, now appeared not; neither the brasse balles of artificiall fire, to be shott with

[1] The greater part of the powder on board men-of-war is made up into cartridges, to avoid delay in filling during action, and danger from using loose powder in a ladle.

slurbowes (whereof I had sixe bowes, and two hundreth bals, and which are of great account and service, either by sea or land); he had stowed them in such manner, though in double barrels, as the salt water had spoyled them all; so that comming to use them, not one was serviceable. Some of our company had in him suspition to be more friend to the Spaniards then to us; for that he had served some yeares in the *Tercera*, as gunner, and that he did all this of purpose. Few of our peeces were cleere, when we came to use them, and some had the shott first put in, and after the powder. Besides, after our surrendery, it was laid to his charge, that he should say, he had a brother that served the king in the *Peru*, and that he thought he was in the armado; and how he would not for all the world he should be slaine. Whether this was true or no, I know not; but I am sure all in generall gave him an ill report, and that he in whose hands the chiefe execution of the whole fight consisted, executed nothing as was promised and expected.

Admonitions for commanders.

The griefe and remembrance of which oversights once againe inforceth me to admonish all captaines and commanders hereby to take advice, now and then to survey their officers and store-roomes, the oftener the better; and so their defects and wants may be supplied in time: never relying too much upon the vulgar report, nor giving too much credite to smooth tongues and boasting companions. But to performe this taske, it is requisite that all captaines and commanders were such, and so experimented in all offices, that they might be able as well to controule as to examine all manner of errors in officers. For the government at sea hardly suffereth a head without exquisite experience. The deficiency whereof hath occasioned some ancient sea-men to straighten the attribute of marriner in such sort, as that it ought not to be given but to the man who is able to build his shippe, to fit and provide her of all things necessary, and after to carry her about

Who to be accounted a true mariner.

Sect. LIV.

the world: the residue to be but saylers. Hereby giving us to understand, that though it is not expedient that he should be an axe-carpenter, to hewe, cut, frame, and mould each timber piece, yet that he should know the parts and peeces of the shippe, the value of the timber, planke, and yron-worke, so to be able as well to build in proportion, as to procure all materialls at a just price. And againe, though it be not expected that he should sowe the sayles, arme the shrowds, and put the tackling over head, yet is it requisite that he should knowe how to cut his sayles, what length is competent to every roape, and to be of sufficiency to reprehend and reforme those who erre and doe amisse. In providing his shippe with victualls, munition, and necessaries, of force it must be expected that he be able to make his estimate, and (that once provided and perfected), in season, and with expedition to see it loden and stowed commodiously, with care and proportion. After that, he is to order the spending thereof, that in nothing he be defrauded at home; and at sea, ever to know how much is spent, and what remaineth unspent.

His knowledge for materialls.

For provisions.

In the art of navigation, he is bound also to know so much as to be able to give directions to the pilote and master, and consequently to all the rest of inferiour officers.

For navigation.

SECTION LIV.

My meaning is not that the captaine and governour should be tyed to the actuall toyle, or to intermeddle with all offices, for that were to binde him to impossibilities, to diminish and debase his authoritie, and to deprive the other officers of their esteemes, and of that that belongeth unto them, which were a great absurditie: and my opinion is,

Sect. LIV.

that he should be more then superficially instructed and practised in the imployments. Yea, I am verily perswaded that the more absolute authoritie any commander giveth to his under officers, being worthy of it, the sweeter is the command, and the more respected and beloved the commander.

Office of the master.

For in matter of guide and disposing of the saylers, with the tackling of the shippe, and the workes which belong thereunto, within bourd and without, all is to be committed to the masters charge.

Office of the pilot.

The pilote is to look carefully to the sterridge of the shippe; to be watchfull in taking the heights of sunne and starre; to note the way of his shippe, with the augmenting and lessening of the winde, etc.

The bote-swaine.

The boateswayne is to see his shippe kept cleane; his mastes, yards and tacklings well coated, matted and armed; his shroudes and stayes well set; his sayles repayred, and sufficiently prevented with martnets, blayles, and caskettes; his boate fitted with sayle, oares, thougts, tholes danyd, windles and rother; his anchors well boyed, safely stopped and secured, with the rest to him appertaining.

The steward.

The steward is to see the preservation of vittayles and necessaries committed unto his charge; and by measure and weight to deliver the portions appointed, and with discretion and good tearmes to give satisfaction to all.

The carpenter.

The carpenter is to view the mastes and yards, the sides of the shippe, her deckes, and cabines, her pumpes, and boate; and moreover to occupie him selfe in the most forceible workes, except he be otherwise commanded.

The gunner.

The gunner is to care for the britching and tackling of his artilery; the fitting of his shott, tampkins, coynes, crones,[1] and lin-stockes, etc. To be provident in working his fire-workes; in making and filling his cartreges; in accommodating his ladles, sponges, and other necessaries;

[1] Crows or crow-bars?

Sect. LV.

in sifting and drying his powder; in cleaning the armes, munition, and such like workes, intrusted unto him.

In this manner every officer, in his office, ought to be an absolute commander, yet readie, in obedience and love, to sacrifice his will to his superiors command. This cannot but cause unitie; and unitie cannot but purchase a happie issue to dutifull travelles.

Directions in secret.

Lastly, except it be in urgent and precise cases, the head should never direct his command to any but the officers, and these secretly, except the occasion require publication, or that it touch all in generall.

Such orders would be, for the most part, in writing, that all might know what in generall is commanded and required.

SECTION LV.

Parts requisite in a good husbandman.

And as the wise husband-man, in walking from ground to ground, beholdeth one plowing, another harrowing, another sowing and lopping; another pruning, one hedging, another threshing, and divers occupied in severall labours; some he commendeth, others he reproacheth; others he adviseth, and to another he saith nothing, for that he seeth him in the right way; and all this, for that he knoweth and understandeth what they all doe, better then they themselves, though busied in their ordinary workes: even so a worthy commander at sea, ought to have the eyes, not only of his body, but also of his understanding, continually set (with watchfull care) upon all men, and all their workes under his charge; imitating the wise husband-man; first to know, and then to command: and lastly, to will their obedience voluntary, and without contradiction. For who knoweth not that ignorance many times commandeth that which it understandeth not; which the artist perceiving, first dis-

The like in a good chieftaine.

daineth, afterwards disteemeth, and finally in these great actions, which admit no temporizing, either he wayveth the respect of dutie, or faintly performeth the behest of his superiour upon every slight occasion, either in publike opposing, or in private murmuring: the smallest of which is most pernicious. This much (not amisse) for instruction.

SECTION LVI.

Why the Spanish admirall came to lee-wards.

THE reason why the admirall came to lee-wardes, as after I understood, was for that her artillery being very long, and the wind fresh, bearing a taunt sayle to fetch us up, and to keepe us company, they could not use their ordinance to the weather of us, but lay shaking in the wind: and doubtlesse it is most proper for shippes to have short ordinance, except in the sterne or chase. The reasons are many: viz.—easier charging, ease of the shippes side, better traversing, and mounting; yea, greater security of the artillery, and consequently of the shippe. For the longer the peece is, the greater is the retention of the fire, and so the torment and danger of the peece the greater.

But here will be contradiction by many, that dare avouch that longer peeces are to be preferred; for that they burne their powder better, and carrie the shotte further, and so necessarily of better execution; whereas the short artillery many times spend much of their powder without burning, and workes thereby the slenderer effect.

To which I answere, that for land service, fortes, or castles, the long peeces are to be preferred: but for shipping, the shorter are much more serviceable. And the powder in them, being such as it ought, will be all fiered long before the shott can come forth; and to reach farre in fights at sea, is to little effect. For he that purposeth to annoy his enemie, must not shoot at randome, nor at point blanke, if hee purpose to accomplish with his devoire, nether must hee spend his shott nor powder, but where a pot-gun may reach his contrary; how much the neerer, so much the better: and this duely executed, the shorter artillery will worke its effect as well as the long; otherwise, neither short nor long are of much importance: but here my meaning is not to approve the overshort peeces, devised by some persons, which at every shott they make, daunce out of their carriages, but those of indifferent length, and which keepe the meane, betwixt seaven and eight foote.

SECTION LVII.

Intertainement of Spaniards.

The entertainement wee gave unto our contrairies, being otherwise than was expected, they fell off, and urged a head, having broken in peeces all our gallerie; and presently they cast about upon us, and being able to keepe us company, with their fighting sayles, lay a weather of us, ordinarily within musket shott; playing continually with them and their great artillery; which we endured, and answered as we could.

Our pinnace engaged herselfe so farre, as that before shee could come unto us, the vice-admirall had like to cut her off, and comming to lay us aboord, and to enter her men, the vice-admirall boorded with her: so that some of our company entred our ship over her bow-sprit, as they themselves reported.

The English seventy-five, the Spaniards thirteen hundred.

We were not a little comforted with the sight of our people in safetie within our shippe; for in all we were but threescore and fifteene, men and boyes, when we began to fight, and our enemies thirteene hundred men and boyes, little more or lesse, and those the choise of Peru.

SECTION LVIII.

Sect. LVIII.

The Span'sh discipline.

HERE it shall not be out of the way to discourse a little of the Spanish discipline, and manner of their government in generall; which is in many things different to ours. In this expedition came two generalls: the one Don Beltran de Castro,[1] who had the absolute authoritie and commaund; the other Michael Angell Filipon, a man well in yeares, and came to this preferment by his long and painful service; who though he had the title of generall at sea, I thinke it was rather of courtesie then by pattent; and for that hee had beene many yeares generall of the South sea, for the carriage and waftage of the silver from Lyma to Panama. He seemed to bee an assistant, to supply that with his counsell, advice, and experience, whereof Don Beltran had never made tryall (for hee commanded not absolutely, but with the confirmation of Don Beltran), for the Spaniards never give absolute authoritie to more then one. A custome that hath beene, and is approoved in all empires, kingdomes, common-wealths, and armies, rightly disciplined: the mixture hath been seldome seene to prosper, as will manifestly appeare, if we consider the issue of all actions and journeys committed to the government of two or more, generally.

Two chieftains joyned in commission, dangerous.

The famous victory of Hannibal against the Romane consuls Paulus Emilius and Terrentius Varro, was attributed to their equalitie of government. The unhappie overthrowe given by the Turke Amurate, to the Christian princes, in the journey of Nicopolis, is held to have proceeded from the difference betwixt the heads, every one leaning to his owne opinion. The overthrow in recoverie of the Holy land, undertaken by king Richard of England, and king Philip of France, sprang from the like differences

[1] See note at page 256.

Sect. LVIII. and dissentions. The victory of the emperour Charles the Fifth, against the Protestant princes of Germanie, is imputed to their disfractures arising from parity in command. If we looke into our owne actions, committed to the charge of two generals, the effects and fruits which they have brought forth, for the most part, will be found to be little better: yea, most of them, through emulation, envie, and pride, overthrowne, and brought to nought; though to cover their confusions, there have never beene wanting cloakes and colours. The most approoved writers reproove, and call it a monster with two heads, and not without reason. For if the monarchy be generally approoved, for strongest, soundest, and most perfect, and most sufficient to sustaine it selfe; and the democracie and aristocracie utterly reprooved, as weake, feeble, and subject to innovations and infirmities; it cannot be but errour, confusion, and imperfection, to differ or dissent from it. For where the supreame government is divided betwixt two or more, the authoritie is diminished, and so looseth his true force; as a fagget of stickes, whose bond being broken, the entire strength is easily dissolved: but all under correction.

The Spaniards, in their armadoes by sea, imitate the discipline, order, and officers, which are in an army by land, and divide themselves into three bodies; to wit, souldiers, marriners, and gunners.

The souldier. Their souldiers ward and watch, and their officers in every shippe round, as if they were on shoare; this is the only taske they undergoe, except cleaning their armes, The gunner. wherein they are not over curious. The gunners are exempted from all labour and care, except about the artillery.

And these are either Almaynes, Flemmings, or strangers; for the Spaniards are but indifferently practised in this art.

The mariner. The marriners are but as slaves to the rest, to moyle,[1] and to toyle day and night; and those but few and bad, and not

[1] *To moil* has been supposed to be derived from the French *mouiller*.

suffered to sleep or harbour themselves under the deckes, For in faire or fowle weather, in stormes, sunne, or raine, they must passe voyde of covert or succour. Sect. LVIII.

There is ordinarily in every shippe of warre, a captaine, whose charge is that of our masters with us, and also a captaine of the souldiers, who commandeth the captaine of the shippe, the souldiers, gunners, and marriners in her; yea, though there be divers captaines, with their companies in one shippe (which is usuall amongst them), yet one hath the supreme authoritie, and the residue are at his ordering and disposing. They have their *mastros de campo*, seargant, master, generall (or captaine) of the artillery, with their alfere major, and all other officers, as in a campe.

Officers in a shippe of war. Captaine of the shippe. Captaine of the souldiers.

Mastros de campo, &c.

If they come to fight with another armado, they order themselves as in a battell by land; in a vanguard, rereward, maine battell, and wings, etc. In every particular shippe the souldiers are all set upon the deckes; their forecastle they account their head front, or vanguard of their company; that abaft the mast, the rereward; and the wayste the mayne battell; wherein they place their principall force, and on which they principally relye, which they call their *placa de armas*, or place of armes: which taken, their hope is lost.

The gunners fight not but with their great artillery: the marriners attend only to the tackling of the shippe and handling of the sayles, and are unarmed, and subject to all misfortunes; not permitted to shelter themselves, but to be still aloft, whether it be necessary or needlesse. So ordinarily, those which first fayle, are the marriners and saylers, of which they have greatest neede. They use few close fights or fire-workes; and all this proceedeth, as I judge, of errour in placing land captaines for governours and commanders by sea; where they seldome understand what is to be done or commanded.

Sect. LVIII.

Prying of the Spaniards into our discipline.

Some that have beene our prisoners, have perfitted[1] themselves of that they have seene amongst us; and others, disguised under colour of treaties, for ransoming of prisoners, for bringing of presents, and other imbassages, have noted our forme of shipping, our manner of defences, and discipline. Sithence which espiall, in such actions as they have beene imployed in, they seeke to imitate our government and reformed discipline at sea: which, doubtlesse, is the best and most proper that is at this day knowne or practised in the whole world, if the execution be answerable to that which is knowne and received for true and good amongst us.

Their imitation of our discipline.

In the captaine (for so the Spaniards call their admirall) was an English gunner, who to gain grace with those under whom hee served, preferred himselfe, and offered to sinke our shippe with the first shott he made; who, by the Spaniards relation, being travesing of a peece in the bowe, to make his shott, had his head carryed away with the first or second shott made out of our shippe. It slew also two or three of those which stood next him.

Which may be a good and gentle warning for all those who mooved either with covetousnesse, or with desire of revenge, or in hope of worldly promotion, or other respect whatsoever, doe willingly and voluntarily serve the enemie against their owne nation: *nulla causa iusta videri potest, adversus patriam arma capiendi.*

The ends of fugitives.

And if we consider the end of those who have thus erred, wee shall finde them, for the most part, lamentable and most miserable. At the least, those whom I have knowne, have lived to be pointed at with detestation, and ended their lives in beggary, voyde of reputation.

[1] Profited.

SECTION LIX.

THE fight continued so hott on both sides, that the artillery and muskets never ceased playing. Our contraries, towards the evening, determined the third time to lay us abourd, with resolution to take us or to hazard all. The order they set downe for the execution hereof, was, that the captaine (or admirall) should bring himselfe uppon our weather bowe, and so fall abourd of us, upon our broad side: and that the vice-admirall should lay his admirall abourd uppon his weather quarter, and so enter his men into her; that from her they might enter us, or doe as occasion should minister. Sect. LIX.

The captaine of the vice-admirall being more hardy then considerate, and presuming with his shippe and company to get the price and chiefe honour, wayted not the time to put in execution the direction given, but presently came abourd to wind-wards upon our broad side. Which, doubtless, was the great and especiall providence of Almightie God, for the discouraging of our enemies, and animating of us. For although shee was as long, or rather longer then our shippe, being rarely[1] built, and utterly without fighte or defences; what with our muskets, and what with our fire-works, wee cleered her decks in a moment, so that scarce any person appeared. And doubtlesse if we had entred but a dozen men, we might have enforced them to have rendred unto us, or taken her; but our company being few, and the principall of them slaine or hurt, we durst not, neither was it wisedome, to adventure the separation of those which remained: and so held that for the best and soundest resolution, to keepe our forces together in defence of our owne. The Spaniards pay decrely for their rashnesse.

[1] Slightly—or perhaps what we now call "deep-waisted".

Sect. LIX.

The vice-admirall seeing himselfe in great distresse, called to his admirall for succour; who presently laid him abourd, and entred a hundreth of his men, and so cleered themselves of us.

In this bourding, the vice-admirall had at the least thirtie and sixe men hurt and slaine; and amongst them his pilote shot through the body, so as he died presently. And the admirall also received some losse, which wrought in them a new resolution, onely with their artillery to batter us; and so with time to force us to surrender, or to sinke us; which they put in execution: and placing themselves within a musket shott of our weather quarter, and sometimes on our broad side, lay continually beating upon us without intermission; which was, doubtlesse, the best and securest determination they could take; for they being rare shippes, and without any manner of close fights, in bourding with us, their men were all open unto us, and we under covert and shelter. For on all parts our shippe was musket free, and the great artillery of force must cease on either side (the shippes being once grapled together), except we resolved to sacrifice our selves together in fire. For it is impossible, if the great ordinance play (the shippes being bourded), but that they must set fire on the shippe they shoote at; and then no surety can be had to free himselfe, as experience daily confirmeth. For a peece of artillery most properly resembleth a thunderclap, which breaking upwards, or on the side, hurteth not; for that the fire hath scope to dispence it selfe without finding resistance, till the violence which forceth it taketh end, and so it mounts to its center: but breaking down right or stooping downwards, and finding resistance or impediment, before the violence that forceth it take end, being so subtill and penetrable a substance, passeth and pierceth so wonderfully, as it leaveth the effect of his execution in all points answerable to his levell and nighnesse. For if the

And take a new resolution.

clouds be nigh the earth (as some are higher, some lower), and breake down-wards, the violence wherewith the fire breaketh out is such, and of so strange an execution, that men have beene found dead without any outward signe in their flesh, and yet all their bones burnt to dust. So the blade of the sword hath beene found broken all to peeces in the scabard, and the scabard whole without blemish; and a cristall glasse all shivered in peeces, his cover and case remaining sound: which commeth to passe for that in the flesh, in the scabard, and in the case, the fire being so subtile of nature, findeth easie passage without resistance; but the bones, the blade, the cristall, being of substance more solide, maketh greater resistance, and so the fire with the more fury worketh the more his execution in its objects. As was seene in the Spanish admirall (or captaine), after my imprisonment, crossing from Panama to Cape San Francisco, a rayo (for so the Spaniards call a thunder clappe), brake over our shippe, killed one in the fore-toppe, astonished either two or three in the shroudes, and split the mast in strange manner: where it entred it could hardly be discerned, but where it came forth, it drave out a great splinter before it; and the man slaine, was cleane in a manner without signe or token of hurt, although all his bones turned to powder; and those who lived and recovered, had all their bodies blacke, as burnt with fire: which plainly declareth and confirmeth that above said, and may serve to judge in such occasions of persons hurt with thunder; for if they complaine of their bones, and have little signe of the fire, their hazard of death is the greater, then when the fire hath left greater impressions outward. The fire out of a cloude worketh like effect, only where it leveleth directly, as experience daily teacheth; killing those who are opposite, hurting those who are neere, and only terrifying those who are further distant.

In like manner the peece of ordinance hurteth not those

Sect. LIX. which stand aside, nor those which stand a slope from his mouth, but those alone which stand directly against the true point of his levell: though sometimes the winde of the shott overthroweth one, and the splinter (being accidents), mayne[1] and hurt others. But principally where the peece doth resemble the thunder clappe, as when the ships are bourded: for then, although the artillery be discharged without shott, the fury of the fire, and his piercing nature is such, as it entreth by the seames, and all parts of the ships sides, and meeting with so fit matter as pitch, tarre, ocombe, and sometimes with powder, presently converteth all into flames.

For avoyding whereof, as also the danger and damage which may come by pikes and other inventions of fire, and if any shippe be oppressed with many shippes at once, and subject by them to be bourded; I hold it a good course to strike his foure and mayne yards close to his decke, and to fight with sprit-saile and myson, and top-sayles loose: so shall he be able to hinder them from oppressing him.

Pollicies to avoid bourdings.

Some have thought it a good pollicy to launce out some ends of mastes or yards by the ports or other parts: but this is to be used in the greater shippes; for in the lesser, though they be never so strong, the waight of the bigger will beate out the opposite sides and doe hurt, and make great spoyle in the latter. And in bourding, ordinarily the lesser shippe hath all the harme which the one shippe can doe unto the other.

Disputes concerning ships of trade.

Here is offered to speake of a point much canvassed amongst carpenters and sea captaines, diversly mainetained but yet undetermined: that is, whether the race or loftie built shippe bee best for the merchant, and those which imploy themselves in trading? I am of opinion that the race shippe is most convenient; yet so as to that every perfect shippe ought to have two deckes, for the better

[1] Maim.

strengthening of her; the better succouring of her people; the better preserving of her merchandize and victuall; and for her greater safetie from sea and stormes. Sect. LIX.

Concerning the prince his shippes.

But for the princes shippes, and such as are imployed continually in the warres, to be built loftie I hold very necessary for many reasons. First for majestie and terrour of the enemy; secondly, for harbouring of many men; thirdly, for accommodating more men to fight; fourthly, for placing and using more artillery; fiftly, for better strengthening and securing of the shippe; sixtly, for overtopping and subjecting the enemy; seventhly, for greater safeguard and defence of the ship and company. For it is plaine, that the ship with three deckes, or with two and a halfe, shewes more pomp than another of her burthen with a decke and a halfe, or two deckes, and breedeth greater terror to the enemy, discovering herselfe to be a more powerfull ship, as she is, then the other; which being indeed a ship of force, seemeth to be but a barke, and with her low building hideth her burthen. And who doubteth that a decke and a halfe cannot harbour that proportion of men, that two deckes, and two deckes and a halfe can accommodate to fight; nor carry the artillery so plentifully, nor commodiously. Neither can the ship be so strong with a decke and a halfe as with two deckes; nor with two, as with three; nor carry her mast so taunt; nor spread so great a clue; nor contrive so many fightes, to answer one another for defence and offence. And the advantage the one hath of the other, experience daily teacheth.

All ships of warre are not to be low built.

In the great expedition of eightie eight, did not the *Elizabeth Jones*, the *Triumph*, and the *Beare*, shew greater majestie then the *Arke Royell* and the *Victorie*, being of equal burthens? did they not cause greater regard in the enemy? did they not harbour and accommodate more men, and much better? did they not beare more artillery? And

Sect. LIX. if they had come to boord with the Spanish high-charged ships, it is not to be doubted but they would have mustred themselves better, then those which could not with their prowesse nor props, have reached to their wastes. The strength of the one cannot be compared with the strength of the other: but in bourding, it goeth not so much in the strength, as in weight and greatnesse. For the greater ship that bourdeth with the lesser, with her mastes, her yardes, her tacklings, her anchors, her ordinance, and with her sides, bruseth and beateth the lesser to peeces, although the lesser be farre stronger according to proportion.

The *Foresight* of his Majesties, and the *Daintie*, were shippes in their proportions farre more stronger then the carake which was taken by them and their consorts, anno 92: for she had in a manner no strong building nor binding, and the others were strengthened and bound as art was able to affoord; and yet both bourding with her, were so brused, broken and badly handled, as they had like to have sunke by her side, though bourding with advantage to weather-wards of her. But what would have become of them if she should have had the wind of them, and have come aboord to wind-ward of them? In small time, no doubt she would have beaten them under water.

Anno 90, in the fleet under the charge of Sir John Hawkins, my father, comming from the south-wards, the *Hope*, of his Majesties, gave chase to a French ship, thinking her to be a Spaniard. She thought to have freed her selfe by her sailing, and so would not availe, but endured the shooting of many peeces, and forced the *Hope* to lay her abourd; of which issued that mischiefe which before I spake off. For in a moment the French ship had all her mastes, yards, and sailes in the sea, and with great difficultie the *Hope* could free herselfe from sinking her.

In the self-same voyage, neere the ilands of Flores and Corvo, the *Rainbow* and the *Foresight* came foule one of another; the *Rainbow,* being the greater shippe, left the *Foresight* much torne; and if God had not beene pleased to seperate them, the lesser, doubtlesse, had sunke in the sea; but in these incounters they received little or no hurt. The boording of the *Rainbow* and *Foresight,* as I was enformed, proceeded of the obstinacie and self will of the captaine or master of the *Foresight,* who would not set sayle in time, to give sea roome to the other, comming driving upon her, for that she was more flotie.[1] This pride I have seene many times to be the cause of great hurt, and is worthy of severe punishment: for being all of one company, and bound every one to helpe and further the good of the other, as members of one body, there ought to be no strayning of courtesie; but all are bound to suppress emulation and particular respect, in seeking the generall good of all, yea, of every particular more ingeniously then that of his owne.

Sect. LIX.

Particular respects must give place to the generall.

But in equitie and reason, the le-ward shippe ought ever to give way to the weather most, in hulling or trying, without any exception. First, for that shee advantageth the other in hulling or trying; which is manifest, for that shee to wind-wards drives upon her to le-wards. Secondly, for that the windermost shippe, by opening her sayle, may be upon the other before shee be looked for, either for want of steeridge, not being under way, or by the rowling of the sea, some one sea casting the shippe more to le-wards then ten others. And thirdly, for that the windermost shippe being neere, and setting sayle, is in possibilitie to take away the winde from her to le-wards comming within danger. And this by way of argument, for a hull and under-sayle in stormes and fayre weather, in harbour, or at sea.

Humanitie and courtesie are ever commendable and bene-

[1] Did not hold so good a wind, or drove more easily to leeward.

Sect. LIX. ficiall to all, whereas arrogancie and ambition are ever accompanied with shame, losse, and repentance.

Arrogancy of a Spanish generall.

And though in many examples, touching this point, I have beene an eye witnesse, yet I will record but one, which I saw in the river of Civill,[1] at my comming out of the Indies amongst the galleons loaden with silver. For their wafting, the king sent to the Tercera, eight new galleons, under the charge of Villa Viciosa, who entring the barre of Saint Lucar joyntly, the shippes loaden with silver, anchored in the middest of the river in deeper water, and the wafters on either side, neere the shoare. The admirall of the wafters rode close by the galleon in which I was, and had moored her selfe in that manner, as her streame, cable, and anchor, overlayed our land-most. And winding up with the first of the flood, shee her selfe in one of her cables, which together with the great currant of the ebbe, and force of the winde which blewe fresh, caused her to drive, and to dragge home her anchors; and with that which overlay ours, to cause us to do the like. Whereupon, on both sides was crying out to veere cable: we, for our parts, had lost all our cables in the Terceras, saving those which were a-ground, and those very short, and vered to the better end. The admirall strained courtesie, thinking the other, though loaden with silver, bound to let slippe one, so to give him way; and the generall standing in his gallery, saw the danger which both shippes ranne into, being in a manner bourd and bourd, and driving upon the point of the shoare: yet he commanded to hold fast, and not to vere cable, till he was required and commanded in the kings name, by the captaine of our shippe; protesting the damage which should ensue thereof to the king and merchants, to runne upon the admirals accompt;

[1] Seville was formerly the emporium of the trade of the new world: since the Guadalquiver has become unnavigable for large vessels, its trade has been transferred to Cadiz.

Sect. LIX.

and that in his shippe he had no other cable but those which were aground, and that they had vered as much as they could: which the generall knowing, and at last better considering, willed to vere his cable end for end, and so, with some difficultie and dispute, the punto was remedied; which if he had done at first he had prevented all other danger, inconvenience, and dispute, by only weighing of his cable and anchor after the gust was past, and letting it fall in a place more commodious: whereas, his vaine glory, stoutnesse, and selfe-will, had put in great perill two of the kings shippes, and in them above two millions of treasure. And it may be, if he had beene one of the ignorant generalls, such as are sometimes imployed, whereas he was one of best experience, I doubt not but they would have stood so much upon their puntos, as rather then they would have consented to vere theyr cables (for that it seemed a diminution of authoritie), they would rather have suffered all to goe to wracke, without discerning the danger and damage.

Doubts and objections resolved.

But to returne to my former point of advantage, which the greater shippe hath of the lesser, I would have it to be understood according to occasion, and to be understood of ships of warre with ships of warre; it being no part of my meaning to mainetaine that a small man of warre should not bourd with a great shippe which goeth in trade. For I know, that the war-like shippe that seeketh, is not only bound to bourd with a greater, but were shee sure to hazard her selfe, shee ought to bourd where any possibility of surprising may be hoped for. Witnesse the Biscaine shippes of five hundreth tunnes, taken by shippes of lesse than a hundreth. Such were those which were taken by captaine George Reymond, and captaine Greenfield Halse; both wonne by bourding and force of armes. And did not Markes Berry, with a shippe of four-score tunnes, by bourding and dent of sword, take a shippe which came from the Nova Hispania, of neere foure hundreth tunnes?

And the duty of a small ship against a greater.

Sect. LIX. To recount all such as have beene in this sort taken by our countreymen, as also those of great worth they have lost, for not hazarding the bourding, were never to make an end. Yet discretion is ever to be used; for a man that in a small barke goeth to warre-fare, is not bound to bourd with a carake, nor with a shippe which he seeth provided with artillery and other preventions far above his possibilitie.

Vain-glory of the Spanish.

The Spaniards confesse us to advantage them in our shipping, and attribute all our victories to that which is but a masse of dead wood, were it not managed and ordered by art and experience; affirming, that if we came to handie strokes and bourding, they should goe farre beyond us, which to any person of reasonable understanding, cannot but seeme most vaine-glorious; for we leave not to bourd with them upon occasion, when otherwise we cannot force them to surrender: but I conclude it to be great errour, and want of discretion in any man, to put himselfe, his shippe, and company in perill, being able otherwise to vanquish his enemy.

This imagination, so vaine and so voyde of ground, hath growne from the ignorance of some of our common sort of marriners and vulgar people, which have beene prisoners in Spaine: who being examined and asked, why her Majesties shippes in occasions bourd not, have answered and enformed that it is the expresse order of her Majestie and counsell, in no case to hazard her shippes by bourding; yea, I have knowne some captaines of our owne (to colour their faint proceedings), have averred as much, which is nothing so. For in the houre that her majestie or counsell committeth the charge of any of her shippes to any person, it is left to his discretion to bourd or not to bourd, as the reason of service requireth. And therefore let no man hereafter pretend ignorance, nor for this vanitie leave to doe his duty, or that which is most probable to redound to the honour and service of his prince and countrey, and to the damage of his enemy. For in case he excuse himselfe with this allegation, it cannot but redound to his condemnation and disreputation. And I assure all men, that in any reasonable equalitie of shipping, we cannot desire greater advantage, then we have of the Spaniards by bourding. The reasons why, I hold it not convenient to discourse in particular; but experience and tract of time, with that which I have seen amongst them, hath taught me this knowledge; and those who have seene their discipline, and ours, cannot but testifie the same.

Sect. LX.

SECTION LX.

Courses for artillery after bourding.

AGAINE, all that which hath beene spoken of the danger of the artillery in bourding, it is not to be wrested nor interpreted, to cut of utterly the use of all artillery after bourding, but rather I hold nothing more convenient in shippes of warre, then fowlers and great bases in the cage workes, and murderers in the cobridge heads; for that their execution and speedie charging and discharging, is of great moment.[1]

Disuses of engines of antiquitie.

Many I know have left the use of them, and of sundry other preventions, as of sherehookes, stones in their toppes, and arming them; pikebolts in their wales, and divers other engines of antiquitie. But upon what inducement, I cannot relate, unlesse it be because they never knew their effects and benefit; and may no doubt be used without the inconveniences before mentioned in great ordinance. As also such may be the occasion, that without danger some of the great artillery may be used, and that with great

[1] Fowlers, murderers, etc., were pieces of cannon of the nature of swivels, adapted to close combat. The "cobridge heads" seem to have been bulk heads across the fore and after parts of the vessel.

Sect. LXI. effect, which is in the discretion of the commanders and their gunners, as hath beene formerly seene, and daily is experimented. In the *Revenge* of her Majesties good experience was made, who sunke two of the Spanish armado lying abourd her.

SECTION LXI.

In these bourdings and skirmishes, divers of our men were slaine, and many hurt, and myselfe amongst them received sixe wounds: one of them in the necke, very perillous; another through the arme, perishing the bone, and cutting the sinewes close by the arme-pit; the rest not so dangerous. The master of our shippe had one of his eyes, his nose, and halfe his face shott away. Master Henry Courton was slaine. On these two I principally relied for the prosecution of our voyage, if God, by sicknesse, or otherwise, should take me away.

The Spaniards parley. The Spaniards with their great ordinance lay continually playing upon us, and now and then parled and invited us to surrender ourselves *a buena querra*.[1] The captaine of our shippe, in whose direction and guide, our lives, our honour, and welfare now remained, seeing many of our people wounded and slaine, and that few were left to sustaine and maintaine the fight, or to resist the entry of the enemy, if he should againe bourd with us, and that our contraries offered us good pertido,[2] came unto me accompanied with some others, and began to relate the state of our shippe, and how that many were hurt and slaine, and scarce any men appeared to traverse the artillery, or to oppose themselves for defence, if the enemy should bourd

[1] *En buena guerra* means by fair or lawful means: it probably implied offering quarter: which means, that if accepted, a certaine sum was to be given as ransom.

[2] *Partido* (Spanish), favour or protection.

with us againe; and how that the admirall offered us life and libertie, and to receive us *a buena querra*, and to send us into our owne countrey. Saying, that if I thought it so meete, he and the rest were of opinion that we should put out a flagge of truce, and make some good composition. The great losse of blood had weakened me much. The torment of my wounds newly received, made me faint, and I laboured for life, within short space expecting I should give up the ghost. Sect. LXI.

But this parley pearced through my heart, and wounded my soule; words failed me wherewith to expresse it, and none can conceive it but he which findeth himselfe in the like agonie. Yet griefe and rage ministered force, and caused me to breake forth into this reprehension and execution following.

"Great is the crosse which Almightie God hath suffered to come upon me: that, assaulted by our professed enemies, and by them wounded, as you see, in body, lying gasping for breath, those whom I reputeth for my friends to fight with me; those which I relyed on as my brethren to defend me in all occasions; those whom I have nourished, cherished, fostered and loved as my children, to succour me, helpe me, and to sustaine my reputation in all extremities; are they who first draw their swords against me, are they which wound my heart, in giving me up into mine enemies hands. Whence proceedeth this ingratitude? whence this faintnesse of heart? whence this madnesse? Is the cause you fight for unjust? is the honour and love of your prince and countrey buried in the dust? your sweet lives, are they become loathsome unto you? will you exchange your liberty for thraldome? will you consent to see that which you have sweat for and procured with so great labour and adventure, at the dispose of your enemies? can you content your selves to suffer my blood spilt before your eyes, and my life bereft me in your presence, with the blood and

Sect. LXI. lives of your deere brethren to be unrevenged? Is not an honourable death to be preferred before a miserable and slavish life? The one sustaining the honour of our nation, of our predecessors, and of our societie: the other ignominious to our selves, and reproachful to our nation. Can you be perswaded that the enemy will performe his promise with you, that never leaveth to breake it with others, when he thinketh it advantagious? And know you not, that with him, all is convenient that is profitable? Hold they not this for a maxime: that, *nulla fides est servanda cum hereticis?* In which number they accompt us to be. Have you forgotten their faith violated with my father, in Saint John de Ulua, the conditions and capitulations being firmed by the viceroy and twelve hostages, all principall personages given for the more securitie of either party to other? Have you forgotten their promise broken with John Vibao and company, in Florida, having conditioned to give them shipping and victuals, to carry them into their countrey; immediately after they had delivered their weapons and armes, had they not their throats cut? Have you forgotten how they dealt with John Oxnam and his company, in this sea, yeelded upon composition; and how after a long imprisonment, and many miseries, being carried from Panama to Lyma, and there hanged with all his company, as pyrates, by the justice? And can you forget how dayly they abuse our noble natures, which being voyde of malice, measure all by sinceritie, but to our losse; for that when we come to demand performance, they stoppe our mouthes, either with laying the inquisition upon us, or with delivering us into the hands of the ordinary justice, or of the kings ministers. And then urged with their promises, they shrinke up to the shoulders, and say, that they have now no further power over us; they sorrow in their hearts to see their promise is not accomplished: but now they cannot doe us any good office, but to pray to God for us, and to entreat the ministers in our behalfe.

"Came we into the South sea to put out flags of truce? And left we our pleasant England, with all her contentments, with intention or purpose to avayle our selves of white ragges, and by banners of peace to deliver ourselves for slaves into our enemies hands; or to range the world with the English, to take the law from them, whom by our swords, prowesse, and valour, we have alwaies heretofore bin accustomed to purchase honour, riches, and reputation? If these motives be not sufficient to perswade you, then I present before your eyes your wives and children, your parents and friends, your noble and sweete countrey, your gracious soveraigne; all of which accompt yourselves for ever deprived, if this proposition should be put in execution. But for all these, and for the love and respect you owe me, and for all besides that you esteeme and hold dear in this world, and for Him that made us and all the world, banish out of your imagination such vaine and base thoughts; and according to your woonted resolution, prosecute the defence of your shippe, your lives, and libertie, with the lives and libertie of your companions; who by their wounds and hurts are disabled and deprived of all other defence and helpe, save that which lyeth in your discretions and prowesse. And you, captaine,—of whom I made choise amongst many, to be my principall assistant, and the person to accomplish my dutie if extraordinary casualtie should disable me to performe and prosecute our voyage,—tender your obligation; and now in the occasion give testimony, and make proofe of your constancie and valour, according to the opinion and confidence I have ever held of you." Sect. LXI.

Whereunto he made answere: "My good generall, I hope you have made experience of my resolution, which shall be ever to put in execution what you shall be pleased to command me; and my actions shall give testimonie of the obligation wherein I stand bound unto you. What I have done, hath not proceeded from faintnesse of heart, nor from

Sect. LXI. a will to see imaginations put in execution; for besides the losse of our reputation, liberty, and what good else we can hope for, I know the Spaniard too too well, and the manner of his proceedings in discharge of promises: but only to give satisfaction to the rest of the company, which importuned me to moove this point, I condiscended to that which now I am ashamed of, and grieve at, because I see it disliking to you. And here I vowe to fight it out, till life or lymmes fayle me. Bee you pleased to recommend us to Almightie God, and to take comfort in him, whom I hope will give us victory, and restore you to health and strength, for all our comforts, and the happy accomplishing and finishing of our voyage, to his glory."

I replyed: "This is that which beseemeth you; this sorteth to the opinion I ever held of you: and this will gaine you, with God and man, a just reward. And you the rest, my deere companions and friends, who ever have made a demonstration of desire to accomplish your duties, remember that when we first discryed our enemy, you shewed to have a longing to proove your valours against him: now that the occasion is offered, lay hold of the fore-locke; for if once shee turne her backe, make sure accompt never after to see her face againe: and as true English men, and followers of the steppes of our forefathers, in vertue and valour, sell your bloods and lives deerely, that Spaine may ever record it with sadnesse and griefe. And those which survive, rejoyce in the purchase of so noble a victory, with so small meanes against so powerfull an enemy."

Hereunto they made answere: that as hitherto they had beene conformable to all the undertakings which I had commanded or counselled, so they would continue in the selfe same dutie and obedience to the last breath; vowing either to remaine conquerours and free-men, or else to sell their lives at that price which their enemies should not willingly consent to buy them at. And with this resolution, both captaine and company tooke their leave of me, every one particularly, and the greater part with teares and imbracings, though we were forthwith to depart the world, and never see one the other againe but in heaven, promising to cast all forepassed imaginations into oblivion, and never more to speake of surrendry.

In accomplishment of this promise and determination, they persevered in sustaining the fight, all this night, with the day and night following, and the third day after. In which time the enemy never left us, day nor night, beating continually upon us with his great and small shott. Saving that every morning, an hower before the breake of day, he edged a little from us, to breath, and to remedie such defects as were amisse, as also to consult what they should doe the day and night following.

They resolve to fight it out.

The enemy breatheth.

This time of interdiction, we imployed in repayring our sayles and tacklings, in stopping our leakes, in fishing and wolling our masts and yards, in mending our pumpes, and in fitting and providing our selves for the day to come. Though this was but little space for so many workes, yet gave it great reliefe and comfort unto us, and made us better able to endure the defence: for otherwise, our ship must of force have suncke before our surrendry, having many shot under water, and our pumpes shot to peeces every day. In all this space, not any man of either part tooke rest or sleepe, and little sustenance, besides bread and wine.

The English repaire their defects.

In the second dayes fight, the vice-admirall comming upon our quarter, William Blanch, one of our masters mates, with a luckie hand, made a shot unto her with one of our sterne peeces; it carried away his maine mast close by the decke: wherewith the admirall beare up to her, to see what harme shee had received, and to give her such succour as shee was able to spare; which we seeing, were in good hope that they would have now left to molest us

Sect. LXI. any longer, having wherewithall to entertaine themselves in redressing their owne harmes. And so we stood away from them close by as we could; which we should not have done, but prosecuted the occasion, and brought our selves close upon her weather gage, and with our great and small shot hindered them from repairing their harmes: if we had thus done, they had been forced to cut all by the bourd; and it may bee, lying a hull or to le-wards of us, with a few shot we might have suncke her. At the least, it would have declared to our enemies that wee had them in little estimation, when, able to goe from them, we would not; and perhaps bin a cause to have made them to leave us.

Advantages omitted.

But this occasion was let slip, as also that other to fight with them, sayling quarter winds, or before the winde; for having stood off to sea a day and a night, we had scope to fight at our pleasure; and no man, having sea roome, is bound to fight as his enemie will, with disadvantage, being able otherwise to deal with equalitie; contrariwise, every man ought to seeke the meanes hee can for his defence, and greatest advantage, to the annoyance of his contrarie.

Now wee might, with our fore saile low set, have borne upp before the winde, and the enemie of force must have done the like, if he would fight with us, or keepe us company: and then should wee have had the advantage of them. For although their artillery were longer, waightier, and many more than ours, and in truth did pierce with greater violence; yet ours being of greater bore, and carrying a waightier and greater shot, was of more importance and of better effect for sinking and spoyling: for the smaller shot passeth through, and maketh but his hole, and harmeth that which lyeth in his way; but the greater shaketh and shivereth all it meeteth, and with the splinters, or that which it encountreth, many times doth more hurt then with his proper circumference: as is plainely seene

The difference of shot.

in the battery by land, when the saker, the demy-colverin, the colverin, and demi-cannon (being peeces that reach much further point blanke then the cannon), are nothing of like importance for making the breach, as is the cannon; for that this shot being ponderous, pierceth with difficultie, yea worketh better effects, tormenting, shaking, and overthrowing all; whereas the others, with their violence, pierce better, and make onely their hole, and so hide themselves in the wooll or rampire.[1]

Sect. LXI.

Their effects.

Besides, our ship being yare[2] and good of steeridge, no doubt but we should have played better with our ordinance, and with more effect than did our enemies; which was a great errour, being able to fight with lesse disadvantage, and yet to fight with the most that could be imagined, which I knew not off, neither was able to direct though I had knowne it, being in a manner senselesse, what with my wounds, and what with the agony of the surrendry propounded, for that I had seldome knowne it spoken of, but that it came afterwards to be put in execution.

Errors in fight.

The generall not being able to succour his vice-admirall, except he should utterly leave us, gave them order to shift as well as they could for the present, and to beare with the next port, and there to repayre their harmes. Himselfe presently followed the chase, and in short space fetched us up, and beganne a fresh to batter us with his great and small shott. The vice-admirall, having saved what they could, cutt the rest by the bourd, and with fore-sayle and myson came after us also; and before the setting of the sunne, were come upon our broad side, wee bearing all our sayles, and after kept us company, lying upon our weather quarter, and annoying us what shee could.

Here I hold it necessary, to make mention of two things which were most prejudiciall unto us, and the principall

[1] *Wool* probably means the covering or planking. *Rampire* (for rampart?) what is now termed the bulwark.

[2] Ready.

Sect. LXI.

learned from the Flemings and Easterlings.

causes of our perdition; the errours and faults of late dayes, crept in amongst those who follow the sea, and learned from the Flemings and Easterlings. I wish that by our misfortunes others would take warning, and procure to redresse them, as occasions shall be offered.

1. To fight unarmed.
2. To drinke to excesse.

The one is, to fight unarmed, where they may fight armed. The other is, in comming to fight, to drinke themselves drunke. Yea, some are so madd, that they mingle powder with wine, to give it the greater force, imagining that it giveth spirit, strength, and courage, and taketh away all feare and doubt. The latter is for the most part true, but the former is false and beastly, and altogether against reason. For though the nature of wine, with moderation, is to comfort and revive the heart, and to fortifie and strengthen the spirit; yet the immoderate use thereof worketh quite contrary effects.

In fights, all receipts which add courage and spirit, are of great regard, to be allowed and used; and so is a draught of wine, to be given to every man before he come to action, but more then enough is pernicious; for exceeding the same, it offendeth, and enfeebleth the sences, converting the strength (which should resist the force of the enemy) into weaknesse: it dulleth and blindeth the understanding, and consequently depraveth any man of true valour; for that he is disenabled to judge and apprehend the occasion which may be offered, to assault and retyre in time convenient; the raynes of reason being put into the hands of passion and disorder. For after I was wounded, this *nimium* bred great disorder and inconvenience in our shippe; the pott continually walking, infused desperate and foolish hardinesse in many, who blinded with the fume of the liquor, considered not of any danger, but thus and thus would stand at hazard; some in vaine glory vaunting themselves; some other rayling upon the Spaniards; another inviting his companion to come and stand by him, and not to budge a foote from him; which indiscreetly they put in execution, and cost the lives of many a good man, slaine by our enemies muskettiers, who suffered not a man to shew himselfe, but they presently overthrew him with speed and watchfullnesse. For prevention of the second errour, although I had great preparation of armours, as well of proofe, as of light corseletts, yet not a man would use them; but esteemed a pott of wine a better defence then an armour of proofe. Which truely was great madnesse, and a lamentable fault, worthy to be banished from amongst all reasonable people, and well to be weighed by all commanders. For if the Spaniard surpasseth us in anything, it is in his temperance and suffering: and where he hath had the better hand of us, it hath beene, for the most part, through our own folly; for that we will fight unarmed with him being armed. And although I have heard many men maintaine, that in shipping, armour is of little profit: all men of good understanding will condemne such desperate ignorance. For besides, that the sleightest armour secureth the parts of a mans body, which it covereth from pike, sword, and all hand weapons, it likewise giveth boldnesse and courage: a man armed, giveth a greater and a waightier blow, then a man unarmed; he standeth faster, and with greater difficultie is to be overthrowne.

Sect. LXI.

The Spaniard surpasseth us in temperance.

And I never read, but that the glistering of the armour hath beene by authors observed, for that, as I imagine, his show breedeth terror in his contraries, and despayre to himselfe if he be unarmed. And therefore in time of warre, such as devote themselves to follow the profession of armes, by sea or by land, ought to covet nothing more then to be well armed; for as much as it is the second meanes, next Gods protection, for preserving and prolonging many mens lives.

The use and profit of arming.

Wherein the Spanish nation deserveth commendation above others; every one, from the highest to the lowest,

exactly observed by the Spanish.

Sect. LXI. putting their greatest care in providing faire and good armes. He which cannot come to the price of a corslet, will have a coat of mayle, a jackett, at least a buffe-jerkin, or a privie coate. And hardly will they be found without it, albeit they live and serve, for the most part, in extreame hott countries.

Whereas I have knowne many bred in cold countries, in a moment complaine of the waight of their armes, that they smoother them, and then cast them off, chusing rather to be shott through with a bullet, or lanched through with a pike, or thrust through with a sword, then to endure a little travaile and suffering. But let me give these lazie ones this lesson, that he that will goe a warre-fare, must resolve himselfe to fight; and he that putteth on this resolution, must be contented to endure both heate and waight: first for the safeguard of his life, and next for subduing of his enemie; both which are hazarded, and put into great danger, if he fight unarmed with an enemy armed.

Armes more necessary by sea, then at land.

Now for mine owne opinion, I am resolved that armour is more necessary by sea then by land, yea, rather to be excused on the shore then in the shippe. My reason is, for that on the shore, the bullet onely hurteth, but in the shippe I have seene the splinters kill and hurt many at once, and yet the shott to have passed without touching any person. As in the galeon in which I came out of the Indies, in anno 1597, in the rode of Tercera, when the Queenes Majesties shippes, under the charge of the Earle of Essex, chased us into the rode, with the splinters of one shott, were slayne, maymed, and sore hurt, at the least a dozen persons, the most part whereof had beene excused, if they had beene armed.

And doubtlesse, if these errours had beene foreseene, and remedied by us, many of those who were slaine and hurt, had beene on foote, and we inabled to have sustained and maintained the fight much better and longer, and perhaps at last had freed our selves. For if our enemy had come to bourd with us, our close fights were such, as we were secure, and they open unto us. And what with our cubridge heads, one answering the other, our hatches upon bolts, our brackes in our deckes and gunner room, it was impossible to take us as long as any competent number of men had remained: twentie persons would have sufficed for defence; and for this, such ships are called impregnable, and are not to be taken, but by surrender, nor to be overcome but with bourding or sinking, as in us by experience was verified. And not in us alone, but in the *Revenge* of the Queenes Majestie, which being compassed round about with all the armado of Spaine, and bourded sundry times by many at once, is said to have sunke three of the armado by her side.[1] Sect. LXI.

And in this conflict, having lost all her mastes, and being no other then a logge in the sea, could not be taken with all their force and pollicie, till she surrendred her selfe by an honourable composition.

By these presidents,[2] let governours by sea take speciall care, above all, to preserve their people, in imitation of the French; who carrie many souldiers in their shippes of warre, and secure them in their holdes, till they come to entring, and to prove their forces by the dint of sword.

But here the discreete commaunders are to put difference, betwixt those which defend, and those which are to offend, and betwixt those which assault, and those which are assaulted. For, as I have sayd, no government whatsoever, better requireth a perfect and experimented commaunder then that of the sea. And so no greater errour can be committed, then to commend such charges to men unexperimented in this profession. A difference for commanders.

A third and last cause, of the losse of sundry of our men, most worthy of note for all captaines, owners, and carpen- Race-ships of warre disliked.

[1] See page 102.

[2] Precedents.

Sect. LXI. ters, was the race[1] building of our shippe, the onely fault shee had; and now a-dayes, held for a principall grace in any shippe: but by the experience which I have had, it seemeth for sundry reasons verie prejudiciall for shippes of warre. For in such, those which tackle the sayles, of force must bee upon the deckes, and are open without shelter or any defence: yet here it will be objected, that for this inconvenience, wast clothes are provided, and for want of them, it is usuall to lace a bonnet, or some such shadow for the men; worthily may it bee called a shadow, and one of the most pernitious customes that can be used; for this shadow, or defence, being but of linnen or wollen cloth, emboldeneth many, who without it would retire to better securitie; whereas, now thinking themselves unseene, they become more bould then otherwise they would, and thereby shot through when they least think of it. Some captaines observing this errour, have sought to remedie it in some of his Majesties shippes; not by altering the building, but by devising a certaine defence, made of foure or five inch planckes, of five foote high, and sixe foote broad, running upon wheeles, and placed in such partes of the shippe as are most open. These they name blenders, and made of elme for the most part; for that it shivers not with a shot, as oake and other timber will doe, which are now in use and service: but best it is, when the whole side hath one blender, and one armour of proofe, for defence of those which of force must labour and be aloft.

Wast clothes not so useful

as other devises.

This race building, first came in by overmuch homing[2] in of our shippes, and received for good, under colour of making our shippes thereby the better sea-shippes, and of better advantage to hull and tyre: but in my judgement,

[1] The term "race" is here repeated: if not a misprint for *rare*, can "a race ship" mean one built for speed?

[2] Tumbling home (?); applied to the inclination inward, given to a ship's topsides.

it breedeth many inconveniences, and is farre from working the effect they pretend, by disinabling them for bearing their cage worke correspondent to the proportion and mould of the shippe, making them tender sided, and unable to carry sayle in any fresh gaile of winde, and diminishing the play of their artillery, and the place for accommodating their people to fight, labor, or rest.

And I am none of those who hold opinion that the overmuch homing in, the more the better, is commodious and easier for the shippe; and this out of the experience that I have learned, which with forcible reasons I could prove to be much rather discomodious and worthy to be reformed. But withall, I hold it not necessary to discourse here of that particularitie, but leave the consequence to men of understanding, and so surcease.

SECTION LXII.

All this second day, and the third day and night, our captaine and company susteined the fight, notwithstanding the disadvantage where with they fought; the enemie being ever to wind-ward, and wee to lee-ward, their shott much damnifying us, and ours little annoying them; for whensoever a man encountreth with his enemie at sea, in gayning the weather gage, hee is in possibilitie to sinke his contrary, but his enemy cannot sinke him; and therefore hee which is forced to fight with this disadvantage, is to procure by all meanes possible to shoote downe his contraries masts or yards, and to teare or spoyle his tackling and sayles; for which purpose, billets of some heavy wood fitted to the great ordinance, are of great importance. And so are arrows of fire, to bee shott out of slur-bowes, and cases of small shott, joyned two and two together, with

The disadvantage of ships to lee-ward.

And the best remedie.

Sect. LXII.

peeces of wyer, of five or sixe ynches long, which also shot out of muskets are of good effect, for tearing the sayles or cutting the tackling.

Some are of opinion that crosse barres and chaine-shot are of moment for the spoyling of masts and yards; but experience dayly teacheth them not to be of great importance, though neere at hand, I confesse, they worke great execution; but the round shott is the onely principall and powerfull meane to breake mast or yard.

The Spaniards fore-mast thrice shot through.

And in this our fight, the admirall of the Spaniards had his fore-mast shot through with two round shott, some three yardes beneath the head; had either of them entred but foure ynches further into the heart of the mast, without all doubt it had freed us, and perhaps put them into our hands. The third day, in the after-noone, which was the 22nd of June 1594, according to our computation, and which I follow in this my discourse, our sayles being torne, our mastes all perished, our pumpes rent and shot to peeces, and our shippe with fourteene shott under water and seven or eight foote of water in hold; many of our men being slaine, and the most part of them which remayned sore hurt, and in a manner altogether fruiteles, and the enemie offering still to receive us *a buena querra*, and to give us life and libertie, and imbarkation for our countrey;—our captaine, and those which remayned of our company, were all of opinion that our best course was to surrender our selves before our shippe suncke. And so by common consent agreed the second time to send a servant of mine, Thomas Sanders, to signifie unto mee the estate of our shippe and company: and that it was impossible by any other way to expect for hope or deliverance, or life, but by the miraculous hand of God, in using his Almighty power, or by an honourable surrender: which in every mans opinion was thought most convenient. So was I desired by him to give also my consent, that the captaine might capitulate with the Spanish generall, and to compound the best partido he could by surrendring our selves into his hands, upon condition of life and libertie. This hee declared unto me, being in a manner voyd of sence, and out of hope to live or recover; which considered, and the circumstances of his relation, I answered as I could, that hee might judge of my state, readie every moment to give up the ghost, and unable to discern in this cause what was convenient, except I might see the present state of the shippe. And that the honour or dishonour, the welfare or misery was for them, which should be partakers of life. At last, for that I had satisfaction of his valour and true dealing in all the time hee had served me, and in correspondence of it, had given him (as was notorious) charge and credit in many occasions, I bound him, by the love and regard hee ought me, and by the faith and duty to Almighty God, to tell me truely if all were as he had declared. Whereunto he made answere, that hee had manifested unto mee the plain and naked truth, and that hee tooke God to witnesse of the same truth; with which receiving satisfaction, I forced my selfe what I could to perswade him to annimate his companions, and in my name to intreate the captaine and the rest to persevere in defence of their libertie, lives, and reputation, remitting all to his discretion: not doubting but he would be tender of his dutie, and zealous of my reputation, in preferring his liberty, and the liberty of the company, above all respects whatsoever. As for the welfare hoped by a surrender, I was altogether unlikely to be partaker thereof, death threatning to deprive me of the benefit which the enemie offered; but if God would bee pleased to free us, the joy and comfort I should receive, might perhaps give me force and strength to recover health.

Which answere being delivered to the captaine, hee presently caused a flagge of truce to be put in place of our

Sect. LXII. ensigne, and began to parley of our surrendry, with a Spaniard, which Don Beltran appointed for that purpose, from the poope of the admirall, to offer in his name, the conditions before specified; with his faithful promise and oath, as the king generall, to take us *a buena querra*, and to send us all into our owne countrey. The promise hee accepted, and sayd that under the same hee yeelded, and surrendred himselfe, shippe, and company. Immediately there came unto me another servant of mine, and told me that our captaine had surrendred himselfe, and our shippe; which understood, I called unto one Juan Gomes de Pineda, a Spanish pilote, which was our prisoner, and in all the fight we had kept close in hold, and willed him to goe to the generall Don Beltran de Castro from mee, to tell him that if he would give us his word and oath, as the generall of the king, and some pledge for confirmation, to receive us *a buena querra*, and to give us our lives and libertie, and present passage into our owne countrey, that we would surrender ourselves and shippe into his hands; otherwise, that he should never enjoy of us nor ours, any thing but a resolution every man to dye fighting.

With this message I dispatched him, and called unto me all my company, and encouraged them to sacrifice their lives fighting and killing the enemie, if he gave but a fillip to any of our companions. The Spaniards willed us to hoise out our boate, which was shott all to peeces, and so was theirs. Seeing that, he called to us to amaine our sayles, which we could not well doe, for that they were slung, and we had not men inough to hand them. In this parley, the vice-admirall comming upon our quarter, and not knowing of what had past, discharged her two chase peeces at us, and hurte our captaine very sore in the thigh, and maimed one of our masters mates, called Hugh Maires, in one of his armes; but after knowing us to be rendred, hee secured us: and we satisfying them that wee

The English surrender.

could not hoise out our boate, nor strike our sayles, the admirall layd us abourd; but before any man entred, John Gomes went unto the generall, who received him with great curtesie, and asked him what we required; whereunto he made answere that my demand was, that in the Kings name, he should give us his faith and promise to give us our lives, to keepe the lawes of fayre warres and quarter, and to send us presently into our countrey; and in confirmation hereof, that I required some pledge; whereunto the generall made answere: that in the Kings Majesties name, his master, hee received us *a buena querra*, and swore by God Almightie, and by the habit of Alcantara (whereof he had received knighthood, and in token whereof hee wore in his breast a greene crosse, which is the ensigne of that order), that he would give us our lives with good entreatie, and send us as speedily as he could into our owne countrey. In confirmation whereof, he took of his glove, and sent it to mee as a pledge. Sect. LXII.

With this message John Gomes returned, and the Spaniards entred and tooke possession of our shippe, every one crying, *Buena querra, buena querra! oy por mi, maniana por ti:*[1] with which our company began to secure themselves.

The generall was a principall gentleman of the ancient nobilitie of Spaine, and brother to the Conde de Lemos,[2]

[1] *Hoy por mi, manana por ti:* which may be freely translated, "My turn to-day, yours to-morrow".

[2] Don Pedro Alvarez Osorio, first Count of Lemos, served in all the wars of John II and Henry IV. His wife, Beatriz de Castro, was heiress of the estate of Lemos. He died in 1483, and was succeeded by his grandson, Don Rodrigo de Castro Osorio, as second Count of Lemos. He served in the war of Granada, and dying, left the title and estates to his daughter Beatriz, who married Denis, the third son of the Duke of Braganza, who was son of the Portuguese Prince Fernando. Their son, Fernando Ruiz de Castro, was the fourth Count of Lemos. His son, Don Pedro Fernandez de Castro Andrada, fifth Count of Lemos, married Leonora, daughter of Don Baltran de la Cueva, Duke of Albuquerque; and their second son was Don Beltran de Castro, a Knight of

Sect. LXIII. whose intention no doubt was according to his promise; and therefore considering that some bad intreaty, and insolency, might be offered unto me in my shippe, by the common souldiers, who seldome have respect to any person in such occasions, especially in the case I was, whereof hee had enformed himselfe: for prevention, hee sent a principall captaine, brought up long time in Flaunders, called Pedro Alveres de Pulgar, to take care of me, and whilest the shippes were one abourd the other, to bring me into his ship; which he accomplished with great humanitie and courtesie; despising the barres of gold which were shared before his face, which hee might alone have enjoyed if he would. And truely hee was, as after I found by tryall, a true captaine, a man worthy of any charge, and of the noblest condition that I have knowne any Spaniard.

The mildnes of a generall after victorie. The generall received me with great courtesie and compassion, even with teares in his eyes, and words of great consolation, and commaunded mee to bee accommodated in his owne cabbine, where hee sought to cure and comfort mee the best he could: the like hee used with all our hurt men, six and thirtie at least. And doubtlesse, as true courage, valour, and resolution, is requisit in a generall in the time of battle, so humanitie, mildnes, and courtesie, after victorie.

SECTION LXIII.

WHILST the shippes were together, the maine-mast of the *Daintie* fell by the bourd, and the people being occupied in

Alcantara, and Governor of Callao. His sister, Teresa, was the wife of Don Garcia Hurtado de Mendoza, fourth Marquis of Cañete and Viceroy of Peru.

At the time of the surrender of Sir Richard Hawkins, the Marquis of Cañete was Viceroy of Peru (1590 to 1599), and his brother-in-law, Beltran de Castro, was governor of Callao and General of the Fleet.

Sect. LXIII.

ransacking and seeking for spoile and pillage, neglected the principall; whereof ensued, that within a short space the *Daintie* grew so deepe with water, which increased for want of prevention, that all who were in her desired to forsake her, and weaved and cryed for succour to bee saved, being out of hope of her recoverie.

The *Daintie* in danger of perishing.

Whereupon, the generall calling together the best experimented men hee had, and consulted with them what was best to bee done; it was resolved that generall Michaell Angell should goe abourd the *Daintie*, and with him threescore marriners, as many souldiers, and with them the English men who were able to labour, to free her from water, and to put her in order if it were possible; and then to recover Perico the port of Panama: for that, of those to wind-wards, it was impossible to turne up to any of them, and neerer then to le-ward was not any that could supply our necessities and wants; which lay from us east north-east, above two hundreth leagues.

Michaell Arckangell recovereth the ship.

Michaell Angell being a man of experience and care, accomplished that he tooke in hand; although in clearing and bayling the water, in placing a pumpe, and in fitting and mending her fore-saile, he spent above six and thirtie howers.

During which time the shippes lay all a hull; but this worke ended, they set sayle, and directed their course for the iles of Pearles. And for that the *Daintie* sayled badly, what for want of her maine-sayle, and with the advantage which all the South-sea shippes have of all those built in our North-sea, the admirall gave her a tawe;[1] which notwithstanding, the wind calming with us as we approached neerer to the land, twelve dayes were spent before we could fetch sight of the ilands; which lye alongst the coast, beginning some eight leagues, west south-west from Panama, and run to the south-wards neere thirtie leagues. They

[1] Tow or tug.

Sect. LXIII. are many, and the most unhabited; and those which have people, have some negroes, slaves unto the Spaniards, which occupie themselves in labour of the land, or in fishing for pearles.

Fishing for pearles. In times past, many inriched themselves with that trade, but now it is growne to decay. The manner of fishing for pearles is, with certaine long pinaces or small barkes, in which there goe foure, five, sixe, or eight negroes, expert swimmers, and great deevers,[1] whom the Spaniards call *busos;* with tract of time, use, and continuall practise, having learned to hold their breath long under water, for the better atchieving their worke. These throwing themselves into the sea, with certaine instruments of their art, goe to the bottome, and seeke the bankes of the oysters in which the pearles are ingendred, and with their force and art remouve them from their foundation; in which they spend more or lesse time, according to the resistance the firmnes of the ground affordeth. Once loosed, they put them into a bagge under their armes, and after bring them up into their boates. Having loaden it, they goe to the shoare; there they open them and take out the pearles: they lie under the uttermost part of the circuite of the oyster, in rankes and proportions, under a certaine part, which is of many pleights and folds, called the ruffe, for the similitude it hath unto a ruffe.

The pearles increase in bignes as they be neerer the end or joynt of the oyster. The meate of those which have these pearles is milkie, and not very wholesome to be eaten.

In anno 1583, in the island of Margarita, I was at the dregging of pearle oysters, after the manner we dregge oysters in England: and with mine owne hands I opened many, and tooke out the pearles of them, some greater, some lesse, and in good quantitie.

How the pearle is ingendred in the oyster, or mussell,

[1] Divers.

for they are found in both, divers and sundry are the opinions, but some ridiculous: whereof, because many famous and learned men have written largely, I will speake no more then hath beene formerly spoken, but referre their curious desires to Pliny, with other ancient and moderne authors. Sect. LXIII.

They are found in divers parts of the world, as in the West Indies, in the South sea, in the East Indian sea, in the Straites of Magellane, and in the Scottish sea. The places where pearles are found.

Those found neere the pooles[1] are not perfect, but are of a thick colour; whereas such as are found neere the line, are most orient and transparent: the curious call it their water: and the best is a cleare white shining, with fierie flames. And those of the East India have the best reputation, though as good are found in the West India; the choice ones are of great valew and estimation; but the greatest that I have read or heard of, was found in these ilands of Pearles; the which king Phillip the Second of Spaine gave to his daughter Elizabeth, wife to Albertus, arch-duke of Austria, and governour of the states of Flaunders; in whose possession it remaineth, and is called *la peregrina*,[2] for the rarenes of it; being as bigge as the pomell of a poinard.

[1] Poles.

[2] The *Peregrina*, *Huerfana*, or *Sola* (as having no equal), was a pearl which the King of Spain had in the royal crown. It was fished up in 1515, in the island of Terarequi (?), and was bought by Pedrarias, the first Governor of Tierra Firma. After his death it became the property of Doña Isabel de Bobadilla, of the house of the Counts of Chinchon, from whom it passed to the Empress Isabel. From that time it was in the royal crown of Spain, until it was burnt, with other precious treasures, when there was a fire in the palace at Madrid in 1734. It was highly prized for its size, its orient lustre, its whiteness, and pellucidness. It was pear-shaped, and weighed 550 carats. In 1691 a pearl was procured at the Darien fishery, as large as the *Peregrina*, which belonged to Don Pedro de Aponte, Conde de el Palmar, a native of the Canaries, who gave it to King Charles II of Spain. Latterly, the two were worn by the Queens of Spain as ear-rings.

SECTION LXIV.

Sect. LXIV.

The generall continueth his honourable usage towards the sicke and wounded.

In this navigation, after our surrender, the generall tooke especial care for the good intreaty of us, and especially of those who were hurt. And God so blessed the hands of our surgians (besides that they were expert in their art), that of all our wounded men not one died that was alive the day after our surrendry: the number whereof was neere fortie; and many of them with eight, ten, or twelve wounds, and some with more. The thing that ought to move us to give God Almighty especiall thankes and prayses, was that they were cured in a manner without instruments or salves. For the chests were all broken to peeces, and many of their simples and compounds throwne into the sea; those which remained, were such as were throwne about the shippe in broken pots and baggs; and such as by the Divine Providence were reserved, at the end of three dayes, by order from the generall, were commaunded to be sought and gathered together. These, with some instruments of small moment, bought and procured from those who had reserved them to a different end, did not onely serve for our cures, but also for the curing of the Spaniards, being many more then those of our company.

For the Spanish surgians were altogether ignorant in their profession, and had little or nothing wherewith to cure. And I have noted, that the Spaniards, in generall, are nothing so curious in accommodating themselves with good and carefull surgeans, nor to fit them with that which belongeth to their profession, as other nations are, though they have greater neede then any that I do know.

At the time of our surrender, I had not the Spanish tongue, and so was forced to use an interpreter, or the Latine, or French, which holpe me much for the understanding of those which spake to me in Spanish, together with a little smattering I had of the Portugall.

Through the noble proceding of Don Beltran with us, and his particular care towards me, in curing and comforting me, I began to gather heart, and hope of life, and health; my servants, which were on foote, advised me ordinarily of that which past. But some of our enemies, badly inclined, repined at the proceedings of the generall, and sayd he did ill to use us so well: that we were Lutherans; and for that cause, the faith which was given us, was not to be kept nor performed. Others, that wee had fought as good souldiers, and therefore deserved good quarter: others nicknamed us with the name of *corsarios*, or pirats; not discerning thereby that they included themselves within the same imputation. Some were of opinion, that from Panama, the generall would send us into Spaine: others sayd that he durst not dispose of us but by order from the vice-roy of Peru, who had given him his authority. This hit the nayle on the head. Sect. LXIV.

To all I gave the hearing, and laid up in the store-house of my memory that which I thought to be of substance; and in the store-house of my consideration, endeavoured to frame a proportionable resolution to all occurants, conformable to Gods most holy will. Withall I profitted my selfe of the meanes which should be offered, and beare greatest probabilitie to worke our comfort, helpe, and remedie. And so as time ministered opportunitie, I began, and endevoured to satisfie the generall and the better sort in the points I durst intermeddle. And especially to perswade, by the best reasons I could, that we might be sent presently from Panama; alleaging the promise given us, the cost and charges ensuing, which doubtles would be such as deserved consideration and excuse: besides, that now whilest he was in place, and power and authority in his hands, to performe with us, that hee would looke into his honour, and profit himselfe of the occasion, and not put us into the hands of a third person; who perhaps being

Sect. LXIV. more powerfull then himselfe, he might be forced to pray and intreate the performance of his promise: whereunto hee gave us the hearing, and bare us in hand that hee would doe what hee could.

The generall, and all in generall, not onely in the Peru, but in all Spaine, and the kingdomes thereof, before our surrendry, held all English men of warre to be corsarios, or pirats; which I laboured to reforme, both in the Peru, and also in the counsels of Spaine, and amongst the chieftaines, souldiers, and better sort, with whom I came to have conversation: alleadging that a pirate or corsario, is hee, which in time of peace or truce, spoyleth or robbeth those which have peace or truth with them: but the English have neyther peace nor truce with Spaine, but warre; and therefore not to be accounted pirats. Besides, Spaine broke the peace with England, and not England with Spaine; and that by ymbargo,[1] which of all kindes of defiances is most reproved, and of least reputation; the ransoming of prysoners, and that by the cannon being more honorable; but above all, the most honorable is with trumpet and herald to proclaime and denounce the warre by publicke defiance. And so if they should condemne the English for pirats, of force they must first condemne themselves.

What a pirat is.

Three sorts of defiances.

Moreover, pirats are those who range the seas without licence from their prince; who when they are met with, are punished more severely by their owne lords, then when they fall into the hands of strangers: which is notorious to be more severely prosecuted in England, in time of peace, then in any of the kingdomes of Christendome.

But the English have all licence, either immediately from their prince, or from others thereunto authorised, and so cannot in any sence be comprehended under the name

[1] Imbargo—embargo: laying on an embargo means issuing an order to prevent the sailing of vessels.

of pirats, for any hostility undertaken against Spaine or the dependencies thereof.

The custom of Spaine in warre.

And so the state standing as now it doth; if in Spaine a particular man should arm a shippe, and goe in warre-fare with it against the English, and happened to be taken by them; I make no question, but the company should bee intreated according to that manner, which they have ever used since the beginning of the warre, without making further inquisition.

Then if hee were rich or poore, to see if hee were able to give a ransome, in this also they are not very curious. But if this Spanish shippe should fall athwart his Kings armado or gallies, I make no doubt but they would hang the captaine and his company for pirates. My reason is, for that by a speciall law, it is enacted, that no man in the kingdomes of Spaine, may arme any shippe, and goe in warre-fare, without the King's speciall licence and commission, upon paine to be reputed a pirate, and to bee chastised with the punishment due to *corsarios*. In England the case is different: for the warre once proclaimed, every man may arme that will, and hath wherewith; which maketh for our greater exemption from being comprehended within the number of pirates.

The custome of England.

With these, and other like arguments to this purpose, (to avoid tediousnoss, I omitt): I convinced all those whom I heard to harpe upon this string: which was of no small importance for our good entreatie, and motives for many, to further and favour the accomplishment of the promise lately made unto us.

SECTION LXV.

A disputation concerning *buena guerra*.

One day after dinner, as was the ordinary custome, the generall, his captaines, and the better sort of his followers,

Sect. LXV. being assembled in the cabbin of the poope in conference, an eager contention arose amongst them, touching the capitulation of *buena querra*, and the purport thereof. Some sayd that onely life and good entreatie of the prisoners was to be comprehended therein: others enlarged, and restrained it, according to their humors and experience. In fine, my opinion was required, and what I had seene and knowne touching that point: wherein I pawsed a little, and suspecting the worst, feared that it might be a baite layd to catch me withall, and so excused my selfe, saying: that where so many experimented souldiers were joyned together, my young judgement was little to be respected: whereunto the generall replied, that knowledge was not alwayes incident to yeares, though reason requireth that the aged should be the wisest, but an art acquired by action and management of affaires; and therefore they would be but certified what I had seene, and what my judgment was in this point. Unto which, seeing I could not well excuse myselfe, I condiscended; and calling my wits together, holding it better to shoot out my boult by yeelding unto reason, although I might erre, then to stand obstinate, my will being at warre with my consent, and fearing my deniall might be taken for discourtesie, which peradventure might also purchase me mislike with those who seemed to wish me comfort and restitution; I submitted to better judgement, the reformation of the present assembly, saying: "Syr, under the capitulation of *buena querra*, or fayre warres, I have ever understood, and so it hath beene observed in these, as also in former times, that preservation of life and good entreatie of the prisoner have beene comprehended; and further, by no means to be urged to any thing contrary to his conscience, as touching his religion; nor to be seduced or menaced from the allegeance due to his prince and country; but rather to ransome him for his moneths pay. And this is that which I have knowne prac-

The resolution, etc.

tised in our times, in generall, amongst all civill and noble nations. But the English have enlarged it one point more towards the Spaniards rendred *a buena guerra* in these warres; have ever delivered them which have beene taken upon such compositions, without ransome: but the covetousnes of our age hath brought in many abuses, and excluded the principall officers from partaking of the benefit of this privilege, in leaving them to the discretion of the victor, being many times poorer then the common souldiers, their qualities considered; whereby they are commonly put to more than the ordinary ransome; and not being able of themselves to accomplish it, are forgotten of their princes and sometimes suffer long imprisonment, which they should not."

Sect. LXV.

The noble usage of the English,

but abused in these dayes.

With this, Don Beltran sayd: "This ambiguitie you have well resolved;" and, like a worthie gentleman, with great courtesie and liberalitie, added: "let not the last point trouble you, but bee of good comfort; for I here give you my word anew, that your ransome, if any shall be thought due, shall be but a cople of grey-hounds for mee, and other two for my brother, the Conde de Lemos: and this I sweare to you by the habit of Alcantara. Provided alwayes, that the King, my master, leave you to my dispose, as of right you belong to me."

Don Beltran satisfied, and answereth.

For amongst the Spaniards in their armadoes, if there bee an absolute generall, the tenth of all is due to him, and he is to take choise of the best: where in other countries, it is by lot that the generalls tenth is given. And if they be but two shippes, he doth the like: and being but one, shee is of right the generalls. This I hardly believed, until I saw a letter, in which the King willed his vice-roy to give Don Beltran thankes for our shippe and artillerie, which he had given to his Majestie.

I yeelded to the general most heartie thankes for his great favour, wherewith hee bound mee ever to seeke how to serve him, and deserve it.

SECTION LXVI.

Sect. LXVI.

Short arrowes for muskets.

In this discourse, generall Michael Angell[1] demanded for what purpose served the little short arrowes which we had in our shippe, and those in so great quantitie. I satisfied them that they were for our muskets. They are not as yet in use amongst the Spaniards, yet of singular effect and execution, as our enemies confessed: for the upper worke of their shippes being musket proofe, in all places they passed through both sides with facilitie, and wrought extraordinary disasters; which caused admiration, to see themselves wounded with small shott, where they thought themselves secure; and by no meanes could find where they entred, nor come to the sight of any of the shott.

Hereof they proved to profit themselves after, but for that they wanted the tampkins, which are first to be driven home before the arrow be put in; and as they understood not the secret, they rejected them as uncertaine, and therefore not to be used: but of all the shott used now a-dayes, for the annoying of an enemie in fight by sea, few are of greater moment, for many respects, which I hold not convenient to treat of in publique.

SECTION LXVII.

John Oxman's voyage to the South sea.

A little to the south-wards of the iland of Pearle, betwixt seven and eight degrees, is the great river of Saint Buena Ventura. It falleth into the South sea with three mouthes, the head of which is but a little distant from the North sea. In anno 1575, or 1576, one John Oxman,[2] of Plymouth, going into the West Indies, joyned with the Symarons.

[1] See page 340.

[2] Oxenham.

These are fugitive negroes, and for the bad intreatie which their masters had given them, were then retyred into the mountaines, and lived upon the spoyle of such Spaniards as they could master, and could never be brought into obedience, till by composition they had a place limmitted them for their freedome, where they should live quietly by themselves. At this day they have a great habitation neere Panama, called Saint Iago de Los Negros, well peopled, with all their officers and commaunders of their owne, save onely a Spanish governour.

Sect. LXVII.

What the Symarons are.

Their habitation.

By the assistance of these Symarons, hee brought to the head of this river, by peecemeale, and in many journeys, a small pinnace; hee fitted it by time in a warlike manner, and with the choice of his company, put himselfe into the South sea, where his good hap was to meete with a cople of shippes of trade, and in the one of them a great quantitie of gold. And amongst other things, two peeces of speciall estimation: the one a table of massie gold, with emralds, sent for a present to the King; the other a lady of singular beautie, married, and a mother of children. The latter grewe to bee his perdition; for hee had capitulated with these Symarons, that their part of the bootie should be onely the prisoners, to the ende to execute their malice upon them (such was the rancor they had conceived against them, for that they had beene the tyrants of their libertie). But the Spaniards not contented to have them their slaves, who lately had beene their lords, added to their servitude, cruell entreaties. And they againe, to feede their insatiable revenges, accustomed to rost and eate the hearts of all those Spaniards, whom at any time they could lay hand upon.

Their assistance.

John Oxman capitulateth with them.

John Oxmann, I say, was taken with the love of this lady, and to winne her good will, what through her teares and perswasions, and what through feare and detestation of their barbarous inclinations, breaking promise with the Symarons, yeelded to her request; which was, to give the prisoners

His folly and breach of promise.

Sect. LXVII. liberty with their shippes, for that they were not usefull for him: notwithstanding, Oxman kept the lady, who had in one of the restored shippes eyther a sonne or a nephew.

His pursuit. This nephew, with the rest of the Spaniards, made all the hast they could to Panama, and they used such diligence, as within fewe howers some were dispatched to seek those who little thought so quickly too bee overtaken. The pursuers approaching the river, were doubtfull by which of the afore-remembred three mouthes they should take their way.

And evill fortune. In this wavering, one of the souldiers espied certaine feathers of hennes, and some boughs of trees, which they had cut off to make their way, swimming down one of the outlets. This was light sufficient to guide them in their course; they entred the river, and followed the tracke as farre as their frigats had water sufficient; and then with part of their souldiers in their boates, and the rest on the bankes on eyther side, they marched day and night in pursuite of their enemies; and in fine came uppon them unexpected, at the head of the river, making good cheare in their tents, and devided in two partialities about the partition, and sharing of their gold. Thus were they surprised, and not one escaped.

He flyeth to the Symarons. Some say that John Oxman fled to the Symarons, but they utterly denyed to receive or succour him, for that he had broken his promise; the onely objection they cast in his teeth was, that if he had held his word with them, hee had never fallen into this extremitie.

In fine, hee was taken, and after, his shippe also was possessed by the Spaniards, which he had hid in a certaine cove, and covered with boughes of trees, in the guard and custodie of some foure or five of his followers. All his company were conveyed to Panama, and there were ymbarked for Lyma; where a processe was made against them by the justice, and all condemned and hanged as pirates.

This may be a good example to others in like occasions: first to shunne such notorious sinnes, which cannot escape punishment in this life, or in the life to come: for the breach of faith is reputed amongst the greatest faults which a man can committ. Secondly, not to abuse another mans wife, much lesse to force her; both being odious to God and man. Thirdly, to beware of mutenies, which seldome or never are seene to come to better ends; for where such trees flourish, the fruite, of force, must eyther bee bitter, sweete, or very sower. And therefore, seeing wee vaunt ourselves to bee Christians, and make profession of His law who forbiddeth all such vanities; let us faithfully shunne them, that wee may partake the end of that hope which our profession teacheth and promiseth.

Sect. LXVIII.

Breach of faith never unpunished.

SECTION LXVIII.

COMMING in sight of the ilands of Pearles, the wind began to fresh in with us, and wee profited our selves of it: but comming thwart of a small iland, which they call la Pacheta, that lyeth within the Pearle ilands, close abourd the mayne, and some eight or ten leagues south and by west from Panama, the wind calmed againe.

La Pacheta.

This iland belongeth to a private man; it is a round humock,[1] conteyning not a league of ground, but most fertile. Insomuch, that by the owners industrie, and the labour of some few slaves, who occupie themselves in manuring it; and two barkes, which he imployeth in bringing the fruit it giveth to Panama, it is sayd to bee worth him every weeke, one with another, a barre of silver, valued betwixt two hundreth and fiftie or three hundreth pezos; which in English money, may amount to fiftie or three-

[1] Mound or hillock.

Sect. LXVIII. score pounds: and for that which I saw at my being in Panama, touching this, I hold to be true.

In our course to fetch the port of Panama, wee put our selves betwixt the iland and the maine: which is a goodly channel, of three, foure, and five leagues broad, and without danger, except a man come too neare the shoare on any side; and that is thought the better course, then to goe a sea-boord of the ilands, because of the swift running of the tydes, and the advantage to stop the ebbe: as also for succour, if a man should happen to bee becalmed at any time beyond expectation, which happeneth sometimes.

The generall certefieth the *Audiencia* of his successe.

The seventh of July wee had sight of Perico: they are two little ilands which cause the port of Panama,[1] where all the shippes used to ride. It is some two leagues west northwest of the cittie, which hath also a pere[2] in itselfe for small barkes; at full sea it may have some sixe or seaven foote water, but at low water it is drie.

The great joy of the Spaniards.

The ninth of July wee anchored under Perico, and the generall presently advised the *Audiencia* of that which had succeeded in his journey: which, understood by them, caused bonfires to be made, and every man to put lumina-

[1] Sir Richard Hawkins was at old Panama, the city destroyed by Morgan in 1671. When it was rebuilt the site was removed about four miles. The tower of the church of San Geronimo, in the ruins of the old town, still rises above the forest, but the place is entirely abandoned and overgrown. The harbour is formed by several islands called Isla de Naos, Perico, and Flamencos, and the anchorage is called Perico because it is in front of the second island.

Old Panama was one of the richest cities in Spanish America. It had eight monasteries, two splendid churches and a cathedral, a fine hospital, 200 richly furnished houses, nearly 5000 houses of a humbler kind, a Genoese chamber of commerce, 200 warehouses, and was surrounded by delicious gardens and country houses, now all covered by a dense and impervious forest. After three weeks of rapine and murder, the buccaneer marched out of the ruined city on February 24th, 1671, with 175 laden mules and over 600 prisoners. In 1673 Don Alonzo Mercado de Villacosta founded the present city of Panama.

[2] Pier.

ries in their houses. The fashion is much used amongst the Spaniards in their feasts of joy, or for glad tidings; placing many lights in their churches, in their windowes, and galleries, and corners of their houses; which being in the beginning of the night, and the cittie close by the sea-shore, showed to us, being farre of, as though the cittie had been on a light fire. Sect. LXVIII.

About eight of the clocke, all the artillery of the citty was shott off, which wee might discerne by the flashes of fire, but could not heare the report; yet the armado being advised thereof, and in a readinesse, answered them likewise with all their artillery; which taking ende, as all the vanities of this earth doe, the generall settled himselfe to dispatch advise for the King, for the vice-roy of Peru, and for the vice-roy of the Nova Spana, for hee also had beene certified of our being in that sea, and had fitted an armado to seeke us, and to guard his coast.

But now for a farewell (and note it), let me relate unto you this secret, how Don Beltran shewed mee a letter from the King, his master, directed to the vice-roy, wherein he gave him particular relation of my pretended voyage; of the ships, their burden, their munition, their number of men, which I had in them, as perfectly as if he had seene all with his own eyes: saying unto me, "Heereby may you discerne whether the King, my master, have friends in England, and good and speedie advice of all that passeth." Note.

Whereunto I replyed: "It was no wonder, for that hee had plentie of gold and silver, which worketh this and more strange effects: for my journey was publique and notorious to all the kingdome." Whereunto hee replyed, that if I thought it so convenient, leave should be given mee to write into England to the Queens Majestie, my mistresse, to my father, and to other personages, as I thought good; and leaving the letters open, that he would send some of them in the King's packet, others to his uncle Don Rodrigo

Sect. LXVIII. de Castro,[1] cardinall and archbishoppe of Sevill, and to other friends of his; not making any doubt but that they would be speedily in England." For which I thanked him, and accepted his courtesie; and although I was my selfe unable to write, yet by the hands of a servant of mine, I wrote three or foure coppies of one letter to my father, Sir John Hawkins; in which I briefly made relation of all that had succeeded in our voyage.

The dispatches of Spaine and New Spaine, went by ordinary course in ships of advise; but that for the Peru, was sent by a kinseman of the generalls, called Don Francisco de la Cueva.[2]

Which being dispatched, Don Beltran hasted all that ever hee could to put his shippes in order, to returne to Lyma. Hee caused the *Daintie* to be grounded and trimmed; for in those ilands it higheth and falleth some fifteene or sixteene foote water.

And the generall with his captaines, and some religious men being aboord her, and new naming her, named her the *Visitation*, for that shee was rendred on the day on which they celebrate the visitation of the blessed Virgin Mary.[3] In that place, the ground being plaine and without vantage, whereby to helpe the tender sided and sharpe ships, they are forced to shore them on either side. In the midest of their solemnity, her props and shores of one side fayled, and so shee fell over upon that side suddenly, intreating many of them which were in her, very badly; and doubtlesse, had shee bin like the shippes of the South sea, shee had broken out her bulge:[4] but being without mastes and empty (for in

[1] The Cardinal Rodrigo de Castro was a son of Beatriz, Countess and sole Heiress of Lemos, by her second husband, Don Alvaro Osorio, of the house of Astorga. Rodrigo entered holy orders, became Bishop of Zamora, then of Cuenca, and was Cardinal of the Basilica and of the Twelve Apostles. Finally, he became Archbishop of Seville. His mother, by her first husband, Dionis of Portugal, had a son, Fernando Ruiz de Castro, Count of Lemos, the father of Don Beltran de Castro.

[2] See page 337. [3] The 2nd of July. [4] Bilge.

the South sea, when they bring a-ground a shippe, they leave neither masts, balast, nor any other thing abourd, besides the bare hull), her strength was such as it made no great show to have received any damage; but the feare shee put them all into was not little, and caused them to runne out of her faster than a good pace. Sect. LXVIII.

In these ilands is no succour nor refreshing; onely in the one of them is one house of strawe, and a little spring of small moment. For the water, which the shippes use for their provision, they fetch from another iland, two leagues west north-west of these, which they call Taboga,[1] having in it some fruite and refreshing, and some fewe Indians to inhabite it.

What succeeded to mee, and to the rest during our imprisonment, with the rarities and particularities of the Peru and Terra Firme, my voyage to Spaine, and the successe, with the time I spent in prison in the Peru, in the Tercera, in Sevill, and in Madrid, with the accidents which befell me in them, I leave for a second part of this discourse, if God give life and convenient place and rest, necessary for so tedious and troublesome a worke: desiring God, that is Almightie, to give his blessing to this and the rest of my intentions, that it and they may bee fruitefull to His glory, and the good of all: then shall my desires be accomplished, and I account myselfe most happie. To whom be all glory, and thankes, from all eternitie.

---

[1] A charming island about twelve miles from Panama, which belonged to the Canon Fernando Luque, the partner with Pizarro and Almagro in the project for the conquest of Peru.

A SPANISH ACCOUNT

OF

THE NAVAL ACTION

BETWEEN

SIR RICHARD HAWKINS

AND

DON BELTRAN DE CASTRO.

A

SPANISH ACCOUNT OF THE NAVAL ACTION

BETWEEN

SIR RICHARD HAWKINS AND DON BELTRAN DE CASTRO.

[From the *Hechos de Don Garcia Hurtado de Mendoza, Cuarto Marques de Cañete; por Dr. Don Christobal Suarez de Figueroa* (Madrid, 1614), Lib. v.]

SEVERAL ships, commanded by English pirates, entered the South Sea in the time of former Viceroys, whose audacity was rewarded with success in the shape of prizes and notable plunder. The first who, entering by the Strait of Magellan, coasted along the land from south to north, was Francisco Draque. His Queen, Isabel, sent him with three ships well armed and provisioned. Each ship had a crew of two hundred men, besides ten young gentlemen, who wished to perform the voyage with the object of seeing the world, and of showing their valour on such occasions as might offer themselves. He left the port of Plemua[1] to pass into the South Sea, and seek the above strait.

Having reached the strait after various events which have already been related by others, he passed it alone in the *Capitana*.[2] While he was ranging over those seas and before he arrived at Callao, the port for which he was making, he fell in with a ship of Arica, the port of Potosi. She was coming from Callao, unarmed, and not expecting the appearance of pirates, laden with bars of iron and some gold. Draque boarded her,[3] and giving good treatment to all, he

[1] Plymouth. [2] The Admiral's ship. [3] February 1578.

asked the master, named San Juan de Anton, for the invoice of the cargo; who delivered up what he had got, item by item, without omitting anything, for which he received from Draque a receipt in full as his discharge. Observing that the others were sad, he consoled them by saying that they should cast off all care, seeing that they lived in so good and rich a land. With this he left them in their vessel, and went to Callao,[1] where he came to amongst the other ships. Being there unknown, the people rose in arms, in consequence of which he made sail and proceeded to the coast of Nicaragua. On an island called Del Caño, on the coast of Costa Rica, there is abundance of wood and water. Here he careened the ship, and, without hurrying himself,[2] he then shaped a course towards the west.

Owing to this incursion, which the Englishman made with such promptitude and audacity, Don Francisco de Toledo,[3] then Viceroy of Peru, and in all time an able administrator, whose orders, as being both just and convenient, still retain observance in those parts as municipal laws, despatched ships under the command of Pedro Sarmiento de Gamboa, with Anton Paulo Coros, as chief pilot, who had already fought with the English pirate on other occasions; that they might despoil him, if possible, of the great plunder he had taken from the lands and ships of the king. They set sail in search, with suitable instructions, on a Sun-

[1] February 15th, 1579.

[2] He was at the Isla del Caño from March 16th to 24th, 1579. For mention of this island, see Funnel's account (Dampier, iv, p. 89). It lies S.E. of the Gulf of Nicoya.

[3] Francisco de Toledo was a younger son of the Count of Oropesa, and a relation of the Duke of Alva. He became Viceroy of Peru in 1569, and held the office till 1581. Toledo was an able administrator, and his *Ordenanzas* formed the basis of the code of Peruvian laws during Viceregal times. He especially attended to legislation respecting the mines and coca plantations. But his memory is execrated in Peru, because, from motives of policy, he ordered the judicial murder of the gallant young Tupac Amaru, the last of the Yncas.

day, the 11th of October, 1579. After having traversed the straits, and tarried a little in unknown ports, describing and surveying them with care, they proceeded (according to orders) on their way to Spain, to give a complete and full account of the position and character of the strait, of its narrow parts, and of all that navigation. Thus laden with new information, they reached Cape San Vicente.[1]

Draque continued his voyage, and arrived at the Malucos. He anchored at Ternate,[2] where he had trade in cloves, and made a treaty of perpetual friendship with the king and queen. He then sailed for the coast of Guinea and Cape Verde, and continuing his course to his native land, he arrived there in triumph,[3] with two ships laden with silver, gold, spices, and other riches. He delivered all to the Queen, without being richer by his robberies nor more esteemed by reason of his acts.

After this, in the time of Don Fernando de Torres, Conde de Villar and Viceroy of Peru,[4] the Englishman, Thomas

[1] Sarmiento first went in chase of Drake as far as Panama, but, supposing that the English ship was returning by the way he came, the Spanish commander then made for the Straits of Magellan. Sarmiento had orders to make a minute and careful survey of the straits and of all the approaches. The instructions were drawn up with minute care by the Viceroy Toledo, and journals were kept in accordance with them. One of these journals was published in 1768—*Viaje al estrecho de Magallanes por el Capitan Pedro Sarmiento de Gamboa en los años* 1579 *y* 1580. Sarmiento sighted Cape St. Vincent on August 15th, 1580, and on his arrival in Spain he proposed to Philip II that the straits should be fortified, to prevent the English from passing. His plan was approved. A great fleet was despatched from Seville, under the command of Diego Flores de Valdes, and Sarmiento went in one of the ships to plant a colony in the straits. It was not until 1584 that Sarmiento landed with four hundred men and thirty women; but he was soon afterwards driven out of the strait by a gale, leaving the colonists on shore. He was taken prisoner by the English and brought to London in 1585, but was liberated by order of the Queen. Sarmiento was afterwards serving in the Philippine Islands.

[2] November 3rd, 1579. [3] September 26th, 1580.

[4] Don Fernando Torres y Portugal, Count of Villar, succeeded to the

Candi, entered by the same strait.[1] He anchored in the port of Valparaiso (which is the principal port of the kingdom of Chile), and was attacked by a troop of Spaniards.[2] They caught the English off their guard, and, killing fourteen, obliged Tomas to continue his voyage with much despite. He seized some vessels at anchor, on whose crews he avenged himself for the recent attack. The Viceroy was presently informed of his arrival, and he armed three good ships, which were sent in chase. Other precautions were taken for the pursuit of the pirates, and for giving notice by land and sea. The Audiencia of Quito sent soldiers to Guayaquil, where, finding the enemies on shore, six more were killed.[3] This ship departed full of alarm at this second misfortune, and the ships of Lima, after a fruitless search, arrived at Panama. The Englishman sailed along the coast of Nicaragua, and went thence to the Cape of San Lucas of California, in a height of 22⅓° N.[4] There he waited for the ship *Santa Ana*, that was coming from the Filipinas with a rich cargo. He found her (that sea being pacific) without a sword, and quite secure from such a mishap. Candi went

viceregal chair in 1586, and was succeeded by the Marquis of Cañete in 1590.

[1] Thomas Cavendish sailed from Plymouth on July 21st, 1586, with three ships, the *Desire* (120 tons), *Content* (sixty tons), and *Hugh Gallant* (forty tons). Cavendish found the colony left in the straits by Sarmiento, but all were dead except eighteen. He cruelly left the survivors to their fate, and proceeded on his voyage. On March 18th, 1587, he arrived at Quintero, close to Valparaiso.

[2] It was on the 1st of April that the watering party of Cavendish was attacked by two hundred Spanish horsemen; and the English acknowledged to the loss of twelve men.

[3] Cavendish was at anchor off the island of Puna, in the Gulf of Guayaquil. Twenty of his men were on shore, scattered about, when they were suddenly attacked by Spanish soldiers who had landed on the other side of the island. Seven of the English were killed, two were drowned, and three taken prisoners. This was on June 2nd, 1587.

[4] Cape San Lucas, the southern point of California, is in 22° 52′ N. and 109° 53′ W.

on board, seized on everything, and landed all the crew except a priest whom he hanged.[1] He then examined all the cargo, item by item. He found a large sum in gold, and, selecting the most valuable part of the cargo, he threw the rest into the sea. Lastly, he set fire to the ship, and sailed on towards the Filipinas, where he seized an Indian who showed him a passage by which he passed between the two islands of Taprobane and Java Major, a strait called Fundia.[2] Finally, he arrived at London with his sails made of green damask, and all his sailors dressed in silk, to the general delight of that city.[3]

Such were the results of the two first entries of these pirates whom (envious of their good luck) Ricardo Aquines, also an Englishman, desired to imitate. This man, with a famous ship called the *Linda*,[4] entered by the strait, in the narrows of which he lost two other vessels which came with him, in the year 1594. He arrived at Valparaiso in need of provisions and other necessaries. Here he found five vessels off their guard, laden with provisions, cordage, and other stores. They surrendered without offering any resistance. He enjoyed himself for some days in this port, and at the

[1] The English accounts say nothing about hanging priests.

[2] Sunda.

[3] According to the English account, the prize, taken off Cape San Lucas by Cavendish, made a gallant resistance. She was captured on November 14th, 1587. Her cargo consisted of 122,000 pesos of gold, satins, silks, and musk. Cavendish landed the crew and passengers, numbering 190 souls, at Aguada Segura, a port near Cape San Lucas. He then set the ship on fire and sailed away, but the unfortunate people, who had been put on shore, managed to extinguish the flames, and they escaped in her to Acapulco. (See Torquemada, *Monarquia Indiana*, v, cap. 48.) The *Content* parted company with Cavendish's ship, the *Desire*, soon afterwards, and was never heard of again. The *Desire* sighted the Philippines on January 14th, 1588. Cavendish returned to Plymouth on June 20th, 1588. The English account of the voyage of Cavendish is written by F. Pretty (Hakluyt, iii, p. 800). Nautical remarks were also made by T. Fuller (Hakluyt, iii, p. 827).

[4] The *Dainty*.

end of them, wishing to depart, he came to an agreement with the people regarding the ransom of their vessels; without considering that he was setting those at liberty who could give notice of his arrival. Such was the opinion he had of his ship (as being so well armed and manned), and so cheap did he hold the maritime resources of all Peru. The Viceroy, Don Garcia, received news of this with all despatch, and although the tidings found him in bed, suffering from an attack of illness, he rose up at once, his first care being to send orders to collect the guards of lances and arquebuses at the port of Callao, to the end that it might be secure. He also gave commissions, as captains, to three soldiers who were experienced in martial affairs. Their names were Pulgar, Manrique, and Plaza. They had orders to raise a hundred soldiers each, and to man the ships which were being fitted out with all despatch. The Marquis, not altogether relying upon the diligence of the officers whom he had sent, went himself with a few attendants, on the following day, to see after everything, in spite of a fit of gout which he was suffering from at the time.

He made arrangements, on his arrival, for all necessary stores being provided for the equipment of the ships, and caused a packet to be despatched at once to convey the news, with all diligence, from port to port, so that the enemy might take no one unawares, and then to proceed onward to Guatemala and Mexico. He sent another vessel to Panama, that Don Fernando de Cordova might be ready with his squadron to hinder the Englishman if he should attempt to pass that way. Having made these arrangements by sea, the Viceroy sent various *chasquis* (who are very swift Indian couriers on foot) up the coast, ordering them also to go inland, so that all people might be on the look out for the pirate, and that he might not be able to escape by any means.

He then put Lima in a state of defence, for he desired

above all things to take advantage of this occasion to prove his power. Callao was left, by the Viceroy, in charge of Doctor Alonzo, a native of Castile, and senior Judge of the Royal Audience of Lima, as his lieutenant. The Doctor was distinguished for his learning and virtue, and fit for any charge that might be entrusted to him, careful, active, and efficient. Every afternoon two companies of guards entered the city, the recruits being exercised in the use of arms almost every day. Besides these and other important preparations, three strong ships were fitted out with everything necessary for the work they were to do. Sixty bronze pieces were divided between the *Capitana* and the *Almiranta;* four others being assigned as a broadside for the galleon *San Juan.* The three above-named captains, having raised their men, proceeded with them to the port, ready to embark the moment the order was given. Besides this body of three hundred men, several young gentlemen volunteered for the service, among whom were Lorenzo de Heredia, who embarked with ten soldiers maintained at his own cost; and Don Francisco de la Cueva,[1] with almost as many raised on the same terms.

The Viceroy nominated Don Beltran de Castro y de la Cueva,[2] as commander of the expedition, a son of the Count of Lemos, and his own brother-in-law. Don Beltran was an officer of distinguished talent and capacity equal to the greatest undertakings; as was proved by his former services. He was at Milan in the days when that province was governed, with so much ability, by his uncle, Don Gabriel de la Cueva, Duke of Albuquerque.[3] Knowing his

[1] A kinsman of the General Don Beltran de Castro. See p. 326.

[2] Castro was his paternal surname, and La Cueva that of his mother.

[3] Don Beltran's mother, the Countess of Lemos, was Doña Leonora de la Cueva, a daughter of Don Beltran de la Cueva, third Duke of Albuquerque; and sister of Francisco, the fourth Duke. The wife of the fourth Duke was Constance de Leyva, daughter of Antonio de

talent, the Duke appointed him, when only twenty-two years of age, to the command of an army which was sent by order of His Majesty to take Final. The selection of Don Beltran, by the Viceroy, as General of the expedition, was approved by all, and he was not long before his deeds justified the appointment. He was scarcely appointed before he set out for the port, and devoted himself to the preparation of the fleet, without ever leaving the sea shore, morning or evening.

He completed the fitting out with marvellous rapidity, so that in the course of eight days all was ready, a thing almost incredible when the amount of work to be done is considered. The Viceroy was of opinion that, of the two kinds of war, the offensive is always better than the defensive. He was accustomed to say that the assailant finds himself prepared, and provided with everything necessary for the encounter; while he who waits to be attacked is generally unready, because he has to make preparations and defend himself by force. He would add too that, after a long march, there is deterioration in all the equipment of soldiers, in provisions, artillery, and stores, and everything else necessary for defence; while the men on the defensive, are not working of their own accord but from necessity. Moreover, the towns that are threatened suffer infinitely from constant fear of life, without any hope of gain.

At last the three galleons were ready and well provided with soldiers, priests, arms, stores, and provisions, and they only waited for favourable weather to make sail. In the meanwhile the Marquis wished to honour the expedition with his presence. He, therefore, went to Callao and, getting into his baot, pulled towards the ships. On his approach the ships fired off all their pieces, and very high mountains of smoke ascended, while cheers resounded on all sides.

Leyva, Prince of Asculi, Governor of Milan, and Captain-General of Italy.

The Viceroy visited them all, inciting the men and cheering them with his speeches. Finally, he returned to the shore, and, according to custom, the last gun was fired, and the ships sailed shortly afterwards, the three keeping company until they were out of sight.

Don Beltran had scarcely disappeared when the Viceroy received the news that Ricardo had appeared off Arica, with three ships. A fisherman brought this intelligence, from whom the pirate had taken a supply of fish, and then given him his liberty.[1] It was supposed that the two other vessels might be the *Almiranta*, and another that was reported to have been lost in the straits. It, therefore, seemed good to the Viceroy to take some further precautions. He, therefore, prepared a "galizabra",[2] built by his orders at Callao, together with another galleon and a brigantine. These were supplied with all necessaries, and their duty was to protect the thirty ships and packet boats that were in that port, so entirely without defence that one small vessel might almost have taken them all. The new vessels would also be in a position to reinforce the first fleet, and to fill up vacancies caused by any accidents. The coast was garrisoned, and all watched with such diligence that the pirate had scarcely been seen before the news had been announced to each port, being sent from one to the other by means of flaming beacons.

This constant vigilance was the reason why Aquines did not venture on shore, being fearful of destruction, as he saw the beaches crowded with cavalry, which was what caused most dismay to the enemy. Thus he had to continue his voyage without being able to do any harm, until he arrived

[1] Sir Richard gives an account of the capture of this fisherman. See p. 251.

[2] The Dictionary of the Spanish Academy describes a "zabra" as a kind of small frigate used in the Bay of Biscay. The compound word, "galizabra" is not given.

off Chincha,[1] which is a place at a distance of thirty leagues from Lima. Thence a runner set out to the Viceroy with the news, which was at once forwarded to his brother-in-law. During the twelve days that he had been at sea Don Beltran had not been able to obtain any news of Ricardo: so that, when the intelligence reached him, he altered his course with great joy, and steered towards the land. It was at dawn, one day, that he discovered the pirate under the land; but the enemy had got the first sight of our fleet, and strove to escape with all speed, by hauling his wind. Don Beltran wished to get the wind, but it was impossible, because a storm arose almost at the same time. Nevertheless he did his best to follow in spite of a heavy sea, until the gale increased and, losing sight of the chase, it was as much as he could do to save his own ships. This storm was considered to have been the greatest that had ever been encountered in those parts. It obliged the fleet, which was to follow Ricardo, to return to the port whence they had sailed, where they arrived in a very damaged condition. Nor did the tempest spare the fugitive, for those on board were obliged to throw part of the cargo overboard in order to save her.

On his arrival at Callao, Don Beltran was easily able to refit, owing to the preparations that had been made by the Viceroy. He got ready to sail again without loss of time, but it was necessary to make some change in the vessels. The ship which had previously been the *Almiranta* was selected for *Capitana*, while the *Galizabra*, a small but beautiful vessel, was chosen for *Almiranta*. To these was added a launch for use in seeking out creeks and anchorages. Miguel Anjel Filipon accompanied the General. He was a famous pilot and, although a stranger, was a man of great trust. On the day when the embarkation commenced there

[1] The rich coast valley of Chincha is between those of Cañete and Pisco. The distance from Lima is correctly stated in the text.

was a heavy sea, so that the work was performed with difficulty, as the beach is full of large pebbles. There were many accidents, and people were killed and hurt in going off to the ships. The Viceroy, in great anxiety, rode up and down the seashore on horseback, watching the embarkation, and he saw one man in extreme peril. His humanity would not allow him to neglect his accustomed office, so, getting off his horse, and rushing into the water up to his knees, he strove to save the man. Fired by his example, others dashed into the sea without regard to their costly clothes, and the soldiers of the guard doing the same with their halberds, the man was rescued from his perilous position. The embarkation was completed at a distance of two musket shots above the port.

At the first favorable wind the fleet sailed again, approaching the shore whenever there was a chance, to see whether Aquines was cruising under the land, or was at anchor in any bay or creek. A point had scarcely been doubled on a certain day, being the vespers of Santa Isabel,[1] at about four in the afternoon, when the enemy was discovered in the bay of San Mateo, which is on the coast of Esmeraldas.[2]

Aquines saw the two ships and, supposing that they were not men of war, but suited for plunder, he prepared to capture them. He only had one ship and a launch, for con-

[1] This is a mistake. Sir Richard tells us that the surrender took place on the day of the Visitation of the Virgin Mary, which is the 2nd of July. This, no doubt, is correct; but, in other respects, Sir Richard, when he wrote his book, had lost account of the dates. He gives the date of the action as June 22nd. Suarez de Figueroa is wrong about the vespers of Santa Isabel, which are on the 18th of November.

[2] On the coast of the province of Quito. Cape San Francisco is a high bluff, clothed with tall trees. The land then trends north to Galera Point, and thence N.N.E. Atacames is a small town, twelve miles from Point Galera, in 0° 57′ 30″ N., and fourteen miles N.E. is the entrance to the Esmeraldas river. Verde Point is a cliffy bluff, thirteen miles east of Esmeraldas, and the intervening coast forms the bay of San Mateo, in about 1° 10′ N. latitude.

sidering that the two other ships, with which he appeared at Arica, would be a hindrance to his voyage, he had brought them no further.[1] The pirate, without leaving his position, sent his captain to reconnoitre the vessels that had come in sight. He did so, and approached within a little less than a cannon shot. Don Beltran, at the same time, had ordered his Admiral Lorenzo de Heredia to advance with the *Galizabra* to meet the enemy. He also gave instructions that, as his vessel was small, he should take up a position inshore, while, at the same time, Don Beltran selected a station to seaward of the enemy. The *Almiranta* fired off three pieces which, without doing any harm to the reconnoitring vessel, merely served to warn him that the strangers were enemies. The English captain returned, with sails and oars, to where Ricardo was waiting for him; and delivered a brief report of what had happened. Instantly weighing his anchors, and sounding a loud trumpet, Ricardo then came forth to do battle with the strangers. As he approached, the *Capitana* discharged the guns on the port side, and then going about fired two guns, from the poop, the shot from which hit the English ship. Presently the *Galizabra* came up, and discharging six guns at one time, the mizen was cut away and fell into the sea. The pirate sheered off, and again opening fire, two negros and two sailors on board the *Capitana*, who were on the poop hauling aft the sheet, were cut in two near the bitts. This discharge was followed up so quickly by another that the ship of Don Beltran de Castro was hardly pressed. At this time the *Galizabra*, which had been chasing the launch, came up with the intention of running into the enemy, but the attempt turned out badly; for Ricardo defended his ship with renewed valour, shooting away the main mast of his assailant and killing fourteen men.

The ships then sheered off from each other somewhat and,

[1] This is a mistake. He had no other ships with him at Arica.

the night coming on, those of the King followed Aquines, keeping a good look-out, and firing off their guns from time to time. At dusk they began the work of attending to the wounded, and of throwing the dead into the sea. The *Galizabra* rigged a jury main mast, and in the morning (being the day of the Visitation), she opened fire on the enemy, with all her guns and muskets. Presently Don Beltran came up, also firing off his pieces, but the enemy replied with so terrible a discharge that one ball shot away the figure head and another entered the dead wood, passing out on the other side without doing any harm. Having exchanged these shots, the vessels came along side each other and were so close that the gallant Hawkins himself seized the royal standard by means of a bowline knot which he threw over it. But the attempt failed, as Diego de Avila, Juan Manrique, Pedro de Reinalte, Juan Velazquez, and others came to the rescue, and defended it valorously. The Englishman paid for his audacity by two wounds, one in the neck and the other in the arm, both received from gun shots. At this moment the *Galizabra* attempted to run alongside, but the enemy hurled two harpoons into her sails, and four inboard, killing the *Condestable* and two sailors. The men in the *Galizabra* were not, however, dismayed; but, persevering in their attempt, they grappled the enemy and boarded her. The first to reach her deck were Juan Bantista Montañes and Juan de Torres Portugal, both valiant soldiers. The captain of the ship opposed the entry of Torres with a shield and sword, but, after some blows and wounds dealt on both sides, the Englishman fell on his back, giving place to the Spaniard to pass onwards. Meanwhile, Juan Bantista had killed two and driven others backwards until they were forced into the cabin under the poop, where they continued their resistance with signal courage. Finally they received quarter, the *Capitana* having also boarded, and sent her men into the enemy's ship.

The prize was a ship of 400 tons, most beautiful in all her parts. She carried for arms on the stern a negress with gilt ornaments. Miguel Anjel Filipon repaired her that night, lest she should go to the bottom, as she was badly damaged, for this purpose heaving her to. Captain Pulgar[1] captured Ricardo, who was sent on board the *Capitana* with others of highest rank. They arrived at Panama on the following day,[2] where they were well received by Don Francisco de Cardenas,[3] the President of that Chancery. The wounded were brought into the city, some in litters and others on horseback, while those who were unhurt remained with the prisoners, in the street of the caulkers.[4]. The victorious Don Beltran caused the refit of the ships to be hurried forward, and he sent forward the news of his success to the Viceroy. Finally, he departed for Lima and, on arriving at Payta, he received an order from the Marquis that Captain Plaza should bring the English prisoners to Callao in a ship that was waiting there. In all there were 120. Out of these ninety escaped out of the battle, and of these seventeen were wounded. In the *Capitana* there were five killed and four wounded. In the *Galizabra* twenty-three were killed, twelve wounded, and six burnt or scorched.

In this action two things happened which are worthy of memory. One was that while the enemy was playing on the *Capitana* with his artillery, a ball hit the port main tack and then killed a gunner who was loading a piece, and

[1] Pedro Alvarez de Pulgar, "a principal captain brought up long time in Flanders", as Sir Richard tells us.

[2] The distance from the bay of San Mateo to Panama is five hundred miles; and the passage must have occupied nearer a fortnight than a day. San Mateo is in 1° 10′ N. and 80° 35′ W. Panama in 9° N. and 79° 28′ W. Sir Richard tells us that they did not sight the Pearl Islands until the twelfth day. They anchored off Panama on July 9th.

[3] The Licentiate Francisco de Cardenas was the tenth President and Governor of Tierra Firme. He died at Panama in 1594.

[4] Calle de los calafates.

passing onwards it struck another and carried away nearly all the skin of his belly. This last man was a Biscayan of the age of sixty years, named Encinel. Undismayed by seeing his own intestines lost to him, and without assistance, he gathered them back, fastened them in with a pocket handkerchief, and turning to finish the duty on which he was engaged, he fired off the piece with as much spirit and vigour as if he had not been wounded. The other was that, when they were boarding the enemy's ship a certain Italian, named Jorje, received a musket wound in the left hand. He looked on the hand with indignation, and without desisting from his intention, he entered the ship, where he fought desperately with his right hand, and dashed the socket of the left against those he encountered, covering the bodies and faces of the enemy with blood.[1]

All Peru rejoiced at this victory, and that the enemies of our holy faith should have been captured in that sea, a thing which had never before happened. The general dread in which the enemy used to be held was lost, and all the good fortune was attributed to the wonderful promptitude and resolution displayed by the Marquis. He at once sent a report of the victory to his Majesty, who replied in a letter, also containing other matters, the tenor of which was as follows:—

"The King.

"Marquis of Cañete,—The letters which you have written to me on the 15th of May, 1590, and the 20th of January of the present year, both on subjects relating to war, have been received, and in this I shall reply to them.

[1] These two memorable acts are celebrated by Doctor Pedro de Peralta Barneuvo, in his *Lima Fundada*, I, Canto v-lx, p. 193 (Lima, 1732):—

"Assaltara sin manos la osadia
Peleară descubiertas las entrañas."

"I have felt much satisfaction on receiving the news of the success which Don Beltran de Castro obtained over the English General Ricardo who entered that sea by the strait of Magellan. The event is of great importance, as well because his designs were frustrated, as that from this time the enemy will hesitate to undertake similar enterprises from dread of loss and punishment. I highly appreciate the diligence with which you caused him to be followed, and sent the news to me; and I also approve of the good service of Don Beltran, and that which he did for me in foregoing the claim he might have to a share of the ship and artillery. You will say this to him from me, and that I will keep the one and the other in memory, for showing him favor when an opportunity occurs.

"As regards the punishment of the General and of the others who were captured in the said ship, you inform me that they have been claimed by the Inquisition, but that as you had no instructions from me as to their disposal, you have put off compliance with the requisition of the Holy Office, and the delivery of the said General to tho 'auto'.[1] You understand that he is a person of quality. In this matter I desire that justice may be done conformably to the quality of the persons.

"You inform me that, on this occasion of the capture of the English ship, the gunners who were in the fleet performed their duties very well. You should arrange to retain their services. With reference to the General Miguel Angel Filipon, whom you also report to have worked well on the above occasion, I shall give orders that a note may be made with a view to rewarding him when an opportunity

[1] Tribunals of the Inquisition were established at Lima and Mexico in 1571, on the model of the Tribunal in Spain. The Royal Order, signed by Philip II, was dated at Madrid on August 16th, 1570. Another was afterwards formed at Carthagena. For an account of these Tribunals, see *Solorzano Polit. Ind.*, lib. IV, cap. xxiv.

offers. Touching the other captains and soldiers who, as you say, distinguished themselves in the action, you will send me a special report as to their various merits, that I may make such arrangements concerning them as may seem convenient.

"You say that, it being necessary to repair the *Capitana*, being the ship to which the English surrendered, you have ordered the Captain Andres Gomez, the master of her (who fought well and was among the first who boarded the enemy's ship), to repair her. Although he made an agreement respecting this work, yet he produced a very strong galleon on which he spent his own money and that of his friends. The great expense to which he has been put was represented to you, to the Audience, and to the royal officers, but you have not determined to grant the remuneration he seeks. You, therefore, apply for orders. In this matter you will, jointly with the Audience, ascertain what grant it will be just to make to the said Andres Gomez, and report to me, that I may, on receiving a statement of the merits of the case, grant the reward that may be proper. From Madrid on the 17th of December, 1595.

"I, THE KING.

"By order of the King, our Lord, JUAN DE IBARRA."

THE JOURNALS

OF

CAPTAIN WILLIAM HAWKINS

(JUNR.)

I.—JOURNAL OF THE VOYAGE UNDER CAPTAIN FENTON, 1582

(MS., OTHO, E viii).

II.—JOURNAL IN THE *HECTOR*, IN THE THIRD E.I.C. VOYAGE, 1606

(MS., EGERTON, 2100).

III.—RELATION OF OCCURRENCES DURING HIS RESIDENCE IN INDIA, 1608

(PURCHAS).

I.

Journal of William Hawkins, Lieutenant-General in Fenton's Voyage, intended for the East Indies, 1582.

[*British Museum MS., Otho E. viii. Manuscript much mutilated by fire.*]

............x]ixth of Maye 1582 we departed from..............

The seconde of Juyñ 1582 wee departed out of............ into wch porte wee came by meanes of a contra[rie........... theare the generall wolde have left behind hym Mr. T. .... Blackcoller Pilatte wth Capiteyne Drake, Willyam .... and the barke ffrancys: saying that he had better ma............... wyth imborde then auny of those, and that yf neede weare .... put in wth ffalmo^uth for as good as they. The company .... sayed, that they wold not go to sea wythout them, by .... knewe the voyage must be perfourmed, and made mar .... Then they seeing the Bark ffranncys comyng towardes .... they did cast about.

After my comyng aborde agayne, because I lefte Kyrkman .... me for querelling I had not from that tyme till my comyng .... any good countenaunce.

The xvi^th of Juyñ 1582 wee had sight of the Canaries.

The xxvi^th of the same monethe we fell with Bonavista one of the Islandes of Cape de Verde wheare we might haue watered, but they wolde not staye.

The xx^th of Julye 1582 we fell wth the coast of Guynny: the wether was heave, so fowle as for foure or fyve daies we colde not take the heigthe.

The xth of August 1582 we ankered in Soraleon Riuer[1] at night and the seconde of September we departed out of this harborough.

The fourthe of Septembre 1582 we came in agayne to the same harbrough *(sic)* the pretence whearof as yet not knowen to me (I was not made acquaynted wyth our comyng yn). All the buesines w[ch] wee did in this place might haue been doon in lesse than xx[te] daies, Mr. Walker preacher, Mr. Evans marchant, Mr. Fayrewether, and Willyam Hawkins were more enuied at then annye of the rest wth daylie reproache of spightfull wourdes.

.... the xxvi[th] of Septembre 1582 .... [Mr. Wa]lker tolde me that he had a matter to let me .... wolde not make it knowen: saying that the voya[ge] .... in was broken cleane, and that from oure first depa[rture .... they weare determyned not to proceede in that acc .... in: but in an other w[ch] sholde be more profytable .... and of theire owne devising. I aunswering saied that .... be a good voyage of their device w[ch] never weare out of the .... owne chymbneys, or from their mothers pappes in respect of .... In replie whearof he sayed that the generall was determyn .... in St. Helena and to possesse the same, and theare to be p............... kyng, promysing great rewardes to all the well willers .... consent to the same: as first Cap[en] Warde 10,000*l*. C... .... 5,000, Com[r] Walker 2,000 Com[r] Maddocks 2,000 .... payment of this money he was determyned to haue taken the .... Armathos yf he colde.

I aunswered, will the generall make so light of o[r] artycles as .... in this ordre w[ch] weare set down by so many good vertuous .... and those w[ch] we aught, wyth all reverence to follow and obey in .... dements for that they are for the benefyte and profyte of the cōmon

[1] Sierra Leone.

w............... also oure profyts. (Let vs travayle thearin as honest men : and .... to the dyscredyt of others that do the contrarye.)

Walker (replying) aunswered : well there is nowe no remedie .... must be content as wee all are : but wth gods assistaunce I w[ill] .... wythin thiese two daies what I can do wth my Cap[n] toching this ma[tter].

Mr. Walker being in great agonye aboutes this matter, came to his Cap[n] .... the daye following being in his Cabyon, and fell downe upon his knees and besought hym for god sake that he wolde not geeve his consent to thi[s] determynacon, and with teares made Mr. Warde to promyse him, that he wolde proceede in the voyage wee weare sent in let generall do what he wolde. Saied Cap[n] Warde to morrowe I will go to the generall and knowe his minde what he meaneth to do and will tell hym playne my mynde.

The generall being not hable to do this feat w[th]out Cap[en] Warde, saied then that he wolde go back agayne to the Islands of Cape de Verde to fetche some wyne, w[ch] was onelye a device to pick and steale.

.... seconde of October 1582 we departed............

The first of Nouembre we past the equinoctiall lyne ....

The first of Decembre we Ankered in a Baye in .... to the Southwardes of the lyne. Theare oure generall .... a Barck to be taken w[ch] we sawe at sea.

The xii[th] of the same moneth they departed out of that .... determynacon (in outwarde shewe) of the generall and .... for the Straightes. But in verye deede (as it afterwards .... nothing at all ment, but dissembled for a further pollycye .... blynde their companye).

For in truthe, this maketh the sayinge of some of our companye .... thought true, which saied that this honourable voyage (the more .... the pyttie) was baught and solde by the Spanyards frendes or sp.............. themselfes before oure comyng out of Englande. Wee think tha[t] they canne scarce aunswere it at their comyng home w[ch] did it : .... but some of them care not whether ever they see England, or no.

The xix[th] of Decembre 1582 we weare in 33 degrees ½.

The same xix[th] of Decembre the generall called Cap[en] Warde wth the rest to thinck what was best to be doon in o[r] proceedings : the matter being longe before determyned by thre or foure of them. Then casting a doubt of the Spanyshe Fleete, and of meeting them being as wee afterwardes vnderstoode to be to the northewarde of us 150 legues. This they made a suffycyent cawse to breake of the voyage, alleaging also that they wanted many things the w[ch] they wolde supplye in St. Vincents. This color of oure want and to refreshe, it was nothing but becawse they wolde go back agayne (as we after found it most true) for traffique for sugar, and being in St. Vincents he was not hable longer to deteyne the matter, but it all bu[r]st out what myne opynyon was toching oure going back agayne.

For my parte (the wants of our victuells every way considered, as of water-casks, wyne, and other necessaryes) we are inforced with gods assistaunce to geeve th' adventure through the Straigtes of Magalan into the South Sea, in hoape of a good releefe for our money : whereas going by Cap Bona speransa, or back agayne for Brasel. There was no hoape to speed for money or love, becawse the contrey .... also the chiefe time of the yeare .... gods help, and in his feare to proceede .... obiection to the contrarye to be alleaged .... Bon speransa or back home agayne, I thinke .... and other defaltes we as neyther waye hable to ....

The names of those w[ch] semed willing .... of Decembre to go through the Straights .... in two dayes weare cleane turned the .... yet to vs unknown: are

The Generall.	The Edwards two ....
Luke Warde.	The M[r] of the E ....
Nich[as] Parker	
Richard Maddock Preacher	
Chr[st]ofer Hall M[r] of the Gallyon	

The names of such as gaue not their consen[t] .... go back: becawse they knewe that yf the oport.............. and time of the yeare weare neglected: .... not possible oure voyage sholde be made for .... Molocos; becawse o[r] men and victuells weare .... everye daye to decaye.

Willm. Hawkins
John Walker mynyster
Thomas } Pilots
Thomas Blackoller } Pilots
Mathew Talbuthe
John Drake
Richard Farewether M[r] of the ffrancys.

The xx[th] of Decembre 1582 oure Generall Bare vp wth St. Vincents being in heigth 33 degrees ½. The next daye the wynde was contrarye to go to the northwardes and so contynued three .... xi[th] and xii of the clock .... xx[th] of Januarye we ankered in ....

In the harbrough the Portingales daylie reported .... that they weare nowe the King of Spayne his Subjects ....fore they durst not neyther wolde they traffique wyth v............... Notwythstanding the vice Roye promysed vs soche loves .... as sholde be a good refresshing: But this fell out in the .... but delayes for a further myschief: we had nothing heere .... hogge and a small Bullock.

The xxiiiith theare came into vs Thre Spanysh shippes w............... determyned to have taken vs wch afterwardes we vnderstoode .... of theire owne menne: Thiese shippes were sent from Don .... generall of the Spanysh Fleete to searche the coast, and yf they .... fynde vs to take vs.

Theare weare in thies three shippes .670 and odde menne, and they weare in burthen as followeth. The Admyrall .500 tonnes. The vice admyrall 400. The thirde being in burthen .600 tonnes was worthe bothe the other: she was a newe ship. They began to fight wyth vs aboutes tenne of the clock at night, and contynued verye extreame till noone the next daye: Their vice admyrall wee did sink: Theare weare of our menne slayne in bothe shippes six or eight; and more then twenty hurte. They had of theirs slayne above Cth (100) menne and manye wounded. This we vnderstoode at Spirito Sancto of the Portingales when we watered theare.

Being afterwardes at Sea our Generall wrauget soch ordre bearing vp before euerye wynde that blewe: His mynde was so trobled that wee weare 25 dayes and more ere wee did get to the northwards 200 leagues, wch wolde not haue required halfe the tyme (he tooke this on hym for a vayne glorye, being laughed at of every man almost becawse all knewe that he vnderstoode not what he did).

The xxiith of ffebruarye we ffell wyth lande being the Lande of Spirito Sancto.

The same night we ankered in the mouth of the River.

.... dayes after wee weare .... for King Phillip: yet they span .... of thre halfe-pence the pounde: ffor .... things we had theare, the marchants saied that w.............. tymes the vallewe good marchants to bring a m..............

When we weare reddy to departe the proffered .... for 500 *Rooves* of Sugar, but no more w[ch] was .... pollycye to deferre the tyme till the Spanyardes sh[oulde] .... vs: and some of their companye did tell vs as moche tha[t] .... wolde be thre shippes wythin foure dayes w[ch] sholde come .... Januarie. This tretcherye was like to that w[ch] they sh[ewed] vs in St. Vincent.

They also did tell vs that theare was of late killed in .... Vincent .100 Spanyards, w[ch] indeed was true, for ....selves had done it though we made no boast thearof theare ....

Sugar was worth in Spirito Sancto 2 ducats ½ .... *Roove*, being for the most parte in poulder.

The iiii[th] of marche theare came a Portingale bark .... the Roade by vs from Januarie as they saide, but .... from San Eta in St. Vincent as afterwards they confessed ....

The same daye the Generall received two sheetes of pap[er] full wrytten from the vice Roye of Sancto Spirito subscrib[ed] wyth the handes of six or seuen severall men w[ch] I judge to [be] the Assistants of the saide vice Roye: but what it toched I do not knowe. Albeit the Portingales forewarned vs to looke to our selfes.

The fyveth of march in the morning we departed out of Spirito Sancto Roade heigthe .20[d] and ½.

In this harbrough what our generall did he kept to hymselfe many [let]tres weare sent, received, and aunswered. The second day of this march I craved leave of the Generall to go a shore to the watering-place to take the Soone, but he denyed me, and at ....

The xiiiith of Juyñ 1583 we arryved in Ireland .... stayed ten dayes in Kynsale, and theare was I d............... being requested by divers noble men of the contr[ie] .... them for the space of one howre: and also wrytten for by .... Sent leger, and required by Capen Bartlet and xiiiien more gentlemen of good credyt.

The xxvii of Juyñ we ankered in the downes wheare I wa[s] .... reserved wyth Irons from the shore least I sholde go to my lorde .... the letter wch I had wrytten to my lorde in that place was opened a............... kept from sending by the generall. And two dayes before that [the] generall coming from the poope comaunded me in his anger to the Bilbowes wythout any cawse whye: at wch manyfest wrong .... shewed, perceiving hym to have no reason in hys dealinge, kneeling uppon my knees I appealed to the Queenes matie praying hym also to followe her mats Comyssion or ells I said vnto hym that he must looke to aunsweare this wronge: at wch appeale I called the whole ship to wytnes: whearat he made but a tushe, neyther putting of his cap or vsing anny other reverence at all: but with vile speches towardes me sayed That yf I spoke one worde more he wolde dashe me in the teethe, and called me villeyn sclave, and errant knave, wyth many more vile wourdes, the wytnessing whearof I referre to the whole companye.

The same xxvii of Juyñ the generall went into my cabban and tooke from me all my Daggs, one of them being charged uppon an occasion of two shippes wh gaue vs chace in lyklihoode to laye us aborde: comaundement being geven xii howres before both by the generall and Parker that everye man sholde be in a reddynes. The great ordynaunces being prymed, and all or small shot being reddye.

.... dynner .... of his gentrie abusing as good as .... it was borne. The generall taking .... was more busyer then I needed I aunswered

.... this buesines I do nothing but my ductie, for I ... . doth belynge to thys voyage then those such as he is .... was I sent in yt. The generall aunswering, sayd .... a companyon. I knowe yo^w welynough I knowe the .... make the voyage, and go neyther by Cape Bonsperansa .... by the straites of Malegan *(sic)* and said in further choller .... had three strings to his Bowe wch I knewe not of. I .. .. I did not knowe one string (yet is it none of yo^rs). Let vs .... oure comyssion, and those directions wch we have to follow .... Counsell and wee shall do welynough: but as for yo(ur) .... I feare me they will fall out to be made of rotten stuffe .... think. Naye S^r saide he: ffor S^r ffrancys Drake .... knows it as well as he himselfe or anny of yo^u that are h[is] .... and I knowe that he is not hable to do the like againe. He played the Pirate and Thiefe, do you think I will .... Naye I knowe howe to make my voyage wythout anny of .... advise, thearto saide I yf yo^u string that waye I care .... lesse for yor strings and the sequell showeth that one of .... Imagyned stringes was like to be the dystructyon of vs .... yf god had not been on owre sides: The Gallyons sides to [wit] .... of it, and some of our menne are slayne, and many wounded. And before that being at the Sea he asked me: what is the .... Molocos? I saied those things wch wee are sent for, ... sortes of spices, but specyally cloues. Q^d he, will yo^u and yor companyons assure me w^e shal be hable to lade our shippes when we come thither. Nay (q^d I) that is more then I was demanded of in Englande. Q^d he except yo^u and the rest will insure it me, I will not go thither. Q^d I: Then do .... not that yo^u weare sent for, and I think that it will not be so easelie aunswered as yo^u make accompt of.

[*Gen*]*eral*. Do thies matters trouble ye ....

Hawkins. Generall yor ordre is good I .... made it at the begynnyng: but being doon .... weare home it makes the companye in an vproar .... is an honourable accõn overthrowen, yet I thank God that .... lyeth not in me but wheare as it is, when wee come .... the Counsell will pearcive it welynough. *Gen*. Yea .... It is overthrowen because I wolde not play the theefe as .... the last voyage. *Haw*. When God sendeth vs home .... ffrauncys and yo^u must ende that matter, for I haue .... to do wyth it howbeit I gaue more in action than ... . perhaps yo^u knowe of, and that maketh me to speake, for .... undoon by the overthrowe of it: but heare for yor place .... I do reverence yo^u, but when we come home, yf yo^u call .... Theefe, I will see howe you canne justyfie it: for when we .... came both fourthe wee weare gentilemen alike. *Gen*. Th[ou] shalt not be so good as I, so long as thou lyvest. *Hawkins*. What make yo^u of me then? *Gen*. A knave, villeyn, and a Boye. *Haw*. If I weare at home, I wolde not be afearde to followe you in anny grounde in Englande: but heare in this place for quyetness sake I let it passe and will beare every wronge be it never so great. *Gen*. Wilt thowe so? *Haw*. Yea, truelye. Then the general wolde have drawen his longe knyfe and have stabbed Hawkins, and intercepted of that, he tooke vp his longe staffe and thearwith was ronnying at Hawkins, but the M^r (Master), Mr Bannester, Mr Cotton, and Symon Fernando stayed his ffurye. *Haw*. Truely generall in this place yo^re a justice, and this becommeth a governo^r to be a dysordre to the hole. If you canne fynde anny just cawse agaynst me punysh me by yo^re ordre whiche is prescribed, and let yo^re weapons passe tille till wee come in place wheare: for he that cannot holde his handes heare is not wourthie of the place, I knowe this is but yo^re olde quarrell renewed, and so let it go.

... .
had for the perform .... ffor wch speache the gouer .... haue and whensoeuer he did see .... to absent hymself out of the Generall .... quyetness of the hole as all the compa[n]ye .... will wytnes of my side I doubt not.

Wrytten by me willyam hawkins this vi d[ay] ....1583, wch do not desire of myselfe to be justy .... do willingly reserue myselfe to the report of the companyes of the Gallion, and of the other two shipp[es].

By me William Ha[wkins].

II.

"A Journal kept by m[e William Hawkins in] my voyage to the East I[ndies, beginning the 28 of] March a° 1607, concerning all [that happened vnto] the good Ship called the [Hector in the saied] Viag^{e}, I being Captaine t[hereof]."

[*Egerton MS.*, 2100.]

1607. MARCH 28. The ship wherin I was Captaine was [anchored in the downs] wth the dragon Admirall for that viage, [where we rode till the] 1st day of Aprill and then wth an Easterly winde we [weighed anchor] and put to sea; and vpon the 13th of Aprill we [arrived in Plymouth] sound, and there anchored till the 16th of Aprill: [when the Dragon] came thither vnto vs, of whom before we had [lost the sight].

Aprill 16. The 16th of Aprill at 2 of the clock we sett saile wth [a prosperous] and faire winde wch blew Easterly, and hauing sayld clere out of [the] sound, 2 or 3 houres after we hoysted in o^{r} boates and vpon [the] 17th of Aprill we lost the sight of the landes end, the wind north wth a small gale.

Apr. 20. We had a West and north west winde and found o^{r}selues to be in the height of the north cape and then held o^{r} course South west and by south.

Apr. 21. We obserued the sonne and found o^{r} selues to be 24 degrees and steered S.S.W.

Apr. 22. We steered S. and by W. wth a N. and N.W. wynde and then found o^{r} selues to be 40 degrees od minutes.

Apr. 27. We wth a N. winde steered S. and by W. and found the sunne to be 55 degrees and 25 minutes.

Apr. 28. We wth a N. winde and a small gale obserued the sunne and found it in 31 degrees and 26 minutes and helde S.S.W.

Apr. 29. Saluages. We had sight of a small Island called the Saluages and upon the sight wherof we altered o^r course and steered S. and by E.

Apr. 30. Tenerife. We had a sight of Tenerife and held S. [and about] evening we found [the] grand canaries to be on o^r broad side.

May 1, 2, 3. We steered S.W. and by S. and S.S.W. and obseruing .... about t[hat] .... at noon we found o^r selves to be entered the [tropic of cancer].

May 6. We still continuing our course in the m[ornin]g .... we saw an Island called bona Vista and about 4 of the clock [the same day] we saw Mayo, and the 7th day w^e anchored there to see if there w[e could] find any fresh water and victalles as goates wch that Island only affordeth to refreshe o^r men, where we bought some, but found no water to serve our turns.

May 8. We set sayle and continued in o^r course wth variable wind and severall ....

May 25. Course held as tyme served till the 25th of May and then o^r course S.W. wth a small E. wynde we observed the sonne to be .... the equinoctiall line.

May 29. W^{th} a scant winde, so that we could hold but E. and E. [by North] and tooke the sonne and found o^r selves to be und[er 2 degrees].

Jun^e 2. W^{th} an E. wynde as before we found that we [had p] ....

June 6. We had a calme wth a small E. wynde and th^t day [we passed a] small Island called Firnando Larania at sight [whearof] ....

June 7. We observed the sunne and found o^r selves to

.... he un[der] .... minutes to the Southward of the equinoctiall ....

June 8. Were in 5 degrees and 48 minutes.

June 10. The winde scanting came up to the .... found that we held o[r] course to mu[ch] .... to the coast of Brasill and so ta[ckt about] .... close E.N.E. till 4 of the clock and .... [coming] more Easterly and steering S. and by East wth a gusty wynde and [much] rayne w[ch] made us spring o[r] maine top mast and fowle weat[her] all that night and so sayling forward till the [morning] wth a slack S.W. wynde we sayled so long till we spyed a small [sail] bearing S.E. of us, so th[t] we were in good hope th[t] it had bin o[r] [pinnace], but at last toward night she left us and stood in for the shoare of Brasill. [We had] the winde E[ly] and layd S. and by W. and about evening we saw land w[ch] by o[r] observacon we thought to be cape St. Augustine[s] upon the coast of Brasill, bearing on o[r] broade side, and the winde being scant we tackt about at night and stood to seaward.

June 16. Having stood 10 howers to seaward at 4 of the clock in the morning we tackt about agayne; the wynde still at E.S.E. and at 12 of the clock the generall sounded and had ground at 21 fadome whereupon he p[r]esentely tackt about finding that to try to windward upon that coast of Brasill was dangerous by reason of the currant and the winde likely to continew.

June 17. There was no hope to advantage o[r] selves, and the 17 or 18 dayes holding to seaward agayne, upon the 18 day we found o[r] selves to be in 8 degrees and 13 minutes.

June 19. The next day in 7 degrees 31 minutes.

June 20. The 20 day we plyed to gett o[r] selves more to the Eastward because upon the coast of Brasill, and from there all the way hitherto, we have a mighty currant w[ch] setteth to the N.W.

June 23. The wynd continewing S.E. and E.E. we plyed to windward and were under 4 degrees.

June 25. The generall and we consulted about o$_{r}$ course and in regard of the west windes and great currant wch had drawn us farre to leeward of the small Island called Larania where o^{r} generall fully intended to water and to refresh o^{r} men we consulted what course we were best [to hold] for recouery thereof because the winde being likely to continue [the want of] water and refreshing for our men would compel us [to some extr]emity before we could gett the cape w^{h} considered we determi[ned] upon o^{r} course for recouery thereof if it were possible. .... sayle till the 30th of June and held Southward, the wind scanting upon us and that morning we lookt out to descry the Island being by observation in the latitude and longitude thereof [and observing] the sunne found o^{r} selves in 4 degrees 25 minutes and [so continued] till night but could not find the Island being yet to southwardes of it 17 minutes whereby we found that the great currant haddrawen us more westerly then we expected, and that night about [6] of the clock we tackt about to bring o^{r} selves to the latitude of the Island againe and so stoode that night. In the morning we cast about againe to Southward the wind E. and by N. and we laye S.E. and by S. and about 10 of the clock not being able to weather Larania, we tackt about eastward, the wind at S.E. and S.E. and by S. and held o^{r} course so till the 7th day.

July 8. The winde continewing found o^{r}selves then to be in 10 minutes to the southward of the equinoctiall, and the 8th day the wind [S.E.] and by E. we stood eastward and found o^{r}selves to be 40 minutes [to the] northward of the equinoctiall.

July 14. 14th day the wind at S. and S. by E. The generall and we .... wth the M^{r} and M$^{r's}$ mates what course was fittest [to be ta]ken, who finding themselves wthin 140 leagues or there [about from the s]holes of St. Anne gave their opinions that to stande .... did 24 howers could not be preiudiciall but gainfull unto them, the wind hanging as it did, wh[ereunto we assented and then to] stand againe to sea was o^r^ determinacon, and the next day the wind continewing as it did we found o^r^selves in 4 degrees and 40 minutes. Whereby we perceaved that wee were entered into currant wch setteth into the barre of Ethiopia, and it being very dangerous for us to continue upon that tack, finding the currant very strong we tackt about p[rese]ntly and layd close by S.W.

July 16. We layd close by plying to the eastward, and obtaining the sunne found that we were in 4 degrees 46 minutes of the north latitude; whereupon we cast about and layd close by S.W.

From the 16th day to the 30th day of July we continued o^r^ course as wind and wether served still sayling to and fro, and were under 3 degrees 15 minutes, 4 degrees 36 minutes, 4 degrees 8 minutes, 4 degrees 11 minutes, and 3 degrees 56 minutes, 3 degrees 50 minutes, 4 degrees 53 minutes, 4 degrees 46 minutes, and upon the 29 and the 30 day the wind being still flatt against us, and having little hope, the wynde continewing still in that place to find Larania, or any other good place of refreshm^t^ of o^r^ weak men being then in 5 degrees and 24 minutes, we consulted wth the generall about the weakness of o^r^ men and o^r^ want of water, and after councill taken amongst us, the generall opinion was, that to stand long[er] for Larania was in vaine, for that though the wind should somthing favo^r^ us, and should take the benefitt thereof in hope to recover Larania, and then should find the winde southerly, wch is the generall expected wind, as we find by experience, then that course would p^e^iudice the viage, and extend to o^r^ utter overthrow, in regard whereof after we had nominated and thought upon divers places, we all agreed that Sera Lion[1] if it might [be] obtained wth any posible safety, were the fittest place of refreshment, w^h^ lyeth in the latitude of 8 de[grees] wch place if it might be obtayned, according to expect[ation] wee sayd

[1] Sierra Leone.

would prove more convenient th[an] the Isl[and of Larania] becaus if we gott to Larania, we could not h[ave] a wynd [for] o^{r} turns till October, but if we found refreshment at Sera [Lion] we might from thence put to Sea at pleasure and take the benefit [of] the first winds, for that o^{r} ship drew much water we determined to sound wth a boate, before o^{r} ship at the entr[ance] thereof for avoyding of dangers, but if it so fell ou[t that] we should be taken short wth a wind off the shoare [stormy] and tempestuous wch that shoare is subject unto .... we might be frustrate of o^{r} purpose, we determi[ned to steer] for Cape Verde where there is an Island called [the Island of] safety where all ships both english and french [come, so our] trust was that we should find releife at these [places ?] but because we were in doubt that we were [the] .... shoales of St. Anne then they made account of [we thinking it] dangerous for us to stand longer in being in [the latitude] that the shoales lye, we thought it fitt to sou[nd] .... and found no ground at 8 score fadoms and the[refore we stood in] still that night, and the 31st we observed [the sunne and found o^{r}selves] to be in 5 degrees 15 minutes, and thereupon [wanting room for] avoyding the shoales of St. Anne [we steered N.E. and by N. ?].

August 1. Wth the wind at S. we were in 6 degrees 25 minutes and sounded [and] found no ground and lying by the lee we iudged o^{r}selves to be clear to the Northward of the shoales of St. Anne, and then we hove in for Sera Leon and steered E.N.E.

Aug. 2, 3, 4. The wind somewhat westerly we were under 7 degrees 15 minutes and then altering 2 points and steered E. and sounded but found no ground, and being in 7 degrees and 45 minutes and sounded twice, at last wee found 27 fadoms ground, and continuing o^{r} course as before wth more leades out, we found it to shoale very fast upon us.

Aug. 5. The 5 of August being a league a head of o^r^ Admirall, wee made land, wch rising not in that form as formerly it had risen at o^r^ comming to that place, we bore hard in to make the land more certaine, in wch Roming we had 17, 15, and 12 fadoms and at last but 7 fadoms, then having made the land certain we found it to be a small Island bearing of us N.E. rising like a sugar loafe, then coming by the lee to stay for o^r^ Admirall we steered in for the porte of Sera Leon, and steered N.E. and by N. and as we neared the land we haled more Northerly. In this roming we found diversity of depthes, for between a cast of lead we found 3 fadoms shoaling, in this roming we had from 7 to 14 fadoms, then we found o^r^selves to be upon the edge of a sandy bank, lying to the southward of us, and the Channell lyeing to the northward, and having brought o^r^selves into 14 fadoms, we steered N. and N. and by E. and never had lesse than 10 fadoms, and having brought the Islands on o^r^ broade sides we came to an anchor in 17 fadoms, where we ridd very well all night.

Aug. 6th. The 6th day we weighed, the wind at S., a fine top sayle gale and steered 15, 11, 12, and 13 fadoms, and coming w^th^in 2 leagues of the head land we descryed the breach of a rock, lying a mile to seawards of the point, here our pinnaces being mannd and under sayle sounded before o^r^ ship and we boare w^th^in 2 cables lenght of the rock having right against it 12 fadoms. Then we shott w^th^in the point, and never had less than 14 fadoms untill we came to an anchor wch was at 13 fadoms, w^th^in 2 cables lenght of the shoare, where staying [until] the 13th of Septemb^r^ we bought certen henns, lymes to make water, and nothing els for there was nothing els there to be had for refreshm^t^ of o^r^ men, only some fish which we fished for, and having had some conference divers tymes wth the contry people and laden as much fresh water as served o^r^ turne wch being done we hoysted ankers, and before we went from thence,

We anchor in Sera Leon.

upon a faire stone at the watering place, where all ships water that come to that place, we graved o^{r} names, the yeare of the Lord, and the month wherein we departed, as we had sene S^{r} ffran^{s} drake and Capt Candish that had been there before us had don,[1] and being under sayle the winde at E., we put to Sea steering W. and W.S.W., untill the tide of flood was come, and then came to anchor at 10 fadoms, having sayled about 7 leagues.

September 14. We weighed anchor and sayled from morning till 4 a clock in the afternoon the wind N.N.E. and anchored at 13 or 15 fadoms wth a [var]iable wind, we sayled to and fro holding divers courses as the [wind served and] at last sounded and found 25 and 23 fadoms and then [30 and 35] fadoms and at the evening we could find no ground, and then [held ....] divers courses with variable winds, we steered S.S.W. [we then] found o^{r}selves upon the 23th day to be under 9 degrees.

Sept. 29. Upon the 29 we sterred S.S.W. with a northerly winde and were [in] 6 degrees 33 minutes.

Sept. 30. We were in the latitude of 6 degrees with the winde southerly.

October 2. The wynd a little at large we held our course S.S.W. and by S. and under 5 degrees 40 minutes and the 3 day the wynd slacking we were under 5 degrees 49 minutes and sayling still with variable windes.

Oct. 7. Till the 7th day we found o^{r}selves to be under 4 degrees 34 [minutes], from the 7th day to the 20th day we had still variable wyndes and were forced to hold severall courses, and found o^{r}selves out of sight of the Dragon, upon the day, but not long after had the sight of her againe, and then found o^{r}selves to be under 4 degrees 33 minutes, the next day under 4 degrees 5 minutes, the 14th 3 degrees 44 minutes, the 15th in 3 degrees 23 m^{ts}, the 17th in 2 de-

[1] See Captain Keeling's account of this stone, at page 114 of the Hakluyt Society's volume of 1877 (*Voyages of Sir James Lancaster*, etc.)

grees 17 m^ts^, the 18th in one degree 33 m^ts^, the 19 in one degree 6 minutes, and the [20th] day lyeing S. and S. and by W. we were under 16 m^ts^ N. latitude and that evening we crost the lyne about 9 of the clock being the third tyme between England and the Cape bona Speranca, and we had 6 degrees ½ variation and the Dragon had a degree lesse.

Oct. 24. The 24th day the wynde at E. and by S. we lay S. and were in 3 degrees.

Oct. 25. 35mts and the next day 4 degrees 15mts, the same course the 26th we were in 5 degrees 11mts, the same course, the 27, in 6 degrees 30mts our course S.E.

Oct. 28. The 28 having an E. and by N. winde and lying as before, the Dragon came unto us, to speake with us, the reason was for that we were then drawing into a colder climate, which would preiudice [the health of or men, if provision of warme clothes were not made [for] them whereof some of his men had allready complayned, and then he opened a packe of clothes of the lowest prizes for to [serve] the mens turnes, and willed me to do the like, that day [we were] in 7 degrees 46mts.

A colder climate.

Oct. 30. The 30th day the wynd at N.E. we sterred S.E., and by [E. being in] the latitude of 9 degrees 50mts.

November 1. The first day the wynd at N.E. we sterred as before and [were in the] latitude of 12 degrees.

Nov. 2. We were in the latitude of 12 degrees 50 minutes.

Nov. 3. We were in 14 degrees 28 mts, the winde N.E.

Nov. 4. We were in 15 degrees 40mts, easterly winde.

Nov. 5. Had 17 degrees.

Nov. 12. The winde at N.E., we sterred S.E., and had the latitude [of 24 degrees] 8 minutes.

Nov. 19. The winde at N.N.W., we layd E. and by S. and E. among .... the latitude of 31 degrees 11mts.

Nov. 23. The wynd N.W., we sterred E. and were in 33 degrees ....

Nov. 24. We were in 33 degrees 42 mts.

Nov. 25. We were in 34 degrees 54 m^{ts}.

Nov. 27. Having a calm the generall dined with me, and there order was by us taken, that in regard that our viage was like to prove somewhat long, to avoyd scarsity of victualls homeward bound from that day forward 2 meales of flesh every week should be abated and in steed thereof other meat allowed, which would not so well keepe as the fleshe. Abatement of 2 meales of flesh in a weeke.

Nov. 29. The wynde being northward, we bare E.S.[E., and] E. and by S., and were in 33 degrees 42 m^{ts}.

Nov. 30. We were in 34 degrees.

December 5. We were in 35 degrees 24 m^{ts}.

Dec. 11. We sterred for the Cape E. and by N., the wind westerly.

Dec. 14. It was calm this day the generall and I consulted together what was fitt to be don in so much as we esteemed o^{r}selves to be about 130 leagues from the Cape, and we agreed by consent, that if the wind were likely to favour us we would go forward and not touch at any place till we came to the Island of St. Laurence, although our long continuance at Sea required speedy meanes of refreshment for strenghtning of o^{r} men, which we purposed to do at Saldania if the wind favoured us not, but in regard of the former consideration, as also for supply of water and expectac̃on of hearing somewhat of the pinnasse.

Dec. 15. The wynde being at W.N.W., we steered E. and by S.

Dec. 17. We had a fresh gale of wind at W., and we were under 34 degrees and 32 minutes, and steered E. and by N., and that day at 2 of the clock we saw land Land. bearing E. of us, and we steered in to make the land, and having don, we steered in to double the Cape E.S.E., whereupon the men of the Admirall were desirous to put into Saldania, which the generall hearing, he bare up the helme, and stood in for the shore. The Master of the ship seeing that comended his course iudging it to be the safest course for the good of the viage, his reasons were that if in case standing alongst we should meete with S.E. wyndes, which that time of the yeare usually blow and so be forced to lye to and againe or men already weake with overlong being at Sea and having expected refreshment there, would in one fortnight, partly by reason of discontent for not putting in there and by the scanting of our allowance which our small spare of water, wold enforce us to be so cast downe, as it might worke the utter overthrow of the viage.

Dec. 18. Saldania. In the morning we put into Saldania bay, and came to an anker in 4 fadoms and a halfe water, the Sugerloffe bearing of us W.S.W. and the table S.S.W., in that Roade we found Capt Middleton's name graven upon a stone, who had bene there in that roade the 24 of July last past before our coming thether 1607, where remaining for the space of 14 dayes we refreshed or men with fresh victualles, for there while we lay attending wind and weather, and filling or vessels with fresh water, we bought 453 sheepe, 2 oxen, 8 calves, 18 steres, and 47 cowes, and all for 200 Iron hoopes, which cattell were equally divided between both our Shipps, which don and our people well refreshed, upon the

January 1. The first of January the wind being southerly, fitt to cary us forth of the baye, we hoysted anker and sett sayle.

Jan. 3. The wind being large we sterred S.S.E., and were in 34 degrees 50mts latitude.

Jan. 4. We were under 35 minutes 53 degrees.

Jan. 5. The wind scanted and we were lying close by N.E., were in latitude of 35 degrees 50mts.

Jan. 6. Were in the latitude of 35 degrees 44mts.

Jan. 8. The wynd S.W., we were in the latitude of 36 degrees 4mts.

Jan. 10. The wynde Easterly we lay close by the N., and were in latitude of 35 degrees, in the afternoone land was descryed, which bare N. of us, and it was very high land, this land our Master iudged to be St. Brassé, other sayd no, the master's reason was that a currant had sett us to the westward, and there we tackt about to the Southward and S.S.E.

Jan. 12. With a hard W. wynd we steered E. and E. and by North, and were under 36 degrees 20 minutes.

Jan. 13. We were in 35 degrees 41 m^te^ latitude.

Jan. 14. We were in 35 degrees 45 m^te^ latitude.

Jan. 15. We were in 36 degrees latitude.

Jan. 16. The wynd continewing westerly we were in 35 degrees 16 minutes latitude.

Jan. 17. The wynd being E., we stood to the northward and lay N.N.E. and after noone we sounded and had ground at 65 fadoms, after that, we tackt about and lay S.E. and S.S.E., and that night we had 6 degrees ½ variation. 6th ½ variation.

Jan. 18. The wynd northerly, we lay E.S.E. being in the latitude of 34 degrees 56 m^te^ and had 6 degrees ½ variation.

Jan. 19. We were in 35 degrees ½, the wynd W^ly^ our ship labouring extreamly by reason of the great Seas.

Jan. 20. We held our course N.E., and toward night we saw lande and thereupon we sterred E.N.E., the land bearing of us N.E.

Jan. 21. From the top of our ship we descryed 2 head landes, the one bearing N.W., th'other N.E., from us we held a course E. and by N., and E.N.[E.] 6th ¾ variation.

Jan. 22. The wynd at S. we were in the latitude of 34 degrees 11 m^te^ [sterring] E.N.E., that euening we had variation 6 degrees ¾ wherby we understood the currant hindered us very much.

Jan. 23. The 23 in the morning it was calme and we had sight of land againe which bare of us N.N.W., we were then in the latitude of 34 degrees 14^mts^, and 6 degrees 9^mte^ 6th 9m. variation.

[variation]: This land was iudged to be Punto Primero, or els Baia del Agua.

Jan. 24. We were in 34 degrees 44 m^{ts}.

Jan. 25. Being under 34 degrees 51 m^{ts} latitude our variation was 6^{ds} 33 m^{ts}.

Jan. 26. We were in 35^{ds} 45^{mts} latitude.

Jan. 29. Being under 36^{ds} 5^{mts} latitude stering E. and by N. we had 8^{ds} variation.

Jan. 30. With a variable winde, we were under 36^{ds} 34 m^{s} latitude.

February 2. With a S.S.W. wynde, we layd E., and by N. we were in the [latitude of] 35^{ds} 57 m^{s}.

Feb. 3. With a small gale northerly we layd E. and by S., and were in [latitude] of 35^{ds} 57 m^{s}.

Feb. 4. The wynde at S. and by W., we held E.N.E. and N.E. and by E. and ....

Feb. 5. The wynde continewing thereabout, we sterred as before and were in [latitude] of 33^{ds} 37^{ms}.

Feb. 6. The wynde N.E. and by N., and sterring as before we were in 32^{ds} [56^{mts}].

Feb. 7. The wynde N^{ly}, we held N.E., and were in 31^{ds} 4^{ms} latitude..

Feb. 8. The wynd small and E^{ly} we layd close S.E., and were in [the latitude] of 30^{ds} 49^{ms} in our course before when we kept nere the s[hore we had] a currant against us which hindered us much so that [when we thought] o^{r} selves farre from the land, we were in sight [thereof .... having stood of and meeting with a faire wynd [which .... a weeke: we gest we had found a currant that [furthered us much] .... having found by tryall, that he which standeth nere the shore .... and is bound to the eastward worketh in vayne.

Feb. 9. The wynd E^{ly} we stood southward till noone lyeing S.E., southerly and S.E. and by S., and being aboord the Admirall we conferred about keeping o^{r}selves in a good birthe. The wyndes contrary lest we should hinder o'selves, by meeting with a contrary currant, at noone, we went about to the northwarde and lay N. and N. and by E.

Feb. 10. We lay Southward with a E'y wynd and were in the latitude of 29ds 50m.

Feb. 11. The wynd E'y we were in 29ds 5m and lay N.E.

Feb. 12. The wynd E'y we were in 27ds 22ms.

Feb. 13, 14, 15. We with an E'y wynd, sometymes calm, we sterred Southwards S.E., and then N.E., for St. Laurence, having before sounded often but could find no ground.

Feb. 16. With a S'y wynd we sterred N.E. and by E. till noone and then being under 25ds 25ms latitude we sterred E. and E. by N., and sounded but found no ground.

Feb. 17. The wynde continowing with a stiffe gale we lay E. and E. and by N. about 4 of the clock after dinner we descryed land, bearing of us E. and by S., which we iudged to be the land lyeing between St. Justa and cape Augustin, and having stood in to make the land, we tackt about and stoode of till one of the clock, and then stood in for the land againe.

Feb. 18. The wynd continewing a faire gale, and having borne in with the land and haling the Admirall went rome for the bay of St. Augustin, and about noone lay by the Lee, and the Admirall stood in nere the shore, where there was a litle Island, of which Island dew N. lyeth a great breach or rise, and E.N.E. of the Island lyeth a Sandy Shoale or Island, and having made the land and being the latitude of 23ds 37ms we came to an anchor. (The Admirall first springing his loofe, and which observing stood out againe.) In the offining the Island bearing of us S. and by W. we stood as we had anchored, we consulted with the generall, whether they iudged us to be in the latitude of St. Augustin, and whether the going in that we saw was in their iudgmte the port; all of us agreed in one that it was the same place, the Admirall after our opinions whether it was best to touch there, or to go forwarde, the tyme of the yeare being then come, that S.E. windes do ordinarily blow, the answere was that some write, the wyndes may yet favo[r] us 2 monthes, other that they may continew a month, but sayd we because we have hitherto found no certenty in reporte, but rather wyndes favoring us at such tymes as all mens opinions were contrary, and because we were not certaine how to find the wyndes standing to the northward, therefore having fallen with that place in faire weather, we thought it very necessary (both for knowledge of the place to the intent we might have it to frend if need required us, also for supply of water and other things we stood in need of) to put into the baye, these reasons considered, we concluded to weigh anchor betymes in the morning, and to stand in if wynd favored. And as we then lay at anker, a hummockle lyeing upon the head land to the Northward, rysing like Westminster Abbey, boare of us N.E. and by E. and the bay whether we intended to put in boare of us E. and by N. here we haue 16 variation.

Feb. 19. The wind at E.N.E. we lay at anker till noone, about which tyme we had the breese of the Sea, and then we waighed aud stood in for the baye in 8 and 10 fadome awhile, but more wythin we had a greater depth in some places 100 fadome, and after we anchored in the Bay where we had ozie ground, and very uncertaine depthes, for in some places we had 2 and 23 fadome and hard by 60, in some places more, and there we stayed and bought of the countrie people, 5 calves, 2 sterres, 3 cowes, 3 sheep, and 1 lambe, which was all we could get, and those cost us 19[s], there we gott water and wood to serve o[r] turnes as well as we could, and in the meane tyme the Admirall lost an anker and a new cable, being galled asunder, and by reason of the deepe water, the anker lay in the oze and could not be recouered. This place spent us 2 ankers, such benefitt did it afford us, which was so highly coīīended and had we not touched at Saldania out of doubt our viage had ben in great hazard.[1]

Feb. 28. We weighed anker having a very small gale of the shoare wherewith we stood to seaward, till the breese came, and the 29, we sterred N. and N. and by W. before the winde.

March 1, 2, 3, and 4. With variable wynd and wether stormy, we kept to and fro at Sea.

March 5. In the morning, the wynd large, we lay N. and by E., and then we saw land, bearing of us E. and by S. and then we observed the sonne and found [our]-selues in 22^{ds} 26^{ms} which was but a small distance from St. Augustin for [6 days] sayling.

March 6. We stered N. and by E. the winde S., and were under 21^{ds} 4^{ms}.

March 7. The wynd S^{ly} we were in 18^{ds} 47^{ms} and stered N. and by W.

March 8. The wynd S^{ly} we steered N. and W. and N. and were in the latitude of 16^{ds} 47^{ms} and then we stered N. and by E., and by o^{r} recouring the Island of John de Nova,[2] was some 20 leagues Eastward of us on our broad side.

March 9. The winde S^{ly} we stered N.N.E. and N.E. and were in the latitude of 16^{ds} 40^{ms}. That day w^{h} (we) lookt into o^{r} plots, our Master's plot being a portingale plot, which generall and Mr Shippon desired to see, because of certaine shoales that appeared in it, which were not sett downe in theirs, which being viewed, we agreed to hold our course N.N.E., and N. and by E. and not to touch any where, before we came [to] Sokotora, unless need required, but allwayes provided to haue Zanzibar and the Islands of Comoro to frend.

March 10. With a S^{ly} wynd we steerd as before o^{r} latitude, being 15^{ds} $\frac{1}{3}$ variation and then we found 15^{ds} 23^{ms} variation.

[1] This was the Bay of St. Augustine on the S.W. coast of Madagascar.

[2] Johanna.

March 12. The wynd at N.E. we lay close by N.W. and N. and by W., and in the morning we descryed land, being the coast of Mozambike, and after none we nered the same, which lay on o^{r} broad side. Then we consulted with [the] generall, that if we wanted wynde to carry us of we would stand nere the shoare, and come to anker, untill such tyme as we should haue wyndes to serve o^{r} turne, and after that we sounded, and had no ground in 180 fadome, and anone after within to (two) houres we had ground at .... Then we stood of expecting a land turne to set us to .... night we lay to and againe, nere the shoare the wynd [being easterly].

March 13. With litle wynd, we were in the latitude of 15^{ds} 45^{ms} .... wynd S.E., a small gale, and yet we went againe to the .... as we p[er]ceived, the cause whereof we iudged to be a tyde in as much [as] we were nere the shoare.

March 14. With a storme at S.E., but not long, we were under [15]^{ds} 30^{m} lati[tude].

March 15. The wynd S^{ly} we were in 15^{ds} 56^{ms} having ben strangely hin[dered] by a currant, for we had a fresh gale of wynde f[or] t[he last] 24 howers, and gained nothing, but rather gon a sterne.

March 16. With a S^{ly} wynd, we saw land bearing of us N.W., wh[ereupon we] agreed to steere N.W., and now in 15^{ds} 15^{ms} Mr Ship[pon iudged] the land to be the first we had se(e)n upon that C[oast].

March 17. We were in latitude of 15^{ds} 3^{ms} and brought the land .... to beare of us, N.W. and by W., and now we iudged o[urselves to be out of the] currant, and lay close by N.W. and by W. and W.N.W.

March 18. The wynd N.W. and by N., we lay close N.E. and by N., with [our larboard] a bord, some dozen leagues Northward of the high land we had seen 2 dayes before. This day we saw 6 hommocks, and being in the latitude of

14 degrees and a halfe, we iudged the land we saw, to be the going into Mozambike.

March 19. We were in latitude 14^{ds}.

March 21. The wynd S^{ly} we stered N. and by E., and being in the latitude of 11^{ds} [30^{ms}] we descryed 3 or 4 Islands, nere the maine, the Southerlyest of them boare of us W. ½ point Southerly.

March 22. The wind S^{ly} we were in the latitude of 9^{ds} 58^{ms}.

March 24. We determined to put into Zanzibar hoping there to find some good $refreshm^{t}$, which having missed at St. Augustins, and o^{r} men being weake and standing in great need thereof, we thought it most expedient to do, as well for recovery of some sicke men as also setting up o^{r} pinnasse.

March 26. We found our selves in the latitude of 5^{ds} 20^{ms} and we descryed the Island of Pemba a head, the Southerlyest point thereof, boare of us N.W. and by W. wherefore p'cieving o^{r} selves shot to the northward of Zanzibar, and the wynd Southerly, we boare up and stered away N.E. and by E. for the Island of Sokotora.

March 27. We were in the latitude of 3^{ds} 19^{ms} whereby we iudged o^{r} selves entered into a currant which helped us.

March 28. We were in latitude of 2^{ds} 4^{m} and had 11^{ds} 24^{ms} variation. 11 ds. 24m. variation.

March 29. We were becalmed, and found o^{r} selves to be in 1^{d} 16^{m}.

April 1. The wind calme we descryed the coast of Maggadoza along on o^{r} broad side, and after that we were in 27^{m} of the N. latitude, and having nered the shoare, the wynd dulling, we stered E.

April 2. Being calme, we out of sight of land, we stered N.W. and were in 44^{m}.

April 3. We were in the latitude of 1^{d} 20^{m} and we againe had sight of the coast.

April 4. A S^{ly} wynd we went E.N.E. and were in sight of the Shoare, o^{r} latitude 1^{d} 54^{m}.

April 5. The wynd S^{ly} o^{r} course as before, o^{r} latitude was 2^{ds} 14^{ms}.

April 6. The wynd as before, we stered N.E. and by E. o^{r} latitude 3^{ds} 55^{m}.

April 7. As before the wether very calme.

April 8. O^{r} latitude was 4^{ds} 57^{m}.

April 9. The 9th we were in 5^{ds} 23^{m} with a S.E. wynd.

Variation. April 10. The wynd W^{ly} we had 6^{ds} 18^{m} latitude, and that evening o^{r} variation was 17^{ds} 23^{ms}.

April 11. The wynd at S.W., o^{r} course N.E. and by E., o^{r} latitude was 7^{ds} 4^{m} [our] variation was 17^{ds} 50^{m}.

April 12. The wynd N^{ly} we held N.W. o^{r} latitude 7^{ds} 34^{m}.

April 13. The wynd E^{ly} we lyeing N. and by W. we had 17^{ds} 29^{m} variation.

April 14. O^{r} latitude was 7^{ds} 24^{m} the wynd S^{ly}.

April 15. We agreed to steere more W^{ly} because we could not see the coast, so that we doubted that a currant had put us to Leaward, and then towards night we steered N.W., and then o^{r} latitude was 7^{ds} 49^{ms}.

April 16. The wynd S^{ly} we steered N.W., standing for the coast, o^{r} latitude was then 8^{ds} 33^{m}.

April [17]. We stered N.W., the wynd S^{ly}, o$_{r}$ latitude 9^{ds} and 3^{m}, then againe stering W.N.W. to haue the coast, which we descryed about 2 of the clocke bearing W.N.W. with us, and then we sterred away N.N.E. and N.E. and by E., for the Island of Socotora. This evening we had 17^{ds} 16^{m} variation.

April 18. The wynd S.W., we held o^{r} course as before, and were in the latitude of 9^{ds} 51^{m}, and not long after we saw land, which bare of us N.N.W., which we iudged to be some point of the cape Dortny,[1] the southern point thereof

7 ds. 15m. variation. did rise like the lizard upon the coast of England, we being

[1] Dorfu, in the Journal of the *Dragon*, p. 116.

then some 7 leagues S.E. from it, and had 17^{ds} 15^{m} variation.

April 19. The wynd S.S.E., we stered N.E. and by E., and then descryed an Island to the northward, which we iudged to be Adelcuria, and being in the latitude of 11^{ds} 30^{m} we saw another Island, bearing of us N.E. and by E., and after that another that bare E. and by N., northerly, and then we lay up E. and by S. and when we came nere the Islands called Los Hermanos,[1] between them we had sight of Socotora, then we kept our loofe awhile purposing to wether the westerlyest point of the Hermanos, but could not and therefore bore up and went to leeward thereof, and being westward thereof about a league, had 17^{ds} 16^{m} variation. 17 ds. 16 m. variation.

April 20. Being to the northward of the westerlyest of the Hermanos, and with all near Socotora, we lay close E.S.E. with a S.W. wynd, seeking to wether Socotora but could not, and therefore we hove up and went to the westward thereof, between Socotora and a rocke lyeing to the westward thereof, between Socotora and a rocke lyeing to the Westward with [3] hummocks, and about noone came to an anker to the northward of the westerlyest point of the Island, in 10 fadoms water; in an open Roade, the rocke with 3 hummocks called Savoniza bearing of us N.W. and by W. There we finding no fresh water, we ankered there all night.

April 21. We set sayle againe along the N. side of the Island and stered N.E., and then there opened another bay wherein apeared some low land and we stood in with o^{r} ships, and there had 5 fadoms and 4 fadoms and a halfe; and about 5 a clock we ankered in the bay right against the towne wherein there was a Churche with a Portingall Crosse.

April 23. We lay at anker but could gett no refreshing,

[1] The Brothers: two islands S.W. of Socotra.

at night the wind E^{ly}, we weighed and stood to Seaward, stering N. and N. and by E., the latitude of this roade was 12^{ds} 39^{m}.

April 24. With a northerly wynd we standing eastward, we opened a very deepe bay, and having stood in a while to make searche for fresh water and could find none but 2 ponds of brackysh water, in that bay we saw a Church with a portingall Crosse upon it.

April 25. The wynd E^{ly} we lay close E.S.E., then the wynd coming W^{ly} we still stood E. for the point, and when we had weighed we opened some low land to the Eastward thereof, upon which was a building like unto a fort, between the Sea side and it was a grove of trees and a town.

April 26. We ankered against the Towne which we took for the fort bearing of us $S.W^{ly}$ in 11 fadoms water. There we had 10 goates given us.

April 27. We had fresh water brought by slaves from the shoare upon [their] backes. There we spake with a Guzerat ship and understood [them to say] that if we had run 10 or 20 leagues to the Southward we should haue fayled of wyndes either to carry us to Aden or .... gotten to that Island againe: The Guzerat .... Moonesone began there the 5th or 10th of May .... 4 monthes at least, and therefore wished us [not to staye] .... at the furthest there.

April 28. We took in fresh water, and bought 20 goates, 15 shepe [and 2 cowes of the] Arabians.

April 29. We weighed anker, and put to Seaward with a land tour[ne, the wind] at W.S.W. and were close by N.W.

May. From the first of May to the 15th we kept to and fro at [sea] .... divers windes, and the 13th day the wynd continewing .... and we lyeing at anker before Socotora in the westerlyest .... place, we tooke counsell with us whether it was best for .... continew there at anker or to weigh, and to go to sea and

.... Deliza,[1] which is a good roade lyeing to the Eastward .... place where we had watered, and I was of advice .... our best way to ryde it out, that we might be ready to take .... slent of wynd when it came, but or generall was of an[other] opinion, and sayd if we ryde it out, it would danger him anoth[er] cable and an anker, and or Master sayd it would do as much to us if the wynde wexed more westerly. And for these reason, as also for that or shipe grew light and we must take in more ballast, the next morning we weighed, and sett sayle for Deliza.

May 14. The wynd Sly we put to Sea and that day ankoured before the towne of Tamery,[2] there we were aduised not to ryde in that place, for the violence of wyndes euery day expected, but as [soon] as we had watered, to put for Deliza the next baie.

May 19. We hoysted saile, and made to Deliza where the same day we anchored at 9 fadoms water not farre from the shoare. The point of the land to us westward, bearing N.W. and by W. of us, and the point of land to the eastward, bearing S.E. and by E. of us and there we bought 24 or 25cwt. of alloes, and there we stayed till the 4 of August, and then weighed anker, the wynd Wly we took or course for Cambaya N.E. and by N. and being out at Sea we sterred N.E. and by E.

August 5. We stered N.E. by E. with the same wynd.

Aug. 6. The wind continewing we held or former course, the wynd still encreasing, we took in or maine saile and went under or foresayle, thereby to spend that forcible weather and bad gale before we came upon the Coast of Cambaya.

Aug. 7. By reason the sunne, the daye before, was our Zeneth, and the wether such as or Master could niether observe sunne nor starre, I askt the Master and his mates

[1] Bandar Delishi. [2] Tamarida.

advice, how they thought it best to work. They sayd considering the weather, it was best to spend some tyme at Sea, before we came nere the Lee shoare; whereupon the Master put the ship a hull, that night we came into white water.

Aug. 10. Continewing our course as before, we found o[r] selves to be in 19[ds] 23[m] latitude, and then we layd S. and S. and by E., with a strong gale of wynd at S.W. and the weather hasie, so as the Master durst not put the ship any nerer a Lee shoare till he saw cleare weather and more temperate windes, and because at Surat, we were to ride without the barre, and by all likelyhood open to the Sea and wynde, which being there we feared would be uneasy ryding, being heavy laden with lead and Iron, and the ship not able to endure it, we went to spend some tyme at Sea, till the weather broke up.

Aug. 11, 12. We continewed o[r] course as before.

Aug. [14]. Then we observed the sunne, and found that we were under 20[ds] 12[m] latitude, then we altered our course, and stered for Diu, E.S.E., and at night E. and by N., and sounding found no ground.

Aug. 16. The same wynd we stered E. for Diu, and sounding found 22 fadoms water, and then stood in to see the land, N. and by E., but saw it not, then we ran in till we came at 17 fadoms, and then held of S.E. and by E. sounding all night and 16 or 17 fadoms.

Aug. 17. We came to an anker about 2 leagues from the shoare, in 9 fadoms and ½ ozie ground, but presently o[r] cable brake and o[r] ship drove a mile before we had another ready, the land we fell withall was low land at the sea shore and full of trees, and within high land.

Aug. 19. We weighed anker, and went up with the tide of flud about 5 leagues, and the flud being spent we came again and anchored, then when floud came we weighed and had 13 or 14 fadoms. And as we nered the shoare 10, 11, or 12 fadoms at last we came into 8 fadoms, and saw [on] the shoare [a] white building which we tooke to be the Banians Church the Guzerat told us of, the which seeing in 8 fadoms water was the tokens they told us of by which we should know when we were nere the barre and where they advised us to anchor, and because at 8 fadoms we found hard and rough ground, we stood of till we came in 9 fadoms and ½ ozy ground, where we anchored safely, there I caused a peece of Ordinance to be shot of, for a boate to come from the shoare [to us] as the Guzerat had informed me was the manner in that place. That don, we saw the breach from the shoare to Leaward .... we could see, which we surely thought to be the barre of [Surat] according to the quantity of leagues the boate told us which was [12 leagues]. Then the Master said it was a dangerous place, and sayd that he durst [not] stire with the ship, till he had a pilott from Surat.

Aug. 20. I sent o[r] Pinnas to Suratt with direc̃ons to keepe aloofe to Leaward and to sound all the way, and when he had the depth of the Barre then to shape his course to the shoareward for Suratt, which by estimac̃on as it was told us was 6 leagues.

Aug. 21. We saw a boate at sea, and out of her gott a pylott, which told us, that there we roade in a most dangerous place; among shoales and sande and that we were 30 leagues short of the barre of Suratt, and advised us to put to Sea into 20 fadoms water, where we should haue good ground and be in faire way to ply for Surat, as the tides would give leave, whereupon we weighed, and at night anchored againe at 17 fadoms water.

Aug. 22. We weighed and plyed up the flud within 5 leagues of Damon and anchored at 15 fadoms water.

Aug. 23. We anchored with a N.W. wynde in 11 fadoms water.

Aug. 24. The wynd scant, we sayled till we came in

sight of the pa[goda] or Banians Idoll, being 4 leagues of us a head, our ship came to anker in 7 fadoms water, the land at our broadside being 2 leagues from us. The pylott told us that there was the place where all our great ships did lade and unlade. The pylott having brought us to the place where we should ryde bad me shoot of a peece or 2 of ordenance for a boate to come aboard us, o[r] pylott tolđ us for o[r] better directions, that we should have a speciall care to fall with the point of Diu, and then to shape o[r] course E. for Daman which [must] be the first land we must see, coming from Socatora [but] contrary to directions, hauing the wynd allways large [we went] to Leeward very nere 8 leagues, and were in danger of a [wreck ?] which caused the Infidell to say, that o[r] God loued vs [in giuing vs such ?] an escape in so dangerous a place, at th[at time of the year].

Aug. 28. I embarked my selfe for Suratt in our pinnace .... from thence where we anchored, was thought .... the downes, which cost vs 2 tydes, being deceа[ved by the directions we] took.

III.

Captaine Williame Hawkins, his Relations of the Occurrents which happened in the time of his residence in India, in the County *(sic)* of the Great Mogoll, and of his departure from thence; written to the Company.

[*From Purchas*, "*His Pilgrimes*", *Lib. III*, *Chap. vii* (*p.* 206).]

§ I.

His barbarous usage at Surat by Mocrebchan: The Portingals and Jesuits treacheries against him.

At my arrivall vnto the Bar of Surat, being the foure and twentieth of August, 1608, I presently sent vnto Surat Francis Buck, Merchant, with two others, to make knowne vnto the Gouernour, that the King of England had sent me as his Embassadour vnto his King, with his Letter and Present: I received the Gouernour's answere, both by them, and three of his Seruants sent me from Surat, that he and what the Country afoorded, was at my command: and that I should be very welcome, if I would vouchsafe to come on shore. I went accompanied with my merchants, and others, in the best manner I could, befitting for the honour of my King and Country. At my comming on shore, after their barbarous manner I was kindly receiued, and multitudes of people following me, all desirous to see a new come people, much nominated, but neuer came in their parts. As I was neere the Gouernours house, word was brought me that he was not well, being I thinke, rather drunke with affion or opion, being an aged man. So I went vnto the chiefe Customer, which was the oncly man that Sea-faring causes

Captain Keeling and he had kept company together at the voyage before related (and not needfull to bee repeated) to the Roade of Delisa in Socatora, whence on June 24th Captaine Keeling departed in the Dragon, as you haue heard; the other in the Hector for Surat (the meane while built a Pinnasse) on the fourth of August, hauing receiued from the Generall a duplicate of the Commission vnder the Great Seale. He commeth on shoare the 28 of August, 1608. belonged vnto (for the gouernment of Surat belonged vnto two great Noblemen; the one being Vice-Roy of Chanchana. Decan, named Chanchana; the other Vice-Roy of Cambaya Mocrebchan. and Surat, named Mocrebchan, but in Surat hee had no command, saue onely ouer the Kings Customes) who was the only man I was to deale withall. After many complements done with this chiefe Customer, I told him that my comming was to establish and settle a Factory in Surat, and that I had a Letter for his King from His Maiesty of England, tending to the same purpose, who is desirous to haue league and amitie with his King, in that kind, that his Subiects might freely goe and come, sell and buy, as the custome of all Nations is: and that my ship was laden with the commodities of our land, which by intelligence of former trauellers, were vendible for these parts. His answere was, that he would dispatch a Foot-man for Cambaya, vnto the Nobleman his Master: for of himself he could doe nothing without his order. So taking my leaue, I departed to my lodging appointed for mee, which was at the Custome-house: In the morning, I went to visit the Gouernour, and after a Present giuen him, with great grauity and outward shew of kindnesse, he entertained me, bidding me most heartily welcome, and that the Countrey was at my command. After complements done, and entring into the maine affaires of my businesse, acquainting him wherefore my comming was for these parts: he answered me, that these my affaires did not concerne him, because they were Sea-faring causes, which did belong vnto Mocrebchan, vnto whom hee promised me to dispatch a Footman vnto Cambaya, and would write in my behalfe both for the vnlading of my shippe, as also concerning a Factorie. In the meane while, he appointed me to lodge The Captaine of the ship that Sir Edward Michelborne tooke. in a Merchant's house, that vnderstood the Turkish, being at that time my Tronch-man, the Captaine of that shippe which S[r] Edward Michelborne tooke.

It was twentie daies ere the answer came, by reason of the great waters and raines that men could not passe. In this time, the Merchants, many of them very friendly, feasted me, when it was faire weather that I could get out of doores: for there fell a great raine, continewing almost the time the Messengers were absent, who at the end of twenty daies brought answer from Mocrebchan, with Licence to land my goods, and buy and sell for this present voyage: but for a future Trade, and setling of a Factorie, he could not doe it without the Kings Commaundement, which he thought would be effected, if I would take the paines of two monthes trauell, to deliver my Kings Letter. And further, he wrote vnto his chiefe Customer, that all, whatsoeuer I brought, should be kept in the Custome-house, till his Brother Sheck Abder Rachim came, who should make all the hast that possibly could bee, for to chuse such goods as were fitting for the King: (these excuses of taking goods of all men for the King, are for their owne private gaine). Vpon this answere, I made all the hast I could, in easing our shippe of her heauy burthen of Lead, and Iron, which of necessitie must be landed. The goodes being landed, and kept in the Customers power, till the comming of this great man; perceiuing the time precious, and my ship not able long to stay, I thought it conuenient to send for three Chests of Money, and with that to buy Commodities of the same sorts, that were vendible at Priaman and Bantam, which the Guzerats carry yearely thither, making great benefit thereof. I began to by against the will of all the Merchants in the Towne, whose grumbling was very much, and complaining vnto the Gouernour and Customer, of the leaue that was granted me, in buying these Commodities, which would cut their owne throates at Priaman and Bantam, they not suspecting that I would buy Commodities for those parts, but onely for England.

Excessive rain.

At the end of this businesse, this great man came, who

gaue me licence to ship it: before the shipping of which I called a Councell, which were the Merchants I had, and those that I thought fitting for the businesse I pretended, demanding euery ones opinion according to his place, what should be thought conuenient for the deliuery of his Maiesties Letter, and the establishing of a trade. So generally it was agreed and concluded, that for the effecting of these waighty affaires, it neither would, nor could be accomplished by any, but by my self, by reason of my experience in my former trauels and language: as also I was knowne to all, to be the man that was sent as Embassadour about these affaires. After it was concluded, and I contented to stay, I made what hast I could in dispatching away the ship, and to ship the goods. This done, I called Master Marlow, and all the company that was on shore before mee, acquainting them with my pretence, and how they should receiue for their Commander Master Marlow: willing them that they obey and reverence him, in that kind as they did me. This done, I brought them to the water side, and seeing them imbarke themselues, I bad them farewell.

The next day, going about my affaires to the great mans brother, I met with some tenne or twelue of our men; of the better sort of them, very much frighted, telling me the heauiest newes, as I thought, that euer came vnto me, of the taking of the Barkes by a Portugal Frigat or two; and all goods and men taken, onely they escaped. I demanding in what manner they were taken, and whether they did not fight, their answer was no: Mr. Marlow would not suffer them, for that the Portugals were our friends: and Bucke, on the other side, went to the Portugall without a pawne, and there he betrayed vs, for he neuer came vnto vs after. Indeed, Bucke went vpon the oath and faithfull promise of the Captaine, but was neuer suffered to returne. I presently sent a letter vnto the Captaine Maior, that he release my men and goods, for that we were Englishmen, and that our

Our two Barks taken by the Portugals, and thirtie men in them.

This not fighting was vpbrayded to our men by the Indians with much disgrace.

since recouered with interest by our Sea fights with the Portugals.

Kings had peace and amity together. And that we were sent vnto the Mogols countrey by our King, and with his letter vnto the Mogol, for his subiects to trade in his Countrey: and with his Maiesties Commission for the gournment of his subiects. And I made no question, but in deliuering backe his Maiesties subiects and goods, that it would be well taken at his Kings hands: if the contrary, it would be a meanes of breach. At the receit of my letter, the proud Rascall braued so much, as the Messenger told me, most vilely abusing his Maiestie, tearming him King of Fishermen, and of an Island of no import, and a fart for his Commission, scorning to send me any answer.

The intolerable pride of the Portugall Captaine.

It was my chance the next day, to meete with a Captaine of one of the Portugal Frigats, who came about businesse sent by the Captaine Maior. The businesse as I vnderstood, was that the Gouernour should send me as prisoner vnto him, for that we were Hollanders. I vnderstanding what he was, tooke occasion to speake with him of the abuses offered the King of England and his subiects: his answer was, that these Seas belonged vnto the King of Portugall, and none ought to come here without his license. I told him, that the King of Englands license was as good as the King of Spaines, and as free for his Subiects, as for the King of Spaines, and he that saith the contrary, is a traytor, and a villaine, and so tell your great Captaine, that in abusing the King of England, he is a base villaine, and a traytor to his King, and that I will maintaine it with my sword, if he dare come on shore. I sending him a challenge, the Mores perceiuing I was mooued, caused the Portugal to depart. This Portugal some two houres after, came to my house, promising me that he would procure the libertie of my men and goods, so that I would be liberall vnto him. I entertained him kindly, and promised him much, but before he departed the Towne, my men and goods were sent for Goa.

The English prisoners sent for Goa.

I had my goods readie, some fiue dayes before I could be cleare, and haue leaue, for they would not let them be shipped vntill this great man came, which was the third of October: and two dayes after, the ship set sayle; I remaining with one Merchant William Finch, who was sicke the greater part of his time, and not able to stirre abroad to doe any businesse: the rest were two seruants, a Cooke, and my Boy. These were the companie I had to defend our selues from so many enemies, which lay lurking to destroy vs: aiming at me for the stopping of my passage to the great Mogol. But God preserued me, and in spight of them all, I tooke heart and resolution to goe forwards on my trauels. After the departure of the ship, I vnderstood that my goods and men were betrayed vnto the Portugal, by Mocreb-chan, and his followers: for it was a plot laid by the Jesuite and Mocreb-chan to protract time till the Frigats came to the Bar, and then to dispatch me: for till then, this dogge Mocreb-chan his brother came not: and the comming of these Frigats was in such secrecy, that till they had taken vs, we heard no newes of them.

The third of October. The ship departeth leauing M. William Hawkins and his seruants in the Countrey.

The perfidy and treason of Mocreb-chan and the Jesuite Peniero.

After the departure of my ship, I was so misused, that it was vnsufferable, but so long as my ship was at the Bar, I was flattered withall. But howsoeuer, well vsed or ill, it was not for mee to take thought for anything, although remaining in a heathen Countrey, inuironed with so many enemies, who daily did nothing else but plot to murther me, and cosen me of my goods, as hereafter you shall understand. First, misused by Morcreb-chan, as to haue possession of my goods, taking what he pleased, and leauing what he pleased, giuing me such a price as his owne barbarous conscience afforded: that from thirtie fiue he would giue but eighteene, not regarding his brothers bil, who had full authoritie from him: and how difficult it was to get money from his chiefe seruant, after the time expired, as it is best knowne to vs, who tooke the paines in receiuing a small part thereof, before his comming to Surat: and after his comming, I was barred of all: although he outwardly dissembled, and flattered with me almost for three moneths, feeding me with faire promises, and other kindnesses. In the mean time, he came to my house three times, sweeping me cleane of all things that were good, so that when he saw that I had no more good things left, he likewise by little and little degraded me of his good lookes. Almost all this time, William Finch was extreame sicke of the Fluxe, but thankes be to God recouered past all hope, I, on the other side, could not peepe out of doores for fear of the Portugals, who in troops lay lurking in by-wayes, to giue me assault to murther me, this being at the time that the Armada was there.

The first plot laid against me, was: I was inuited by Hogio Nazam to the fraughting of his ship for Mocha, as the custome is, they make at the fraughting of their ships great feasts, for all the principallest of the Towne. It was my good hap at that time, a great Captaine belonging to the Vice-Roy of Guzerat resident in Amadauar,[1] being sent about affaires vnto Surat, was likewise inuited to this feast, which was kept at the water side: and neere vnto it, the Portugals had two Frigats of their Armada, which came to receiue their tribute of the shippes that were to depart, as also refreshment. Out of these Frigats, there came three gallant fellowes to the tent where I was, and some fortie followers Portugals, scattering themselues along the Sea side, ready to giue an assault when the word should be giuen. These three Gallants that came to the tents, armed with coats of Buffe downe to the knees, their Rapiers and Pistols by their sides, demaunded for the English Captaine: vpon the hearing of which, I arose presently, and told them that I was the man, and perceiuing an alteration in them, I laid hand vpon my weapon. The Captaine Mogol perceiuing treason towards me, both he and his followers drew

The first plot of the Portugals to kill me.

[1] Ahmedabad.

their weapons: and if the Portugals had not boon the swifter, both they and their scattered crew (in retiring to their Frigats) had come short home.

The second plot.

Another time, they came to assault me in my house with a Friar, some thirty or fortie of them: the Friars comming was to animate the soldiers, and to giue them absolution. But I was alwaies wary, hauing a strong house with good doores. Many troopes at other times, lay lurking for me and mine in the streetes, in that kind, that I was forced to goe to the Gouernour to complaine, that I was not able to goe about my businesse, for the Portugals comming armed into the Citie to murther me: which was not a custome at other times, for any Portugals to come armed as now they did. He presently sent word to the Portugals, that if they came into the city armed againe, at their owne perils be it. At Mocreb-chan his comming, with a Jesuite named Padre Pineiro in his company (who profered Mocreb-chan fortie thousand Rials of eight, to send me to Daman, as I understood by certaine aduise giuen me by Hassun Ally, and Ally Pommory) I went to visit him, giuing him a Present, besides the Present his brother had: and for a time, as I haue aboue written, I had many outward shewes of him, till the time I demanded my money. After that his dissembling was past, and he told me plainely, that he would not giue mee twentie Mamadies per Fare, but would deliuer me back my cloath. Vpon which dealings, I dissembled as well as I could with him, intreating leaue for Agra, to the King, telling him that William Finch was the man that I left as my chiefe in this place: and in what kind soeuer his pleasure was to deale with me, he was the man to receiue either money or ware. Vpon which answer, he gaue me his license and letter to the King, promising me fortie horsemen to goe with me, which hee did not accomplish. After license receiued, the Father put into Mocreb-chan his head, that it was not good to let me passe: for that I would

Padre Peneiro a Jesuite, a paterne of Jesuiticall sanctitie. How franke would the Jesuites haue bin to Judas, beyond those Priests which gaue but thirty pieces for the price of bloud, and those but of two shillings (and) six pence the piece? whereas this Jesuite offers forty thousand Royals (who can deny them Royall Merchants?) at foure shillings (and) six pence the piece.

complaine of him vnto the King. This he plotted with Mocreb-chan to ouerthrow my iourney, which he could not doe, because I came from a King: but he said, that he would not let me haue any force to goe with me. And what else hee would haue him to doe, either with my Treuchman and Coachman, to poyson or murther me, if one should faile, the other to doe it: this inuention was put into Mocreb-chans head by the Father. But God for his mercie sake, afterward discouered these plots, and the Counsell of this Jesuite tooke not place. Before the plotting of this, the Jesuite and I fell out in the presence of Mocreb-chan, for vile speaches made by him of our King and Nation, to bee vassals vnto the King of Portugall: which words I could not brooke, in so much, that if I could haue had my will, the Father had neuer spoken more, but I was preuented.

Jesuites policy. Just Jesuitisme.

---

§ II.

His Journey to the Mogoll at Agra, and entertay(n)ment at Court.

Now finding William Finch in good health, newly recouered, I left all things touching the Trade of Merchandizing in his power: giuing him my rembrance and order, what he should doe in my absence. So I began to take vp Souldiers to conduct mee, being denyed of Mocreb-chan, besides Shot and Bow men that I hired. For my better safety, I went to one of Chanchanna his Captaines, to let mee haue fortie or fiftie Horsemen to conduct me to Chanchanna, being then Vice-Roy of Decan, Resident in Bramport, who did to all his power all that I demanded, giving me valient Horsemen Pattens,[1] a people very much feared in these parts: for if I had not done it, I had beene ouer-throwne. For the Portugals of Daman had wrought with an ancient friend of theirs a Raga, who was absolute Lord of a Prouince, (betweene Daman, Guzerat and Decan) call Cruly,

[1] Patans.

to be ready with two hundred Horsemen to stay my passage: but I went so strong and well prouided, that they durst not incounter with vs: so likewise that time I escaped. Then at Dayta, another Prouince or Princedome, my Coachman being drunke with certaine of his kindred, discouered the Treason that hee was hiered to murther me: he being ouer-heard by some of my Souldiers, who at that present came and told me, and how it should be done in the morning following, when we begin our trauell: (for wee vse to trauell two houres before day) vpon which notice, I called the Coachman vnto me, examining him, and his friends, before the Captaine of the Horsemen I had with mee: who could not deny; but he would neuer confesse who hired him, although hee was very much beaten, cursing his fortune that he could not effect it: for he was to doe it the next morning, so I sent him Prisoner vnto the Gouernour of Suratt.

Dayta another province.

They vse to trauell two houres before day.

But afterward by my Broker or Truchman, I vnderstood that both hee and the Coachman were hired by Mocreb-chan, but by the Fathers perswasion, the one to poyson me, and the other to murther me: but the Truchman receiued nothing till he had done the deed, which hee neuer meant to doe, for in that kind hee was alwayes true vnto mee: thus God preserued me. This was fiue dayes after my departure from Suratt, and my departure from Suratt was the first of February 1608. So following on my trauels for Bramport, some two dayes beyond Dayta, the Pattans left me, but to be conducted by another Pattan Captaine, Gouernour of that Lordship, by whom I was most kindly entertained. His name was Sherchan, being sometime a Prisoner vnto the Portugal, and hauing the Portugall Language perfect, was glad to doe mee any seruice: for that I was of the Nation that was enemie vnto the Portugall. Himselfe in person, with fortie Horse-men, went two dayes iourney with mee, till he had freed mee from the dangerous places: at

The Jesuites bloudie plot discouered. Virtus an virus, quis in Jesuita requirat?

M. Hawkins departeth from Suratt the first of February 1608.

which time he met with a troupe of Out-lawes, and tooke some foure aliue, and slew and hurt eight, the rest escaped. This man very kindly writ his Letter for me, to haue his house at Bramport, which was a great curtesie, otherwise I could not tell where to lodge my selfe, the Towne being so full of Souldiers: for then began the Warres with the Decans. The eighteenth of the said Moneth, thankes be to God, I came in safetie to Bramport, and the next day I went to the Court to visit Chanchanna, being then Lord Generall and Vice-Roy of Decan, giuing him a Present; who kindly tooke it: and after three houres conference with him, he made me a great Feast, and being risen from the Table, inuested me with two Clokes, one of fine Woollen, and another of Cloth of Gold: giuing mee his most kind Letter of favour to the King, which aualyed much. That done he imbraced me, and so we departed. The Language that we spoke was Turkish, which he spake very well. I remained in Bramport vnto the second of March; till then I could not end my businesse of Monies that I brought by exchange, staying likewise for a Carrauan; hauing taken new Souldiers, I followed my Voyage or iourney to Agra: where after much labour, toyle, and many dangers, I arriued in safety the sixteenth of Aprill, 1609. Being in the Citie, and seeking out for an house in a very secret manner, notice was giuen to the King[1] that I was come, but not to bee found: He presently charged both Horsemen and Footmen in many troupes, not to leaue before I was found, commanding his Knight Marshall to accompany mee with great state to the Court, as an Embassador of a King ought to be: which he did with a great traine, making such extraordinary haste that I admired much: for I could scarce obtayne time to apparell my selfe in my best attyre. In fine, I was brought before the King, I came with a slight present, hauing nothing but cloth, and

His arriuall at Bramport.

He stayeth in Bramport till the second of March.

His arriuall at Agra the sixteenth of April, 1609.

He came before the King.

[1] The Emperor Jehángír, who succeeded his father Akbar in 1605, and died in 1627.

that not esteemed: (for what I had for the King, Mocreb-chan tooke from me, wher-with I acquainted his Maiestie.) After salutation done, with a most kind and smiling countenance, he bade me most heartily welcome, vpon which speech I did my obeysance and dutie againe. Hauing his Maiesties Letter in my hand, he called me to come neere vnto him, stretching downe his hand from the Seate Royall, where he sate in great Maiestie something high, for to be seene of the people: receiuing very kindly the Letter of me, viewing the Letter a prettie while, both the Seale, and the manner of making it vp, he called for an old Jesuite that was there present to reade it. In the meane space, while the Jesuite was reading it, hee spake vnto mee in the kindest manner that could bee, demanding of mee the contents of the Letter, which I told him; upon which notice, presently granting and promising me by God, that all what the King had there written, he would grant and allow with all his heart, and more if his Maiestie would require it. The Jesuite likewise told him the effect of the Letter, but discommending the stile, saying it was basely penned, writing Vestra without Maiestad: my answere was vnto the King, and if it shall please your Maiestie, these people are our enemies: how can this letter be ill written, when my King demandeth favour of your Maiestie? he said, it was true.

Jesuiticall Charitie.

Perceiuing I had the Turkish Tongue, which himselfe well understood, hee commanded me to follow him vnto his Chamber of Presence, being then risen from that place of open Audience, desiring to haue further conference with me: in which place I stayed some two houres, till the King came forth from his women. Then calling mee vnto him, the first thing that hee spake, was that he vnderstood that Mocreb-chan had not dealt well with mee, bidding mee bee of good cheere, for he would remedie all. It should seeme, that Mocreb-chans enemies had acquainted the King with all his

The Mogoll skilfull in the Turkish tongue.

proceedings: for indeed the King hath Spies vpon every Nobleman. I answered most humbly, that I was certaine all matters would goe well on my side, so long as his Maiestie protected me. Vpon which speech he presently sent away a Post for Suratt, with his command to Mocreb-chan, writing vnto him very earnestly in our behalfes: coniuring him to bee none of his friend, if hee did not deale well with the English, in that kind, as their desire was.

Spyes upon euery Nobleman.

This being dispatched and sent by some Messenger, I sent my Letter to William Finch, wishing him to goe with this command to Mocreb-chan: at the receit of which hee wondred that I came safe to Agra, and was not murthered, or poysoned by the way, of which speech William Finch aduertised me afterward.

It grew late, and hauing had some small conference with the King at that time, he commanded that I should daily be brought into his presence, and gaue a Captaine named Houshaberchad charge that I should lodge at his house, till a house was found conuenient for mee: and when I needed anything of the King, that he should bee my Solicitor. According to command, I resorted to the Court, where I had daily conference with the King. Both night and day, his delight was very much to talke with mee, both of the Affaires of England and other Countries, as also many demands of the West Indies, whereof hee had notice long before, being in doubt if there were any such place, till he had spoken with me, who had beene in the Countrey.

M. Will. Hawkins had been in the West Indies.

Many dayes and weekes being past, and I now in great favour with the King, to the griefe of all mine enemies, espying my time, I demanded for his Commandement or Commission with Capitulations for the establishing of our Factory to be in mine owne power. His answere was, whether I would remayne with him in his Court, I replyed, till shipping came; then my desire was to goe home, with the answere of his Maiesties Letter. Hee replyed againe, that his meaning was a longer time, for he meant to send an Embassador to the King of England, at the comming of the next shipping: and that I should stay with him vntill some other bee sent from my King, to remayne in my place, saying this: Thy staying would be highly for the benefit of thy Nation, and that he would giue me good maintenance, and my being heere in his presence, would bee the cause to right all wrongs that should be offered vnto my Nation: and further, what I should see beneficiall for them, vpon my petition made, hee would grant: swearing by his Fathers Soule, that if I would remayne with him, he would grant me Articles for our Factorie to my hearts desire, and would neuer goe from his word. I replyed againe, I would consider of it. Thus daily inticing me to stay with him, alleaging as is aboue written, and that I should doe seruice, both to my naturall King and him, and likewise he would allow me by the yeare, three thousand and two hundred pounds sterling for my first, and so yeerely, hee promised mee to augment my Liuing, till I came to a thousand Horse. So my first should be foure hundred Horse. For the Nobilitie of India haue their Titles by the number of their Horses,[1] that is to say, from fortie to twelue thousand, which pay belongeth to Princes, and his Sonnes. I trusting upon his promise, and seeing it was beneficiall both to my Nation and myself, being dispossessed of that benefit which I should haue reaped, if I had gone to Bantam, and that after halfe a doozen yeeres, your Worships would send another man of sort in my place, in the meane time, I should feather my Neast, and doe you seruice: and further perceiuing great iniuries offered vs, by reason the King is so farre from the Ports, for all which causes aboue specified, I did not think it amisse to yeeld vnto his request. Then, because my

The Kings stipendary wages and honorable Pensions to his Nobles.

[1] The Emperor Akbar established 66 *munsubs* or commands of cavalry, the *Munsubdars* commanding from ten to 10,000; but only the king's sons had *munsubs* above 5,000. (See Gladwin's *Ayin Akbari*, i. p. 210.)

name was something hard for his pronuntiation, hee called me by the name of English Chan,[1] that is to say, English Lord, but in Persia it is the Title for a Duke, and this went currant throughout the Countrey.

Now your Worships shall vnderstand, that I being nowe in the highest of my fauours, the Jesuites and Portugalls slept not, but by all meanes sought my ouerthrow: and to say the truth, the principall Mahumetans neere the King, enuyed much that a Christian should bee so nigh vnto him. The Jesuite Peneiro being with Mocreb-chan, and the Jesuites here, I thinke did little regard their Masses and Church matters, for studying how to ouerthrow my Affaires: aduice being gone to Goa by the Jesuites here, I meane in Agra, and to Padre Peneiro at Surat or Cambaya, hee working with Mocreb-chan to be the Portugals assistance, and the Vice Roy sending him a great Present, together with many Toyes vnto the King with his Letter. These presents and many more promises, wrought so much with Mocreb-chan, that he writeth his Petition vnto the King, sending it together with the present, aduertising the King, that the suffering of the English in his land, would be the cause of the losse of his owne Countries, neere the Sea-Coasts, as Suratt, Cambaya, and such like: and that in any case he entertaine me not, for that his ancient friends the Portugalls murmured highly at it: and that the same is spread amongst the Portugalls, that I was Generall of ten thousand Horse-men, readie to giue the assault vpon Diu, when our shipping came.

Jesuiticall Christianitie.

The practice of the Portugals against our Trade.

Lying a great stratageme.

The Vice-Royes Letter likewise was in this kind: the Kings answere was; that he had but one English-man in his Court, and him they needed not to feare, for hee hath not pretended any such matter; for I would haue giuen him Liuing neere the Sea ports, but he refused it, taking it neere me heere. This was the Kings answere, upon which

The King answere.

[1] Inglis Khán.

answere, the Portugalls were like madde Dogges, labouring to worke my passage out of the World. So I told the King what dangers I had passed, and the present danger wherein I was, my Boy Steuen Grauoner instantly departing this World, my man Nicholas Vfflet extreame sicke, and this was all my English Company, my selfe beginning to fall downe too. The King presently called the Jesuites, and told them if I dyed by any extraordinary casualtie, that they should all rue for it. This past, the King was very earnest with me to take a white Mayden out of his Palace, who would giue her all things necessary, with slaues, and he would promise mee she should turne Christian: and by this meanes my meates and drinkes should be looked vnto by them, and I should liue without feare. In regard she was a Moore, I refused, but if so bee there could bee a Christian found, I would accept it. At which my speech, I little thought a Christians Daughter could bee found. So the King called to memorie one Mubarique Sha[1] his Daughter, who was a Christian Armenian, and of the Race of the most ancient Christians, who was a Captaine, and in great fauor with Ekbar Padasha,[2] this Kings Father. This Captaine dyed suddenly and without will, with a Masse of Money, and all robbed by his Brothers and Kindred, and Debts that cannot be recouered: leauing the Child only a few Jewels. I seeing she was of so honest a Descent, hauing passed my word to the King, could not withstand my fortunes. Therefore I tooke her, and for want of a Minister, before Christian Witnesses, I marryed her: the Priest was my man Nicholas, which I thought had beene lawfull, till I met with a Preacher that came with Sir Henry Middleton, and hee shewing me the error, I was new marryed agayne: for euer after I liued content and without feare, she being willing to goe where I went, and liue as I liued. After these matters

Nicholas Vfflet.

Mubarique Sha an Armenian Christian.

Ekber Padasha.

He taketh a Christian gentlewoman to Wife. She came ouer with him for England, but he dying by the way, she was after marreyed to M. Towerson.

[1] Mubarik Khan is given in the list of *Munsubdars* of 1,000 in Gladwin's *Ayín Akbori*, i, p. 218.

[2] Akbar.

ended, newes came hither that the Ascention was to come by the men of her Pinnasse, that was cast away neere Suratt, vpon which newes, I presently went to the King and told him, crauing his Licence, together with his Commission, for the setling of our Trade: which the King was willing to doe, limiting me a time to returne, and be with him againe.

The Pinnasse of the Ascention cast away neere Suratt.

But the Kings chiefe Vizir Abdal Hassan, a man enuious to all Christians, told the King that my going would be the occasion of warre: and thus harm might happen vnto a great man who was sent for Goa, to by toyes for the King. Vpon which speech, the Kings pleasure was I should stay, and sent away his Commission to my chiefe Factor at Surat, and presently gaue order, that it should be most effectually written, so firmely for our good, and so free as heart can wish. This I obtained presently, and sent it to William Finch. Before it came there, newes came that the Ascention[1] was cast away, and her men saued, but not supposed to come into the Citie of Surat. Of that likewise I told the King, who seemed to be very much discontented with that great Captaine Mocreb-chan my enemy: and gaue me another Commandement for their good vsage, and meanes to be wrought to saue the goods, if it were possible. These two commandments came almost together, to the great ioy of William Finch and the rest, admiring much at these things. And now continuing these great fauours with the King, being continually in his sight, for one halfe of foure and twentie houre seruing him day and night, I wanted not the greater part of his Nobles that were Mahumetans, to be mine enemies. For it went against their hearts, that a Christian should be so great and neere the King: and the more, because the King had promised to make his Brothers children Christians. Awhile after came some of the Ascen-

The Kings Commission in the fauour of the English vnder his greate Seale with golden Letters.

Ascention cast away.

The greater part of the Kings Nobles are Mahumetans.

Some of the Ascentions Company and M. Alexander Sharpey their Generall came to Agra.

[1] See the *Voyages of Sir James Lancaster to the East Indies*, etc. (Hakluyt Society), pp. 120-130, for an account of the loss of the *Ascension*.

tions Company vnto me (whom I could haue wished of better behaviour, a thing pryed into by the King). In all this time, I could not get my debts of Mocreb-chan, till at length he was sent for vp to the King, to answere for many faults, and tyrannicall In-justice, which he did to all people in those parts, many a man being vndone by him, who petitioned to the King for Justice.

Now this Dogge, to make his peace, sent many bribes to the Kings Sonnes and Noble-men, that were neere the King, who laboured in his behalfe. After newes came that Mocreb-chan was approached neere, the King presently sent to attach all his goods, which were in that abundance, that the King was two moneths in viewing them, every day alloting a certaine quantitie to be brought before him: and what he thought fitting for his owne turne he kept, and the rest deliuered againe to Mocreb-chan. In viewing of these goods, there came those Peeces and Cortlet, and Head-peece, with other Presents, that he tooke from me for the King of mine owne, not suffering mee to bring them my self: at the sight whereof, I was so bold to tell the King what was mine. After the King had viewed these goods, a very great complaint was made by a Banian, how that Mocreb-chan had taken his Daughter, saying she was for the King, which was his excuse, deflowering her himself: and afterwards gaue her to a Brammen, belonging to Mocreb-chan. The man who gaue notice of this Child, protested her to passe all that euer he saw for beautie. The matter being examined, and the offence done by Mocreb-chan found to be true, hee was committed to prison, in the power of a great Nobleman: and commandement was giuen that the Brammene his priuy members should be cut off.

Before this happened to Mocreb-chan, I went to visite him diuer times, who made me very faire promises, that he would deale very kindly with mee, and be my friend, and that I should haue my right. Now being in this disgrace, his friends daily soliciting for him, at length got him cleere: with commandement, that he pay euery man his right, and that no more complaints be made of him if he loved his life. So Mocreb-chan by the Kings command, paid euery one his due, excepting me, whom he would not pay, but deliuer me my cloath, whereof I was desirous, and to make, if it were possible, by faire meanes and end with him: but he put me off the more, delaying time till his departure, which was shortly after. For the King had restored him his old place againe, and he was to goe for Goa, about a faire ballace Ruby,[1] and other rare things promised the King.

---

§ III.

The Mogols inconstancie, and Captaine Hawkins departure with Sr Henrie Middleton to the Red Sea: Thence to Bantam, and after for England.

All my going and sending to Mocreb-chan for my Money or Cloath was in vaine, I being abused so basely by him, that I was forced to demaund Justice of the King, who commanded that the money be brought before him; but for all the Kings commaund he did as he listed, and doe what I could, he cut me off twelve thousand and five hundred Mamadies.[2] For the greatest man in this Kingdome was his friend, and many others holding on his side, murmering to the King, the suffering of English to come into his Countrey: for that we were a Nation, that if we once set foot, we would take his Countrey from him. The King called me to make answere to that they said: I answered his Maiestie, that if

[1] Balas ruby; or a ruby from Balakhsh or Badakshan. (See Yule's *Marco Polo*, i, 169.)

[2] The *Mahmudi* was a gold coin of Gujrát. The Muhammadan Dynasty of Gujrát flourished from A.D. 1376 to 1572, when that country was annexed to Akbar's empire. (See Thomas's *Pathan Kings*, p. 352.)

any such matter were, I would answere it with my life: and that we were not so base a Nation, as these mine enemies reported. All this was because I demaunded my due, and yet cannot get it. At this time those that were neere fauourites, and neerest vnto the King, whom I daily visited, and kept in withall, spake in my behalfe: and the King holding on my side, commanded that no more such wrongs be offered me. So I thinking to vse my best in the recouery of this, intreting the head Vizir that he would be meanes that I receiue not so great a losse: answered me in a threatening manner: that if I did open my mouth any more, hee would make me to pay an hundred thousand Mamadies, which the King had lost in his Customes, by entertaining me, and no man durst aduenture by reason of the Portugall. So by this meanes I was forced to hold my tongue, for I know this Money was swallowed by both these Dogges. Now Mocreb-chan being commaunded in publicke, that by such a day he be ready to depart for Guzerat, and so for Goa, and then come and take his leaue, as the custome is: in this meane time, three of the princi-pallist Merchants of Surat were sent for by the Kings commaundement, and come to the Court about affaires wherein the King or his Vizir had imployed them, being then present there when Mocreb-chan was taking his leaue; this being a plot laid both by the Portugals, Mocreb-chan, and the Vizir. For some six daies before a Letter came vnto the King from the Portugal Vice-roy, with a Present of many rare things. The Contents of this Letter were, how highly the King of Portugall tooke in ill part the entertaining of the English, he being of an ancient amitie, with other complements: and with all, how that a Merchant was there arriued, with a very faire ballace Ruby, weighing three hundred and fiftie Rotties,[1] of which stone the pattern

A Letter from the Viceroy of the East India to the Mogull against the English.

[1] *Rati* (corruptly *Ruttee*), the seed of *Abrus precatorius*, used as the basis of weights for gold and silver. 8 *Rati* = 1 *Masha*, 12 *Masha* = 1 *Tola*, 5 *Tola* = 1 *Chitak*, 16 *Chitak* = 1 *Sír*, a *Sír* = 2 lbs. 6 oz.

was sent. Upon this newes Mocreb-chan was to be hastened away, at whose comming to take his leaue together with Padre Pineiro, that was to goe with him, the aboue named Merchants of Surat being then there present, Mocreb-chan began to make his speech to the King, saying, that this and many other things he hoped to obtaine of the Portugall, so that the English were disanulled: saying more, that it would redound to great losse vnto his Maiestie and Subiects, if hee did further suffer the English to come into his parts. Vpon which speech he called the Merchants before the King, to declare what losse it would be, for that they best know. They affirmed, that they were like to be all vndone because of the English, nor hereafter any toy could come into this country, because the Portugal was so strong at sea, and would not suffer them to goe in or out of their Ports: and all their excuse was, for suffering the English.

A speech of Mocreb-chan to the King against the English.

These speeches now and formerly, and lucre of this stone, and promises by the Fathers of rare things, were the causes the King overthrew my affaires; saying, Let the English come no more: presently giuing Mocreb-chan his commandment, to deliuer the Viceroy to that effect, that he would neuer suffer the English to come any more into his ports.

The Kings commandment vpon false information against the English.

I now saw that it booted me not to meddle vpon a sudden, or to make any petition vnto the King, till a prety while after the departure of Mocreb-chan; and seeing my enemies were so many, although they had eaten of me many Presents. When I saw my time, I made my petition vnto the King. In this space I found a toy to giue, as the order is: for there is no man that commeth to make petition, who commeth empty handed. Vpon which petition made him, he presently graunted my request, commanding his Vizir to make me another commandement in as ample manner as my former, and commanded that no man should open his mouth

None make petition to the King without some Present.

to the contrary: for it was his pleasure that the English should come into his Ports. So this time againe I was a floate.

Of this alteration, at that instant the Jesuite had notice: for there is no matter passeth in the Mogols Court in secret, but it is knowne halfe an houre after, giuing a small matter to the writer of that day: for there is nothing that passeth, but it is written, and writers appointed by turnes, so that the Father, nor I, could passe any businesse, but when we would we had notice. So the Jesuite presently sent away the most speedy messenger that could be gotten, with his Letter to Padre Pineiro and Mocreb-chan, aduertising them of all that had passed. At the receit of which, they consulted amongst themselues, not to go forward on their voyage to Goa, till I were ouerthrowne againe. Wherefore Mocreb-chan wrote his petition vnto the King, and letters vnto his friend, the head Vizir, how it stood not with the Kings honour to send him, if he performed not what he promised the Portugal: and that his voyage would be ouerthrowne, if he did not call in the commandement he had giuen the Englishman. Vpon the receiuing and reading of this, the King went againe from his word, esteeming a few toyes which the Father had promised him more than his honour.

Now beeing desirous to see the full issue of this, I went to Hogio Tahan, Lord General of the Kings Palace (the second man in place in the Kingdome) intreating him that he would stand my friend. He very kindly, presently went vnto the King, telling him I was very heauy and discontent, that Abdall Hassan would not deliuer me my commandement, which his Maiestie had graunted me. The King answered him (I being present, and very neere him), saying, It was true, that the commandement is sealed, and ready to be deliuered him: but vpon letters receiued from Mocreb-chan, and better consideration by me had on these my affaires in my Ports in Guzerat, I thought it fitting not to let him haue it. Thus was I tossed and tumbled in the kind of a rich Merchant, aduertising all he had in one bottome, and by casualtie of stormes or pirates, lost it all at once. So that on the other side, concerning my liuing, I was so crossed, that many times this Abdall Hassan his answere would be vnto me; I know wel enough you stand not in such need, for your Master beareth your charges, and the King knew not what he did in giuing it to you, from whom he should receiue. My answer was, that it was the Kings pleasure, and none of my request; and seeing it is his Maiesties gift, I had no reason to loose it: so that from time to time he bade mee haue patience, and he would find out a good liuing for me. Thus was I dallied withall by this mine enemie, in so much that in all the time I serued in Court, I could not get a liuing that would yeeld anything, giuing me my liuing still, in places where Out-lawes raigned: only, once at Lahor by an especiall commandement from the King, but I was soone depriued of it: and all that I receiued from the beginning, was not fully three hundred pounds, a great part whereof was spent vpon charges of men sent to the Lordships. When that I saw that the liuing which the King absolutely gaue me, was taken from me, I was then past all hopes: for before, at the newes of the arriuall of shipping, I had great hope that the King would performe former grants, in hopes of rare things that should come from England. But when I made Petition vnto the King concerning my liuing, he turned me ouer to Abdall Hassan: who not only denied me my liuing; but also gaue order, that I be suffered no more to enter within the red rayles: which is a place of honour, where all my time was placed very neere vnto the King, in which place there were but fiue men in the Kingdome before me.

The red Railes a place of Honour.

Now perceiuing that all my affaires were ouerthrowne, I determined with the Councell of those that were neere me, to resolue whereto to trust, either to be well in or well out. Vpon this resolution I had my petition made ready, by which I made known vnto the King, how Abdall Hassan had dealt with me, hauing himselfe eaten what his Maiestie gaue me: and how that my charges for so long time (being by his Maiestie desired to stay in his Court, vpon the faithful promises he made me) were so much, that it would be my vtter ouerthrow: therefore I besought his Maiestie that he would consider my cause, either to establish me as formerly, or giue me leaue to depart. His answere was, that he gaue me leaue, commanding his safe conduct to bee made mee, to passe freely without molestation, throughout his Kingdoms. When this commandment was made, as the custome is, I came to do my obeysance, and to take my leaue, intreating for an answere of my King's Letter. Abdall Hassan comming vnto me from the King, in a disdainfull manner utterly denyed me: saying, that it was not the custome of so great a Monarch, to write in the kind of a Letter, vnto a pettie Prince, or Gouernour. I answered him, that the King knewe more of the mightinesse of the King of England, then to be a petty Gouernour. Well, this was mine answere, together with my leaue taken.

I went home to my house, studying with all my endeauours to get all my goods and debts together, and to buy commodities with those monies that were remayning, vsing all the speed I could, to cleere my self of the countrey: staying only for Nicholas Vfflet, to come from Lahor, with a remainder of Indico, that was in William Finches power, who determined to goe ouer land, being past all hopes for euer imbarking our selues at Surat: which course I also would willingly haue taken, but that as it is well knowne, for some causes I could not trauell thorow Turkie, and especially with a woman. So I was forced to currie fauour with the Jesuites, to get mee a safe conduct, or *Seguro*, from the Vice Roy to goe to Goa, and so to Portugall, and from

Will. Finch determined to returne ouerland for England.

thence to England—thinking, as the opinion of others was, that the Vice Roy giuing his secure Royall, there would be no danger for me. But when my Wifes Mother and kindred saw that I was to carry her away, suspecting that they would neuer see her any more, they did so distaste me in these my trauels, that I was forced to yeeld vnto them, that my Wife go no further than Goa, because it was India: and that they could goe and come and visit her, and that, if at any time I meant to goe for Portugall, or any otherwhere, that I leaue her that portion, that the custom of Portugall is, to leaue to their Wiues when they dye: vnto which I was forced to yeeld to giue them content, to preuent all mischiefes. But knowing that if my Wife would goe with me, all would bee of no effect, I effected with the Jesuites to send for two Secures, the one concerning my quiet being and free liberties of conscience in Goa, and to be as a Portingall in all Tradings and Commerce in Goa: (this was to shew my Wifes Parents). The other was an absolute grant for free passage into Portugall, and so for England, with my Wife and Goods, without any disturbances of any of my Wiues friends: and what agreements I made with them to be void and of none effect, but I should stay or goe, when I pleased, with free libertie of conscience for my self. This last *Seguro* I should receaue at Cambaya, which at my departure for our shippes were not yet come, but was to come with the Carrauan of Frigats.

This and much more the Fathers would haue done for me, only to rid me out of the Country; for being cleare of me, they should much more quietly sleepe. About this time, I had notice of the comming of three English ships that were arriued at Mocha, and without faile their determination was to come for Surat, at the time of the yeare; hauing this Aduertisement by Nicholas Bangham from Bramport, who departed from me some weekes before, both for the recouery of certain Debts, as also with my

Letter to our shipping, if it were possible to send it, aduertising them of my proceedings.

In this time of my dispatching, newes came of Mocreb-chans returne from Goa, with many gallant and rare things, which he brought for the King. But that Ballace Ruby was not for his turne, saying it was false, or at the least, made his excuse for feare, that if he should giue the Portugall his price, and when it came into the King's power, it should bee valued much lesse (which ouerplus he should bee forced to pay, as hee had done in former times for other things), hee left it behind him. And besides, I vnderstood, the Mocreb-chan had not his full content as he expected of the Portugalls. And likewise, at this instant the Vizir, my enemy, was thrust out of his place, for many complaints made of him, by Noblemen that were at great charges and in debt, and could not receiue their liuings in places that were good, but in barren and rebellious places: and that he made a benefit of the good places himselfe and robbed them all. For these complaints and others, he had much ado to escape with life, being out of his place, and sent to the wars of Decan. Now one Gaihbeig[1] being the King's chief Treasurer (a man that in outward shew made much of me, and was always willing to pleasure me, when I had occasion to vse him) was made chiefe Vizir; and his Daughter marryed with the King, being his chiefe Queen or Paramor.[2] The Vizir's sonne and my selfe were great friends, he hauing beene often at my house, and was now exalted to high Dignities by the King. Perceiuing this alteration, and being certified of the comming of shipping, by certain aduice, sundry wayes. Knowing the custom of these Moores, that without gifts and bribes nothing would

[1] Mirza Ghiyas, son of a native of Tehran, who rose from great poverty to a position of trust under Akbar.

[2] The celebrated Núr Jehán. Her father Mirza Ghiyas, was made chief minister by Jehangír.

either goe forward or bee accomplished, I sent my Broker to seeke out for Jewels, fitting for the King's Sister and new Paramour; and, likewise, for this new Vizir, and his sonne.

Now after they had my Gifts, they beganne on all sides to solicite my cause; at which time newes came to Agra, by Banians of Diu, how that off Diu, three English ships were seene, and three dayes after other newes came, that they were at the Barre of Surat. Vpon which newes the great Vizir asked me what toy I had for the King, I showed him a Ruby Ring that I had gotten, at the sight of which he bade me make readie to goe with him at Court time, and he would make my Petition to the King, and told me that the King was alreadie wonne. So once more comming before his Greatnesse, and my Petition being read, he presently granted mee the establishing of our Factorie, and that the English come and freely trade for Surat; willing the Vizir that with all expedition my commandement be made, vpon which grant the Vizir made signe vnto mee, to make obeysance, which I did, according to the Custome. But now what followed?

A great Nobleman and neerest fauourite of the King, being the dearest friend that Mocreb-chan, and likewise Abdall Hassan had, brought vp together from their childhood, and Pages together vnto the King, began to make a speech vnto the King: saying, that the granting of this would be the vtter overthrow of his Sea Coasts and people, as his Maiestie had beene informed by petition from diuers of his Subiects: and besides, that it stood not with his Maiesties honour to contradict that which he had granted to his ancient friends the Portugals, and whosoeuer laboured for the English, knew not what he did; if knowing, hee was not his Maiesties friend. Vpon the speech of this Nobleman, my businesse once againe was quite ouerthrowne, and all my time and presents lost: the King answering, that for my Nation, hee would not grant Trade at the Sea Ports, for the inconuenience that diuers times had been scanned vpon. But, for my selfe, if I would remayne in his seruice he would command, that what he had allowed me should be giuen me to my content: which I denyed, vnlesse the English should come vnto his Ports according to promise, and as for my particular maintenance, my King would not see me want. Then desiring againe answere of thė Kings Letter, he consulted a-while with his Vizirs, and then sent mee his denyall. So I tooke my leaue and departed from Agra, the second of Nouember 1611. Being of a thousand thoughts what course I were best to take: for I still had a doubt of the Portingalls that for lucre of my goods they would poyson me. Againe, on the other-side, it was dangerous by reasone of the Warres to trauell thorow Decan vnto Masulipatan: by land, by reason of the Turkes, I could not goe; and to stay I would not amongst these faithlesse Infidels.

He departeth from Agra the second of Nouember 1611.

I arriued at Cambaya, the last of December 1611, where I had certaine newes of the English ships that were at Surat.[1] Immediately I sent a Footman vnto the ships with my Letter, with certaine aduice, affirmed for a truth, by the Fathers of Cambaya, unto me, that the Vice-Roy had in readinesse prepared to depart from Goa, foure great ships, with certaine Gallies, and Frigats for to come vpon them, and Treasons plotted against Sir Henry Middletons person: of which newes, I was wished by the Fathers to aduise Sir Henry: which I found afterwards to bee but their policie, to put him in feare, and so to depart, and withall, I wished them to be well aduised. And as for me my shifts were to goe home, by the way of the Portugalls, for so I had promised my Wife and her Brother, who at that present was with me: and to delude him and the Fathers till I had notice for

A fained policie of the Jesuites.

[1] See the *Voyages of Sir James Lancaster to the East Indies*, etc. (Hakluyt Society, 1877), p. 195.

certaine, that I might freely get aboord without feare, which I was assured to know at the returne of my Letter; in the meane time I did all I could to dispatch her Brother away: who within two dayes after departed for Agra, not suspecting that I had any intent for the ships. Nicholas Ufflet now departing from mee to survey the way, beeing two dayes iourney on his way, met with Captaine William Sharpeigh, Master Fraine, and Hugh Greete, sent by Sir Henry to Cambaya vnto mee, which was no small ioy vnto mee. So vnderstanding of the place (which was miraculously found out by Sir Henry Middleton, and never knowne to any of the countrey) I admired and gaue God thankes: for if this place had not beene found, it had been impossible for mee to haue gotten aboord with my goods. Wherefore making all the haste that I could, in dispatching my self away, I departed from Cambaya, the eighteenth of January 1611, and came vnto the ships the six and twentieth of the said moneth, where I was most kindly receaued by Sir Henry Middleton. From this place we departed the eleuenth of February 1611, and arriued at Dabul the sixteenth of the same: in which we tooke a Portugall ship and Frigat, out of which we tooke some quantitie of goods. And from thence we departed the fift of March 1611 for the Red Sea, with an intent to revenge vs of the wrongs offered vs, both by Turkes and Mogols: at which place wee arriued the third of Aprill 1612. Here we found three English ships, their General was Captaine John Saris. Hauing dispatched our businesse in the Red Sea, wee set sayle from thence the sixteenth of August 1612, and arriued in Tecu in Sumatra the nineteenth of October 1612, and hauing ended our businesse there, we departed in the night, the twentieth of November 1612, and came on ground the same night, three leagues off, vpon a Bed of Corall, in three fathome water, or thereabouts, and by the great mercie of God we escaped: but were forced to returne backe againe to stop

Hee came aboord the English Fleet.

They depart with the English Fleet from Surat to Dabull.

A Portugal ship taken.

They arriue at the mouth of the Red Sea.

The Fleet of M. John Saris.

They arriue at Tecoo in Sumatra.

her leakes, the goods being taken out, and some damage receiued.[1] Now her leakes being somewhat stopped, and her goods in, not losing an houre of time, wee departed from thence the eight of December 1612, and arriued at Bantam the one and twentieth of the same: where Sir Henry Middleton not finding the Trade sufficient to goe home that yeare, was forced to stay and carine her. Hauing ended account with him, as himselfe liked best, I tooke my goods and shipped them in the Salamon, which came for our Voyage, for sauing of a greater Fraight: but I could not be admitted to goe in her myselfe; Captaine Saris, I thank him, accommodated me in the Thomas, and it was agreed, that the Salamon and wee should keepe company together.[2]

They arriue at Bantam December, 1612.

From thence we set saile on the thirtieth of January 1612, and arriued in Saldania Road, the one and twentieth day of April 1613, and comming neere some two hundred leagues from the Cape, we had much foule weather and contrary windes. Here we found foure sayle of Hollanders that departed Bantam a moneth before vs. There was great kindnesse betwixt vs, especially to me, in regard that they had heard much of my great estate in India, by an Agent of theirs, that was Lieger at Masulipatan. Some eight dayes after the Expedition came in, and brought mee a Letter from your Worships, and deliuered it vnto mee two days after their arriuall. The wind comming faire, we departed from Saldania the one and twentieth of May 1613.

The Expedition arriued in Saldania.

Many aduises of the Authour touching Forts, Indian Factories, etc. I haue omitted as not so fitting euery Eye.

Their departure from Saldania.

[1] See page 209 of the *Voyages of Sir James Lancaster to the East Indies* (Hakluyt Society's vol., 1877). Tiku (Tecu) was one of the principal Sumatran ports for pepper on the west coast.

[2] See *Voyages of Sir James Lancaster, etc.*, p. 218. The *Thomas* was a ship in the fleet of Captain Saris.

§ IV.

A briefe Discourse of the strength, wealth, and Gouernment, with some Customes of the great Mogol: which I haue both seene and gathered by his chiefe Officers, and Ouer-seers of all his Estate.

First, I begin with his Princes, Dukes, Marquesses, Earles, Viscounts, Barons, Knights, Esquires, Gentlemen, and Yeomen. As Christian Princes vse their degrees by Titles, so they haue their Degrees and Titles by their number of Horses: vnlesse it bee those that the King most fauoureth, whom he honoureth with the Title of Chan and Trumirza. None haue the title of Sultan but his Sonnes. Chan in the Persian Language, is as much as Duke, Trumirza is the title of the King's Brother's Children.

They that be of the Fame of twelve thousand Horsemen belong to the King, and his Mother, and eldest Sonne, and one more, who is of the blood Royal of Vybeck, named Chan Azam. Dukes be nine thousand Fame, Marquesses fiue thousand Fame, Earles three thousand, Viscounts two thousand, Barons a thousand, Knights four hundred, Esquires an hundred, Gentlemen fifty, Yeomen from twenty down wards. All they that haue these numbers of Horsemen are called Mansibdars,[1] or men of Liuings or Lordships. Of these there are three thousand, that is to say, foure be of twelve thousand Horse a-piece, and they be the King, his Mother, Sultan Peruis, Prince and Chan Azam. Of nine thousand Horsemen there bee three, that is to say, Sultan Choran, the King's third Sonne, Chanchanna, and Kelich Chan. Of fiue thousand there be eighteene, named Hasuff Chan, Chan Tchan, Abdula Chan, Raga Manzing Ray Durga, Raga Sursing, Ramadus Rechuna, Raga Bassu, Emirel Vinera, Mahabet Chan, Chan Dowran, Sedris Chan, Hogio Bey Mirza, Mirza Cazi, Etlebar Chan, Abulfet De-

Vybeck.

Mansibdars.

[1] See Gladwin's *Ayín Akbari*.

kenny Selem Cully Chan, Sheik Serid. Of three thousand there be two and twentie, to wit, Chan Alem Mirza Ereg, Mirza Doreb, Hogio Sahan, Hogio Abdal Hassan, Mirza Gaysbey, Mirza Shemchadin, Mirza Chadulla, Seffer Chan, Kazmy Chan, Mirza Chin Kelich, Saif Chan, Lalla Bersingdia, Mirza Tyeady, Mirza Ally Ecberchuly, Terbiat Chan, Mirza Laschary, Mirza Chamcogly, Mirza Rustem, Ally Merdon Badur, Tasbey Chan, Abulbey. The rest bee from two thousand downwards till you come to twentie Horses, two thousand nine hundred and fiftie. Of Horsemen, that receiue pay monethly, from sixe Horse to one, there bee fiue thousand, these bee called Haddies. Of such Officers and men as belong to the Court and Campe, there be thirtie sixe thousand, to say, Porters, Gunners, Watermen, Lackeyes, Horse-keepers, Elephant-keepers, Small shot, Trasses, or Tentmen, Cookes, Lightbeares, Gardiners, Keepers of all kind of Beasts. All these be payd monethly out of the King's Treasure, whose Wages be from ten to three Rupias.

All his Captaines are to maintaine at a seuen-nights' warning, from twelue thousand to twentie Horse, all Horsemen three Leckes,[1] which is three hundred thousand Horsemen: which of the Incomes of their Lordships allowed them, they must maintayne.

The Kings yeerely Income of his Crowne Land is fiftie Cror of Rupias, every Cror is an hundred Leckes, and every Leck is an hundred thousand Rupiæ.

The compasse of his countrey is two yeares trauell with Carrauan, to say, from Candahar to Agra, from Loughtare in Bengala to Agra, from Cabul to Agra, from Deccan to Agra, from Surat to Agra, from Tatta in Sinde to Agra. Agra is in a manner in the heart of all his kingdomes.

Candahar.

His Empire is diuided into fiue great Kingdomes, the

[1] Lakhs.

first named Pengab, whereof Lahor is the Chiefe Seate ; the second is Bengala, the Chiefe Seate Sonargham : the third is Malwa, the Chiefe Seate is Ugam :[1] the fourth is Decan, the Chiefe Seate Bramport: the fifth is Guzerat, the Chiefe Seat is Amadauer :[2] The Chiefe Citie or Seat Royall of the Kings of India is called Delly, where hee is established King: and there all the Rites touching his Coronation are performed.

There are sixe especiall Castles, to say, Agra, Guallier,[3] Neruer, Ratambore, Hassier, Roughtaz. In euery one of these Castles he hath his Treasure kept.

In all his Empire there are three Arch-enemies or Rebels, which with all his Forces cannot be called in, to say, Amberry Chapu[4] in Decan: in Guzerat, the Sonne of Muzafer, that was King, his name is Bahador of Malwa, Raga Rahana. His Sonnes be fiue, to say, Sultan Coussero,[5] Sultan Peruis,[6] Sultan Chorem,[7] Sultan Shariar,[8] and Sultan Bath. Hee hath two yong Daughters, and three hundred Wiues, whereof foure be chiefe as Queenes, to say, the first, named Padasha Banu, Daughter to Kaime Chan: the second is called Noore Mahal, the Daughter of Gais Bijge :[9] the third is the Daughter of Seinchan : the fourth is the Daughter of Hakim Hamann, who was Brother to his Father Ecber Padasha.

His Treasure is as followeth: The first is his seuerall Coine of Gold.

In primis, of Seraffins Ecberi, which be ten Rupias a piece, there are sixtie Leckis. Of another sort of Coyne, of

[1] Ujain. [2] Ahmedabad. [3] Gwalior.

[4] Malik Amber, the famous Minister of Ahmadnagar.

[5] Khuzru, who rebelled and passed the rest of his life in captivity.

[6] Parwíz, a drunkard.

[7] Khurram, who succeeded as Shah Jehan. [8] Shahryar.

[9] See note at p. 414.

a thousand Rupias a piece, there are twentie thousand pieces. Of another sort, of halfe the value, there are ten thousand pieces. Of another sort of Gold, of twenty Tolas[1] a piece, there are thirtie thousand pieces. Of another sort of five Tolas, which is this Kings stampe, of these there be fiftie thousand pieces.

Of Siluer as followeth:

In primis, of Rupias Ecbery, thirteene Cror (euery Cror is an hundred Leckes, and every Lecke an thousand Rupias) or one thousand three hundred Leckes. Of another sort of Coine of Selim Sha this King, of an hundred Tolas a piece, there are fortie thousand pieces. Of twentie Tolas a piece, there are thirtie thousand pieces. Of ten Tolas a piece, there are twentie thousand pieces. Of fiue Tolas a piece, there are fiue and twentie thousand pieces. Of a certaine Money that is called Sauoy, which is a Tola ¼, of these there are two Leckes. Of Sagaries, whereof fiue make sixe Toles, there is one Lecke. More should haue beene coyned of this stampe, but the contrary was commanded.

Here followeth of his Jewells of all Sorts.

In primis, Of Diamantes 1½ Battmann, there be rough, of all sortes and sizes, great and small; but no lesse than 2¾ Caratts. The Battman is fiftie pound waight, which maketh eightie two pounds ½ weight English. Of Ballace Rubies little and great, good and bad, there are single two thousand pieces. Of Pearle of all sorts, there are twelue Battmans. Of Rubies of all sorts, there are two Battmans. Of Emeraudes of all sorts, fiue Battmans. Of Eshime, which stone commeth from Cathaia, one Battman. Of stones of Emen, which is a red stone, there are fiue thousand pieces. Of all other sorts as Corall, Topasses, etc., there is an infinite number.

Eshime a precious stone comming from Cathaya.

[1] See note at p. 408.

Here followeth of the Jewells wrought in Gold.

Of Swords of Almaine Blades, with the Hilts and Scabbards set with diuers sorts of rich stones, of the richest sort, there are two thousand and two hundred. Of two sorts of Poniards, there bee two thousand. Of Saddle Drummes, which they vse in their Hawking, of these there are very rich ones of Gold, set with stones, fiue hundred. Of Brooches for their heads, whereinto their Feathers be put, these be very rich, and of them there are two thousand. Of Saddles of Gold and Siluer set with stones, there are one thousand. Of Teukes there be fiue and twentie; this is a great Launce couered with Gold, and the Fluke set with stones, and these instead of their colours, are carryed, when the King goeth to the warres, of these there are five and twentie. Of Kittasoles[1] of state, for to shaddow him, there bee twentie. None in his Empire dareth in any sort haue any of these carryed for his shadow but himself, of these, I say, there are twentie. Of Chaires of Estate there bee fiue, to say, three of Siluer, and two of Gold: and of other sorts of Chaires, there bee an hundred of Siluer and Gold, in all an hundred and fiue. Of rich Glasses, there bee two hundred. Of Vases for Wine very faire and rich, set with Jewels, there are an hundred. Of Drinking Cuppes fiue hundred, but fiftie very rich, that is to say, made of one piece of Ballace Ruby, and also of Emerods, of Eshim, of Turkish stone, and of other sorts of stones. Of Chaines of Pearle, and Chaines of all sorts of precious stones, and Ringes with Jewels of rich Diamants, Ballast Rubies, Rubies and old Emerods, there is an infinite number, which only the keeper thereof knoweth. Of all sorts of Plate, as Dishes, Cups, Basons, Pots, Beakers of Siluer wrought, there are two thousand Battmans. Of Gold wrought, there are one thousand Battmans.

Eshim stones of Cathay.

[1] Quitasoles—State umbrellas.

Here followeth of all sorts of Beasts.

Of Horses there are twelue thousand. Whereof there bee of Persian Horses foure thousand, of Turkie Horses six thousand, and of Kismire two thousand: all are twelue thousand.

Or Kismire.

Of Elephants there bee twelue thousand, whereof fiue thousand bee teeth elephants, and seuen thousand of shee ones, and yong ones, which are twelue thousand. Of Camels there be two thousand. Of Oxen for the Cart, and all other seruices, there bee tenne thousand. Of Moyles[1] there be one thousand. Of Deere, like Buckes, for game or sport, there be three thousand. Of Ounces for Game, there be foure hundred. Of Dogges for hunting, as Greyhounds and other, there be foure hundred. Of Lions tame there be an hundred. Of Buffaloes, there be fiue hundred. Of all sorts of Hawkes there bee foure thousand. Of Pidgeons for sport of flying, there bee ten thousand. Of all sorts of Singing Birds, there be foure thousand.

Of Armour of all sorts at an houres warning, in a readinesse to arme fiue and twentie thousand men.

His daily expense for his owne person, that is to say, for feeding his Cattell of all sorts, and amongst them some few Elephants Royall, and all other expences particularly, as Apparell, Victuals, and other petty expenses for his house amounts to fiftie thousand Rupias a day.

The expenses daily for his Women by the day, is thirtie thousand Rupias. All this written concerning his Treasure, Expenses and monethly pay is in his Court or Castle of Agra: and euery one of the Castles above nominated, haue their seuerall Treasure, especially Lahor, which was not mentioned.

The Mogoll heire to euery man.

The Custome of this Mogoll Emperour is to take possession of his Noblemens Treasure when they dye, and to

[1] Mules.

bestow on his Children what he pleaseth: but commonly he dealeth well with them, possessing them with their Fathers Land, diuiding it amongst them; and vnto the eldest Sonne, hee hath a very great respect, who in time receiueth the full title of his Father. There was in my time a great Indian Lord or Prince, a Gentile named Raga Gaginat, vpon whose goods the Kings seizing after his death, he was found (besides Jewels and other Treasure) to haue sixtie Maunes in Gold, and euery Maune is fiue and fiftie pound waight. Also his custome is, that of all sorts of Treasure, excepting Coine, to say of all sorts of Beasts, and all other things of value, a small quantitie is daily brought before him. All things are seuerally diuided into three hundred and sixtie parts, so that hee daily seeth a certaine number, to say, of Elephants, Horses, Camels, Dromedaries, Moyles, Oxen, and all other: as also a certaine quantitie of Jewels and so it continueth all the yeere long: for what is brought him to day is not seene againe, till that day twelue moneth.

Raga Gaginat his wealth.

He hath three hundred Elephants Royall, which are Elephants whereon himselfe rideth: and when they are brought before him, they come with great iollitie, hauing some twentie or thirtie men before them with small Stremers. The Elephants Cloth or Couering is very rich, eyther of Cloth of Gold, or rich Veluet: hee hath following him his shee Elephant, his Whelpe or Whelpes, and foure or fiue yong ones, as Pages, which will be in number some sixe, some seuen, and some eight or nine. These Elephants and other Cattell, are dispersed among his Nobles and men of sort to ouer-see them, the King allowing them for their expenses, a certaine quantitie: but some of them will eate a great deale more then their allowance commeth vnto. These Elephants Royall eate tenne Rupias euery day in Sugar, Butter, Graine, and Sugar Canes. These Elephants are the goodliest and fairest of all the rest, and tame withall, so

Elephants Royall.

managed, that I saw with mine eyes, when the King commanded one of his young Sonnes named Shariar (a Childe of seuen yeeres of age) to goe to the Elephant to bee taken vp by him with his snout: who did so, deliuering him to his keeper that commanded him with his hooke: and hauing done this vnto the Kings Sonne, he afterwards did the like to many other Children. When these Elephants are shewed, if they who haue the charge of them bring them leane, then are they checked and in disgrace, vnlesse their excuse bee the better: and so it is with all things else in that kinde, that euery man striueth to bring his quantitie in good liking, although hee spend of his owne.

The Kings Tents as large in compasse as London.

When hee rideth on Progresse or Hunting the compasse of his Tents may bee as much as the compasse of London and more, and I may say, that of all sorts of people that follow the Campe, there are two hundred thousand: for hee is prouided, as for a Citie. This King is thought to be the greatest Emperour of the East, for Wealth, Land, and force of Men: as also for Horses, Elephants, Camels, and Dromedaries. As for Elephants of his owne, and of his Nobles, there are fortie thousand, of which the one halfe are trayned Elephants for the Warre: and these Elephants of all beasts, are the most understanding. I thought good here to set downe this one thing, which was reported to me for a certainty, although it seemed very strange. An Elephant hauing iourneyed very hard, being on his trauell, was misused by his Commander, and one day finding the fellow asleepe by him, but out of his reach, hauing greene Canes brought him to eate, split the end of one of them with his teeth, and taking the other end of the Cane with his snowt, reached it toward the head of the fellow, who being fast asleepe, and his turbant fallen from his head (the vse of India being to weare their haire long like Women), he tooke hold with the Cane on his haire, wreathing it therein, and withall, haling him vnto him, vntill he brought him

Forty thousand Elephants.

within the compasse of his snowt, he then presently killed him. Many other strange things are done by Elephants.

He hath also infinite numbers of Dromedaries, which are very swift, to come with great speed, to giue assault to any Citie, as this Kings Father did: so that the enemies thought he had been in Agra, when he was at Amadauar: and he came from Agra thither in nine daies, vpon these Dromedaries, with twelue thousand choyce men, Chan-channa being then his Generall. The day being appointed for the battell, on a suddaine newes came of the Kings arriuall, which struck such a present feare into the Guzerats, that at that time they were ouerthrowne and conquered. This King hath diminished his chiefe Captaines, which were Rasbootes,[1] or Gentiles, and naturall Indians, and hath preferred Mahumetans (weak spirited men, void of resolution) in such sort, that what this mans Father, called Ecber Padasha, got of the Decans, this King Selim Sha, beginneth to loose. He hath a few good Captaines yet remaining, whom his father highly esteemed, although they be out of fauor with him, because that vpon his rebellion against his father, they would not assist him, considering his intent was nought: for he meant to haue shortened his Fathers daies, and before his time to haue come to the Crowne. And to that purpose, being in Attabase, the regall seate of a Kingdome called Porub, hee arose with eighty thousand horse, intending to take Agra, and to haue possession of the Treasury, his Father being then at the warres of Decan: who vnderstanding of his Sonnes pretence, left his conquering there, and made hast to come home to saue his owne. Before the Kings departure to the warres, hee gaue order to his Sonne to goe with his Forces vpon Aranna, that great Rebel in Malwa, who comming to parle with this Rebel, he told the Prince, that there was nothing to bee gotten by him but blowes: and it were better for him, now

Dromedaries swiftness.

From Agra to Amadauar in nine dais.

Selims rebellion.

Or Rabanne.

[1] Rajputs.

his Father was at Decan, to goe vpon Agra, and possesse himselfe of his Fathers treasure, and make himselfe King, for there was no man able to resist him. The Prince followed his counsell, and would haue prosecuted it, but his Fathers hast before, vpon notice being giuen, preuented his purposes: at whose arriual at Agra hee presently sent unto his Sonne, that he make choyce either to come and fall at his feete, and be at his mercie to doe with him as he pleased, or to fit himselfe for the battell and fight it out. He well considering the valour of his Father, thought it meetest to submit himself, and to stand to his Fathers mercy: who after affronts shewed him and imprisonment, was soone released and pardoned, by reason of many friends, his Mother, Sisters, and others.

Sultan Cossero proclaimed.

This Selim Padasha being in rebellion, his father dispossessed him, and proclaimed heire apparent, his eldest Sonne Cossero[1] being eldest Sonne to Selimsha:[2] for his owne Sonnes younger Brothers to Selim, were all dead in Decan and Guzerat: yet shortly after his Father dyed, who in his death-bed had mercy on Selim, possessing him againe. But Cossero, who was proclaimed heire apparent, stomached his father, and rose with great troopes, yet was not able to indure after the losse of many thousand men on both sides: but was taken, and remaineth still in prison in the Kings Pallace, yet blinde, as all men reporte: and was so commanded to be blinded by his father. So since that time, being now eight yeares after, he had commanded to put all his sonnes confederates to death, with sundry kinds of death; some to be hanged, some spitted, some to haue their heads chopped off, and some to bee torne by Elephants. Since which time hee hath raigned in quiet, but ill beloued of the greater part of his Subiects, who stand greatly in feare of him. His custome is euery yeare to be out two moneths on hunting, as is before specified. When he

Hee was not blinded and is since (as you shall see in Sir Tho. Roe's relations) deliuered out of prison.

[1] Khuzru.

[2] Jehanghir.

meaneth to begin his iourney, if comming forth of his Pallace, hee get vp on a Horse, it is a signe that he goeth for the warres: but if he get vpon an Elephant or Palankine, it will bee an hunting voyage. My selfe in the time that I was one of his Courtiers, haue seene many cruell deeds done by him. Fiue times a weeke, he commaundeth his braue Elephants to fight before him: and in the time of their fighting, either comming or going out, many times men are killed, or dangerously hurt by these Elephants. But if any be grieuously hurt (which might very well escape) yet neuerlesse that man is cast into the Riuer, himselfe commanding it, saying: dispatch him, for as long as he liueth, he will doe nothing else but curse me, and therfore it is better that he dye presently. I haue seene many in this kind. Againe hee delighteth to see men executed himselfe, and torne in pieces with Elephants. He put to death in my time his Secretary, onely vpon suspicion, that Chan-channa should write vnto the Deccan King, who being sent for and examined about this matter, denied it: whereupon the King not having patience, arose from his seate, and with his sword gaue him his deadly wound, and afterwards deliuered him to bee torne by Elephants.

Likewise, it happened to one who was a great friend of mine (a chiefe man, hauing vnder his charge the Kings Wardrobe, and all Woollen Cloath, and all sorts of mercery, and his China dishes) that a faire China dish (which cost ninetie Rupias, or fortie fiue Rials of eight) was broken, in this my friends time, by a mischance (when the King was in his progresse) being packed amongst other things, on a Cammell, which fell and broke all the whole parcell. This Nobleman knowing how dearly the King loued this dish aboue the rest, presently sent one of his trusty seruants to China-machina, ouer land to seeke for another, hoping that before he should remember the dish, he would returne with another like vnto it: but his euill lucke was contrarie. For

Seuerity.

China-machina.

the King two yeares after remembered the dish, and his man was not yet come. Now, when the King heard that the dish was broken, he was in a great rage, commanding him to be brought before him, and to be beaten by two men, with two great whips made of cords: and after that he had receiued one hundred and twenty of these lashes, he commanded his Porters, who he appointed for that purpose, to beate him with their small Cudgels, till a great many of them were broken: at the least twenty men were beating of him, till the poore man was thought to bee dead, and then he was haled out by the heeles, and commaunded to prison. The next day the King demaunded whether he was liuing, answer was made, that he was: whereupon he commanded him to be carried vnto perpetuall prison. But the Kings Sonne being his friend, freed him of that, and obtained of his Father, that he might bee sent to his owne house, and there be cured. So after two moneths, he was reasonably well recouered, and came before the King, who presently commanded him to depart the Court, and neuer come againe before him, vntill he had found such a like dish,
China-machina. and that hee trauell for China-machina to seeke it: the King allowed him fiue thousand Rupias towards his charges; and besides, returning one fourth part of his liuing that he had before, to maintaine him in his trauell. He being departed, and fourteene moneths on his trauell, was not yet come home: but newes came of him, that the King of Persia had the like dish, and for pitties sake hath sent it him, who at my departure was on his way homeward.

Likewise, in my time it happened that Pattan, a man of good stature, came to one of the King's Sonnes, named
Sultan Peruis. Sultan Peruis, to intreat him to bestow somewhat on him, by petition deliuered to one of the Princes chief men, at the deliuery whereof, the Prince caused him to come neere: and demanding of him whether hee would serue him; he answered, No, for he thought that the Prince would not

grant him so much as he would aske. The Prince seeing him to be a pretty fellow, and meanly apparelled, smiled, demanding what would content him: hee told him plainly, that hee would neither serue his Father nor him, vnder a thousand Rupias a day, which is 100 pound sterling. The Prince asked him what was in him that he demanded so much; he replyed, make tryall of me with all sorts of weapons, either on horsebacke, or on foote, and for my sufficient command in the warres, if I doe not performe as much as I speake, let mee dye for it. The houre being come for the Prince to go to his Father, he gaue ouer his talk, commanding the man to be forth comming. At night the kings custome being to drinke, the Prince—perceiuing his Father to be merry, told him of this man: so the King commaunded him to be brought before him. Now while he was sent for, a wilde Lyon was brought in, a very great one, strongly chained, and led by a dozen men and keepers: and while the King was viewing this Lyon, the Pattan came in, at whose sight the Prince presently remembered his Father. The King demanding of the Pattan whence he was, and of what parantage, and what valour was in him, that he should demand so much wages: his answer was, that the King should make tryal of him. That I will, saith the King, goe wrastle and buffuet with this Lyon. The Pattans answere was, that this was a wild beast, and to goe barely vpon him without weapon, would be no triall of his man-hood. The King not regarding his speech, commanded him to buckle with the Lion, who did so, wrastling and buffeting with the Lyon a pretty while: and then the Lyon being loose from his keepers, but not from his chaines, got the poore man within his clawes, and tore his body in many parts: and with his pawes tore the one halfe of his face, so that this valiant man was killed by this wilde beast. The King not yet contented, but desirous to see more sport, sent for ten men that were of his horse-men in pay, being that night on

Proud demand.

Cruell command.

the watch: for it is the custome of all those that receiue pay, or liuing from the King, to watch once a week, none excepted, if they be well, and in the Citie. These men, one after another, were to buffet with the Lyon, who were all grieuously wounded, and it cost three of them their liues. The King continued three moneths in this vaine, when he was in his humors, for whose pleasure sake many men lost their liues, and many were grieuously wounded. So that euer after, vntill my comming away, some fifteene young Lyons were made tame, and played one with another before the king, frisking betweene mens legs, and no man hurt in a long time.

Bloody experiments.

Likewise, he cannot abide, that any man should haue any precious stone of value, for it is death if he know it not at that present time, and that he hath the refusall thereof. His Jeweller, a Banian named Herrauand, had bought a Diamond of three Mettegals, which cost one hundred thousand Rupias: which was not so closely done, but newes came to the King: Herrauand likewise was befriended, beeing presently acquainted therewith, who before the King sent for him, came vnto him, and challenged the King that he had often promised him that he would come to his house: the King answered that it was true. Herrauand therefore replyed, that now was the time, for that he had a faire Present to bestow vpon his Maiestie: for that he had bought a stone of such a weight. The King smiled and said, Thy lucke was good to prevent me. So preparation was made, and to the Bannians house he went. By this meanes, the King hath ingrossed all faire stones, that no man can buy from fiue Carats vpwards,—without his leaue: for he hath the refusall of all, and giueth not by a third part so much as their value. There was a Diamant cutter of my acquaintance, that was sent for to cut a Diamant of three Mettegals and a halfe, who demanded a small foule Diamant to make powder, wherewith to cut the other Diamant. They brought

Costly entertainment.

him a Chest, as he laid, of three spannes long, and a spanne and a halfe broad, and a spanne and halfe deepe full of Diamants of all sizes and sorts: yet could he find neuer any one for his purpose, but one of fiue Rotties, which was not very foule neither.

An inestimable rich coffer of Diamonds.

He is exceeding rich in Diamants, and all other precious stones, and vsually weareth euery day a faire Diamant of great price, and that which he weareth this day, till his time be come about to weare it againe, he weareth not the same; that is to say, all his faire Jewels are diuided into a certaine quantitie or proportion to weare euery day. He also weareth a chaine of Pearle, very faire and great, and another chaine of Emeralds, and ballace Rubies. Hee hath another Jewell that commeth round about his turbant, full of faire Diamants and Rubies. It is not much to bee wondered, that he is so rich in Jewels, and in Gold and Siluer, when he hath heaped together the Treasure and Jewels of so many Kings, as his forefathers haue conquered, who likewise were a long time in gathering them together; and all came to his hands. Againe, all the money and Jewels which his Nobles heape together, when they die come all vnto him, who giueth what he listeth to the Noblemans wiues and children; and this is done to all them that receiue pay, or liuing from the King. India is rich in siluer, for all Nations bring Coyne, and carry away commodities for the same; and this Coyne is buried in India, and goeth not out: so it is thought, that once in twentie yeeres it commeth into the Kings power. All the lands in his Monarchie are at his disposing, who giueth and taketh at his pleasure. If I haue lands at Lahor, being sent vnto the warres at Decan, another hath the lands, and I am to receiue mine in Decan, or thereabouts, neere the place where I am, whether it be in the warres, or that I be sent about any other businesse, for any other countrey. And men are to looke well vnto their doings; for if they be

Cause of so great wealth.

Those lands which are let pay to the King two thirds of the profit: and of those which he giueth in fee, one third remaineth to the King. In all the world is not more fertile land than in some part of his Dominions.

found tardie in neuer so little a matter, they are in danger of loosing their lands; and if complaints of Iniustice which they doe bee made vnto the King, it is well if they escape with losse of their lands.

He is very seuere in such causes, and with all seueritie punisheth those Captaines who suffer out-lawes to giue assault vnto their Citie, without resisting. In my time there were some eight Captaines, who had their liuing vpon the borders of Bengala, in a chiefe Citie called Pattana,[1] which was suffered to be taken by out-lawes, and they all fled; but that Citie was againe restored by a great Captaine, who was Commander of a Countrey neere thereabouts, who took all those Captaines that fled, and sent them to the King, to vse punishment vpon them at his pleasure. So they were brought before the King in chaines, and were presently commanded to be shauen, both head and beard, and to weare womens apparel, riding vpon asses, with their faces backwards, and so carried about the Citie. This being done, they were brought before the King againe, and there whipped, and sent to perpetuall prison; and this punishment was inflicted vpon them in my sight. He is seuere enough, but all helpeth not, for his poore Riats or Clownes complaine of Iniustice done them, and cry for Justice at the Kings hands. They come to a certaine place, where a long rope is fastened vnto two pillars neere vnto the place where the King sitteth in Justice. This rope is hanged full of Bels, plated with gold, so that the rope beeing shaken the Bels are heard by the King; who sendeth to know the cause, and doth his Justice accordingly. At his first comming to the Crowne, he was more seuere then now he is, which is the cause that the Countrey is so full of outlawes and theeues, that almost a man cannot stirre out of doores, throughout all his Dominions, without great forces; for they are all become Rebels.

Punishment of Cowards. A chiefe Citie called Pattana.

[1] Patna.

There is one great Ragane[1] betwixt Agra and Amadavar, who commandeth as much land as a good Kingdome: and all the forces the Mogol hath cannot bring him in, for his forces are vpon the mountains. He is twentie thousand strong in Horse, and fiftie thousand strong in Foote, and many of these Rebels are in all his Dominions: but this is one of the greatest. There are many risen at Candahar, Cabul, Moldun,[2] and Sinde, and in the Kingdome of Boloch: Bengala likewise, Decan, and Guzerat are full, so that a man can trauell no way for out-lawes. Their Gouernment is in such a barbarous kind, and cruell exacting vpon the Clownes, which causeth them to be so head-strong. The fault is in the Chiefe, for a man cannot continue half a yeere in his liuing, but it is taken from him and giuen vnto another: or else the King taketh it for himselfe (if it be rich ground, and likely to yeeld much) making exchange for a worse place: or as he is befriended of the Vizir. By this meanes he raketh the poore, to get from them what he can, who still thinketh euery houre to be put out of his place. But there are many, who continue a long time in one place, and if they remaine but sixe yeeres, their wealth which they gaine is infinite, if it be a thing of any sort. The custome is, they are allowed so much liuing to maintaine that Port which the King hath giuen them, that is to say, they are allowed twentie Rupias of euerie horse by the Moneth, and two Rupias by the Moneth for euery horse Fame, for the maintenance of their Table. As thus: A Captaine that hath fiue thousand horse to maintaine in the warres, hath likewise of Fame other fiue thousand, which he is not to maintaine in the warres, but onely for his Table, allowed vpon euery horse by the Moneth two Rupias, and the other fiue thousand, twenty Rupias by the Moneth: and this is the pay which the greater part of them are allowed.

He calleth rebels (as the Mogols did) those that refused subiection, though perhaps some of them were free Kings, as this Ragane or Ranna, supposed the true successor of Porus, whom Alexander conquered. He is now brought, or bought rather (as they say) peaceably to acknowledge tribute to the Mogol.

[1] The Rana of Udaipur.

[2] Multan.

The great Mogol his deuotions. Some suppose him author of a new sect.

Now here I meane to speake a little of his manners and customes in the Court. First, in the morning about the breake of day, he is at his Beades, with his face turned to the Westward. The manner of his praying when he is in Agra, is in a priuate faire roome, vpon a goodly set stone, hauing onely a Persian Lambe-skinne vnder him: hauing also some eight chaines of Beads, euery one of them containing foure hundred. The Beads are of rich Pearle, ballace Rubyes, Diamonds, Rubyes, Emeralds, Lignum Aloes, Eshern, and Corall. At the vpper end of this Jet stone the Picture of our Lady and Christ are placed, grauen in stone: so he turneth ouer his Beads, and saith three thousand two hundred words, according to the number of his Beads, and then his Prayer is ended. After he hath done, he sheweth himselfe to the people, receiuing their Salemes or good morrowes, vnto whome multitudes resort euery morning for this purpose. This done, hee sleepeth two houres more, and then dineth, and passeth his time with his Women, and at noone hee sheweth himselfe to the people againe, sitting till three of the clocke, viewing and seeing his Pastimes, and sports made by men, and fighting of many sorts of beasts, euery day sundry kinds of Pastimes. Then at three of the clocke all the Nobles in generall (that be in Agra, and are well) resort vnto the Court, the King comming forth in open audience, sitting in his Seat-Royall, and euery man standing in his degree before him, his chiefest sort of Nobles standing within a red Rayle, and the rest without. They are all placed by his Lieutenant Generall. This red Rayle is three steppes higher then the place where the rest stand: and within this red Rayle I was placed, amongst the chiefest of all. The rest are placed by Officers, and they likewise be within an other uery spacious place rayled: and without that Rayle, stand all sorts of horseman and souldiers that belong vnto his Captaines and all other commers. At these Rayles there are many doores

The great Mogol spending his time.

The red rayle.

kept by many Porters, who haue white rods to keepe men in order. In the middest of the place, right before the King, standeth one of his Sheriffes, together with his Master Hangman, who is accompanied with forty hangmen, wearing on their heads a certaine quilted cap, different from all others, with an Hatchet on their shouldiers: and others with all sorts of Whips, being there readie to do what the King commandeth. The King heareth all causes in this place, and stayeth some two houres euery day (these Kings of India sit daily in Justice euery day, and on the Tuesdayes doe their executions). Then he departeth towards his priuate place of Prayer: his Prayer beeing ended, foure or fiue sorts of uery well dressed and roasted meats are brought him, of which as he pleaseth, he eateth a bit to stay his stomache, drinking once of his stronge drinke. Then hee commeth forth into a priuate roome, where none can come but such as himselfe nominateth (for two yeeres I was one of his attendants here). In this place he drinketh other fiue cupfuls, which is the portion that the Physicians alot him. This done, he eateth opium, and then he ariseth, and being in the height of his drinke, he layeth him downe to sleepe, euery man departing to his owne home. And after he hath slept two howres they awake him, and bring his Supper to him, at which time he is not able to feed himselfe; but it is thrust into his mouth by others, and this is about one of the clocke: and then he sleepeth the rest of the night.

Captaine Hawkins, two yeeres together neere about the great Mogol.

Now in the space of these sixe cups, he doth many idle things: and whatsoeuer he doeth, either without or within, drunken or sober, he hath writers, who by turnes set downe euery thing in writing which he doth: so that there is nothing passeth in his life time, which is not noted; no, not so much as his going to the necessary; and how often he lieth with his women, and with whom: and all this is done vnto this end, that when he dieth, these writings of al his actions and speeches, which are worthy to be set downe, might be recorded in the Chronicles. At my being with him, he made his brother's children Christians; the doing whereof was not for any zeale he had to Christianitie, as the Fathers, and all Christians thought; but upon the prophecie of certaine learned Gentiles, who told him that the sonnes of his body should be disinherited, and the children of his brother should raigne. And therefore he did it to make these children hatefull to all Moores, as Christians are odious in their sight: and they being once Christians, when any such matter should happen, they should find no subiects: but God is omnipotent, and can turne the making of these Christians vnto a good ende, if it be his pleasure.

The Mogol makes his brothers children Christians.

This Christianitie is since disclaymed, and was then but a tricke, rather of sensualitie, than of deuotion or state.

This King, amongst his children, hath one called Sultan Shariar, of seuen yeeres of age, and his Father on a day being to goe some whether to solace himself, demanded of him whether hee would goe with him: the child answered, That if it pleased his Highnesse, he would either goe or stay, as the Pleasure of his Father was. But because his answer was not that with all his heart he would waite vpon his Maiestie, he was very well buffeted by the King, and that in such sort, that no child in the world but what would haue cryed; which this child did not. Wherefore his Father demanded why he cryed not; he answered, that his Nurses told him that it was the greatest shame in the world for Princes to cry when they were beaten: and euer since they nurtured me in this kind, saith he, I neuer cryed, and nothing shall make me cry to the death. Vpon which speech, his Father being more vexed, stroke him againe, and caused a bodkin to bee brought him, which he thrust through his cheeke; but all this would not make him cry, although he bled uery much, which was admired of all, that the Father should doe this vnto his child, and that he was so stout, that hee would not crie. There is great hope of this child to exceed all the rest.

Two feasts.

This Emperour keepeth many feasts in the yeare, but two

feasts especially may be nominated; the one called the Nourous,[1] which is in honour of the New Yeares day. This feast continueth eighteene daies, and the wealth and riches are wonderfull, that are to be seene in the decking and setting forth of euery mans roome or place where he lodgeth, when it is his to watch: for euery Nobleman hath his place appointed in the Palace. In the middest of that spacious place I speake of, there is a rich Tent pitched, but so rich, that I thinke the like cannot bee found in the world. This Tent is curiously wrought, and hath many Seminans ioyning round about it, of most curious wrought Veluet, embroidered with Gold, and many of them are of Cloath of Gold and Siluer. These Seminans be shaddowes to keepe the Sunne from the compasse of this Tent. I may say, it is at least two acres of ground, but so richly spread with Silke and Gold Carpets, and Hangings in the principall places, rich as rich Veluet imbroydered with Gold, Pearles, and precious stones can make it. Within it fiue Chaires of Estate are placed, most rich to behold, where at his pleasure the King sitteth. There are likewise priuate rooms for his Queenes, most rich where they sit, and see all, but one not seene. So round about this tent, the compasse of all may bee some fiue Acres of ground. Euery principall Nobleman maketh his roome, and decketh it, likewise euery man according to his ability, striueth who may adorne his roome richest. The King, where he doth affect, commeth to his Noblemens roomes, and is most sumptuously feasted there: and at his departure is presented with the rarest Jewels and toyes that they can find. But because he will not receiue any- thing at that time as a present, he commandeth his Treasurer to pay what his praysers valew them to bee worth, which are valewed at half the price. Euery one, and all of his Nobles prouide toyes, and rare things to giue him at this feast: so commonly at this feast euery man his estate is aug-

An exceeding rich Tent.

[1] Nau Rôz. The Persian New Year's Day, at the vernal equinox.

mented. Two daies of this feast, the better sort of the Women come to take the pleasure thereof: and this feast beginneth at the beginning of the Moone of March. The other feast is some foure moneths after, which is called the feast of his Birth-day: This day euery man striueth who may be the richest in apparell and Jewels.

The feast of his Birth-day.

After many sports and pastimes performed in his Palace, he goeth to his mothers house, with all the better sort of his Nobles, where euery man presenteth a Jewell vnto his Mother, according to his estate. After the bancket is ended, the King goeth into a uery faire roome, where a ballance of beaten Gold is hanged, with one scale emptie for him to sit in; the other scale being filled with diuers' things, that is to say, Siluer, Gold, diuers sorts of Grain a little, and so of euery kind of Mettall a little, and with all sorts of precious stones some: In fine, he weigheth himself with these things, which the next day are given to the poore, and all may be valued to be worth ten thousand pounds. This day, before he goeth vnto his mothers house, euery man bringeth him his present, which is thought to be ten times more worth, than that which he giueth to the poore. This done, euery man departeth vnto his home.

See hereof Sir Thom. Roe.

His custome is, that when you petition him for any thing, you must not come empty handed, but giue him some toy or other, whether you write or no: by the gift you giue him, he knoweth that you would demand some thing of him: so after enquiry is made, if he seeth it conuenient, he granteth it.

The custome of the Indians is to burne their dead, as you haue read in other Authors, and at their burning, many of their Wiues will burne with them: because they will bee registred in their bookes, for famous and most modest and louing Wiues, who leauing all worldly affaires, content themselues to liue no longer then their Husbands. I haue seene many proper Women brought before the King, whom (by

Voluntary burning of women with their dead husbands.

his commandement) none may burne without his leaue and sight of them, I meane those of Agra. When any of these commeth, hee doth perswade them with many promises of gifts and liuing if they will liue: but in my time no perswasion could prevaile, but burne they would. The King seeing that all would not serue, giueth his leaue for her to be carried to the fire, where she burneth her selfe aliue with her dead husband. Likewise his custome is, when any great Nobleman hath been absent from him two or three yeares, if they come in fauour, and haue performed well, he receiueth them in manner and forme following.

First, the Noble-man stayeth at the gate of the Pallace, till the Vizir and Lieutenant Generall, and Knight Martiall come to accompany him vnto the King: then he is brought to the gate of the outermost rayles, whereof I haue spoken before, where hee standeth in the view of the King in the middest betweene these two Nobles; then he toucheth the ground with his hand and also with his head, very grauely, and doth this three times. This done, he kneeleth downe touching the ground with his fore-head, which being done, he is carried forward towards the King, and in the midway he is made to do this reuerence againe: then he commeth to the doore of the red rayles, doing the like reuerence the third time: and hauing thus done, he commeth within the red rayles, and doth it once more vpon the Carpets. Then the King commandeth him to come vp the staires or ladder of seauen steppes, that he may embrace him; where the King most louingly embraceth him before all the people whereby they shall take notice, that he is in the Kings fauour. The King hauing done this, he then commeth downe, and is placed by the Lieutenant Generall according to his degree. Now, if he come in disgrace, through exclamations made against him, he hath none of these honours from the King, but is placed in his place till he come to his tryall. This King is very much adored of the Heathen Com-

Fauourable entertainment of the Grandees.

monality, insomuch, that they will spread their bodies all vpon the ground, rubbing the earth with their faces on both sides. They vse many other fopperies and superstitions, which I omit, leauing them for other Trauellers, which shall come from thence hereafter.

Funerall feast or Obit for his Father?

After I had written this, there came into my memory another Feast, solemnized at his Fathers Funerall, which is kept at his Sepulchre, where likewise himselfe, with all his posterity, meane to be buried. Vpon this day there is great store of victualls dressed, and much money giuen to the poore. This Sepulchre may be counted one of the rarest Monuments of the world. It hath beene this foureteene yeeres a building, and it is thought it will not be finished these seuen yeares more, in ending gates and walls, and other needfull things, for the beautifying and setting of it forth. The least that worke there daily, are three thousand people: but thus much I will say, that one of our Workemen will dispatch more then three of them. The Sepulchre is some ¾ of a mile about, made square: it hath seauen heights built, euery height narrower then the other, till you come to the top where his Herse is. At the outermost gate before you come to the Sepulchre, there is a most stately Palace building: the compasse of the wall ioyning to this gate of the Sepulchre and garding, being within, may be at least three miles. This Sepulchre is some foure miles distant from the Citie of Agra.[1]

Sumptuous Sepulchre.

[1] Mr. Fergusson says that Akbar's tomb at Secundra is quite unlike any other tomb built in India either before or since, and of a design borrowed from a Buddhist model. The tomb stands on a raised platform, of pyramidal form. The lower storey is pierced by ten great arches on each face, and is thirty feet high. On this terrace stands another far more ornate, and a third and fourth stand on this, all of red sandstone. The tomb itself is a splendid piece of the most beautiful Arabesque tracery.

INDEX.

T. RICHARDS, 37, GREAT QUEEN STREET.

Ingram Content Group UK Ltd.
Milton Keynes UK
UKHW020659200323
418846UK00006B/560

9 781376 349849